POLICY *and* OPINION *in the* GULF WAR

John Mueller

THE UNIVERSITY OF CHICAGO PRESS · CHICAGO AND LONDON

John Mueller is professor of political science at the University of Rochester. He is the author of *Retreat from Doomsday* (1989), *Astaire Dancing: The Musical Films* (1985), and *War, Presidents, and Public Opinion* (1973).

The University of Chicago Press, Chicago 60637
The University of Chicago Press, Ltd., London
© 1994 by The University of Chicago
All rights reserved. Published 1994
Printed in the United States of America
03 02 01 00 99 98 97 96 95 94 5 4 3 2 1

ISBN (cloth): 0–226–54564–4
ISBN (paper): 0–226–54565–2

Library of Congress Cataloging-in-Publication Data

Mueller, John E.
    Policy and opinion in the Gulf War / John Mueller.
       p.   cm. — (American politics and political economy series)
    Includes index.
    ISBN 0-226-54564-4. — ISBN 0-226-54565-2 (pbk.)
    1. Persian Gulf War, 1991—Public opinion. 2. Persian Gulf War, 1991—United
States. 3. Public opinion—United States. I. Title.
II. Series: American politics and political economy.
DS79.724.U6M84   1994
956.704′42—dc20
                                        93-21226
                                          CIP

To JAM and ESM,
to Karl, Michelle, Karen, Erik, and Susan,

and to the memory of
BILL RIKER,
colleague, mentor, and friend

CONTENTS ....

FIGURES ....

PREFACE ....

When the crisis in the Persian Gulf erupted on August 2, 1990 with Iraq's invasion of neighboring Kuwait, American public opinion quickly became a major consideration.

President George Bush sought public backing as he attempted to deal with the invasion and as he led his country into war against what many feared might prove to be a formidable enemy. And, as well, he needed public backing as he pursued the war itself. Those who opposed his war policies also appealed to public opinion and, like Bush, they sought to influence it in their favor.

Meanwhile, on the other side of the world, Iraq's president, Saddam Hussein, tried several times (with singularly counterproductive results) to influence the American public, and he seems to have hoped that if war—the "mother of all battles," as he called it—were to break out, popular support in the United States would quickly fade as his forces inflicted substantial casualties on American forces, leading to effective demands to end the conflict on terms congenial to Iraq. As he put it to U.S. Ambassador April Glaspie before the war, "Yours is a society which cannot accept ten thousand dead in one battle" (Stein 1992, 175). He also apparently had another theory about American public opinion. When Americans became aware of the enormous damage being done to Baghdad by air raids, he told several people, support for the war would quickly crumble: "We will only have to face two air strikes, then it'll be ended." Accordingly, he never evacuated his capital city, and he carefully kept America's Cable News Network wired in to report the consequences of falling bombs (Simpson 1991, 273, 281–82).

The crisis and ensuing war came to preoccupy not only CNN, which may well have been the war's only unqualified winner, but the media as a whole. Indeed, it quickly became, as Craig LaMay has put it, "the mother of all media events." In the five months of the crisis leading up to the war, one analysis found that it had generated 2,334 television news stories, "the most intensive coverage that we have ever logged." Other data show that from December 1990 through the war's conclusion at the end of February 1991, television devoted 2,658 minutes to the episode while, by contrast, affording no other story more than a total of 56 (LaMay 1991, 44, 47). In all, television transmitted 4,383 stories on the crisis and war in the Persian Gulf over seven months; by comparison, the 22-month-long presidential campaign of 1988 yielded only 2,301 stories (Lichter 1992, 224).

The importance of public opinion in all this was fully apparent, of course, to the polling agencies and to the newspapers, magazines, and television networks that sponsor them. Accordingly, the agencies overran their budgets on telephone surveys asking hundreds of questions seeking to assess the reaction of the American public to the crisis and war in the Persian Gulf. In fact, the episode may well be the most extensively polled in history: the mother of all polling events.

This book grapples with this mass of data. Focusing primarily on opinion trends, it seeks to assess how the American public related to the crisis and to the war that ensued. It is also concerned with policy during the period and particularly with the interaction between opinion and policy.

Much of the public opinion analysis is, I'm afraid, rather untidy. The data it relies upon were created prodigiously, but not always very systematically, by the polling agencies, who were chiefly trying, of course, to generate data for short-range journalistic purposes, not for longer-range academic ones. However, although there are many places where the polls failed to ask what a latter-day analyst might consider to have been the right question at the right time, they did manage to create a considerable amount of semi-redundant data on many aspects of the issue, and these redundancies can be highly instructive: if several polls in different ways show the same opinion pattern to have taken place, one can begin to believe that something like that actually happened. Moreover, as will be seen quite often in this study, the results of one poll often shed additional, and sometimes correcting or importantly embellishing, light on the results of another, similar one.

The book begins with a chapter discussing what public opinion surveys measure. It stresses the importance of paying close attention to question wording—a concern developed often in the analysis—and it urges the value of using a comparative approach when analyzing poll data.

The rest is archaeology—an effort to sort through and discern patterns in the shards and artifacts left behind by the polling agencies.

Throughout, an effort is made to put the data in broader political and military context, to evaluate policy options, and where appropriate to compare the Gulf episode to such earlier experiences as Panama, Vietnam, Korea, the Falklands, World War II, and even the War of 1812.

I assess opinion on the Gulf crisis in three chronological chunks. The first, comprising chapters 2 and 3, deals with public opinion in the period up to the beginning of the war on January 16, 1991. Since Bush successfully started the war and since the public enthusiastically rallied to him after it began, quite a few analysts, sometimes using selective data, have retrospectively concluded that Bush convinced the public of the war's wisdom before he began it. A more thorough assessment of poll data, however, suggests that, while policy in the Gulf increasingly became a partisan affair, opinion during the prewar period, quite remarkably perhaps, generally changed rather little, particularly during the two-month period before the war when the debate was at its height. Although the President was leading the country to war and was able to keep it high on the public's agenda of issues to worry about, he was not notably successful at generating increased support for war, nor were his opponents able to sway public opinion to their side. Among other things, the exercise helps to illustrate the value of dealing comprehensively with poll data and applying information from a variety of sources.

It appears that Bush, not usually noted for his charismatic persuasiveness, was able, despite determined political opposition, to lead the country to war not because he notably convinced a growing number of Americans of the wisdom of war, but because of his position as foreign policy leader; because he and his aides enjoyed what appears to have been a fair amount of trust in this matter; because Saddam Hussein played the villain role with such consummate skill; and because people generally anticipated that the war would be beneficial in resolving a pressing and important issue and that it would be comparatively quick and low in casualties. The opinion dynamic that probably helped Bush most, however, was a growing fatalism about war—as time went by the public became increasingly convinced not that war was particularly wise, but that it was inevitable. In that sense, the public, as well as a great deal of officialdom, felt entrapped and was willing to be led to war: for many, the attitude was, "Let's get it over with." But it was a close call: war was by no means predestined or inevitable. The opposition was not without resources or persuasive arguments, and the public seems to have been quite willing to embrace a compromise settlement to avoid war. In some important respects, it seems that Bush was able to pull off the war before his opposition could get fully organized.

The second section evaluates public opinion during the six-week war itself and occupies chapter 4. Predictably, public support rallied to the President and to the war once hostilities began, and this led to a sort of boosterism within the media. However, the public's tolerance for American casualties appears to have been quite low, and if there had been substantial costs to American forces, support would probably have dwindled quickly. Indeed, even though the war was remarkably brief and low in U.S. casualties, some measures suggest that support did decline during its duration.

The third section, comprising chapters 5 and 6, deals with public and electoral opinion after the war. As it happened, the war's aftermath delivered a number of surprises. In its first Sunday edition after the war (March 3, 1991), the *New York Times* published in adjacent columns two confident and entirely sensible predictions. In one, James E. Atkins, a career foreign service officer and Middle East specialist, asserted, "There is little reason to concern ourselves with Saddam. He has been defeated and humiliated and will soon be dead at the hands of his own people unless some unlikely country gives him refuge." In the other, *Times* columnist Anna Quindlen predicted with "reasonable" sureness that "George Bush will be re-elected President in 1992."

Chapter 5 considers public opinion after the war. It observes that even before the war the public had come to feel that removing Saddam Hussein should be a central war aim, and this desire was, if anything, heightened by the war itself. After the war, accordingly, the public became somewhat disillusioned with the war and the euphoria faded, though there was less of a diminution in the numbers who approved the decision to go to war in the first place. Mostly, however, people promptly turned their attention to other issues, especially to the economy. As Bush came to seem distanced from these concerns and ineffectual in dealing with them, his various approval ratings, which stood at stupendous highs at the war's end, quickly dropped—some of them within *days* of the war—and then underwent a descent that is virtually unprecedented historically.

Then, chapter 6 assesses the Gulf War's electoral consequences. While initial punditry, like Quindlen's, held that the war would help the Republicans, both contemporary polling data and historical comparison suggest there was reason to expect that it might not have all that much impact as voters turned to other, more immediate concerns. The war's influence, or lack thereof, on the 1992 elections is assessed. The chapter also includes a comparison with the War of 1812 and speculates that if the Gulf War had gone awry there might have been short-range, but not necessarily long-range, benefits for the opposition Democrats.

With this as background, chapters 7–9 deal more broadly with policy issues of the Gulf War and with the war's longer-range impact, if any, on history and on opinion.

Chapter 7 considers several issues concerning the interaction of policy and public opinion. It begins by evaluating how the public opinion polls affected the war and planning for it. In the fall of 1990, the polls inspired in the administration a sense of urgency about resolving the crisis that seems unjustified. They also influenced the arguments used in the debate—in particular, they encouraged the administration to emphasize Hussein's nuclear efforts. And the polls also suggest that the administration was unduly anxious in its concerns about American troop vulnerability to Iraq in the early days of the buildup and about public reaction to stories of Iraqi casualties at the end of the war—indeed, although the public displayed very little animosity toward the Iraqi people, Americans were remarkably insensitive to reports of Iraqi civilian or military casualties. The chapter also investigates the widespread belief that the public had turned favorable to war by January 1991 and argues that the data do not support this conclusion.

The public, as the administration correctly assumed, appears to have been quite sensitive to American casualties—though not so sensitive as the administration apparently believed. Accordingly, had the Iraqis managed to fashion a strategy—there were feasible ones—that could cause notable U.S. losses, support for the war would in all probability have declined even if the eventual result were still a clear victory. This decline would have been led by Democrats who would forcefully point out that Bush, against their advice, had turned against a policy that promised to achieve the war's ends without the costs in American lives.

The chapter also considers the relation between the war and the media, arguing that the media, far outdistanced by major players and by the force of events, probably had little independent impact. Principally, the agenda was set by events, by central decision-makers, and ultimately by the customers: the public itself. The Gulf War episode also suggests that pictures of a major event are not necessary to convey the event's impact.

Chapter 8 speculates about how the war will be viewed in retrospect, and it deals particularly with the postwar efforts of Bush and others to put a congenial and politically helpful spin on it. The continued postwar existence of the troublesome Saddam Hussein and of Mideast instability undercut some of the war's glow for Bush. And the chapter reflects, in retrospect, on the feasibility of a strategy of punitive containment as a method for dealing with Iraq's invasion. It also assesses the economic impact of the crises and war on the recession in the United States. Finally, it argues that, because enemy forces were probably far less numerous than assumed and because the enemy was utterly demoralized before the war ever took place, the chief achievement of the American military may not have been in its armed wizardry or in the slaughter it carried out, but rather in its ability to gain its goals with so little damage to the other side's military personnel—a perspective unappreciated at the time of the war by the public, by the military, or by the media.

Chapter 9 concludes the book with some reflections on the remarkably limited impact this seemingly cataclysmic event had on public and electoral opinion a year or less after it was over. It also seeks to put the war in broader historical context. As the most impressive aspect of post–World War II history is a non-event—the war that never took place between the heavily armed and intensely hostile United States and USSR—so perhaps the single most notable aspect of the relation between public opinion and the Gulf War was how the war, like last month's Big Game, soon faded as a notable and motivating event. In this, opinion may be reflecting the judgment of history. On the eve of hostilities, Secretary of State James Baker declared that the war would be "a defining moment in history" (Atkinson 1991), and George Bush grandly suggested as he launched it that the war would "chart the future of the world for the next hundred years" (1991b, 314). But the war, despite its drama and seeming importance at the time, failed to a remarkable degree to live up to this advance billing. Bush seems, in fact, to have inflated its impact by a factor of something like 365.

Presented in the second half of the book are several figures and nearly three hundred tables displaying public opinion poll results, the principal data source for the analysis. The tables are grouped by subject matter and can be read independent of the analysis. They will, I hope, provide a useful compendium of public opinion data from this most heavily polled of events.

For generous assistance in supplying data, I would like to thank Michael R. Kagay of the *New York Times,* William C. Stratmann and John Palmerini of the Gordon S. Black Corporation, and Thomas W. Graham and the Institute on Global Conflict and Cooperation at the University of California, San Diego. I would also like to thank Marc Maynard and Lois Timms-Ferrara of the Roper Center for assistance. Valued allies at the University of Chicago Press have been editor John Tryneski, production editor Claudia Rex, copy editor Peter Daniels, and designer Michael Brehm.

A PERSPECTIVE ON PUBLIC OPINION

The application of public opinion polls to issues of public concern often seems to be a reasonably straightforward process. An issue of current interest is seized upon by the polling agencies; they formulate a poll question that seems to get at the issue in a sensible, direct manner; the question is asked of a reasonably representative sample of the population; and the results are presented as the public's opinion on the matter.

This has sometimes been called the "pulse of democracy" and put forward as a scientific referendum of public sentiment on the issue at hand. In this way questions like these are probed: What percentage of the public favors increases in defense spending? approves the job the president is doing? favors abortion? trusts the government? thinks there is too much violence on television? has a warm and generous feeling toward Saddam Hussein?

It turns out, however, that public opinion polls are essentially incapable of answering questions like these with any reasonable degree of reliability. Accordingly, reports and analyses that parade such results as tangible reflections of public attitudes and then soberly draw larger implications from them are often substantially meaningless.

QUESTION WORDING AND CONTEXT

This observation stems not from discontent about sampling procedures or from a dark suspicion that the polling agencies may be "biased" toward some political or ideological position. Rather, it is based on the well-known, but under-appreciated, fact that the response to a poll question is generally very sensitive to the wording of the question and sometimes to its context. Measured opinion may not be infinitely variable by changes in question wording, but the variations that do occur

1

can often be far larger than those likely to be obtained by almost any variability—the poll's published "margin of error"—caused by sampling problems.[1]

Thus it is essential to pay close attention to the precise nature of the question, because on many issues seemingly minor changes in the wording of the question can notably alter the response. Respondents often seem to react as much to the tone or context of the question, or to key words in it, as they do to its objective content.

This is hardly a new discovery. A 1941 investigation found in comparing matched samples that 46 percent of the population were in favor of "forbidding" public speeches against democracy while 62 percent were in favor of "not allowing" such speeches. Obviously, many people were reacting as much to the tone of the questions as to its content: "forbidding" something is more difficult than "not allowing" it even though the expressions are essentially synonymous. That was still true in 1976 when the experiment was repeated: 19 percent then said they were in favor of forbidding those kinds of speeches while 42 percent were now in favor of not allowing them (Mueller 1988, 11).

How then can one determine what percentage of the population is in favor of free speech for opponents of democracy? Results 16 to 23 percentages points apart were generated by entirely reasonable poll questions designed to answer this query.

Another example concerns question context as much as question wording. In a 1974 survey the *same respondents* were twice asked whether they wanted defense spending expanded, cut back or kept the same. At one point in the interview they were asked about defense spending by itself; at another, they were asked about defense spending immediately after being asked whether they wanted spending on education expanded, cut back, or kept the same. The second version *implied* a tradeoff and, accordingly, found that people were 10 percentage points more likely to be willing to cut defense spending (Mueller 1977, 324–25; on context effects, see Schuman 1992).

As will be seen, examples of the problem abound in the public opinion data for the Gulf War. For example, people responded quite differently to policies like "go to war," "engage in combat," or "use military force."

Moreover, substantially more people were likely to express a "hawk" sentiment if the question simply asked whether the country should go to war than if the question gave them a choice between war and something else. Question options also made a great difference when respondents assessed the likelihood of war. At various points in the crisis, for example, people were asked, "Do you think the United States is going to get involved in a war with Iraq, or not?" while others were asked, "Do you expect the United States military to end up fighting against Iraq or do you think the situation will be resolved without fighting?" The latter formulation consistently found about 20 percentage points fewer anticipating war. Similarly, the number willing to approve Bush's decision in November to send additional troops to the Gulf area dropped 20 percentage points when the phrase "or should he have waited longer to make that decision" was supplied as an option.

Or consider a set of questions in which people are asked whether the country is going in the right direction or whether it has gotten off on the wrong track. One formulation of the question asks the respondent if the country is "off on the wrong track," while another asks if the country "has pretty seriously gotten off on the wrong track." One might suspect that it would be harder to agree that the country has "pretty seriously" gone off on the wrong track than that it has merely gone off on the wrong track. If so, one would be wrong. As it happens, people apparently are not affected by the "seriously" part of the phrase, but rather by the "pretty" part—and this has the effect of moderating the question. Thus, as a comparison of tables 198 and 199 indicates, Americans find it far more difficult to agree that things in the country "are off on the wrong track" than that things "have pretty seriously gotten off on the wrong track."

Results like these do not only suggest that the exact wording of the question is of vital concern. They also suggest that it is essentially impossible to say reliably what the public's opinion about anything actually *is*—although that is what the polling agencies are usually expected to do. Using a set of differently worded, but entirely reasonable, questions, the "polls show" that, in August 1990, 63 or 66 or 78 or 86 percent of the population supported the President's action in sending American troops to the Persian Gulf (tables 15, 17, 20, 16), even as they "show" that in January 1990 either 29 or 49 percent of the population thought things in the country had gotten off on the wrong track (tables 199 and 198).

Thus, although the polls were often asked during the Gulf crisis to determine what percentage of the population favored war or sanctions or compromise, or approved this or that decision or personality, they are simply incapable of doing so with anything resembling precision.

There may seem to be something of an anomaly here. The poll's estimates of voting results often are quite accurate, particularly in high-visibility, two-candidate races. If they can estimate voting behavior so well, why can't they do the same on other matters? The answer is that there is a major difference between ascertaining a voting preference and asking about opinions. The voting query concerns behavior, not opinion: essentially, it asks, "Which lever will you flip in the polling booth?" It does not ask why a given candidate is supported, or how the respondent feels about relevant issues.

Similarly, assuming proper sampling methods and assuming the respondents' recall and honesty can be relied upon, the polls are quite capable of estimating how many people watch a given television show or drink a certain brand of coffee. But they can't estimate with the same clarity and reliability how many people enjoy the show or the coffee because there are dozens of perfectly reasonable ways to ask about the enjoyment, and this array of questions is likely to generate a series of different numbers.

This is an important distinction because the polls' considerable, if not unrelieved, success at predicting elections is often taken to suggest that the other numbers they come up with—those measuring attitudes—have the same tangible meaning. This is simply not the case.

WHAT PUBLIC OPINION POLLS MEASURE

While the polls' estimates of attitudes are sensitive to the wording of the question, valid analysis can still be done with poll data. But to do so, it is helpful to consider what goes on in the interview situation.

It is a rather odd social arrangement. The respondent—in the living room, on the doorstep, or now most commonly over the telephone— is peppered with a series of questions on a variety of topics by an interviewer who carefully records each response. Some people decline to undergo this ritual—refusal rates on telephone surveys can run upwards of 35 percent—but most go along with it. And many find it a pleasant experience, even a flattering one, as their every utterance is faithfully recorded, if not as some kind of cosmic revelation, at least as a form of valued ephemera.

It is not surprising that many people do not want to seem unprepared at this great moment, and they soon find themselves pontificating in a seemingly authoritative manner on all sorts of issues to which they have never given much thought. Polling agencies usually encourage this; they do not particularly like to have high "no opinion" or "don't know" percentages. They also try to make the opinion-uttering process easy by formulating questions that are as uncluttered and as direct as possible. In the process, however, the issue at hand can get simplified nearly to the point of numbness and, to facilitate analysis, the responses are usually forced into a few rigid categories.

While people will often cheerfully answer poll questions as if they knew what they were talking about, it is reasonably clear that by most standards many people simply cannot be said to have much of an opinion on a great many issues. Consequently, it is not surprising to find their answers swayed by the tone or context of the question or by key words in it.

In the 1960s, polls asked, "Do you happen to know what kind of government most of China has right now—whether it's democratic, or Communist, or what?" If the answer was unclear they were further asked, "Do you happen to know if there is any Communist government in China now?" About a quarter of the respondents *admitted* they didn't know. Yet, on polls conducted simultaneously, a much lower percentage responded "no opinion" to a question asking if Communist China should be admitted to the United Nations (for other examples, see Page and Shapiro 1992, 9–12; Delli Carpini and Keeter 1991).

The interview situation, then, is best seen as a rather primitive stimulus–response situation in which quick and often ill-considered answers are casually fitted to a set of simplistic questions in a rather odd social situation. The results of this process are a set of numbers representing the frequency with which the polled population spewed out certain categorized answers in response to these questions. If 64 percent of the sample put themselves in one box in response to an opinion question, it does not mean 64 percent of the population "think" a certain way about that issue. It simply means 64 percent, faced with a particular stimulus in a particular social environment, came back with a particular response.

COMPARISON

For such numbers to have broader meaning they must be compared to something else. There are at least four ways poll data can be used in a comparative manner: one can compare the results with one's expectations, one can do comparisons over time, one can compare various subgroups of the poll population, and one can compare differently worded questions with each other.

Comparisons with Expectations

The first of these, the comparison of the poll results with one's expectations, is a fairly weak kind of analysis but it sometimes can be helpful to correct misleading stereotypes and assumptions. With many published poll reports it is the only kind of "analysis" that is possible, and some of this will, of necessity, be found in this study.

For example if in 1964 one had assumed one's own interest in international affairs to be universal, one might have been shocked by the large percentage that admitted it had never heard of "Communist China." Or, judging from the rhetoric about the McCarthy era, one might assume that the population during that period was in absolute hysteria about Communism; accordingly, it might be surprising to discover that a 1954 survey found virtually no one even mentioning the issue when asked about their worries and concerns (Stouffer 1955). And when the United States bombed a Baghdad bunker during the Gulf War, killing hundreds of civilians, many people initially assumed that the action would turn people away from supporting the war. They would thus be surprised to find that 79 percent said they blamed Saddam Hussein or Iraq itself for the deaths (table 253B).

But the surprise is mostly related to one's previous conceptions (or misconceptions). Accordingly, this kind of "comparison" is of limited value. But it can be helpful for mellowing simple stereotypes and for generating limited information—for getting a rough feel for where the public stands. For example, an officeholder might poll constituents to ascertain their griefs and may find an issue coming up much more frequently than expected. The numbers may not be taken to have much precise meaning, and they may be quite manipulable by changes in question wording. But the official would be wise to take the issue seriously anyway.

Comparisons over Time

The form of comparison principally applied in this book is trend analysis: comparing responses to the same question asked at various times over the course of the Gulf crisis. This can work because, whatever problems there may be in the way a question is worded, these remain constant and, usually, one can reasonably discuss any changes over time in the response percentages (see also Page and Shapiro 1992, 39).

The problem of question wording does not vanish, however. Sometimes the meaning of the question can change over time even if the precise words don't. For example, when the question "Do you expect the U.S. to be involved in another war within the next 5 years?" was asked in 1947, respondents took it to refer to another *world* war. Asked in 1992, it might be taken to refer as well to a limited war, like that in Korea or Vietnam or the Gulf. In addition, as will be seen at a few points in this study, even though the precise wording may not change, the question context may be altered enough to influence the results.

However, the chief problem for those who study trends in public opinion is a lack of usable data: the polling agencies frequently change their questions, thus rendering trend comparison dubious or impossible; or else they drop key questions entirely as their interests turn to other issues or to new aspects of an old one.

For example, during the 1950s the public was asked dozens of times if it expected World War III to erupt in the near future, but for some reason the question went out of fashion around 1963. Consequently, if one wants to explore how the Vietnam War affected the public's expectations of major war, one has precious little data to work with (see Mueller 1979).

One reason for the absence of good trend data in the polls, besides the pollsters' over-sensitivity to fashionable topics, derives from the fact that public opinion often does not vary much over time (see Page and Shapiro 1992, chap. 2). Since trend lines that do not fluctuate do not make interesting copy, there is little journalistic incentive to create a rich bank of trend data.

Table 266 gives an example of a question tapping attitudes toward internationalism and isolationism. As can be seen, there has not been a great deal of movement in the response to this question over the last half-century, and there were long periods, for example from 1948 to 1956, where it was close to stationary. That's a rather interesting observation, but one can't make too many eye-catching newspaper articles out of it. That is, one can hardly expect the media (who are among the polling agencies' chief clients) to buy a series of articles saying that there's again been no change in isolationism. Better to fill the questionnaires with questions about hotter, if more ephemeral, topics.

This imperturbability of opinion can be found on many topics and should not seem too surprising. After all, those who are essentially responding to the question in a random manner will be "consistent" in the aggregate over time. And those who are responding thoughtfully are likely to answer the same way as long as opinion leaders keep sending the same signals and as long as there are no major opinion-altering events.

Another reason there are often few good trend data available derives from the efforts of the survey organizations (including academic ones) always to "improve" the wording of their questions, to ask the question in a way that "gets at" the issue in the best possible way. As suggested earlier, finding the perfect question is essentially impossible—though efforts to minimize ambiguity and confusion in the questions are generally desirable.

Such "improvements" often undercut efforts at sound trend analysis. For example, if one wanted to trace public sentiment for withdrawal from Vietnam over the course of the war there, one would find that of the dozens of poll questions on that issue, none was repeated consistently enough to be used in trend analysis. The changes in wording were at once subtle and devastating—there are, as it happens, major differences between "withdraw gradually," "begin to withdraw," "withdraw completely," "withdraw immediately," and "withdraw as fast as possible" (see Mueller 1973, chap. 4).

During the crisis period leading up to the Gulf War, many questions were asked about various Gulf policy options—support or opposition for war or for continued reliance on sanctions. As discussed in chapters 2 and 3, the most remarkable aspect of public opinion during that period was that opinion changed very little, particularly during the interval between November 8, 1990, when Bush announced he was increasing troop levels in the Middle East, and January 16, 1991, when the war began—this despite the fact that there was at the same time a very substantial public debate over whether war or continued sanctions should be used to pressure Saddam Hussein out of Kuwait.

This posed the usual dilemma for pollsters seeking to come up with something that can be accepted as news by their journalistic clients. When opinion—rather unexpectedly, perhaps—didn't change very much, there were two methods for generating interesting copy. One was to change the questions all the time, hoping to come up with interesting and topical, if perhaps ephemeral, findings. The other was to stress time series that *did* happen to move. Gallup seems to have succumbed to the latter temptation in this case. Although the agency had asked seven questions that showed little or no opinion change between December and January (tables 8, 20, 34, 40, 57, 58, 76, 126B) and only one that did (table 79), the question that was given big play and portrayed on the cover of the January 1991 issue of *The Gallup Poll Monthly* was the one that did move (see also Mueller 1993a).

Comparisons of Subgroups

One can also validly compare how different subgroups of the population respond to the same question: old versus young, for example, or isolationists versus internationalists, or Democrats versus Republicans. One does not pronounce that a given percentage of the population "thinks" a certain way on the issue but rather, simply that men are more likely to support the issue than women, for example. A limited amount of this sort of analysis will be found in this book.[2]

In these cases the problem of question wording is not usually very important. If there are peculiarities in the question, they are generally the same for all subgroups and hence the bias is held constant.

It should not be assumed, however, that this kind of comparison eliminates the problem of question wording in all cases. Sometimes words in the questions will alter the comparative reactions of the subgroups. For example, a question on "policy X" may find Democrats and Republicans in a substantial degree of agreement. If the question instead asks about "the President's policy X," however, there may be a considerable polarization in the results. During the Vietnam War one was more likely to find a "generation gap" among the age groups if anti-war protesters were referred to as "young people demonstrating against the war" rather than as "demonstrators against the war." Sometimes a question can so simplify an issue in order to be clear to the unsophisticated that it loses all meaning for the sophisticated. And there is a tendency for some people to agree to rather folkloric bromides regardless of their content: the poorly educated may be particularly susceptible to this and consequently one might find them disproportionately inclined to agree *both* that "you should look before you leap" and that "he who hesitates is lost."

Comparisons of Differently Worded Questions

Finally, one can compare differently worded questions that happen to have been asked at the same time to see what sorts of words, cues, and images seem to have affected the response. For example, during the Korean War questions which asked about support for the war were fashioned in three different ways. The simplest question was, "Do you think the war has been worthwhile?" This gained a relatively low support score. A question that achieved support scores some 10 or 15 percentage points higher was, "Do you think the U.S. made a mistake in getting involved in the war?" And higher percentages yet were achieved by "Do you think the U.S. was right to send troops to stop the Communist invasion?" At the same time the words "to defend South Korea" did not notably boost support at all. Clearly, words suggesting support for governmental action actively affected the response, as did the suggestion that the war was anti-Communist in nature, and this phenomenon clearly has substantive implications (Mueller 1973, 44–48).[3]

In this example, questions with substantially different opinion cues in them were compared. It is not that one can casually toss any words into a question and significantly change the response. Generally, the changes must be substantial. On some issues, there may be quite a bit of flexibility—as in the questions about "forbidding" and "not allowing" speeches against democracy. On other issues it may be found that opinion is largely unalterable by wording changes—as, for example, in a 1941 study that posed substantially different questions about Hitler and found that opinion responses did not change much at all (Rugg 1941).

There is quite a bit of opportunity to compare differently worded questions in the poll data from the Gulf crisis because so many different polling agencies so frequently asked questions that tried to get at the same issues. Thus they fortuitously created a set of experiments that can be analyzed.

THE POLLS AND THE REASONABLE RESPONDENT

While this discussion should inspire a healthy skepticism toward those who claim that polls tap the "will of the people," it would be a mistake to be condescending or contemptuous of the respondents. Most people can function perfectly well and be entirely valuable members of society without spending a great deal of time thinking about, much less reaching reasoned conclusions about, issues other people choose to find of great significance.

Anyway, when complex issues are reduced to facile phrases, with all subtlety squeezed out, a random, or near-random, response to them may be as good as any: Is nuclear power a good thing? Are taxes too high? Do you trust the British? Do you support the UN? Is Congress doing a good job? Given all the horrors of human existence on display in this morning's newspaper, which one is the biggest problem facing the country today? Which do you like better, lightning or sand?

Furthermore, it is not at all clear that we should expect people to spend a lot of time worrying about political issues when they do, after all, have plenty of personal concerns to preoccupy them. I happen to be very interested in government and its processes and so, it seems reasonable to assume, are most readers of this book. But it verges on the arrogant to suggest that other people are somehow inadequate or derelict unless they share the same curious passion (on this issue, see Mueller 1992a, 1992b).

For all that, the responses to public opinion surveys generally make quite a bit of sense. As Benjamin Page and Robert Shapiro conclude in their extensive study of poll data, public opinion, seen collectively, is really quite "rational" in the sense that it is "real, stable, differentiated, consistent, coherent; reflective of basic values and beliefs; and responsive (in predictable and reasonable ways) to new information and changing circumstances" (1992, 172; see also Popkin 1991; Holsti 1992).

That is, by and large, poll data hang together rather well. Despite the fundamental social awkwardness, even absurdity, of the polling experience, people do not characteristically react erratically or incoherently. Instead, there is a certain reasonableness and usually even a kind of logic to their collective response. This will, I think, be obvious in the following analysis which seeks to ferret out, and to explain, patterns in the reaction of the American public to the Gulf War.

Part One ....

Opinion during the Approach to the War

CHRONOLOGY

1990 Jul 25	U.S. Ambassador April Glaspie meets with Saddam Hussein
1990 Aug 2	Iraqi forces invade Kuwait; UN Security Council condemns invasion; President Bush condemns Iraq's invasion as "naked aggression" and sends extra warships to the Gulf
1990 Aug 4	Japan joins U.S. and Europe in halting trade with Iraq; blockade begins
1990 Aug 5	Bush announces that Iraq's aggression "will not stand"
1990 Aug 6	UN imposes worldwide trade embargo; Iraq starts taking hostages
1990 Aug 7	Saudis request U.S. troops
1990 Aug 8	Bush announces that troops will be sent to Saudi Arabia
1990 Aug 8	Hussein proclaims annexation of Kuwait
1990 Aug 12	Bush orders naval blockade
1990 Aug 22	Bush calls up Reserve; hostages moved to Iraqi military sites to be used as "human shields"
1990 Aug 23	Hussein appears on television with a group of hostages
1990 Aug 25	UN approves the use of force to carry out embargo
1990 Aug 28	Iraq declares Kuwait to be its nineteenth province
1990 Sep 4	US naval forces intercept an Iraqi cargo ship in the Gulf of Oman, marking the first time that the U.S. Navy forcefully boards an Iraqi ship
1990 Sep 9	Bush and Soviet President Mikhail Gorbachev take tough stand against Hussein
1990 Sep 11	Bush asks Congress for support of his Persian Gulf policy in a nationally televised speech
1990 Sep 21	Iraq's Revolutionary Command Council says "there is not a single chance for any retreat" and promises "the mother of all battles"
1990 Sep 23	Hussein says he will destroy Israel and launch an all-out war before allowing the UN embargo to "strangle" Iraq
1990 Oct 8	Israeli police fire on Palestinians at Temple Mount
1990 Oct 20	Opponents of U.S. involvement in Gulf stage protests in at least fifteen American cities
1990 Oct 20	Bush breaks "read my lips" election pledge on taxes
1990 Oct 24	Budget agreement with Congress
1990 Nov 6	Congressional elections
1990 Nov 8	Bush announces troop increase to attain "adequate offensive military option"

1990 Nov 18   Iraq announces it will free all foreign hostages over a three-month period beginning Christmas Day unless it is attacked

1990 Nov 28   Congressional hearings on Gulf policy begin

1990 Nov 29   UN Security Council authorizes using force against Iraq, sets January 15 withdrawal deadline

1990 Nov 30   Bush proposes meetings between Iraq and U.S.

1990 Dec 6   Hussein releases all hostages in Iraq and Kuwait

1991 Jan 8   Bush asks for Congressional authorization to use force

1991 Jan 9   U.S.–Iraq talks in Geneva fail

1991 Jan 12   Congress approves use of force in Persian Gulf

1991 Jan 13   UN chiefs meet, unsuccessfully, with Saddam Hussein

THE APPROACH TO WAR:

Data

A large amount of public opinion data was generated during the period before the war, and because of its extent and diversity, analysis that seeks to make sense of it must of necessity also be extensive and diverse—some might even say tedious. This chapter is mostly devoted to a display of poll results from the prewar period, while chapter 3 draws conclusions about the relationship between policy and public opinion that derive from these data.

The chapter begins with an overview of the events of the prewar period, and then it supplies a summary of American public opinion trends and patterns during that time. The remainder of the chapter lays out and discusses these patterns in considerable detail. Some readers may decide, after reading the summary, to skim over the detail and head on to the next chapter. They could hardly be faulted.

APPROACH TO WAR: THE EVENTS OF AUGUST 1990–JANUARY 16, 1991

During 1990, Saddam Hussein, the president and resident dictator of Iraq, had become particularly annoyed with his neighbor country, Kuwait. Iraq was in desperate economic straits, and he argued that Kuwait should forgive a debt Iraq had incurred by fighting the mutual enemy, Iran, in an eight-year war that ended in 1988. He also claimed that Kuwait was stealing Iraqi oil by slant-drilling at the border, and he argued that Kuwait was violating agreements by over-producing oil and thus damagingly lowering the world price for a product vital to Iraq's well-being. To signal his anger, he moved troops to the border. In various meetings over the issue, Kuwait, urged on by British Prime Minister Margaret Thatcher, refused to budge, and Kuwait's Crown Prince and Prime Minister reportedly shouted in a meeting on August 1 that if the

Iraqis needed funds they should "send their wives out onto the street to earn money for them" (Simpson, 1991, 20, 107–8).

Iraq's invasion of oil-rich Kuwait the next day caught almost everyone by surprise, including the rulers in Kuwait and other countries in the Middle East—who had brushed off the troop buildup as a bluff (Woodward 1991a, 215–22). This act of war in an area of importance alarmed most world leaders, particularly Thatcher and American President George Bush, who saw it as a form of "naked aggression" comparable in its way to that of Adolf Hitler in the 1930s. To Thatcher it may have also resembled Argentina's 1982 invasion of the Falkland Islands, which led to a small-scale war with Britain that the British won handily, greatly boosting her sagging popularity as well as that of her party.[1]

Encouraged by Thatcher ("Remember, George, this is no time to go wobbly"), Bush led a determined international effort to impose a punishing economic blockade on Iraq, and the Americans and others sent warships to the area. Cooperating in this venture were not only the Western countries, but most Arab ones. Moreover, in the wake of the Cold War, which had been essentially resolved the year before, Iraq's former friend and ally, the Soviet Union, joined the boycott—something that took Hussein by surprise (Simpson 1991, 227). Hussein probably had no intention of further aggression (U.S. News 1992, 98; Hiro 1992, 120–22; Simpson 1991, 197), but, fearing a Western military response, he detained Westerners in Iraq and Kuwait as hostages against an attack by the threatening international coalition.

Then, after boldly announcing that Iraq's aggression "will not stand" and after drawing, as he put it, a "line in the sand," Bush sent emissaries to Saudi Arabia to convince its leaders that Iraq might attack their country as well. The Saudis were reluctant to have foreign troops stationed on their soil, and in launching his invasion Hussein probably counted on this reluctance, anticipating that it would prevent any significant foreign military response to his aggression. However, the Saudis allowed themselves to be persuaded, and the United States and several other nations were permitted to move troops to their country to deter an Iraqi incursion. They and other oil-producing states also agreed to increase their output to compensate for the shortfall in international oil supplies caused by the boycott of Iraq and occupied Kuwait. Meanwhile, Iraq annexed Kuwait as its nineteenth province and proclaimed that "there is not a single chance for retreat . . . this battle is going to become the mother of all battles" (Woodward 1991a, 297).

The situation in the Middle East continued to concern Americans, particularly because of the hostages, but it is important to note that in

October the public's attention shifted from matters in the Persian Gulf to disapproving outrage as Congress and the President engaged in a noisy battle over the budget. This was eventually resolved in a compromise in which Bush notably broke his repeated and dramatically emphasized election pledge, "Read my lips: no new taxes." Although this unseemingly battle fostered considerable hostility toward Washington, almost all incumbents were returned in the Congressional elections on November 6 (Alford and Hibbing 1992).

Because its economy depended so heavily on oil exports, Iraq was peculiarly vulnerable to an economic blockade. Indeed, in short order its economy had been fractured and its export income cut to almost nothing, making these sanctions far more punishing than any others ever imposed (Elliott, Hufbauer, and Schott 1990; Hufbauer, Schott, and Elliott 1990; Hufbauer and Elliott 1991). However, by October Bush had decided that the economic sanctions were not working fast enough. He apparently felt that public support for his venture in the Gulf would decline damagingly and, in addition, he came to believe that the coalition aligned against Iraq probably would eventually become unstuck, making the use of the military force to remove Iraq from Kuwait problematic (Sciolino 1991, 233; Woodward 1991a, 42). Moreover, if sanctions dragged on, observed a sympathetic columnist, "Bush would lose face, popularity, and reelectability" (Barnes 1991a, 11).

Accordingly, shortly after the Congressional elections Bush announced a change of policy: troop levels in the Middle East would be substantially increased in order to attain an "offensive military option." At the end of the month, Bush was able to sharpen the threat by getting the United Nations Security Council to authorize the use of force unless Iraq left Kuwait by January 15, 1991. A few days later, Bush offered to talk, but emphatically insisted there could be no compromise. Meanwhile, the American economy was entering a recession and consumer confidence was plummeting.

The primary goal of the buildup, apparently, was to scare Saddam Hussein out of Kuwait, and even at the end of the year Bush was telling reporters, "My gut says he will get out of there" (Muller and Stacks 1991, 33). Clearly, except for the fact that there would have been no actual test of arms, an excellent solution to the situation for Bush would have come about if Hussein, duly frightened and humiliated by the threat, had pathetically and ignominiously pulled his troops out of Kuwait. That would have been a bloodless triumph for Bush's will and for American arms, and Bush would have been greeted with great adulation.[2]

Bush's earlier policy in the Gulf had been strongly supported by the political leadership of both parties, but his unilateral November escalation, with its apparent rush to war before sanctions would be given a full chance to take effect, alarmed many, including many in the foreign policy establishment and almost the entire leadership of the Democratic party. Beginning in November, then, a debate arose over Gulf policy, and it became substantially partisan.

In early December, Hussein released all the hostages, in part, it appears, to swing Western public opinion in his favor (Karsh and Rautsi 1991, 238; Sciolino 1991, 241; Simpson 1991, 236). Hopes rose that effective negotiations might be possible, but efforts by various parties peacefully to resolve the crisis failed. "Initially," recalled one senior Administration official, "the Iraqis were interested in the offer of meetings, but when they realized we . . . wouldn't negotiate, they backed off" (Drew 1991, 85).

Throughout, Bush became emotionally absorbed, even obsessed, by the crisis (Woodward 1991a; Barnes 1991b) and felt he was being "tested by real fire" (Frost 1991a). And, to some, he seemed to yearn to have a war (Drew 1991, 83; Tucker and Hendrickson 1992, 91; Simpson 1991, 215–16). He insisted that there could be no deals: in his view, Hussein must withdraw unconditionally and ignominiously, suffering maximum humiliation for his aggression. This was expressed most concisely in what Robert Tucker and David Hendrickson call his "four nos": "No negotiations, no compromises, no attempts at face-saving, and no rewards for aggression" (1992, 91; also U.S. News 1992, 199–200; J. Smith 1992, 222; Drew 1991, 85).[3] There were also growing concerns that Iraq might be able to produce a crude atomic bomb, complicating the eventual use of force; and persistent reports about atrocities committed by Iraqi troops within Kuwait deeply outraged Bush (see Drew 1991; Woodward 1991a; and especially Frost 1991a; see also Solarz 1991, 21).[4] Reading reports of what was going on in occupied Kuwait, Bush labeled it "genocide" (Frost 1991a).

Military planners, meanwhile, were concluding that a war against Hussein's forces could easily be won or, as Bush put it, "we're going to kick his ass out" (Barnes 1991b, 9; Drew 1991, 83).[5] Worst case projections were for twenty thousand American casualties, including seven thousand dead, but some senior officers were confident that no more than one thousand Americans would die (Woodward 1991a, 349, 376). An influential supporter of war, House Armed Services Committee Chairman Les Aspin, a Democrat, publicly concluded that "prospects are high for a rapid victory" and suggested that American casualty rates would be between three thousand and five thousand, with five hundred to one thousand dead (Schmitt 1991; Moore 1991a). Although Bush did not get into the numbers game, he continually insisted that a war with Iraq would not be long and drawn out like Vietnam—that it would be, in logical consequences, short and decisive. And in a television interview a few weeks before the war, he expressed the hope that the war "would be over in a matter of days" (Frost 1991a).

The debate continued over whether force should be used after January 15 or whether sanctions would continue to be relied upon, and a Vietnam-style antiwar movement was growing across the country. The administration was of the opinion that the UN vote gave it sufficient authority to use force, and in November Bush had said that he did not want a Congressional vote on the issue unless he was going to receive a substantial vote in his favor (Woodward 1991a, 326). But in January the Democratic leadership in Congress announced a debate on a resolution, and Bush formally asked Congress to authorize him to use force after the deadline. A three-day debate in Congress led to a vote on January 12 authorizing the President to use force, and it was approved by a majority—a rather slim one in the Senate—that substantially followed party lines. From a strictly political standpoint, the vote was a tricky one since it depended on how the war came out. If the war was the walkover Aspin promised, a vote for it would be wise. If it proved to be a mess, as many feared, a vote against it was sensible.

Bush seems to have "stirred Saddam's Arab macho," as one senator put it (Drew 1991, 84). Hussein apparently became convinced that war was inevitable and that a humiliating backdown would be suicidal for him—or, as he put it, "The Iraqi people will not forgive me for unconditional withdrawal from Kuwait" (Freedman and Karsh 1993, 431; see also Viorst 1991a, 67–68; Sciolino 1991, 31; Karsh and Rautsi 1991, 240–41; Freedman and Karsh 1991, 9 n.; Simpson 1991, 17, 228, 231, 274). He may also have concluded from American statements that even if he withdrew his forces from Kuwait the sanctions would never be lifted until he was removed from office (Tucker and Hendrickson 1992, 89–90; Record 1993, 51–55). Accordingly, Hussein called Bush's bluff and refused to move his occupying troops. As James MacGregor Burns observed at the time, Bush "thought he could overpower Saddam psychologically, but it hasn't worked" (Apple 1991). There was a growing sense, too, of helpless fatalism in Washington—a feeling that the United States simply couldn't back down from the expensive and heightened troop commitment that had been unilaterally instituted by the President two months earlier.

Bush, meanwhile, was reported to be "serene" (Seib 1991a), "very composed" (Drew 1991, 88), and "pensive, subdued, preoccupied" (Barnes 1991b, 8). Unleashed now by Congress, he proclaimed that there would be a "great promise of a new world order" in victory (Frost 1991a), announced that "the world could wait no longer" (Bush 1991b, 312), and began the war on the moonless night of January 16, 1991, a few days before huge antiwar demonstrations were scheduled to take place in Washington.

PUBLIC OPINION BEFORE THE WAR: A SUMMARY

Politically, the approach to the Gulf War became particularly contentious; it was characterized by an extensive public debate, beginning in November and continuing until the brink of war in mid-January, that was notably partisan in nature. The public followed the issue quite closely and considered it an important one, though there was some decline of interest during the budget debate in October. The most remarkable aspect of public opinion during the period of debate is that, despite (or perhaps because of) the pointed, dramatic, and noisy discussion that took place, public attitudes toward the issue changed little.

The public rallied to Bush's support in August, but by October there was a notable change: a substantial increase in the number of people who thought involvement in the Gulf was a mistake and a similar decline in the number who supported Bush's policy there. However, after that, as the debate over policy escalated, there was little further change in these measures. Apparently, as the initial heady urgency of the issue faded, fair-weather supporters dropped off and support was maintained by a harder core. Bush's approval score—but not his foreign policy ratings—dropped considerably in October, mainly because of the acrimonious debate with Congress over the budget, but it recovered some in November, and it is likely that the distracting and impending war helped in this.

There was some decline in belief in the efficacy of sanctions, but questions dealing specifically with policy options—support or opposition for war or for continued reliance on sanctions—generally changed very little from the onset of the crisis in August to the initiation of war in January. There are data series which suggest something of a movement toward greater "hawkishness," but other data indicate something of a movement toward "dovishness," and there are considerable data to suggest that there was no change at all. Both hawkish and dovish options had adherents, and support for these options was maintained at fairly consistent levels. If there was a decline in the belief that sanctions could be effective, this disillusion did not, in general, translate into growing support for war. It may be, of course, that quite a few people were changing their minds; but if so, any movement from one side to the other was canceled out by people switching in the opposite direction. In general it seems likely that at any time—even on the eve of war—the public would have bought a reasonable, properly packaged settlement (including even the sort of negotiated compromise Bush held to be totally unacceptable) as an alternative to the initiation of military action.

Thus, although President Bush was leading the country to war, he was not notably successful at generating increased support for that option. Nor, however, were his opponents in the debate able to sway public opinion to their side.

In responding to the debate, the public was clearly gripped differently by different arguments. Comparatively, the public, like the President, was greatly concerned about Iraq's chemical and nuclear capacity and about Iraqi atrocities in Kuwait, and the notion of turning back aggression also enjoyed substantial support. Moreover, the public early on accepted Saddam Hussein as a demon (he scarcely needed the promotional efforts of Bush to achieve that status) and—more so than the administration—it began to see Hussein's removal as an important goal. On the other hand, the public was comparatively unmoved by the notion that it was important to fight for Middle East oil (though it saw that as a major reason the United States had become involved in the crisis) and by sympathy for the Kuwait government. Since the debate was substantially partisan in nature, the public tended to be similarly divided by party.

In three areas, however, there was notable change during the debate period. Because of the continuing uncertainties, presumably enhanced by the fear of war, there was a very considerable drop in consumer and business confidence. In addition, there seems to have been a decline in the number of people who expected the war to be a long one or to be like Vietnam. Finally, people increasingly came to see war as likely, even inevitable.

SUPPORT FOR INVOLVEMENT
AND FOR THE PRESIDENT

Support for involvement in the Gulf and for Bush's handling of the crisis declined between August and October. But thereafter, despite the post-election troop buildup, the UN vote and deadline, the release by Iraq of all hostages, various meetings with Iraqi leaders, a great deal of name-calling between Bush and Hussein, increasingly contentious controversy on the issue, and a major debate and war vote along partisan lines in Congress, these levels of support did not change much until war was initiated.

Support for Involvement in the Gulf

Support for the Gulf effort is measured with very general questions in tables 15–21 and 34–37 and in figure 1. Tables 15–21 supply the responses to questions asking about approval of the decision to send troops to the Middle East, and tables 34–37 variously asks whether involvement there was a mistake or the "right thing." As can be seen from tables 20 and 34, support was highest at the outset, in August and September.

It is possible to argue that support on these measures declined gradually over the course of the five-and-a-half month crisis, but closer inspection suggests, I think, that the decline largely bottomed out in mid-October and suffered little or no movement thereafter. The pattern in table 36—which covers only the October-January period and also shows no change—supports this conclusion. That is, from early highs, there was a decline of about 10 percentage points on these measures by October, after which support remained at much the same level until the war actually began in mid-January.

On these questions, it should be emphasized, there was little or no disagreement within the political establishment. Hawks and doves both found the basic American commitment to the area to be sound policy; the differences that emerged after Bush's November troop escalation came over whether war should be used to resolve the issue.

There are some question-wording patterns of interest in tables 15–21. People appear to have been quite a bit more willing to send troops "as a defense against Iraq" (table 20) and even more "to help defend Saudi Arabia" (table 16) than they were willing, less moderately, to send troops "to protect Saudi Arabia from Iraq" (table 17). The sizable jump in support between tables 15 and 16 seems to reflect something of what I once dubbed the "rally-round-the-flag" effect (Mueller 1970, 21), since the question in table 15 was asked before Bush's announcement of a major troop commitment and the one in table 16 was asked after it.

As can be seen by comparing the items in table 34 with those in tables 35 and 37, little difference was found when the question was put positively (did we do the right thing?) or negatively (did we make a mistake?). A similar comparison is possible with questions asked during the Korean and Vietnam Wars, and the same result is found (Mueller 1973, 44, 55).[6]

Support for Bush

Basically, the same pattern is found in questions that deal with Bush and his handling of the crisis. In polls conducted in the few days after the August invasion, quite a few people withheld judgment one way or the other when they were asked whether they supported the way Bush was handling the crisis. But after August 8, when Bush announced that troops would be sent to Saudi Arabia, the "no opinion" numbers dropped off quickly, and by mid-month the vast majority had rallied to his side and voiced approval (tables 8, 9; see also table 33A). Thereafter, as with the general questions asking about support for U.S. involvement in the Gulf in tables 20 and 34, these approval ratings declined by some 15 percentage points by mid-October and then rambled on at much the same level until Bush launched the war in January (tables 8–13, 33A), at which point they took a sizable rally-round-the-flag jump upward (tables 8, 9, 13, and fig. 2). (The high findings in the instant polls of January 9 and 13 in table 12 are discussed below.)

There is one wrinkle in this pattern. Table 20 suggests that there was no notable drop in support for the decision to send troops to the Gulf after Bush's announcement on November 8 that he planned a troop increase in order to attain an "adequate offensive military option." Similarly, tables 34 and 36 suggest that the announcement did not notably increase the numbers asserting that sending troops to the Gulf had been a mistake or holding that we should have stayed out. However, the November announcement, followed as it was by new concerns and criticisms coming from Democratic leaders, does seem initially to have caused support for the way Bush was handling the situation in the Gulf to decline by several percentage points (tables 8, 9, 10, and 12). Then, by December, probably helped by the UN vote of November 29, support levels had generally recovered to October levels (tables 8, 9, 12).[7]

On a related issue, table 98 traces the result of a question that asks whether Bush has been too quick to get military forces involved and insufficiently willing to try to reach diplomatic solutions. Not surprisingly, it finds that people were more inclined to see him as war-eager in mid-November after his troop escalation announcement, but this soon subsided to previous levels (after he said on November 30 that he would arrange for meetings with the Iraqis) and stayed there into January even as his policies were, in fact, leading the country to war.

Some element of complexity in these results is suggested when the questioners asked those who disapproved of Bush's handling of the situation *why* they did so (table 12). In mid-November it was found that those disapproving because they said they felt Bush was moving too *slowly* against Iraq outnumbered those who disapproved because they felt he was moving too quickly by 44 to 37. Immediately after the UN vote, however, when war seemed more likely, these percentages were reversed—although overall levels of support did not change between the two polls.[8] Despite this intriguing finding, the follow-up question was not repeated in later surveys.[9]

Bush's overall approval ratings, as determined by the Gallup Poll, are given in table 1 and figure 5. These do not trace exactly the same pattern as questions asking specifically about his policy in the Gulf; however, since the Gulf episode was considered important in his general evaluation, there is substantial resemblance.

At the outset of the crisis in early August, Bush's approval ratings jumped upward in a rally-round-the-flag effect. (By comparison, however, tables 197, 198, and 199 and fig. 6 demonstrate that there was no upward surge in the percentage satisfied with the way things were going in the country or holding that the country was on the right track.) This support level began to decline in September and it took a real nosedive in October, reaching its lowest level to date: 53 percent.[10] The October decline was not particularly due to disapproval of Bush's Gulf policy, since his ratings for handling the situation there did not decline nearly as much at the time (table 8). Rather, it stemmed from Bush's acrimonious budget fight with Congress that ended in a deal in which he prominently broke his no-tax pledge. Rather remarkably, by early November Bush's approval ratings had recovered nearly to their levels of July, before the Kuwait invasion (table 1; see also table 33G). As in tables 8, 9, 10, and 12, Bush's approval ratings in table 1 suggest there may have been something of a mid-November dropoff after his troop increase announcement, followed by a recovery again by early December and then rather steady ratings until he launched the war. It seems likely that he was substantially helped in this by his ability to shift attention back to the international crisis in the Gulf and to foreign policy in general. Foreign policy, as table 3A and figure 5 demonstrate, was an area in which Bush enjoyed his highest approval ratings throughout his presidency. And the limited data in tables 6 and 7 certainly suggest that he and his advisers were the repositories of a goodly amount of trust in this area.

The data in table 2 further indicate that Bush was able at the time to shrug off the effects of the "lip-reading" episode with considerable alacrity—and, again, the Gulf crisis must surely have helped in this development. At several points Gallup asked respondents to gauge Bush's sincerity, steadiness, intelligence, confidence, friendliness, strength, leadership quality, and activeness. His ratings on these measures were high in February 1990 because of his successful war on Panama that had taken place a few weeks earlier.[11] (For a comparison of the impact of the Gulf and Panama Wars on public opinion, see chapter 5.) Between February and July, paralleling a decline in Bush's popularity (see table 1), there had been a drop in most of these evaluative measures but, despite the October tax/budget flurry, Bush had suffered no further notable decline when the questions were again asked in November. (Later, the war was to push these ratings skyward.)

THE GULF CRISIS AS AN ISSUE

Somewhat similar patterns are found in various questions asking people about how important they considered the Gulf affair to be and how closely they were following it: a decline from the high levels of August took place in October, and this was followed by a revival after Bush's troop escalation announcement in November. Meanwhile, self-professed understanding of the issue declined after the announcement, but then revived.

Importance

Tables 45, 33E, and 33F and figure 3 furnish the results for repeated questions asking what the respondent feels to be the most important problem facing the country today. In July, the greatest concern had been with the federal government's enormous budget deficit and with the drug problem, but the Gulf crisis quickly distracted attention and immediately became the most important problem (table 45).

Despite the ongoing concern about the issue and about the hostages being held by Iraq, however, the deficit again regained top honors in October during the fight between Congress and the President over the budget. Similarly, a poll conducted from October 23 to November 15 asked not for the single most important problem, as in table 45, but rather for "the two or three biggest problems facing the country today." Only 11 percent mentioned the Middle East on that survey, while 8 percent mentioned oil or energy problems. By contrast, 30 percent named the budget deficit, 30 percent named drug abuse, 18 percent named dissatisfaction with government, 16 percent named crime, and 13 percent named poverty (Rielly 1991, 11).

By late November, however, the Gulf had again clearly taken over first place, and it held that position into the war.

Table 45 also supplies data from earlier periods that put these results in broader context. As can be seen, while the Gulf affair certainly was considered a major problem, it never managed to generate as much concern by this measure as had inflation, drugs, unemployment, or the fear of war at various points in earlier years.

Attention

People were strongly inclined to say they followed the crisis closely throughout the period (tables 46 and fig. 3). Once again, however, there was a noticeable, if less than precipitous, decline in interest in October as attention was distracted by the budget fight (see also table 331). Press attention, not surprisingly, followed a similar trajectory, with a large decline of coverage in October and a resurrection in November when Bush forcefully brought the issue back to center stage (table 48 and fig. 3).

Unlike the importance measure (table 45), these indices are not competitive or comparative—it would be possible for people to continue to follow the issue closely and for the press to report heavily on it even if other concerns also surge into view.

By the time the war came about, people, it seems, were really on edge. A few days before the war began, 22 percent of the public said they thought about the crisis in the Gulf every few minutes, and another 27 percent said they did so at least once an hour. Only 10 percent were so blasé as to claim they thought about it at most once a day (table 47; see also table 46).

Understanding

The Gulf issue, it seems, was quite easy for people to understand. Some 70 or 75 percent regularly said they had a "clear idea" why American troops had been sent to Saudi Arabia (tables 49 and 50 and fig. 3). By contrast, in the midst of war in Vietnam, in 1967, a similar question found only 48 percent expressing such clarity about what American troops were fighting for in that country (Mueller 1973, 63). Even more remarkably, in June 1942—six months after Pearl Harbor—only 53 percent of the people said they had a clear idea of what World War II was about, though that percentage rose toward the 70 percent level shortly thereafter (Cantril and Strunk 1951, 1078; Cantril 1967, 48).

Bush's November announcement about troop increases brought something of a decrease in the number professing an understanding of

American involvement (tables 49 and 50), but by December, that dip had been corrected (table 50 and fig. 3). Similarly, the percentage believing Bush had adequately explained why the United States had sent troops (always lower than the percentage professing a "clear idea" about the issue) dropped in November (table 22), but rose again later (tables 22, 23).[12]

SUPPORT FOR WAR IN THE GULF

Since the United States is a democracy and since it propelled itself into war in January 1991 after a great deal of talk, discussion, and argument over the issue, it would be reasonable to expect that people moved gradually into the "hawk" category over the course of the debate, thus allowing the war to take place. As it happens, however—although there are some polling data to support such a conclusion—for the most part there was little change in the degree to which popular opinion supported the idea of initiating a war in the Gulf during the entire prewar period from August 1990 to January 1991.

Question Wording

Throughout, there was a central concern over the number of Americans who favored war. If the United States went to war, the politicians—particularly those in Congress who were to vote on the issue on January 12, 1991—wanted to know if opinion was behind them.

The polls tried to supply the answer, but essentially it was a hopeless enterprise. As suggested in chapter 1, because of the problem of question wording, polls are simply incapable of measuring with any degree of precision how many people think one way or the other about an issue. Attitudes toward going to war are certainly no exception to this generalization.

For example, a *Washington Post* report at the end of December 1990 concluded at one point that "Persian Gulf hawks currently outnumber doves by better than 2-to-1." This conclusion was based, it said, on "a computer analysis of the public's response to eight key questions." Later in the same article, however, it pointed out that "depending on how questions are framed, support for a hard line can be depressed to the 40 or 50 percent range or increased to 70 or 80 percent" (Morin and Dionne 1990).[13] Actually, it was possible to generate an even wider range of responses.

To start, one might look at the results from two quite general questions posed throughout the period which are documented in tables 40 and 52. The first asks, rather blandly and simply, whether a war in the Mideast would be worth it or not; the second (one of those used in the *Post* analysis) asks if all action necessary, including military force, should be used to get Iraq out of Kuwait. At any point in the approach to war, one could use them either to show that the public was evenly split over whether the United States ought to go to war in the Middle East, or that war enjoyed a substantial advantage. The difference, of course, is in the question wording. The question in table 40 uses the mind-concentrating word "war" and generates comparatively low levels of support for that option. At the same time, the question in table 52 merely asks about the "use of military force" and seems to suggest that it would only be used if all else fails; accordingly, it inspires much greater support.

Meanwhile, those who want to believe that the American public *opposed* war could latch onto table 53 or 54. While the question in table 40 merely asks rather abstractly if it is worth going to a war over the situation in the Mideast, the question in table 53 puts the issue more bluntly—Should the United States go to war or not?—and generates notably lower levels of support (see, similarly, table 57). The question in table 54 gives a specific option to war and uses the more dynamic phrase, "initiate a war," rather than "go to war." Accordingly, it generates even less support for war.

Related questions in tables 54, 53, 126B, and 52 were all asked in mid-November and can be compared. One might conclude from this array of results that at the time these polls were conducted, 28 percent of the population was willing to initiate war, 38 percent was willing to go to war, 46 percent was willing to engage in combat, and 65 percent was willing to use military force—that is, one could as easily argue that doves outnumbered hawks by two to one as the reverse. The question array does not really allow for such precise comparisons, but the dilemma is clear.

In another comparison, table 55 presents the results from a question similar to the one in table 52 except that it asks about "war" rather than "the use of military force." Both questions were asked on the same survey at the end of November; 4 percent of those who had agreed to the use of military force only a few seconds earlier demurred when the question was asked again with the phrase "go to war" (rather vaguely "at some point") inserted. Similarly, table 56 supplies the results of a survey in which 45 percent said they considered forcing Iraq to withdraw to be "worth going to war over," while a survey conducted at the same time (table 52) found 65 percent willing to "use military force" to accomplish the same objective.

Trends

While the polls cannot tell us with any sort of definitiveness how many people supported or opposed war, they can be used productively to trace trends. However differently worded, the questions in tables 40 and 52 do try to get at the same concern. As can be seen, neither moved much at all. One might argue from the Gallup data in table 40 (see also fig. 4) that war support increased a bit after the UN vote on November 29, but after that there was a retreat to levels attained earlier—and no further change even in a poll taken just a few days before the war began in January. From table 52 one might conclude that there was a rise of pro-war sentiment in January as the country moved toward war but, even so, this increase only brought the war support percentage back to levels attained in August and September from lows attained between mid-November and early December. Moreover, as will be discussed shortly, the January 9 and 13 numbers are probably high because of some peculiarities of the polling process: they betray a hawkish bias found on instant, overnight polls in some instances.

In contrast to the data in tables 40 and 52, some data do suggest a rise in support for war.

Table 126B documents the results attained from a question asked over the entire prewar period. The question inspired about the same results between August and November, but there was an apparent 10 percentage point rise in war support by early December and a further rise of 5 or 6 points in January. It is not very easy to reconcile this pattern with the one found in table 52. In both cases the questions are rather similar: neither mentions the word "war," though the lower levels consistently found by the question in table 126B probably derive from its use of the more threatening phrase "engage in combat" instead of the blander "the use of military force" if "necessary." The trend in the question in table 126B, however, may reflect a context effect (see Schuman 1992). When the question was asked before December, it was embedded in a sequence; its more hawkish results in December and January may have been due to the fact that the question was asked on its own and hence in a different context. This is perhaps also suggested when the results are compared to those obtained by the question in table 52 asked at the same time: the table 126B results from August, October, and November find less war willingness by 20 or 25 percentage points than the table 52 results, while those from December and January are in contexts more like those in table 52 and obtain results that differ from them by less than 10 points.[14] (I know this is tedious stuff, but it's not my fault Gallup changed the question format.)

The question in table 57 also shows some movement. Asked in mid-November, 37 percent favored war if the Gulf situation did not change by January. In the wake of the November 29 UN vote establishing a specific January 15 deadline, support for war rose significantly by this measure—to 53 percent. Some questions (table 52, for example) show a decline in war support in mid-November and then a return to earlier levels later. It is possible something like this happened with the question in table 57, but there are no data from earlier periods to test this suspicion. The impact of the UN vote is also suggested in a comparison of tables 57 and 58. They are worded quite similarly, except that one specifically mentions the UN vote, and it registers around 10 percent higher support for war. Most interestingly, however, neither question undergoes further change during all the debates, disputes, and fulminations of December and January.

Other data also suggest something of a UN impact—though it may not have lasted too long. To begin with, people voiced substantial support for the UN decision (tables 62, 64). Then, a comparison of the data in tables 60 and 61—which seem to document a bit of upward creep in the (basically consensual) belief that the United States should "attack militarily" if the economic embargo failed—with that in the first item in table 63 (which mentions the UN vote) suggests the UN vote may have boosted support for war by 9 percentage points. The December questions, moreover, use the dramatic word "war" (albeit vaguely "at some point after January 15"), and thus may be harder to agree with. However, when the table 63 question was again asked a few days later, on December 9, support declined a bit.

Some of the data in table 63 suggest that a fairly notable rise in war support took place in January as the country moved toward military conflict with Iraq. Specifically, the data from the polls of January 9 and 13 reach unprecedented highs on this question.[15] These highs, however, seem to reflect the fact that these were single-evening surveys conducted in the immediate aftermath of failed talks: the ones between foreign ministers James Baker and Tariq Aziz on January 9 and between UN Secretary General Javier Perez de Cuellar and Saddam Hussein on January 13. Other surveys in the field at the same time but not focused on instant reaction obtain results 7 to 9 percentage points lower. As shown in the second part of table 63, the surveys of January 9 and 13 also obtained substantial upward bumps in the percentages wanting the war to take place immediately after the deadline, while the results of other surveys are scarcely different on this dimension from ones achieved in December. Similarly, these two surveys found a considerable bolt upward in the percentages feeling the United States was going to get involved in a war with Iraq (table 231). There are also upward hawkish bumps on these polls alone for approval of the President's Gulf policies (table 12) and, apparently, for support for the use of military force in the Gulf (table 52).[16]

It seems reasonable to infer from these results that events like failed peace talks, which were heavily reported, recent, and disappointing, caused a temporary surge of outrage hawkishness that was essentially ephemeral. It may also be, however, that the sampling peculiarities of the overnight poll—and of the people who can be contacted under such circumstances—contributed to this variability. Whatever the explanation, caution in interpreting overnight polls seems to be in order. With improvements in telephone polling, it is now possible to assess the public's instant reaction to dramatic events, and the journalistic appeal of such data is undeniable. But the numbers these polls generate may substantially distort trends and even imply bogus ones. (See also Mueller 1993a.)

Other data instructive on these matters are provided in table 33. Between August 22 and the end of December 1990, the Wirthlin Group asked a set of questions about the Gulf situation on a daily basis.[17] One question asks for agreement with the statement, "Given everything that has happened, the U.S. is justified in launching an attack against Iraq to drive them out of Kuwait" (table 33D). Agreement with this question might be considered mildly hawkish, though many of those opposed to war might be quite willing to agree as well. At any rate, it shows little change over the course of the period, though its last reading at the end of December is comparatively high. Respondents on these surveys were also asked whether they thought that "The death of American soldiers in a fight with Iraq is too high a price to pay in this Persian Gulf conflict" (table 33C). There was not a great deal of movement in this either, but there may have been a modest increase in agreement with this quite dovish proposition across the period.

Finally, the Wirthlin respondents were also asked whether they thought "the actions the U.S. has taken so far in the Persian Gulf" had been "too tough, not tough enough, or just about right" (table 33B). The data certainly suggest there was no notable increase in the demand for tougher actions. Indeed, between August and November, when the Bush administration was deciding to take tougher actions, the percentage advocating such action actually declined some 15 percentage points or more. Then between November and the end of the year, after the administration had actually taken tougher actions and as it was gearing up for—and trying to build support for—very tough actions indeed, there was little further change in this measure.

Generally, then, poll data on these issues suggest that there was no clear trend one way or the other in the willingness of the American public to go to war during the approach to war in the Gulf.

SUPPORT FOR WAR COMPARED TO SUPPORT FOR SANCTIONS

Except for the question in table 54, all the questions examined in the previous section simply asked the respondent whether the United States should go to war or not. As the debate evolved after Bush's decision in early November to attain "an adequate offensive military option," however, the issue was not whether the United States should go to war, but whether economic sanctions remained a viable alternative to war for obtaining the same result.

Before the escalation, Gallup asked respondents several times between August and early November to choose among three options (table 66): whether the United States should "begin to withdraw," continue present troop levels, or increase troop levels in order "to force Iraq to leave Kuwait." Those supporting the maintenance of present troop levels declined a bit during that period, but the option that gained supporters was not the hawkish one but the "begin to withdraw" option. This may suggest a growing frustration with policy in the Gulf, but it could also reflect the not unreasonable notion that, since the troops had been sent to Saudi Arabia expressly to deter an Iraqi attack, one could now begin safely to reduce their numbers because it had become abundantly clear by November that Iraq was not about to launch a wider war.

Tables 67, 68, and 72 suggest a decline in confidence in the perceived efficacy of sanctions between August and October—though, most interestingly, they don't reveal much further erosion after Bush's November announcement about large troop increases. At the same time, table 74 suggests that between September and October people became *less* willing to use force even if sanctions were found not to work. Table 75 suggests a substantial willingness to keep troops in the area for "years," though later data in a different context (see table 70) suggest less patience.

Tables 76–88 present the results of a set of questions asked at the same points in time during the big debate period of mid-November to mid-January. In various ways, each counterpoises the option of war with the option of sanctions.

The formulation of the nonwar options in the question in table 76 is quite stark. People are asked if they want to withdraw U.S. troops from the area (not "begin to withdraw" as in table 66) or rely on sanctions forever—"no mater how long it takes." Alternatively, they can choose to "initiate a war"—a strong formulation that is, however, substantially softened by the provision that it would be done only "if Iraq does not change its position within the next several months" and by the wistful promise that the war will "draw matters to a close." According to this question there was an erosion of support for sanctions (or at least for endless sanctions) of several percentage points during the month of January—something that appears in part to be corroborated by the question in table 77 which also asks about letting sanctions run on "no matter how long it takes." Additionally, table 78 suggests that frustration over sanctions rose 7 points during November.

The questions in tables 76 and 77 do not really capture the essence of the political debate of the time, however, because war opponents did not favor maintaining sanctions "no matter how long it takes," but rather proposed giving them more time to take effect. Table 79 is better in this respect, although the hawk option is fairly easy to accept because it does not use the word "war" but merely suggests that the time may have come to "take stronger action against Saddam Hussein," including "the use of armed force." In this series there was a substantial decline in support for sanctions, but it occurs between December and January, not in January as in table 76.[18]

Then there is table 80, which also juxtaposes a wait for sanctions to "work" with an option to "start military actions." In contrast to the data in tables 76, 77, and 79, this question shows no change of opinion whatever between December and the initiation of war in mid-January.

Finally, tables 82–88 display a set of somewhat similar questions asked during December and January in which sanctions are variously contrasted with war, attack, and military action. Like the question in table 80, all remind the respondent of the January 15 deadline. And, like that series, it does not appear that one can make out much of a trend one way or the other.

Table 89 is added because it vividly shows the impact of explicitly mentioning the sanctions option. It furnishes the results of a question that was asked at the same time (and apparently on the same poll) as the question in table 83.[19] In table 89, 54 percent of the population support "the U.S. going to war" when sanctions were not mentioned, while in table 83 only 46 percent are willing even to "take military action" when the sanctions option was furnished.

The results of this rather inelegant exercise could be taken to suggest that there was a growing frustration with sanctions and perhaps also that, consequently, a shift of several percentage points from sanctions toward war took place. However, the evidence, particularly for the latter proposition, is tenuous and there is quite a bit of data to suggest that during the whole course of the public and Congressional debate over the relative value and wisdom of sanctions and war, there was no notable shift of opinion at all.

SUPPORT FOR COMPROMISE AND NEGOTIATION

During the approach to war, there were few official voices calling for compromise. Bush adamantly and repeatedly rejected any deals or negotiations that might somehow be taken to reward Iraq for its aggression. To encourage Iraq to leave Kuwait, he was unwilling to consider agreeing even to something as mild as a post-withdrawal Mideast conference that would be unlikely to result in much of anything except empty and quickly forgotten atmospherics. For the most part, his political opponents favored continued reliance on sanctions essentially as a functional equivalent of war, and they were scarcely more open than Bush to cutting deals with Hussein.

However, although no political leader made much of a play for compromise, there seems to have been considerable potential for leadership on this issue. The results of several questions about compromise are tallied in table 103–109 and 90.

The issue was put most starkly in early November: Do you want to start a war, or would you rather compromise with Saddam Hussein? Given that unpleasant choice, most people responded that they liked the sound of compromise (table 103).

When people were asked more specifically if they were willing to give part of Kuwait to Iraq to get it to withdraw, most responded negatively (tables 104, 105). But on the eve of armed conflict in January—even as Congress was voting for war—most people said they were willing to give Iraq a piece of Kuwait to end the crisis if the Kuwaitis agreed, which presumably is the only way it could have happened (table 108). Moreover, a poll in December found most people quite willing to say that giving Iraq "some concessions" was a preferable alternative to using "military force" (table 106).

Table 109 documents the results of a question asked in those two ABC/*Washington Post* single-evening surveys that were conducted immediately after the breakdowns of last-ditch talks—one between Baker and Aziz on January 9, the other between UN chiefs and Saddam Hussein on January 13. Despite the fact that these recent disappointing experiences understandably caused optimism about diplomacy to plummet (table 110), despite the fact that most people said they trusted Bush and his advisors to make the right decision about war (table 6), and despite the fact that the question specifically pointed out not only that Bush opposed any concessions to Iraq, including a Mideast conference, but also that such a concession would "reward Iraqi aggression"—despite all this, most people said they supported just such concessions to prevent war.[20]

These same surveys included other questions about negotiations. Most people said they thought the United States had done enough to seek a diplomatic solution (table 99)—though a different wording of the question (compare table 98) would have pushed this percentage much lower. Nevertheless, the percentage feeling this way actually *declined* between January 9 and 13 (table 99), while the percentage favoring additional talks increased (table 101). Moreover, the percentage willing to link an Iraqi withdrawal from Kuwait with an Israeli withdrawal from the West Bank and Gaza *increased* a bit between December and January (table 107).

Finally, table 90 furnishes the results of a question from the 1990 National Election Study which was in the field during the debate period. The respondents were given a four-part choice concerning policy options. It included a hawkish option that was worded quite mildly: "take tougher military action" (nothing about "war" or "combat"). It also proffered the mildly aggressive "tighten the economic embargo." Yet even when presented with such attractively assertive options, by far the most popular option selected was "try harder to find a diplomatic solution."

Thus it seems that the public could readily have been persuaded to accept compromise over war.

THE REASONS WHY

From time to time the polling agencies asked people why they thought the United States had become involved in the Gulf conflict. More frequently, they tried to discover what reasons people found most persuasive for initiating war against Iraq. It is difficult to sort out trends on these issues because the questions were so often changed, but a few patterns do emerge. As it happens, the two sets of reasons differed in notable ways. Oil loomed large in their explanations about American involvement, but not in their reasons for supporting war.

Reasons the United States Became Involved in the Gulf

One August poll listed five reasons for sending American troops to the Gulf and allowed respondents to select more than one (table 111). Two towered over the others: "To protect our oil supplies" and "To show that countries cannot get away with aggression." Tables 112–120 juxtapose oil with the anti-aggression principle and various other arguments for involvement in the Gulf. In that company, the oil argument is always strong and usually dominant, though table 120 might perhaps be taken to suggest (compared to table 114) that it had faded somewhat by the time of the January war debate in Congress.

Goals in the Gulf

Rather than asking why the United States was in the Gulf, a number of questions asked why the United States *should* be there and what its goals ought to be. A set of queries in August (tables 121 and 122) finds the public willing to accept a whole host of reasons. Most notably, when asked as in table 122, the goal of freeing hostages received easily the most support. In table 123 that goal is juxtaposed with others, and it clearly dominates, both in August and when posed again in mid-November.

Table 124 documents the results from a September query which asked about eleven goals (not including the hostage issue, however). Again, all are quite popular, with relatively weak support for the goals of promoting democracy in the Middle East and for punishing Iraq for the invasion. The goal of "returning the Kuwaiti royal family to govern Kuwait"—a formulation that puts the proposition quite negatively—receives the least support. As can be seen in table 122, that notion is more acceptable if it is framed as "restoring the former government of Kuwait," but it still does comparative poorly as a goal.

The respondents were then forced to pick one of these eleven goals as the most important and also to indicate the one they felt most motivated Bush (table 125). The results of this exercise seem to presage some of the problems Bush was to find in the postwar period. In this list (which, again, does not include an item about freeing hostages), the most popular goals concern neither oil nor aggression nor driving Iraq out of Kuwait. Rather, they call for removing Hussein from power and for producing a lasting peace in the Middle East—precisely the two things the war failed to accomplish. Meanwhile, the notion of punishing

Iraq for its aggression, something the war *did* achieve in huge measure, was picked as the most preferred goal by only one percent. Interestingly, despite Bush's many protestations about confronting aggression, people most commonly suggested that his primary goal, unlike theirs, was to preserve the free flow of oil.

Reasons for Initiating a War

Another set of questions asked not about U.S. "goals," but more specifically about what might be an acceptable reason to go to war.

People may have thought oil was a major reason impelling the United States (and Bush) into the Gulf, but it was not a popular reason for war. In August a couple of polls asked about reasons to go to war, and they juxtaposed the oil argument with the dealing-with-aggressors argument. The latter strongly dominated (tables 127–130).

Although Bush frequently used the can't-let-aggressors-get-away-with-it argument in speeches and discussions about the Gulf crisis and upcoming war, the polling agencies only rarely asked people about this rather central argument as a justification for war after August. The November comparison of table 127 and 129 is one instance, and it continues to show that the aggression theme strongly dominated the oil one, with little change from August.

The same mid-November poll also contained a lengthy sequence of questions about what might justify a "major war" or "limited military involvement" (table 131), but the anti-aggression theme was not included in the list. Of the notions that were asked about, the protection of oil and the restoration of the Kuwait government scored weakest as justifications for "major war." The most popular reasons for war were protecting American hostages, removing Hussein, and destroying Iraq's nuclear and chemical facilities. Tables 133 and 134, reporting questions from November and December, generate similar results: people found oil issues and the restoration of the Kuwait government to be far less compelling reasons to go to war than doing something about Hussein's chemical and nuclear capability. Something similar was found during the wars in Korea and Vietnam. Support for the war was boosted when the respondent was reminded in the question that the war was designed to stop the Communists, but the notion of defending South Korea or South Vietnam had no such impact (Mueller 1973, 44, 58, 100).

Bush often expressed his deep emotional concern over the brutalities committed by the Iraqi occupiers in Kuwait. The January data in table 135 indicate he was far from alone. As usual the weakest reasons for war related to oil and to the restoration of the Kuwait government.

Tables 126 and 136 present some data in which people were asked for circumstances which might provoke them to favor military action. Table 126 finds Americans very willing to go to war if American citizens were killed in Kuwait or Iraq, and overwhelmingly so if the Iraqis were to attack U.S. forces.

Unusually, table 126 finds comparatively high numbers of people willing to engage in combat for oil: specifically, if "Iraq begins to control or cut off oil." It may be that the rather extreme notion of cutting off oil impels this response, or else it may be because the question was asked so early: on August 9 and 10. At any rate, table 136 reports poll results from 10 or 25 days later that find far less support for taking military action if the price of gasoline skyrockets or even if oil shortages threaten an economic recession. (A decline in the appeal of the oil argument is also suggested in table 123.) These polls find strongest support for military action if Saudi Arabia (and hence American troops) were to be attacked or if hostages were to be harmed.

The bank of questions in table 136 was repeated in December, but the wording was crucially changed. Instead of asking whether the United States should take "military action," the question now wanted to know whether the United States should "go to war." This more dramatic presentation of the issue dropped measured support for belligerent action in all categories, and generally by some 10 to 20 percentage points. By and large, however, the same issues inspired, or failed to inspire, support.

During the autumn of 1990, the Kuwait government spent quite a bit of money trying to influence American public opinion in a favorable direction. They hired a public relations firm which sought to publicize the plight of Kuwaitis under the rule of the Iraqi invaders, to spread stories about atrocities (see Sciolino 1991, 217; MacArthur 1992a; MacArthur 1992b, chap. 2), and to bolster the reputation of Kuwait and its government. As indicated, the restoration of the Emir of Kuwait to his throne was one of the most weakly supported reasons for war. There is very fragmentary evidence, however, to suggest that the notion of liberating Kuwait and restoring its government gained a bit in acceptability in the late fall of 1990 (tables 133A and 137). At any rate, there is no evidence that war opponents who were seeking to discredit Kuwait for its undemocratic political and social policies were having an effect.

Assessing the Popularity of Saddam Hussein

In the course of the debate over war, Bush repeatedly characterized Saddam Hussein as the Western equivalent of the Great Satan: he was worse than Hitler, Bush suggested (Freedman and Karsh 1993, 462 n.). Within the United States Bush was preaching to the choir: from the start of the crisis, Hussein's mean rating on a scale from 0 to 100 was less than 10 and it held at the abysmal level for the rest of the year (in most polls his median rating was zero) with a very slight (and very temporary) improvement after he released the hostages in December (table 33H). Table 138 also suggests that Saddam had been pretty well accepted as a demon at least as early as late August.

Hussein was surely George Bush's secret weapon in bringing about the war: with an enemy like that, Bush scarcely needed friends. Indeed, as far as American public opinion was concerned, Hussein's only adept accomplishment during the whole crisis period was his consummate portrayal of the demon role. One of his early efforts to gain favor with the Western public was to appear on television with a group of extremely uncomfortable hostages—or "guests," as he called them. The event, it seems, was singularly counterproductive with the American public (table 139). As noted earlier, he apparently hoped his release of the hostages in December would make Americans less willing to go to war with him. In this, he was 18 percent correct: that proportion of the public said the gesture did make them less willing. However, another 18 percent said that the removal of the hostage problem made them *more* willing to support military action against him (table 140). Bush's reaction was similar: "When you don't have Americans there and if force is required—that's just one less worry I've got" (Bush 1991c, 1773; on this issue, see also Tucker and Hendrickson 1992, 107–10).

While the substantially self-induced demonization of Saddam Hussein may have helped Bush to sell the war, it was also to pose a dilemma for the American president. Bush sometimes suggested or implied that the removal of Hussein was an American war aim (see Tucker and Hendrickson 1992, 77, 90, 194). However, the policy of the United States and of the UN was to limit the war objectives to driving the Iraqis out of Kuwait and, if it came to war, to destroying Iraq's chemical and nuclear capability and rendering it militarily incapable of repeating its aggression. The public, however, came to believe that the ouster of Saddam Hussein should be a major war goal. This was seen quite neatly in tables 124 and 125 from September. It is also clear in table 131 from November when almost as many people said they felt the removal of Saddam was worth a "major war" as said that about protecting hostages or destroying Iraq's chemical and nuclear capability. Table 186, from the same poll, also boded poorly for a limited strategy: 51 percent of the public (up from 37 in August) said it would not consider a war against

Iraq to be a victory unless Saddam Hussein's government were overthrown. As is seen in chapters 5 and 7, this issue was to haunt Bush in the postwar period.

Curiously, while the American public accepted Saddam as a demon and felt that removing him should be a top goal, questions specifically asking in various ways if the United States ought to try to assassinate him find far less than overwhelming support (tables 146–149). Particularly impressive in this regard are the results in table 147: most people said they would consider an assassination to be wrong even if it ended the crisis quickly. During the war, with American lives directly at stake, the assassination of Hussein still did not notably gain in popularity (table 149), nor did it after the war (table 173). The deliberate cold-blooded assassination of foreign leaders, even demonic ones, does not appear to be a policy that plays well with the American public.

Conclusions

Overall, then, the arguments that seem to have most forcefully moved people to support war were concerns about American hostages and about Iraq's chemical and nuclear capacity. In addition, the public strongly accepted the notion that aggression could not be allowed to stand. There were also, it seems, concerns about atrocities going on in Kuwait, while going to war to eject Iraq from Kuwait enjoyed a reasonable amount of support, and efforts to demonize Saddam found very fertile ground indeed. On the other hand, comparatively few people were moved by arguments concerning the protection of oil supplies or by the idea of restoring the Kuwait government.

Thus, those who opposed war were wise to use the slogan, "No blood for oil," and their efforts to heap contempt upon the Kuwait government were likely to find a responsive audience. Over the course of the debate, it does seem that the appeal of the oil argument declined somewhat, but the notion of restoring the government of Kuwait did not; and anyway, it was quite possible for people to agree about oil and about the Kuwait government and still support war for other reasons. War advocates soon found that out.

SOURCES OF SUPPORT AND OPPOSITION TO WAR

There were several notable differences among groups on the way they related to the Gulf issue.

The polls on the Gulf War found that women were notably less likely to support war than men. This finding is nothing new: women were also less supportive of the Vietnam and Korean Wars—and, for that matter, of World War II (see Mueller 1973, 146–47). In some respects the persistence of the "gender gap" is surprising. After Vietnam, women entered the male work world in great numbers and, by some measures, they have become more like men: relatively speaking, they smoke more, commit more crime, use fouler language, and now suffer more from heart disease. But, interestingly, their attitudes toward war do not seem to have changed to become more like those of men. To use old-fashioned terminology, women seem to have become liberated without losing their femininity in this respect.

Polls also show blacks to be more dovish than whites. This difference was also found during the Vietnam War, and some have been led to conclude that it was inspired by Martin Luther King, Jr., and the civil rights movement of the 1960s. Data on black attitudes found in polls conducted before the 1960s should be used only with great care because the agencies did not do a very good job of sampling blacks. But the available data strongly suggest that the differences between the races on war issues presumably go much deeper into the historical black experience: they are found in polls from both Korea and World War II (Mueller 1973, 147–48).

One particularly important demographic difference, which is discussed more fully later, has to do with political party. Because the wars in Korea and Vietnam were begun under Democratic administrations, Democrats tended to support them more than Republicans did. The Gulf situation was begun and engineered by a Republican president, and Republicans, accordingly, are found to be much more supportive of his war-anticipating policies than Democrats. The party difference is far wider than the difference between self-identified liberals and conservatives, and it apparently increased after Bush's controversial escalation announcement in November (Wilcox, Ferrarra, and Allsop 1991).[21]

AREAS OF OPINION CHANGE

Thus far it has been found that, in general, there were few clear, unambiguous changes in public opinion over the course of the prewar period from August 1990 to the middle of January. People did not become consistently more hawkish or dovish, more war-eager or war-averse, or more or less supportive of Bush or his policies. And their perceptions of the reasons behind involvement and the reasons for going to war apparently did not change very much either. The chief exception to this generalization comes from tables 8, 9, 10, 11, 12, 13, 20, and 34, where it is found that questions asking about general support for Mideast involvement and for Bush's policy there declined between August and October or so—and then remained rather constant thereafter.

There were clear signs of change on a few other measures, however. The crisis brought about and sustained a drop in satisfaction with the way the country was going, and there was a related and notable decline in consumer confidence. At the same time, there was growth in the beliefs that a war in the Gulf would be brief and that war was inevitable.

Satisfaction with the Country, Consumer Confidence

During the fall of 1990, the degree to which Americans expressed satisfaction with the way "things are going" reached—and remained at— the lowest levels attained for the better part of a decade (table 197). The slump began by late September, and it hit bottom in October. The drop reflected not so much Gulf policies as disgust with the noisy, acrimonious haggling between the President and Congress over the budget. But the relevant point for present purposes is that satisfaction levels remained at these low levels until the beginning of the Gulf War in January.

A similar phenomenon was traced by various questions asking whether the country was on the right or wrong track. Tables 198 and 199 and figure 6 display an extensive series going back to 1971. By October the percentage willing to say things were going in the right direction had dropped to less than 20 percent, lower than at any time since the Watergate scandal of the early 1970s and among the lowest ever recorded. As with the data in table 197, dissatisfaction remained low throughout the remainder of the period up until the war, though there was a slight rise late in 1990.

Correspondingly, the country suffered a precipitous loss in economic confidence. By October people had become notably more likely to tell Gallup that they felt they were financially worse off than a year earlier (table 200) and that they anticipated they would be worse off a year hence (table 201). The data in these tables—particularly table 201— suggest there may have been a bit of a revival in confidence in the December 13–16 poll at a time when war, it seemed, might be averted because Iraq had only days before released its hostages (something similar may be suggested in table 199). In January, however, as war loomed, these levels slumped again to October levels.

The standard measures of consumer confidence tell a related, but somewhat different story. The consumer confidence indices of both the

University of Michigan (table 202) and the Conference Board (table 203 and fig. 7) dropped sharply in August when Iraq invaded Kuwait. By contrast, the satisfaction, "right track," and Gallup financial measures in tables 197–201 show little change at that time. But like those measures, the consumer confidence indices reached low levels in the fall and held them until the onset of the war.

Anticipations of What War Would Be Like

Questions asked in August, November, and January suggest, not very surprisingly, that overwhelmingly the American public (presumably including most of those who opposed military action) expected the United States to emerge victorious in a war (tables 215–217). That confidence, already high, rose even further between November and the eve of war in January (table 216). But many said they feared that victory might be achieved only after a long war with "many casualties" (table 217).

Several polls variously asked about fears that the country might be in the process of becoming involved in another Vietnam "situation" (tables 218–222). Many expressed that fear, especially after Bush's November announcement about attaining an offensive option (tables 220, 221)—though the concern seems to have subsided considerably by the time war was begun in January (table 220).

Questions of a more specific nature were also asked about how long the war might last and about how many casualties Americans were likely to suffer. The responses suggest that few people really had the Vietnam War—which lasted several years and in which Americans suffered hundreds of thousands of casualties—in mind (tables 223–228 and fig. 4). Apparently, the realities of the situation got through, as did Bush's repeated insistence; "In our country, I know that there are fears of another Vietnam. Let me assure you, should military action be required, this will not be another Vietnam. This will not be a protracted, drawn-out war" (Thomas 1990, 25; also Frost 1991a). Nonetheless, there seems to have been considerable concern that the war would be quite substantial—lasting months and costing thousands of casualties. As usual, the options offered could influence the response considerably. Table 223 gives the respondents a choice only between "a few weeks or months" and "a year or more," and a substantial minority picked the longer of these options. By contrast, the data in table 224 (comparing the October or January figures) suggest that something like a third of these were willing to defect if the option of "several months" was offered.

There is a causal problem in assessing the meaning of these data.

Many people may have opposed war because they felt it would be long and costly, but many of those opposed to war were probably inclined, precisely because of their opposition, to be sympathetic to the supportive notion that the war would be long and costly. And many of those who favored war may have been inclined for that reason to be dismissive of its costs. Thus, in January 1991, a *Washington Post* News Poll found that 74 percent of those who thought it would be "a relatively short war, lasting a few weeks or months" supported going to war when asked the question in table 63, while only 38 percent of those thinking it would last longer than that were so disposed (Morin 1991a). A *New York Times*/CBS News Poll at the time found that 64 percent of those who expected the war to last a few weeks favored starting military actions when asked the question in table 80, as compared to 48 percent of those who expected it to last several months and 30 percent of those who anticipated a war of a year or longer. Similarly, the poll found that 62 percent of those who expected one thousand Americans to die in the war favored military action, as compared to 56 percent of those who anticipated one thousand to five thousand deaths, and 41 percent of those expecting over five thousand dead (Rosenthal 1991a).

This phenomenon is hardly new. In the many years of debate over nuclear policy, for example, there was a tendency for those who were most opposed to the bomb to emphasize, and to exaggerate, its destructiveness. Similarly, after World War I war opponents often anticipated that the next war would bring the end of civilization (see Mueller 1991b, 17–19; Clarke 1966, 167–76).

The data in table 92 are also of interest. Those who favored a military attack on Iraq were asked if they would still support such military action if various levels of casualties might be suffered. It was found that support for war was more than cut in half if it was posited that one thousand U.S. soldiers would be killed or wounded, to less than a third if ten thousand might become casualties, and to less than a quarter if thirty thousand casualties were anticipated. Unusually, the poll also asked about *Iraqi* casualties, and one might extrapolate from the comparative results that support for a war in which a hundred thousand (or more) Iraqis were killed or wounded was about the same as for one in which five thousand Americans became casualties. That is, in the view of the U.S. public, one American life is worth at least twenty Iraqi lives.

Table 93 documents a similar question asked in early January which finds a comparable, though less dramatic, dropoff in support when casualty estimates are posited. Of the 63 percent in the January 4–6 poll who said they support the war, only 70 percent still held that view if it is suggested that one thousand Americans will die and only 55 percent if that number is raised to ten thousand. Table 94 repeats the same basic process as in table 93 except that it applies an experimental approach: instead of asking war supporters sequentially whether they would still support the war if one thousand or ten thousand troops were to die, it divides the sample into thirds and asks for war support in three different ways: without any battle death estimates, with a death rate of one thousand, and with one of ten thousand. Comparing the results to those found in the January 4–6 poll (table 93), the experimental approach finds a smaller dropoff of support: 13 rather than 30 percent of war supporters drop off at the one thousand level, and 38 rather than 45 percent drop off at the ten thousand level.

Casualty numbers undoubtedly mean different things depending on how they are put to the respondent. The notable dropoff in war support as casualty estimates go up is clear in all cases (table 95 furnishes related results from a question asked just after the war had begun). But the response to the numbers themselves depends on how they are framed and presented. It seems likely that people do not respond in any precise way to numbers like 1000 or 10,000: few have a very good feel for what those numbers might mean. This can also be seen by comparing the two sets of follow-up data in table 93. The second finds that 61 percent of hawks remain supportive when it is posited that ten thousand American troops would die; but only 55 percent continue to be supportive at that level if they are asked first about how they would feel if one thousand were to die.[22] But all the data suggest that people can be expected to react to the pain of increasing costs by losing enthusiasm for the war.

The data supply only limited information about trends. Table 223 suggests that fears a war might last more than a year increased a bit between August and October, but both table 223 and table 224 as well as table 220 indicate that those fears declined between October and January as Bush and others promulgated confident predictions that the war would not be long and dragged out like Vietnam (see also fig. 4). With respect to U.S. casualties, on the other hand, the data in table 226 could be taken, perhaps, to suggest that between October and January people became somewhat more concerned that these might number in the thousands rather than in the hundreds.

The Rising Sense of the Likelihood of War

Over the course of the prewar period, a notable change took place in American opinion that seems partially relevant to the oncoming Gulf War: as the debate wore on, and as the United States and Iraq battered each other with invective and jockeyed for position, the public may not have come to view war as more desirable, but it increasingly came to see war as likely, even inevitable. Tables 229–235 and figure 4 supply data.

The trend was not linear. Expectations about the likelihood of war seem to have grown from August to November (found in tables 229, 231, and 232, but not in table 230). Rather surprisingly, it is not at all clear that Bush's escalation announcement on November 8 increased this: tables 229 and 231 suggest people did not become much more likely to anticipate war than they had been in early November, before the announcement. It's possible the UN vote on November 29 boosted war fears a bit (table 231), but they then dropped back approximately to mid-October levels after Hussein released all hostages on December 6 (tables 229, 231, 232, 234, 235). However, war fears had risen again to new highs by the end of December (table 230) and early January (tables 229, 231, 232), and they continued to rise dramatically during that month (tables 229, 230, 231, 232).

Question wording, as usual, made a big difference. Looking at the October figures, for example, it could be concluded from table 229 or 231 that people overwhelmingly felt a war likely at that time. But when the question asked not whether war was likely but whether war or a peaceful resolution was more likely, most people said they expected peace (tables 232 and 233). All questions, however, followed the same general trend patterns toward an increasing belief that war was likely.

Clearly, if people come to think war is inevitable, their resistance to having it happen will diminish, particularly if, as discussed in the previous section, they think their side will be victorious and if they think the costs are likely to be modest. Although the polls never seem to have asked it this way, the sense increasingly came to be, "Let's get it over with." The somewhat unsatisfactory data in table 91 suggest there was real growth in this attitude between August and January. The implications of this are discussed more fully in the next chapter.

3

With the array of public opinion data from the prewar period on display in the previous chapter, it is time to assess the process by which the United States went to war in the Gulf. In addition, this chapter compares the process to that by which the United States went to war against Japan and Germany in 1941 and in Vietnam in 1965.

GEORGE BUSH'S TASK AS LEADER

Data from surveys conducted in the 1980s furnish some rough, rather hypothetical, indication of the opinion atmosphere in which Iraq's invasion of Kuwait took place. In general, these data suggest that Bush had his work cut out for him if he was going to lead the country to war to deal with Iraq's invasion of Kuwait.

In one 1988 survey, respondents were asked what they felt was the strongest action the United States should take if Iran—very much a demon county at the time—were to invade Saudi Arabia. Only 18 percent were willing to go so far as to send American troops to assist Saudi Arabia. Some 34 percent thought the United States should stay out of the conflict entirely, 25 percent were willing to apply diplomatic and political pressure against Iran, and 17 percent would send military supplies and aid to the invaded Saudis. A question on another 1988 survey posited a scenario in which "Iran invades Saudi Arabia to gain control of Persian Gulf oil supplies and Saudi Arabia says it cannot stop Iran without the help of U.S. troops." In this case, 49 percent accepted the somewhat bland notion that "we should be prepared to commit our military strength" (nothing about actually fighting), while 37 percent opted for the only other alternative offered, concluding that such a venture "is not worth the cost in money and lives" (Wittkopf 1990,

49

231–32; Hinckley 1992, 109). A survey conducted in 1986 found only 26 percent favoring "the use of U.S. troops" if "Iran invaded Saudi Arabia" even though 77 percent said on the same survey that they thought the United States had "a vital interest" there (Rielly 1987, 17, 32; Wittkopf 1990, 247–48). Another question posed in late 1988 is instructive. It asked about various lessons one might draw about the war in Vietnam. Of those offered for evaluation, the lesson that was most popular—accepted by over 70 percent, most of whom said they agreed strongly—proposed that the United States "should not send troops to defend an ally that is not supported by its own people" (Wittkopf 1990, 230).

Thus, the American people do not seem to have been notably predisposed to go to war even if a large demonic country like Iran invaded a very important oil-producing state like Saudi Arabia. Their innate enthusiasm for war if a somewhat smaller demonic country like Iraq were to invade a far less important oil-producing state like Kuwait could be expected to be even lower.

Also going against Bush was his apparently quite limited capacity to persuade. In October 1990, Bush tried to sell his domestic budget plan and went on television, pushing it with all his might. The effort was a singular failure, and it was not unreasonable to anticipate that he would have at least as much difficulty selling war to a public that was hardly eager for armed conflict against what was constantly being billed as the world's fourth largest army.

Bush's achievement, accordingly, is all the more remarkable. His threats never sufficiently frightened Saddam Hussein, but they did alarm the American public, and at the time it seemed to me and others that Bush would have great difficulty pulling a war off (Mueller 1990b; Schneider 1990). Yet the great nonpersuader managed to do just that.

CENTRAL ELEMENTS IN THE PROCESS OF GOING TO WAR

In approaching the issue of war with Iraq, six decision concerns seem central: (1) trust in the leadership, (2) the importance of the issue, (3) the benefits of war, (4) the costs of war, (5) the alternatives to war, and (6) fatalism about war.

Trust in the Leadership

Whatever his rhetorical inadequacies and whatever his policy shifts on domestic and economic issues, Bush did have some advantages in the area of foreign affairs. The limited data available suggest that he (and his advisers) enjoyed a considerable amount of trust on the issue at hand: the decision to go to war (table 6).

Some of this is inherent, presumably, in the position of the presidency, designated in the Constitution to be the institution in charge of foreign affairs. But Bush seems to have enjoyed special trust beyond this. During the year and half of his presidency before the Gulf crisis took place, enormous changes had taken place in world affairs, and almost all of these were extremely favorable to the American position. It may be a matter of debate whether Bush had much to do with the dismemberment of the Cold War and of the historic enmity between the United States and the Soviet Union, but he presumably picked up some popular credit for this extraordinarily beneficial development.

At any rate, before the crisis with Iraq took place his ratings on handling foreign policy and for handling the situations in East Europe and Soviet Union were quite high—certainly far higher than his ratings for handling economic problems (table 3). Indeed, before the crisis his foreign policy ratings were about the same as his approval ratings in general (compare table 1), while his economic ratings were quite a bit lower, and this perhaps suggests people were principally using foreign policy to evaluate him. (After the Gulf War, as will be seen, this was to change, with consequent damage to his re-election prospects.) Moreover, while his ratings for handling economic conditions and his presidential approval ratings dropped notably during the budget fight of October 1990 (tables 3B, 1), his ratings for foreign policy and for handling relations with the Soviet Union suffered no decline at all (table 3A, 3E).

In addition, he had pulled off a war with Panama in which he captured an apparent Latin American drug king and brought him to trial in the United States. From the standpoint of most Americans, that venture had gone well.

The Importance of the Issue

At the outset of the crisis in early August, George Bush became convinced that the issue presented by Saddam Hussein's invasion of Kuwait was of paramount importance. He constantly compared it to the situation in the 1930s when adept policy might have prevented one of the most cataclysmic events in history, World War II. As one of his aides observed, Bush was "totally into World War II analogies" (Barnes 1991b).

Throughout, he became deeply committed to—even obsessed by—the crisis. As a White House official put it to a sympathetic journalist,

"Who would have predicted Bush would act like this after a career of compromise? Bush went nuts. It's amazing" (Barnes 1991c, 17). In *The Commanders*, which details the observations of White House intimates in the approach to war, journalist Bob Woodward repeatedly uses language of a related sort: Bush was "betraying the traits of a cornered man," Bush became "emotional," Bush was "deeply, even emotionally, concerned," Bush made a "personal and emotional declaration," Bush was "personally moved," Bush displayed an "obvious emotional attachment," Bush was "visibly riled up," "tension showing in the muscles of his neck," Bush "became very emotional," Bush "was stiff" and his "eyes looked scary" (Woodward 1991a, 229, 255, 260, 298, 302, 317, 318, 337, 350). Elizabeth's Drew's informants use similar language. Bush "is unlike he is on any other issue. . . . Usually he sees the complexities, and doesn't care all that much. . . . But this touches some deep inner core." A senator told her, reluctantly, "We all know instinctively this is not a strong man. It's greatly disturbing. I try not to think about it. I don't know anyone who's honest with himself who doesn't think this." And a congressman said "a good many people" were concerned about Bush's "obsession" with Iraq, his "fixation" on it, "to the exclusion of everything else" (Drew 1991, 82–83; see also Barnes 1991b). Drew suggests there is reason to conclude Bush "was spoiling for a fight with Saddam Hussein for some time," and that he "was proving something to himself and the world—showing what a tough guy he is" (1991, 83).

Bush's rhetoric became very more passionate on the issue. By December he was insisting that standing up to Iraq's aggression promised "a much more peaceful world. . . . It's that big. It's that important. Nothing like this since World War II. Nothing of this moral importance since World War II." And he willingly agreed to the suggestion that in this crisis he was being "tested by fire" (Frost 1991a). Then in launching the war he announced that "We have before us the opportunity to forge for ourselves and for future generations a new world order, a world where the rule of law, not the law of the jungle, governs the conduct of nations," and he suggested, further, that "what we're doing is going to chart the future of the world for the next hundred years" (Bush 1991b).

One could certainly dispute such extreme assessments. For example, Edward Luttwak argued during the pre-war debate that the chief issues in the post–Cold War era were "geoeconomic" rather than "geopolitical," and that the events in the Persian Gulf were a "mere sideshow" (1990, 316). In a postwar analysis, Robert Tucker and David Hendrickson come to the same conclusion (1992, 1). Moreover, as is discussed more fully in chapter 8, insofar as the Gulf was vital to U.S. interests, it could be argued that the problems both of oil and of countering aggression had essentially been handled long before the war every took place since oil was plentiful and since Iraq's aggression had been contained with military encirclement and punished with devastating economic sanctions. And of course, with the benefit of hindsight, it hardly appears that the strenuous American effort in the Persian Gulf brought peace to the Middle East, established an effective new world order, or charted a great deal of history. Nonetheless, although a few of Bush's domestic political opponents considered his assessment of the importance of the Gulf situation to be substantially inflated, most of them agreed that the challenge thrown down by Iraq was an important one that had to be forcefully and directly met.

It seems reasonable to suggest that Bush's emotional state helped him to bring off the war: the sense of drive and determination that resulted from his mindset may have worked to his benefit as a leader as it became transmitted to the American public, which, as suggested in table 45, seems, generally to have accepted his assessment of the importance of the issue. And if an issue is important, it is worth taking some risks over.

It is noteworthy in this regard, however, that in the pre-war period the issue never became as overwhelmingly important to the public as other problems—drugs, nuclear war, unemployment, inflation—had been at times in the past or as the problematic economy would be in 1992. Moreover, it does not seem that the public was demanding that the issue remain at the top of the agenda; interest in and attention to the issue flagged somewhat in October despite the fact that American hostages were still being held. Bush forced it back to the top of the agenda more by actions than by words: by his troop escalation and war brinkmanship (see also Krauthammer 1991).

That is, with the oil and aggression issues essentially under control, Bush could have left the issue on the back burner, focusing attention on other matters, and the public would have followed him, perhaps in relief, as the threat of war subsided. This would have been particularly easy after Hussein released the hostages in early December. A policy like this would probably have required accepting the gradual dismemberment of Kuwait along with that of the Iraqi economy, but the public does not seem to have been eager to push on to war.

However, Bush was apparently driven by the issue, and his presidential actions guaranteed that the issue would continue to be, or at any rate to seem to be, important.

The Benefits of War

From the beginning there was little dispute about the benefits of victory against Iraq: oil would flow freely to the thirsty nations of the world, an innocent country would be liberated from atrocity and hostile occupation, peace would be re-established in the Middle East (at least for a while), a potential nuclear threat would be nipped in the bud, aggression would be countered, and an exasperating, demonic thug and his large, threatening army would get his/its butt thoroughly kicked.

As is discussed more fully in later chapters, the problem as it developed for Bush was that the case became too good, that in a sense he was too effective at selling the war and at personalizing the issue: the public came to see the removal of Hussein from office as a central war aim. However, the dilemma was probably built in. From the beginning, Hussein did a truly masterful job of playing the monster role for the American public. His truculent, defiant language helped to establish this image and so did the atrocities committed by his troops in Kuwait. But his treatment of American hostages, the polls suggest, was enough by itself to generate massive contempt and loathing within the American public. This had also happened in the 1980s when Americans reacted with intense antipathy to Khomeini's Iran. However, Khomeini had hordes of zealots visibly working to do his deeds—including the capture of American hostages in 1979. In the Iraq case, the situation was even more personalized since to a considerable extent Saddam Hussein was directly, even solely, responsible for the misdeeds of his regime.

Thus, when Bush launched his war in January, declaring that "Our goal is not the conquest of Iraq. It is the liberation of Kuwait" (1991b, 313), much of the public was well ahead of him. The American people may not particularly have lusted after the conquest and occupation of Iraq, and they seem to have been quite amenable to a negotiated settlement that would avoid war. But if they were going to go to war, they wanted at least to have the benefit and the satisfaction of experiencing the richly deserved and substantially overdue demise of Saddam Hussein.

The Costs of War

Although official opinion generally concluded that a war with Iraq could easily be won and at quite a low cost, there were no guarantees. War is an extremely uncertain business, and, as discussed more fully in chapter 7, it was not difficult to imagine scenarios in which substantial numbers of Americans would be killed. Indeed, before the war one general, perhaps in part to dampen overconfidence, anonymously told the *Washington Post*, "Many, many people are going to die. And it's important for people to understand that it's not inconceivable we could lose" (Achenbach 1991).

Much of the outcome depended on the skill and determination with which the Iraqis would fight—something that no one, including the Iraqis themselves, could be sure about. There were plenty of reasons to expect that the enemy might not fight very well. Egyptian President Hosni Mubarak had a very low opinion of the Iraqi fighting ability based on his experience with them in the 1973 Arab-Israeli War, and Bush seems to have been impressed by his prediction that a war against the Iraqis would be a "pushover" (Aspin 1991, 11; Woodward 1991a, 360). But some analysts, including the Defense Intelligence Agency's Walter Lang, who had been just about the only person to predict the Iraq invasion in August, anticipated that a war with Iraq would be long and difficult (Woodward 1991a, 216–17, 360). In December, General Schwarzkopf had predicted that the Iraqis would put up a "tough fight" and that the war could last as long as six months (U.S. New 1992, 190). And a study conducted by the U.S. Army War College of Iraq's conduct in its recent war with Iran concluded that Iraq is "formidable" and "superb" on the defense (Pelletiere and Johnson 1991, ix, 61; see also Morrison 1991).

Potentially, the costs even of a highly successful war could be significant. In November 1990, defense analyst Luttwak developed a best-case scenario that in many respects closely resembled the war that was to take place two months later: an extremely effective air offensive; an "elegant" ground offensive, with equipment that works "perfectly," that avoids frontal assault while sweeping around the enemy's flank; and a demoralized enemy largely bent on surrender and incapable of mounting a counteroffensive. By his calculation, in such a "perfect operation" the offensive would still suffer casualties from mines and unexploded munitions, brief fire fights, various accidents, and the remaining Iraqi equipment. Under those conditions Luttwak estimated American losses at "several thousand killed in action or permanently maimed" (1990, 318).[1]

As noted in chapter 2, while official worst-case estimates were for twenty thousand casualties (Schwarzkopf 1991b, 349), the general expectation was that American casualties would number only a few thousand—interestingly, not much different from the estimates Luttwak came up with for his "elegant" and "perfect" case.

Not surprisingly, the American public reflected the prewar opinion of the experts. It clearly expected victory, and while there was no consensus that the war would be a walkover, the general anticipation, despite some fears that the war could become "another Vietnam," was that it would be far shorter and less costly than the earlier conflict. And it may well be that some of those who said they expected the war to run a year or more or to have large numbers of casualties were opponents of the war who were exaggerating their fears for the purpose of advocacy. Finally, during the course of the debate from November to January, there was a notable diminution in the numbers who anticipated that the war would be a long one.

The Alternatives to War

Thus, the public seems generally to have accepted three notions propagated by its President. First, it accepted the idea that the Gulf affair was important and worth taking risks for. Second, it accepted the idea that a war to resolve the crisis would bring substantial benefits—including the elimination of Saddam Hussein, a goal that went beyond the explicit plans of Bush. Third, it accepted the idea that the cost of the war would probably be bearable—and far lower than in Vietnam.

In selling war as a policy, Bush's chief problem was that there was an alternative method which promised to achieve most of the war's benefits at potentially far lower cost, particularly in American lives. Moreover, this point of view was advocated by many important opinion leaders, including almost the entire leadership of the Democratic party.

From November 1990 until the war began in January 1991, the alternatives of war and sanctions were substantially debated. The public's doubts as to whether sanctions would ever work may have increased over the course of the debate, but the urge to go to war did not, and the comparative attraction of sanctions and war did not notably change. Moreover, there seems to have been a considerable willingness to accept a negotiated settlement—even one with substantial concessions—as a way out of the crisis. The result of the debate, therefore, was essentially a standoff.

Fatalism about War

The opinion dynamic that probably helped Bush most was a growing fatalism about war—as time went by the public became increasingly convinced not that war was particularly wise, but that it was inevitable. In that sense, the public was willing to be led to war: for many, the attitude was, "Let's get it over with."

This sense of helpless fatalism was reflected in official thinking as well.

It was commonly argued that the United States simply couldn't back down from the expensive and heightened troop commitment that had been unilaterally instituted by the President two months earlier. Former Secretary of State Henry Kissinger argued that a pullback "would lead to a collapse of American credibility, not only in that area but in most parts of the world," and a war opponent, Admiral William Crowe, concluded, "The decision to augment our forces in Arabia has made it difficult if not impossible to sustain our forces there for a long time" (Peters 1991). War advocate Les Aspin also voiced his concern that there would be a great "loss of credibility" if the United States were to switch policy: "The Administration has brought the coalition along a time line that will bring the crisis to a head on January 15. Walking the Administration back from this policy could spell failure in this crisis. It could send a dangerous message to Saddam Hussein." Moreover, argued Aspin—though without much detail—a backdown could "make war more, not less, likely." But he also seems darkly to have feared that it might make *peace* more likely by leading to an "'Arab solution' or deal brokered by a third party" that would be "unlikely to be to the United States' liking" (1990, 13, 15; see also Sciolino 1991, 234; Dannreuther 1991/92, 39).

The notion that the country was somehow trapped by Bush's "time line" was also expressed on a television news show a day after the Congressional vote. Conservative commentator George Will, after noting "how wrong it was for the President to misdefine this interest as vital, to run up the deployment after November 8th to the point where the deployment itself became the policy," said he supported the resolution even though he thought a war would be "disastrous." Then newsman Sam Donaldson said he would have voted the same way even though he did not believe "we ought to have a war for this purpose," and moderator David Brinkley, who felt "this is not a war we should be in," said he supported the resolution because "we have been on the scene and we can't vote to undercut them" (ABC News 1991). This is even reflected in war opponent Luttwak's testimony as early as November. He argued, "the option of protracted sanctions is now closed. To wait with 200,000 troops or so would have been feasible. To wait with 400,000 and more is quite impossible." And he concluded, therefore, that "war may thus be unavoidable unless Saddam Hussein capitulates" (1990, 325).

Thus many people accepted that the logic of the situation, put into effect unilaterally by Bush in November, somehow demanded that he begin war. The notion that he could simply back down from an overextended position was not commonly seen as an alternative. Bush's chief ally in bringing about the war, Saddam Hussein, apparently also became increasingly convinced that war was inevitable,[2] and war came about. To a considerable extent, it was war by mutual self-entrapment.

However, it should not be concluded that the public would brook no backdown. Even on the brink of war the public was by no means averse to war-avoiding deals, and it could at least as readily be led away from war as it could be led into it. Indeed, in the past it had often followed presidents who had decided to retreat from overextended positions: when Ronald Reagan withdrew policing U.S. troops from Lebanon in 1983 after hundreds of them had been killed by a terrorist, few objected; and the public greeted the collapse of American policy in Vietnam in 1975 with remarkable equanimity (see Mueller 1984b).

TIMING AND THE DEMOCRATS

Overall, then, Bush did not get war because he was able to swing public (or Congressional) opinion toward war—though, conceivably, he was able to arrest a deterioration of support for war. Rather, he managed to lead the country to war because, as President, he was able to keep the issue brewing as an important one; because he could unilaterally commit the country to a path that dramatically increased a sense of fatalism about war and perhaps convinced many that there was no honorable alternative to war; because he could credibly promise a short, beneficial, and relatively painless war; because he and his top aides enjoyed a fair amount of trust in matters of foreign policy at the time; and because Saddam Hussein played the role of a villain with such consummate skill.

The lessons of the episode suggest, then, that a great deal lies in the President's ability to deploy troops and thus to commit the country's honor and destiny. With such moves he can make an issue important and convey a compelling sense of obligation and, in particular, of entrapment and inevitability. Buffeted between the maneuverings of Bush and Hussein, the country, it seems, somehow became increasingly convinced that it was entrapped, and it allowed itself to be led to war.

However, despite such fatalism, there were strong forces in opposition, and war was by no means predestined or inevitable. Indeed, in some important respects, it was a close call.

The move toward war was a sort of duel between the President and his war-opposing, sanctions-preferring opponents, and it lasted up to the initiation of hostilities. In the end, war finally came down to a matter of timing—which in politics, as in comedy, can be everything. Essentially, Bush was able to pull off the war before the opposition could fully get its act together.

In debating the vote for war in the UN, the Bush administration had sought to impose a deadline of January 1 for Iraq to withdraw from Kuwait. The less impatient Soviets, however, suggested January 31, and a compromise of January 15 eventually emerged (Sciolino 1991, 239). The difference of a few days may have been crucial.

Unlike the situation in 1964–65 before the Vietnam War (but partly because of the example of the later Vietnam period), a substantial public antiwar movement was launched in the fall of 1990. Encouraged by many Democrats, it put together protest demonstrations, culminating in marches in Washington in January that were larger than most seen in the Vietnam era. The January 1 deadline came in the midst of a vacation period for colleges (which is where most protesters come from) and would have been hopeless for the protest movement. The January 15 date was only slightly better—and when the big protests, planned weeks earlier, took place in Washington on January 19 and 26, the war was already on. According to police estimates, the January 19 protest (dominated by left-wing groups) drew a crowd of twenty-five thousand, while that of January 26 (much more moderate in tone) drew seventy-five thousand—quite significant numbers, considering their anticlimactic timing (Walsh and Valentine 1991). Held in the heady early days of a successful war, neither drew many establishment politicians as speakers. If the Soviet date had been accepted, the Congressional debate might have been later, and the protests would have been more organized and effective.

It seems to me that much of the antiwar protest in Vietnam, particularly in the first three years of the war, was ineffective, even counterproductive (see Mueller 1973, 164–65; Mueller 1984b; 1991a; but see also Small 1988). A January 1991 protest on the Gulf, however, would have been more like the Vietnam protests after 1968 (during the Nixon administration) when the antiwar movement achieved enhanced impact and respectability because it was now championed by the Democratic party. Furthermore, any protest before the war began could not as readily (and as effectively) be charged with undercutting our heroic troops. It seems quite possible that this combination of factors could have turned enough votes—mainly Democratic ones—in Congress to tip the vote against war, making it far more difficult for Bush to initiate war. The UN debate about the deadline was thus perhaps doubly significant.

It is possible, however, that Bush would have gone to war even without a favorable vote in Congress. He and his advisers held at the time that they did not need Congressional authority to go to war and, in an interview conducted a year after the successful war, Bush told Hugh Sidey of *Time* magazine that he would have sent the troops into combat even if he had not won that authority (Duffy and Goodgame 1992a, 159). However, it was the view before the war of his top security adviser, Brent Scowcroft, that "it would be a disaster to go to Congress and lose" (Woodward 1991, 325).[3] At the very least, a negative vote in Congress would have unleashed a substantial Constitutional crisis and would have massively increased the ranks of those publicly opposing the drive toward war.

In matters of this sort, a trusted, determined president is in a compelling position. Yet the Gulf crisis also suggests that the opposition is by no means powerless, at least if it can promote what appears to be a viable policy alternative. The Democrats launched a determined counteroffensive to Bush's war drive and nearly voted the war down in Congress. Indeed, if the war resolution had required a two-thirds majority like a treaty, it would have failed ignominiously.

In all then, Bush was taking a very substantial political risk in his Gulf venture. The public's tolerance for American casualties was low, and his political opposition was primed for action if the war had become costly. This issue is explored more fully in chapter 7.

COMPARISONS WITH WORLD WAR II AND VIETNAM

Several American wars before the one in the Gulf were preceded by debates over international policy: the War of 1812, the Mexican War, the Spanish–American War, World War I, World War II, and Vietnam. There are public opinion data for the last two of these, and some useful comparisons can be made.

World War II

Unlike the situation in Gulf, polling data generally suggest that American public opinion became increasingly acceptant of war during the year-long period between Roosevelt's 1940 re-election and Pearl Harbor at the end of 1941. The percentage willing to risk war rather than letting Japan take more territory in Asia rose 30 percentage points; the percentage willing to vote to go to war against Germany and Italy rose 15 points, as did the percentage favoring a declaration of war against those countries; the percentage thinking it important to help England even at the risk of war rose (rather jerkily) 10 points; and the percentage considering American entry into the last war to have been a mistake declined some 20 points. While these trends suggesting growing support for war contrast with those found in the approach to the Gulf War, in one aspect there is a similarity: as in the Gulf case, the percentage thinking the United States would eventually get into war rose substantially—some 10 or 15 points (Cantril 1967, 46–47, 173; see also Page and Shapiro 1992, 182–93).

These data suggest that, unlike George Bush fifty years later, Franklin Roosevelt (aided by world events, of course) was successful in gradually moving opinion toward war. Increasingly, Hitler became convinced that Roosevelt would eventually pull the United States into a war with Germany (Rich 1973, chap. 20), and it was his declaration of war upon the United States as well as the Japanese attack on Pearl Harbor a few days earlier that propelled the United States into war in 1941. Whether Roosevelt could have pulled it off without those galvanizing events will never be known.[4]

The war Americans were anticipating in 1941 was, of course, vastly more serious than the one they envisioned in the Gulf. In 1991 Americans anticipated that war in the Gulf might last a matter of weeks or months (tables 223–225); in 1941, they anticipated a war that would last several years (Cantril and Strunk 1951, 1090). Nonetheless, there does not seem to have been much more support for the walkover war of 1991 than for the cataclysmic one of 1941. On the eve of Pearl Harbor some 31 percent said they were willing to vote to go into the war against Germany and Italy (Cantril 1967, 47, 173). There are no strictly comparable questions from the approach period to the Gulf War and, as noted, questions about going to war generate substantially different results depending on how they are worded. But the question that seems most comparable is displayed in table 53, and it finds support for going to war with Iraq to be 38 percent.[5] Presumably, the horrors of the anticipated war in 1941 were compensated for by the value of ridding the world of equally horrible menaces, particularly the real Hitler rather than Iraq's small-time imitation.[6]

Vietnam

The 1990–91 debate over war in the Gulf case has some similarities with the debate that preceded the escalation in Vietnam in 1965. But there are notable differences as well.

For one thing, the enemy in the Gulf War was less significant. In Vietnam (as in World War II) the enemy was seen by the administration,

Congress, and the public to be a global menace, in this case part of a massive international Communist threat which had as its ultimate goal the destruction of the United States itself.[7] Saddam Hussein may have threatened American Middle East interests, and the man himself was eminently demonizable; but it was difficult to see him as that sort of threat.

More importantly, when American troops were sent to Vietnam, there were seen to be only two alternatives: either the troops went in or the enemy would win. In the Gulf, by contrast, there was another potentially viable option for dealing with the enemy: economic sanctions.

Finally, as noted in the previous chapter, there was a considerable difference in partisan support. Democratic leaders represent the party of such war presidents as Wilson, Roosevelt, Truman, and Johnson, but they probably are ideologically more likely to be reluctant to use international force than are Republican leaders. After all, it was from within the Democratic party, not from the opposition Republican party, that opposition to Vietnam policy grew; and when a Republican, Richard Nixon, took over the presidency and the war in 1969, Democrats swung substantially—almost gratefully—to an antiwar position (see Mueller 1973, 116–21).

Thus in the Gulf case, unlike Vietnam, there was a very substantial debate over what Democrats saw as the rush to war, and the war vote was deeply split along party lines with the Democrats supporting the middle-course sanctions policy. By contrast, when a vote was taken in 1964 to authorize the President to take "all necessary steps including the use of armed force" in Vietnam, there were only two dissenting votes in the Senate and none at all in the House.

Curiously, the military often claims that a central lesson from the Vietnam experience is that forces should not be committed to war unless they go in with solid public backing in advance. The troops had that backing in Vietnam, but not in the Gulf War.

World War II, Vietnam, and the Gulf War

These comparisons with World War II and Vietnam suggest that it is the partisanship of the debate, combined with the availability of a viable nonwar option, that explains the curious pattern of opinion before the Gulf War. Poll data clearly suggest that many of the President's concerns about Iraq's aggression, about its nuclear potential, and about its atrocities in Kuwait were widely accepted by the public. Moreover, unlike Roosevelt in 1941 or Johnson in 1965, he could credibly promise a cheap and easy war. Also going for him were the support of the United Nations and the amazingly inept and counterproductive maneuvers and obstinacy of Saddam Hussein. Finally, Bush's drive for war was aided by the rising sense of the inevitability of war, something that evolved from his policies of threat and counterthreat which progressively painted himself and his country into a corner.

All this, combined with his stature as the country's foreign policy leader, should have allowed him gradually to move opinion toward war in the manner of Roosevelt in 1941. The opposition, touting its sanctions option, was able to stalemate his progress—but not to reverse it.

Part Two ....

Opinion during the War

CHRONOLOGY

1991 Jan 16	The air war begins
1991 Jan 19	Antiwar demonstration in Washington
1991 Jan 17	First Iraqi Scud missile hits Israel
1991 Jan 19	Iraq orders foreign journalists out of the country, except Peter Arnett of CNN
1991 Jan 20	Iraqi television broadcasts pictures of battered Allied prisoners of war
1991 Jan 25	Iraq sabotages Kuwaiti Sea Island supertanker terminal, spilling vast quantities of crude oil into the Gulf
1991 Jan 31	Allied forces repel Iraqis at Khafji, Saudi Arabia, in the first major ground battle
1991 Feb 13	U.S. bombs civilians in Baghdad bunker which Iraq claims was a civilian shelter
1991 Feb 15	Iraq offers conditional withdrawal from Kuwait; offer is rejected by allies
1991 Feb 17	Iraqi Foreign Minister Tariq Aziz arrives in Moscow to confer with Soviet President Gorbachev about a possible Iraqi withdrawal from Kuwait
1991 Feb 18	Soviets offer Iraq a peace plan; the next day, President Bush says the plan "falls well short" of the UN demand for an unconditional withdrawal
1991 Feb 22	Hussein orders oil wells to be set ablaze
1991 Feb 23	Allies begin ground attack
1991 Feb 26	Scud hits U.S. barracks in Dhahran
1991 Feb 27	Bush announces ceasefire
1991 Feb 28	Iraqi forces defeated; Bush suspends ground war

4

George Bush launched war on January 16, 1991. In military terms the enterprise was spectacularly successful. The technology, strategy, and training of the forces led by the United States proved far superior, and they easily overwhelmed the Iraqi defenders, who seemed to have little if any stomach for combat: Saddam Hussein promised to wage "the mother of all battles," but his troops delivered instead the mother of all bug-outs.

Several weeks of aerial bombardment of Iraq and of Iraqi positions within Kuwait led, on February 23, to a ground assault which lasted one hundred hours and forced Iraq out of Kuwait and out of positions in southern Iraq. At that point, declaring the contest won and not wishing to risk further American casualties, Bush announced a ceasefire. American losses were lower than anybody even dared hope: total battlefield deaths were 148 (many from "friendly fire"), and 467 were wounded in action. Iraqi military deaths in the brief war (discussed more fully in chapter 8) were never counted carefully and have been placed anywhere from one thousand to two hundred thousand.

War galvanized public attention, and support soared for the war and for the President. And this seems to have led to a sort of boosterism within the media. However, the public's tolerance for American casualties appears to have been quite low. Indeed, on some measures a decline of support for the Gulf War took place despite the war's brevity and its remarkably low American casualty rates. During the war antipathy toward Saddam Hussein increased even further, as did the desire to remove him. The public showed little hostility toward the Iraqi people, but it was not notably impressed (or depressed) by Iraqi casualties. This chapter explores these issues.

69

THE RALLY-ROUND-THE-FLAG EFFECT

It was readily predictable (and predicted: see Mueller 1990c; Mueller 1991b; Doherty 1991, 10) that the war would trigger a very substantial rally-round-the-flag effect. Many of the tables already presented tell the story. Those thinking we had made a mistake sending troops to Saudi Arabia dropped 13 percentage points (table 34, figs. 1 and 4), those approving Bush's handling of the Persian Gulf situation rose 19 points (table 8, fig. 2), those approving his handling of Iraq's invasion of Kuwait rose 24 points (table 9), those approving the way he was handling the Iraq situation rose 28 points (table 13, fig. 2), those approving the job he was doing as president rose 18 points (table 1, fig. 5), those trusting him to make the right decision on war went up 20 points (tables 6–7), those thinking Bush had done a good job explaining why the country was in the Gulf rose over 30 points (tables 23, 25), those thinking the situation in the Mideast worth going to war over rose 25 points (table 40, fig. 4), those favoring going to war rose 16 or 24 points (tables 57–59), those thinking we should wait for sanctions dropped 26 points (tables 80–81; also table 88 as compared to tables 82–87), and those who considered American actions in the Mideast to be morally justified rose substantially (table 96).[1]

These indices generally remained high throughout the war, and Bush's popularity took another bolt upward—to a phenomenal 89 percent—at the time of victory (table 1 and fig. 5). If the war had gone badly it would very likely have ruined Bush's presidency, since he was the war's principal author and salesman. The war went well, however, and it put him on cloud nine initially.

Early military successes in the air war also greatly boosted optimism about its outcome: those anticipating that the war might resemble Vietnam fell precipitously (table 221), those expecting a short war rose 13 points (table 223, fig. 4), and those anticipating there would be a high number of American deaths dropped 26 points (table 227).

As observed in chapter 2, although there had been a notable rally effect on Bush's approval and policy ratings when he sent troops to the Middle East in August, there had been no comparable upward bounce in the percentage satisfied with the way things were going in the country or feeling the country was on the right track. The onset of war, however, triggered a very substantial rise—some 30 percentage points—in these measures (tables 197, 198, 199, and fig. 6).

In questions relating to the economy, when people were asked in February whether they were better off financially than a year earlier, the percentage answering in the affirmative had risen 10 points from prewar levels (table 200), while those thinking they'd be better off a year from now rose 16 percentage points (table 201). Similarly, the onset of war caused consumer confidence to rise notably, and it jumped even higher at the war's end (tables 202 and 203, and fig. 7). Breakdowns indicate that the rise of consumer confidence came from improved anticipations about the future, however, not from improved evaluations of the status quo (table 203, fig. 7).

Nothing in the five and a half months of debate over war changed opinion anything like the way war itself did.

Evaluations of Bush

Table 2 supplies some results documenting public evaluations of Bush at the time of triumph, March 1991. If one compares these numbers with those tapped the previous July, before crisis erupted in the Gulf, it is clear that the war greatly increased—by 15 or 20 percentage points—the numbers of people who would apply to him such words as sincere, steady, intelligent, confident, strong, leader, and active. Moreover, his ratings for "warm, friendly" went up some even though they already stood at 84 percent. One can only regret that Gallup neglected to include "brave," "clean," and "reverent" on its list.

At the war's end the public similarly waxed enthusiastic when it was asked to rate Bush on various performance qualities (table 4). Compared to July 1990, many more people said they thought he was doing an excellent or good job in making appointments, being an efficient manager of government, developing programs to address America's pressing problems, communicating his ideas to the public, following through on his ideas, working with Congress, being a good representative or symbol of the country, and being an inspirational leader.

In both cases (tables 2 and 4), it clearly was the war, not the crisis more generally, that boosted Bush. His ratings in mid-crisis (November 1990) were the same as, or a bit worse than, they had been in July.

However, these results are somewhat less impressive if one looks at figures in the two tables obtained in February 1990 (a month after the invasion of Panama) and compares them to those attained in March 1991 in the wake of his next war. Bush still reached outstanding highs after the Gulf War, but his gains are less impressive in this comparison than they are when one compares them with the deflated July 1990 figures.

Table 5 furnishes the results from a set of questions asking more specifically whether Bush was making progress handling various problems facing the country. The questions were asked in February 1990 (in the wake of the Panama expedition), in November 1990 (in the middle of the Gulf crisis), and then again in March 1991 right after the Gulf War. Between February and November, Bush's ratings on these qualities declined (as did his presidential approval detailed in table 1 and fig. 5, and, as noted, his ratings in the qualities asked about in tables 2 and 4). The successful war in the Gulf generally boosted his progress ratings in table 5 back to their February 1990 levels. On one characteristic, however, "increasing respect for the United States abroad," his approval reached spectacular new heights.

In some ways the most impressive change is at the end of table 5. In October 1990 Bush had raised taxes in a deal with Congress, clearly breaking his emphatic "read my lips: no new taxes" 1988 campaign pledge, and in November the public, not unreasonably, gave him low marks for "making progress" at "avoiding raising taxes." Bush's tax policy was unaffected by the war in the Gulf, but after it was over his ratings on avoiding a tax raise jumped upward by 22 percentage points. Also remarkable is the rating at the beginning of the table: by going to war (and handily winning it), Bush increased his score for "making progress" at "keeping the nation out of war" by 27 percentage points from where it had stood in November (though not back to the levels achieved in the previous February).

Table 3 and figure 5 document approval ratings for the way he was handling various "specific problems facing the country." The war substantially boosted his ratings for handling the economy, and it caused his foreign policy ratings to soar to an all-time high, with less dramatic improvements in his ratings for handling the situations in Eastern Europe and in Central America. His ratings for dealing with the Soviet Union, already very high, inched upward even more. He also registered various improvements, mostly rather modest, for his handling of the drug problem, the abortion issue, the savings and loan crisis, the federal budget deficit, environmental issues, and education policy. Of those issues for which comparative data are available, the only problem area in which Bush's ratings did not rise was for his handling of poverty and homelessness.

Bush's Rally Effect in Historical Comparison

Bush's 18-point jump was not quite the mother of all rally events—it was slightly surpassed by the 19-point jump for Jimmy Carter's approval when hostages were seized in Iran in November 1979 (see Hugick and Gallup 1991). But it was an impressive achievement, and the 89 percent rating he enjoyed at the victorious end of the war was the highest ever recorded.

This is, however, not exactly the same as "an all-time high" (Ladd 1992a) or as a "historic high" (Hugick 1991, 13). With modern telephone polling it is possible to get almost instantaneous reactions to events; face-to-face surveys generally were more delayed. Thus, while it was commented at the time of the Gulf War that Bush was more popular than Franklin Roosevelt had been after the Japanese attack on Pearl Harbor, there are no data to support such a conclusion. Before Pearl Harbor, Roosevelt's approval stood at 72 percent, but there were no polls in the immediate aftermath of the attack, as Roosevelt was making his "date which will live in infamy" speech. Instead his next rating, 84 percent, was measured a month later, in early January 1942, when the war had become an established fact and when some of the Pearl Harbor impact on his approval may have worn off (Cantril and Strunk 1951, 756). It seems quite possible that if his approval had been measured shortly after the attack, it would have surpassed Bush's 89 percent.

Rather surprisingly, Bush's approval was raised much more by the Gulf War than Harry Truman's was boosted by the attack on South Korea in June 1950—though precise data again are not available. Before the attack Truman's rating stood at a low 36 percent; it thus had plenty of room to grow.[2] When measured some two weeks after the attack, his approval ratings had risen only to 45 percent. Even assuming the polls missed an immediate impact, it seems likely that the Gulf effect on Bush's approval was greater than the Korean War's effect on Truman's.

GALVANIZING ATTENTION

War, as pacifist William James once remarked, is "supremely thrilling excitement" and "the supreme theater of human strenuousness" (1911, 282, 288). The sense of theater was certainly not lost on the American people: they were captivated by the war.

Not only did they rally around the flag, but they found the war to be all-consumingly interesting and important. Two weeks into the war, 37 percent called it the most important problem facing the country. This is impressive, though far from a record-breaker: the fear of war had attained that high a rating in 1983, and drugs (in 1989) and unemployment and inflation (variously in 1980–83) had far surpassed it, while concern about the economy was to outstrip it in 1992 (table 45). Similarly, 70 percent said they were following news from the Gulf "very closely," up from 50 percent in the days before the war began (table 46 and fig. 3).

War has a way, as has often been noted, of bringing people together and of cutting away petty differences. It also tends to bring out an intolerance of disagreement and dissent. Tables 236–246 supply some suggestive data on this for the Gulf War—though the numbers of people who gave intolerant responses may seem low to some.[3]

THE EFFECTS OF THE PUBLIC REACTION
ON THE MEDIA

When war broke out, the most common reaction, as table 51 suggests, was to turn on the radio or television set (praying came in second), and the habit stuck. As table 48 and figure 3 document, the media clearly rose to the challenge of supplying their ravenous customers with huge amounts of information about the war. In general, it seems, the media seem very quickly to have grasped two clear lessons about the desire of their customers. The public (1) wanted a great deal of information about the exciting war and (2) it did not want to hear anything critical about the military. The media complied.

This is hardly something new. One of the innumerable myths about Vietnam holds that the press was critical from the start. In fact, for the first years it largely conveyed the official Washington line and was rarely critical even by implication (see Hallin 1986, especially chap. 4). For example, although he became known as a Vietnam War critic, journalist David Halberstam in 1965 called Vietnam a "strategic country in a key area, it is perhaps one of only five or six nations in the world that is truly vital to U.S. interests" (1965, 315). And another future war critic, Neil Sheehan, concluded in 1964, "The fall of Southeast Asia to China or its denial to the West over the next decade because of the repercussions from an American defeat in Vietnam would amount to a strategic disaster of the first magnitude."

Under the intense drama of the brief and hugely successful Gulf War, the media generally reacted with predictable boosterism, even sycophancy. One accounting finds that 95 percent of all television news sources who discussed the performance of the American military praised its effectiveness (Lichter 1992, 227).

And there seems to have been a certain amount of self-censorship in this respect as well. For example, ABC television had managed to purchase satellite pictures of the war zone from the Soviets. These suggested—correctly, as it turned out—that Iraqi forces were far smaller than American military authorities were claiming. ABC decided not to use the information because, they said, they thought maybe the Iraqis had hidden a lot of their equipment and because the satellite images had missed a 15-kilometer band in which perhaps they had cleverly stored great amounts of war materiel. One is entitled to suspect, I think, that ABC did not use the story because it could be taken to be critical of our glorious military (see also MacArthur 1992b, 172–78). Or, the *Wall Street Journal* had a fully developed story about sex in the military during the war and during the five-month period of buildup during which American military personnel were cooped up on ships and in isolated camps in the Saudi desert. It turned out that individual units had established informal areas for sex, and a remarkably large percentage of the female personnel were becoming pregnant. Indeed, it is quite possible that far more Americans were conceived during the Gulf affair than were killed in it—one report puts the number of pregnancies at over twelve hundred (Dunnigan and Bay 1992, 386). The newspaper reportedly decided not to run the story because, it said, it doesn't do stories about sex. Regular readers may be somewhat surprised at that claim and, anyway, the story is not really about sex but about an obvious development (or problem) in a sexually integrated military. One might, then, suspect that the story was suppressed because it could be taken to be critical of our gallant, and presumably virginal, men and women in the service who were doing such a magnificent job for us out there in the Saudi sands.

In contrast to their praise for the military, the media substantially ignored antiwar protest demonstrations during the war. The editors at the *Los Angeles Times* war desk, noting from polls that the public seemed to support the war 80/20, decided that it made sense for their coverage to be similarly "balanced." That proportion would have been generous. According to one study, during the war only one of 878 on-air sources who appeared on newscasts over the major television networks represented a national peace organization (Solomon 1991). And another found that newspapers during the first three weeks of the war devoted 2.7 percent of their space to peace activities, while the comparable figure for television network news was 0.7 percent (LaMay 1991, 50; Lichter 1992, 224, 228).

Had the war gone badly, it is reasonable to suspect that the press would have become critical—though, following the Vietnam experience, it would probably have followed, rather than led, political and public discontent. Without failure in the war, the media remained frozen in advocacy.

The public's response to the media was quite favorable in general, and it gave the press high marks for its coverage both before and during the war and expressed confidence in it. It was also substantially approving of military restrictions on media coverage (FitzSimon 1991).

SUPPORT FOR THE WAR: TOLERANCE OF CASUALTIES

In Korea and Vietnam, popular support, variously measured, followed the same trend: high at first, then declining. It seems clear that it was American casualty rates, not the length of the war, that determined the decline in these wars. Casualties were suffered quite intensely in the early months of the Korean War, and support for the venture dropped rather quickly. In Vietnam, on the other hand, casualties accumulated at a gradual rate and support for the war accordingly declined slowly. Yet, in each case, support followed the same sort of logarithmic pattern in which support dropped some 15 percentage points whenever the casualties increased tenfold—for example, from one thousand to ten thousand or from ten thousand to a hundred thousand (Mueller 1973, 42–157). Essentially, therefore, the wars quickly lost the support of those who were only lukewarm supporters; harder core supporters did not become disaffected until casualty rates became considerably higher. Although Vietnam is often known as America's most unpopular war, it became more unpopular than Korea only after casualty rates there had surpassed those suffered in the earlier war.

When the Vietnam War began in 1965, a "can-do" military generally anticipated—or hoped—that the enemy ("a raggedy-ass third rate country," according to Lyndon Johnson) would break after suffering punishment for some two or three years—about the duration of the Korean War. The public and Congress seem to have accepted that estimate, and they generally supported the war for that long: had victory been achieved by 1967 or 1968, the war would probably have been accepted as a success.[4]

Americans did not expect costs of anything like that magnitude in the Gulf. As discussed in chapters 2 and 3, in their efforts to sell war, the military, the President, and people like House Armed Services Committee Chairman Les Aspin let on that a war of a few weeks, maybe even a few days, could be expected.[5] The President did say that "no price is too heavy to pay" to stand up against Iraq's aggression (Frost 1991a), but he also constantly declared that military action would not lead to a "protracted, drawn out" war like Vietnam, thus effectively promising that it would be short and bearable (Thomas 1990, 25). And, following from such declarations, the public and Congress seem to have envisioned, and to have been prepared to tolerate, something of a walkover war attended by casualty rates more like those suffered in Panama than in Vietnam.

It seems reasonable to suggest from the evidence in tables 92–95 that a dropoff of support would have followed a logarithmic pattern as in Korea and Vietnam. The data in table 92 from late December—less than three weeks before the war began—are particularly helpful for getting a feel for the potential impact of U.S. casualties on American public opinion. As with Korea and Vietnam, support dropped off as a logarithmic function of U.S. casualties: support for war was more than cut in half if it was posited that one thousand U.S. soldiers would be killed or wounded, to less than a third if ten thousand might become casualties, and to less than a quarter if thirty thousand casualties are anticipated. The polls in tables 93–95 find a less dramatic falling off of war support when casualty estimates are incorporated into the question, but the same basic logarithmic pattern of decline is still there.

This low tolerance for casualties was, of course, never put to the test. But, to inspire a decline in war support, the Iraqis did not need to win battles. The only needed to maintain a dedicated fighting force (no easy task) that would be able to push American casualties beyond tolerable levels—and those levels were probably far lower than they were in Vietnam or Korea. The process would have been led by the temporarily silenced, but still war-wary, Democrats. This issue is discussed more fully in chapter 7.

Decline of Support during the War

Actually, there is evidence to suggest that there was some erosion of war support during the course even of the Gulf War with its low casualties. Tables 34 and 38 and figure 1 find that the percentage calling American involvement in the conflict a mistake grew by some 5 percentage points between the beginning of the air war on January 16 and early February. (At the same time, however, table 29 suggests there was no decline in the number who approved of having gone to war.) This erosion was undone by a rally effect when the ground war was initiated on February 23 (table 38) and by the military triumph that quickly followed (table 34; see also fig. 1, as well as tables 39 and 40).

A similar phenomenon is found on other questions. Table 197 documents a decline of 7 percentage points in the numbers satisfied with the way the country was going between the start of the war and mid-

February before the ground offensive began. Similarly, table 198 and figure 6 find a considerable decline at the same time in the percentage considering the country to be on the right track. As with the "mistake" question, these numbers rebounded with the ground offensive and the victory that quickly followed.

OPINION ON SADDAM HUSSEIN AND ON VICTORY

Even before the war, as pointed out in chapter 2, Americans came substantially to feel that the removal of Saddam Hussein should be a central war aim. Polls from September and November (tables 144, 145) find support for his ouster to be about as high as such other popular policies as pushing the Iraqis out of Kuwait, destroying Iraq's nuclear capability, and protecting the country's oil supplies. By late December, the notion of continuing to fight to remove Hussein even after forcing Iraq from Kuwait drew very strong support (table 151; see also the trend in table 186).[6]

That attitude became, if anything, even more firm once the war started (tables 151–156, 158), and people said they anticipated feeling disappointed if Hussein were to survive the war (table 159, 160). Even when the question specifically pointed out that the UN had authorized force only to remove Iraq from Kuwait, most people opted for continuing the fight until Hussein was removed (tables 162, 163), and most of these claimed they were willing to spend several thousand American lives to bring this desirable result about (table 163). Moreover, as the war continued, the antipathy to Hussein seems to have increased (tables 155, 162).

The heightened hostility probably was inspired in part by some of the Iraqi actions during the war, particularly the humiliating and enraging parades before television cameras on January 20 of captured American pilots who were forced to give staged confessions of guiltiness (see Taylor 1992, 104–11). The pilots also appeared to have been beaten— although it turned out that many of their injuries had been sustained during bailing out. The Iraqis also lobbed Scud missiles on civilians in Israel and Saudi Arabia, set off destructive oil fires, and spilled massive amounts of oil into the Persian Gulf.

Similarly, early in the war people were strongly inclined to say that the war could not be considered a victory if Hussein remained in power (table 190, see also 159). However, at the triumphant end of the war, in questions that seem comparable, they had substantially reversed themselves (tables 192, 193). After the war, as is discussed in the next chapter, they were to reverse themselves again (see the trend in table 193).

OPINION ON THE IRAQIS

Americans and their leader may have envisioned Hussein as something of a demon, but the data in tables 247–249 could be taken to suggest that, despite the depredations committed by the Iraqi army in Kuwait and in the war, this animosity did not rub off on the Iraqi people (see also table 124, which finds comparatively low support for "punishing Iraq" as a war goal). In particular, the rather extremely worded question in table 248 managed to get fully 60 percent to hold that the Iraqi people were innocent of *any* blame for their leader's policies. Interestingly, a reporter in postwar Iraq observes that this lack of people-to-people animosity was reciprocated: to his surprise, he found that "Iraqis expressed virtually no anti-American feeling" (Viorst 1991a, 60).

This does not mean, however, that there was a great deal of sympathy among the American public for civilian casualties caused by air attacks; tables 250–252 and 255 are strongly suggestive of this regard. Tables 251 and 252 also indicate that the well-publicized civilian casualties resulting from an attack on a Baghdad bomb shelter on February 13 inspired no notable change in this attitude. Overwhelmingly, Americans said the shelter was a legitimate military target and held Hussein and Iraq responsible for the civilian deaths there (tables 253, 254).

The relevance of these data to Bush's decision to end the war when he did is discussed in chapter 7.

Part Three ....

Opinion after the War

CHRONOLOGY

1991 Mar 3	Iraqi military leaders accept allied terms, formally ending the war
1991 Mar 7	Anti-Hussein uprisings in 15 Iraqi cities
1991 Mar 25	Shiite Muslim rebellions in southern Iraq put down by Hussein
1991 Mar 31	Defeated Kurds swarm into Turkey, Iran
1991 Apr 1	U.S. troops begin withdrawal from southern Iraq
1991 Apr 7	Iraq accepts UN terms for war's end
1991 Apr 13	U.S. troops begin Kurdish relief in Iraq
1991 Jun 8	Huge victory parade held for troops in Washington
1991 Jun 10	Huge welcome-home parade held for troops in New York
1991 Oct	Conference on Mideast in Madrid
1992 Jan 28	State of the Union address
1992 Feb 18	New Hampshire primary
1992 Jun 23	Israeli elections
1992 Jul	Democratic convention: Clinton receives nomination
1992 Aug	Republican convention: Bush renominated
1992 Nov 3	Presidential election, Bush loses

5

As it turned out, the aftermath of victory in the Middle East was rather messy. Egged on by George Bush and by U.S. propaganda, groups opposing Saddam Hussein within Iraq—Kurds in the north, Shiites in the south—seized the opportunity and rebelled, expecting help from the victorious troops (Simpson 1991, 360). Then, even while triumphantly proclaiming the "Vietnam syndrome" to be a thing of the past, Bush proceeded to apply it: after blasting the pathetic Iraqi defenders out of their bunkers, he refused to intervene to get Hussein or to help the rebels because he did not want American troops to become involved in a Vietnam-style quagmire (see Dannreuther 1991/92, 61–67; Freedman and Karsh 1993, 417). As the United States watched from the sidelines, the remnants of Hussein's army put the rebellions down, and a massive and well-publicized exodus of pathetic, fleeing Kurds occurred. Eventually the administration was goaded into movement and it helped to establish a safe zone in the north for the Kurds and, much later, a no-fly zone in the south to help the Shiites. As is discussed more fully in chapter 8, it seems likely that far more Iraqis died from these rebellions and from the breakdowns in hygiene and in health facilities that followed the war than died in the war itself.

In all this, Saddam Hussein remained defiantly in control in Iraq—very much contrary to the confident assumptions by the Bush administration of his early demise (Rosenthal 1991b).[1] Thus, although tens, possibly hundreds, of thousands of Iraqis died in the war and in its aftermath, none of these was the man who started the whole thing. If all Bush wanted was to drive Iraq out of Kuwait and not to topple Saddam, that could have been accomplished at vastly lower human cost, it could be argued, by the judicious sanctions policy advocated by the Democrats, by the Chairman of the Joint Chiefs of Staff, Colin Powell (Woodward 1991a, 300), and by much of the American public—a theme considered more fully in chapter 8.

Before the war, the explicit goal of the sanctions policy was merely to pressure Iraq to leave Kuwait. During and after the war, however, the United States and the UN substantially escalated the requirements for sanctions to be lifted, demanding reparations and an end to repression and insisting that Iraq must allow various inspection teams to probe its military arsenal. It became clear that, at least as long as his arch-nemesis, George Bush, was in office, the sanctions would never be lifted while Hussein remained in control in Iraq. Thus effectively, sanctions required Hussein to commit political and probably personal suicide, and by his standards, "cooperation brings no benefits and defiance has no cost," as one reporter summarized the calculation (P. Lewis 1992a; see also P. Lewis 1993). Accordingly, Hussein obstructed and dragged his feet, the international sanctions remained in place, and the suffering continued in Iraq.

Meanwhile the old order—authoritarian, feudal, and substantially incompetent—was re-established in Kuwait (Viorst 1991b; Ibrahim 1992a, 1992b), and a considerable number of Iraqi-style brutalities were visited upon Palestinians and other Kuwait residents suspected of having collaborated with the invaders (Simpson 1991, 174, 378–79; Middle East Watch 1991b; Lesch 1991, 47–53). Elsewhere, rescued Saudi Arabia showed something less than an overwhelming interest in helping out American Middle East policy even as Bush and his Secretary of State, James Baker, sought to fashion a peace conference to settle Arab–Israeli issues.[2]

The public response to all this could be characterized with two words: "surge" and "decline." Victory brought a euphoria and a glow, and Americans became almost adulatory for a while about the president who had led them into, and then through, the dramatic and successful war in the Gulf. But the glow faded rather quickly—in many cases it took only a few weeks or even a few days. The continued existence in power of Saddam Hussein was responsible for this in part, but in general people continued to think well of the war and of the decision to wage it. Rather, what happened is that the public demonstrated a rather remarkable ability quickly to shift its focus of attention from the distant war to the ailing domestic economy. Mostly, it seems, because of the economy and because of his inability to project an image of leadership on domestic issues, George Bush's popularity went into a descent that is virtually unprecedented historically.

For quite a while, the impact of the war on the Democrats was devastating. For months, it froze them into almost total catatonia, particularly on foreign policy issues. When they did occasionally show signs of life, it was over domestic concerns—which, as it happened, worked for them in the elections of 1992, a subject of the next chapter.

RETROSPECTIVE VIEWS OF THE WAR

Current events can often change or cloud the way one looks at, and remembers, the past—including the way one recalls one's earlier views. The intensely dramatic and hugely successful Gulf War, not surprisingly, provides a case in point. In December 1990, respondents had split about 50/50 on a question asking whether they preferred sanctions or military action. But when asked after the war how they had felt before the war, those inclined to remember that they had supported military action outnumbered those recalling their support for sanctions by nearly four to one (table 83). Before the war, many people said they thought Bush was too quick to get American military forces involved in the Middle East; but after the war begin, far fewer said he had been too eager to wage war (tables 98–102). And, although quite a few people before the war had said they believed sanctions could drive Iraq out of Kuwait, few were of that view at the war's end (tables 67 and 68 vs. 71). In addition, in April 1991, 53 percent told interviewers that they had "always supported the war" (table 97), a number that pre-war poll results suggest is inflated.

People also change their attitudes toward what the conflict was all about. When asked in early December whether the United States was chiefly motivated by a need to keep oil flowing or by the moral principle that invasions could not be allowed, most people picked the oil motivation. When the same question was posed after the war had begun and then again after it had ended, people had come overwhelmingly to prefer morality to oil (table 113). Similarly, when asked after the war about various reasons for going to war against Iraq, respondents liked every reason offered to them more than they had before the war; the oil argument, however, gained only slightly in attractiveness (table 135). And to an open-ended question, people who felt the war to have been worthwhile mainly said it had been about countering aggression and stopping Hussein; relatively few picked oil or the notion of freeing Kuwait (table 185).

SADDAM HUSSEIN AND POSTWAR EVALUATIONS OF THE WAR

At the war's end Americans may have become momentarily more sympathetic to the notion that the war could be considered a victory even if Saddam Hussein survived it (table 190 compared to tables 192 and 193). Less than two months after the war, however, even as huge numbers of people began to welcome the troops home in various "victory" parades, the percentage willing to maintain that victory had in fact been achieved had dropped 19 percentage points, and by mid-1992 it had fallen another 11 (table 193). In a similar fashion, the percentage thinking the war had been ended too soon rose dramatically in the months after the war (tables 164–167, 169, 170 and fig. 4). Moreover, even well after the war the public expressed itself as being strongly of the opinion that the sanctions should never be lifted as long as Hussein reigned—popular support for the American policy that essentially required his death, or the functional equivalent thereof, for the sanctions to be removed (table 184).

Some of these questions mention Hussein's continued presence on the scene while others do not. A comparison of the July figures in tables 166 and 170 with table 171 suggests that the question did not have to remind the public that Hussein was still around to generate large majorities regretting the early end of the war. The use of his name did, however, raise that number a bit higher. However, a comparison of table 168 with the April figures in table 166 or the May ones in table 170 may suggest that, while people were critical of the early ending of the war, they were reluctant to characterize that policy as something other than a "correct decision."

For all that, support for reopening the war to rectify the mistake did not rise in the months after the war (table 172). Moreover, people were quite a bit more willing to suggest the United States ought to "capture" Hussein (table 173) or try to "remove" him from power (table 174), than to "resume military action" to force him out (table 172). And a question about taking "military action against Iraq at this time" that did not mention Hussein generated low enthusiasm (table 175). Americans could, however, be moved into saying they supported resuming military action if the question posited the use by Iraq of chemical weapons or its potential acquisition of nuclear ones (tables 177, 178, 180, 182; see also table 179). But there was less enthusiasm for using force to get Iraq merely to comply with ceasefire terms (table 181). In 1992, after a year or more of frustration, there was some increase in the percentage advocating resuming military action to force Hussein out (table 172).

By some measures retrospective support for the war declined in the months after it was over. The percentage thinking it had been a mistake to get involved in the Gulf or in the war increased by 5 to 9 points between the end of the war and the summer of 1991 (tables 34, 38, 39, fig. 1). Larger declines—14 and 19 points—were tapped by two questions asking whether the war had been worth it or not over the same period (tables 40, 43, fig. 4), while another found a drop of 6 points by summer and further decline of 5 points by fall (table 41).[3] With this decline, however, the trend seems to have bottomed out: when some of these questions were posed again in 1992, none had suffered much further decline (tables 40, 41, 43, fig. 4).

There was no decline in the first months after the war in the percentage who approved the decision to go to war (tables 31, 59) and only an 8 percentage point decline even by the following January (table 31). By June 1991, there had been some increase in the percentage viewing the war as unsuccessful or only partially successful (table 187) and perhaps a small further increase between July 1991 and January 1992 (table 189).

Thus, rather illogically, while the public became somewhat more inclined to view the war as a mistake and quite a bit more inclined to believe the war hadn't been worth the cost and effort, there was a much smaller diminution in the numbers who favored the decision to go to war in the first place. As noted in the previous chapter, something similar happened during the war itself. For the most part, this movement occurred in the few months after the war; although data are sparse, there seems to have been little further decline during the election year of 1992. Thus, although some of the glow wore off, the war continued to be recalled favorably.

POSTWAR EVALUATIONS OF GEORGE BUSH

At the end of the war, George Bush's approval ratings stood at stupendous highs. He was soon, however, to suffer major decline.

Of particular interest in assessing this issue are Bush's ratings in table 3C on the way he was handling the "situation in Central America." His successful war in Panama in late December 1989 boosted his ratings on this item by 26 percentage points and his ratings on handling "the drug problem" by 16 points (table 3G). However, six months later, his ratings on Central America were back down to where they had been before Panama, as were his drug ratings. (The successful war in the Gulf had the somewhat curious effect of boosting both of these ratings a bit, but nowhere back to their earlier highs.) Moreover, although Panama boosted Bush's presidential approval some 9 percentage points, he had lost most of this in a month (table 1 and fig. 5).

From the standpoint of public opinion, the Gulf War, with its big buildup and heavily reported results, was a far more momentous event than the Panama invasion. As Robin Toner observes,

> This was no Panama or Grenada, events that held the public's attention for a matter of days or weeks and then vanished from the television screens. The gulf crisis dominated the nation's psyche for seven months—week after week of People Magazine stories on the troops in the desert, song dedications on the radio to spouses and lovers "in Saudi," yellow ribbons everywhere, and local blood drives. (1991c)

Nonetheless, the Panama precedent regarding Bush's ratings proved to be general. A few weeks after the Gulf War, Bush's presidential approval ratings had declined from the stratospheric 89 percent tapped at the war's end to levels he had attained in the early days of the crisis, and later it fell further (table 1 and fig. 5). More to the point are questions specifically asking about how Bush was handling the "situation" in the Gulf or in the Middle East. His approval ratings on this reached an astronomical high of 92 percent at the end of the war, but a month later it had declined 14 points (table 8 and fig. 2). A few months later—after all the victory and welcome home parades—it had dropped 20 or 30 points (tables 8, 14), quite as much as his Central America rating dropped after the successful invasion of Panama (table 3C). (However, as table 14 documents, two months later, in September 1991, Bush's Gulf ratings had not declined further.)

As he called an end to the war, Bush pointed out that "ahead of us is the difficult task of securing a potentially historic peace" (Bush 1991a, 450–51). One element in his decline, clearly, was the public's increasing belief that the war, contrary to such Presidential hype, did not appear to have made the Middle East more stable and secure (tables 256–259 and fig. 4), and there was rising disappointment with him because Saddam Hussein remained in charge in Iraq (table 160).

Bush's central problem concerning the upcoming election is suggested in table 3A and 3B and in figure 5. His ratings for handling the economy were given a sizable boost by the war, but within *days* of the war's victorious end, his economic rating had dropped 14 percentage points. His foreign policy rating decline bottomed out in June 1991 and then held reasonably firm well into 1992. At the same time, however, his ratings for handling the economy continued to decline. The impact of this on his 1992 reelection campaign is discussed more fully in the next chapter.

Bush's Plunge in Historical Context

As can be seen in table 1, in less than a year and a half George Bush's presidential approval rating dropped from the 89 percent he enjoyed at the end of the Gulf War to a dismal 29 percent. A plunge of that magnitude has not been registered since the days of Harry Truman. In part this is because no one ever reached such heights: Kennedy peaked at 83 percent, Eisenhower and Johnson at 79 percent, Carter at 75 percent, Ford at 71 percent, Reagan at 68 percent, and Nixon at 67 percent. But few have ever dropped so low, either: of these presidents, only Nixon (in the depths of the Watergate scandal) and Carter (in inflation-ridden mid-1979 and then again in inflation-ridden and hostage-humiliated mid-1980) ever received rating scores below 35 percent (Edwards 1990, 165–69).

Bush's only rival in precipitous descent since public opinion polling began was Truman, who achieved ratings in the upper 80s when he came into office in April 1945 and plunged to 27 percent a year and a half later, in October 1946 (Mueller 1973, 198). But Truman's high score was registered as he took office in the wake of Franklin Roosevelt's sudden death while the country was still engaged in World War II: it was almost as if people were afraid to disapprove in those deeply dangerous times. To that degree, his high ratings, unprecedented until Bush, were artificial, a product of sympathy and perhaps even of fear. As the war came to an end and the nation headed into a year of painful readjustment, of labor unrest, and of food shortages, Truman was punished in the polls.

In historical context, then, Bush's decline is really quite remarkable. Unlike Truman, he had *earned* his high ratings. His stupendous high at the end of the Gulf War, after all, was a matter of direct personal achievement: he had led, even dragged, the country to war at great potential political risk, and he had achieved a stunning victory, routing a contemptible enemy at an astoundingly low cost in American lives. Moreover, as documented in chapter 4, this rise in approval was accompanied by dramatic improvement in all sorts of evaluative measures concerning his personality, his leadership abilities, and his policies. In addition, his approval ratings during his first year and a half in office preceding the Gulf crisis were entirely respectable, lingering in the 60s and 70s—as good as, or better than, those the popular Ronald Reagan had achieved in the first portions of either of his terms (table 1 and Edwards 1990,

169). Finally, the war success caused the opposition Democrats almost to vanish from view for several months, giving Bush a very substantial political honeymoon.

Disillusionment with the war, with its bloody aftermath, and with Saddam Hussein's continuing nose-thumbing existence can explain part of this decline, perhaps. But although there was some postwar frustration over the war and although the war's euphoria peak fizzled in rather short order, there is little indication that the American people strongly came to think of the war as an unworthy mistake or blunder: most Americans continued throughout 1992 to remember the war and Bush's decision to enter it favorably. Moreover, although a painful and persistent recession lingered in the aftermath of the war, by most objective measures, it was not exceptionally bitter: unemployment, for example, had been higher in earlier recessions.

It is difficult to avoid the conclusion, therefore, that much of Bush's spectacular postwar decline was self-induced. To a considerable degree, it seems, his demise in the approval ratings can be attributed to his apparent inability to provide leadership on domestic issues; to his frantic, even panicky, arm-waving jolt from issue to issue; and to his inability to project the impression that he knew what was going on domestically, that he cared, and that he had a policy to do something about it. This was, of course, to affect his reelection prospects, a subject of the next chapter.

LESSONS FROM THE WAR

A few poll questions allow for an assessment of broader conclusions that the public might draw from the war.

The war was clearly one against a dictatorship, and it was sometimes billed as a fight for democracy and freedom. However, easy success in the war did not boost popular support for further efforts to intervene to change dictatorship—if anything, the reverse (table 260). Somewhat similarly, people were far more likely to conclude that the war proved the military might of the United States than to accept the rather mildly worded notion that the war demonstrated that the country should "take the lead in protecting democracy in the world" (table 261).

In various questions asked in the month after the war, Americans seem at once to have thought that the country was likely to be more willing to use military force in the future (table 263); to profess less than great concern about this possibility (table 262); and to suggest that, although war was perhaps appropriate in the Gulf case, it ought to be used in the future only as a last resort (table 264). However, at least while it was still on, the war did substantially raise support for the notion that "wars are sometimes necessary to settle differences" (table 265), though it would be difficult for anyone who supported the war logically to disagree with such a statement.

At least in the immediate aftermath, the war seems notably to have reduced the numbers of Americans who said they thought the United States was in decline as a world power (table 204). And it also somewhat increased the number who said they thought the United States would be the top economic power in the next century—but more people still picked Japan (table 205).

In addition, table 266 indicates that the war may have boosted internationalism several percentage points.

SATISFACTION WITH THE UNITED STATES AND ITS ECONOMY

The Gulf War made Americans happy and proud, even euphoric, about themselves for a while. There was a lot of flag-waving, many smiles, and innumerable editorials about a new surge of patriotism. That particular balloon, it seems, began to deflate rather quickly.

As tables 197, 198, and 199 and figure 6 suggest, the war caused a jump of some 30 percentage points in the degree to which Americans registered satisfaction with the way things were going in the country or felt the country was now generally going in the right direction. But satisfaction on these measures dropped quickly, and by the fall of 1991 at the latest it had slumped to about the same level as in July 1990, before the crisis in the Gulf had begun.

Much of the problem seems to have been economic. As table 45 documents, the public very quickly shifted its attention to the state of the economy. And it didn't like what it saw.

While the war may have buoyed the spirits, it didn't seem to improve the economy. Initially it caused people to say they believed themselves to be better off financially than they had been a year ago. Within six weeks of the end of the war, however, this effect had worn off (table 200). Additionally, the indices arrayed in tables 202 and 203 and in figure 7 document a terrific surge in consumer confidence at the end of the war, but this only brought confidence back to where it had been before the crisis, according to the Michigan data (table 202), or only part of the way back, according to the Conference Board reckonings (table 203). By both measures confidence was still lower than at any time during the first year and a half of the Bush administration. And by the fall of 1991, confidence declined until it was at or near the low levels that had been registered in October 1990. The data in table 203 and figure 7 demonstrate that the war-end upward surge in consumer confidence registered by the Conference Board was entirely due to improved confidence in the future; the war caused no upward bound in the percentage holding that the economy was at present in good shape.

Tables 206–212 allow for some longer term comparisons. At the time of the Gulf War, lots of people said they were very proud to be Americans, but pride so measured was actually lower than it had been in 1986 and no higher than in 1981 (table 206). On the other hand, the confidence of Americans in the ability of their country to deal wisely with world problems increased substantially compared to the mid-1980s (table 207), and people were far more inclined to attribute this to recent events (table 208)—although this latter comparison probably mainly reflects the absence of a triggering memorable event in the mid-1980s. By contrast, table 209 suggests that even with triumph in the Gulf War, Americans were actually much *less* likely to express confidence in the future of the country than they had been in the mid-1980s. And, quite astoundingly, they were even less confident in this respect than they had been in 1980 during the lengthy Iran hostage crisis, a phenomenon which they said had lowered their confidence substantially (see table 208).

On other patriotism measures, Americans said they were strongly disinclined to move to another country, but that was nothing new (table 210). There did seem to be a surge in the urge to display the American flag (table 211), but Americans were substantially, and perhaps fortunately, less willing than they had been in the distant 1950s to subscribe to the amazingly unclouded sentiment that "The United States is the greatest country in the world, better than all other countries in every possible way" (table 212).

Crisis and successful war in the Gulf seem to have caused a 15 percentage point surge in the numbers of people thinking that religion was increasing its influence on American life, pushing it back up to mid-1980s levels (table 213). But this belief had sagged back to pre-crisis levels within two months, and it dropped further later in the year. A question asking how important religion was in the respondent's life inched a bit upward during the war and then retreated afterward (table 214). However, this question is not at all volatile, and the chief lesson seems to be that even the dramatic war did not affect it very much.

The yearly General Social Surveys attained rather similar results to the ones discussed here. Between spring 1990 and spring 1991, it found upward bounds in confidence in the military and in the executive branch, but comparable rises in confidence took place as well in major companies, organized religion, education, organized labor, the press, television, and Congress. People became much more likely to say they thought the country would get into a world war within ten years and less likely to support reductions in military spending. But political ideology became, if anything, a bit *less* conservative, and there was little change in the degree to which people expressed cynicism about public officials, felt happy, found life to be exciting, derived satisfaction in their community, or felt satisfied with their own financial condition (*GSS News,* September 1991; see also Ladd 1992a, 2).

At the time, the Gulf War seemed tumultuous and overwhelmingly important. However, the data arrayed in this chapter mostly suggest that the war's long-range impact on public perceptions and attitudes was quite limited. This somewhat surprising conclusion is assessed more fully in chapter 9. Its relation to the 1992 election is discussed in the next chapter.

6

The initial punditry held that the Gulf War would re-
dound very favorably to the Republicans. It had been
their war, after all—they had voted solidly for it in Congress, while the
craven, wimpy, and now terrorized Democrats had mostly opposed it—
and the war had turned out to be a towering success. Moreover, their
standard-bearer, George Bush, had risked all on the venture and had
come out looking like a decisive leader and a certifiable (if "warm" and
"friendly") hero. When Bush spoke to a joint session of Congress a few
days after the war, the members regaled him with standing ovations and
jockeyed to see who could look the most patriotic. To this end the
Democrats came decorated with American flags on their lapels, and the
Republicans countered with small flags they could wave at the television
cameras; the Democrats passed out yellow ribbons to pin on their
chests, and the Republicans trumped with large yellow buttons that
said, "I Voted with the President" (Dowd 1991).

Bush's re-election seemed a certainty. Before the war, the excitable
Democratic hawk, Stephen Solarz, had warned that if Bush triumphed
over Hussein without Democratic backing, voters "will keep us out of
the White House forever" (Barnes 1991a, 11); Republican media con-
sultant Roger Ailes had concluded, "If Saddam Hussein leaves Kuwait
head first or foot first, George Bush wins" (Barnes 1991a, 10–11); and
the President's chief of staff had told people that a short, successful war
would be pure political gold, guaranteeing the President's re-election
(Drew 1991, 83). Now, in the aftermath of triumph, some joked that
Bush might win the nomination of both parties, and a prominent Democrat gloomily concluded, "I will admit that today it looks somewhere
between unlikely and impossible that a Democrat will win the Presidency" (Toner 1991b). Moreover, it surely could be anticipated that his
magic would rub off on his party, and Republican Congressman Newt

Gingrich, after cheerfully suggesting that the Democrats ought publicly to apologize for their votes on the war, urged his party to recruit returning war veterans to run against those Democrats who had had the temerity to vote against the President's triumphal war (Halberstam 1992, 136; Curran 1991). The effects of the traumatic event, some suggested, might even permanently change the party balance by shifting party identification.

As they vanished from sight, Democratic leaders could only mutter hopefully and unconvincingly that it was still a long time until the 1992 elections and that a lot could happen during that time. As it turned out, a lot did.

At the time of the war, Joshua Muravchik opined that "if a large majority of American voters continues to view the gulf war as the most just, necessary and successful our country has fought since World War II, the Democrats will pay a heavy price for having opposed it." He then assessed the political prospects of the Democrats in Congress who had voted against their party and for the war and who, he felt, would accordingly "emerge vastly strengthened." It might well be from their ranks, suggested Muravchik, that the next Democratic Presidential candidate might come, "albeit not before Mr. Bush has had his second term" (1991a).[1]

As the public opinion data discussed in the previous chapter suggest (especially in tables 164, 165, 169, and 193), some voters did eventually come to envision the Gulf War as something less than a total success. However, the war might still be considered to be the most successful since World War II if the comparison is with Vietnam and Korea; and the public generally continued to consider it to have been a good idea. But evidence both from the post–Gulf War polls—including early ones taken before disillusionment with the war had set in—and from the history of other elections suggests that the war might not have all that much of an impact on postwar elections. Thus there was reason to believe war opponents in Congress might not have to "pay a heavy price" for their votes.

This chapter considers that evidence, and it assesses the war's impact—or the lack thereof—on the 1992 elections in which the war's chief author and political beneficiary, George Bush, went down to defeat against an opponent who, on paper at least, did not seem to have the background and qualifications to present a major challenge. Bush tried to wrap himself in his war record, and he was likely to derive benefit from it if he could make it work as an issue. But it seems never really to have clicked for him as the voters focused on domestic concerns and found him lacking on those issues. The chapter concludes with a discussion of the political consequences of the War of 1812 and uses this experience (as well as the Vietnam experience) to speculate about what might have happened politically if the Gulf War had gone awry militarily: the Democrats, it seems, might have gained in the short run, but not in the long run.

THE EVIDENCE FROM POSTWAR POLLS

Although they had voted against the war, the Democrats swung into line as soon as it started, and shortly after the war people seem to have been inclined to see the parties as being equally supportive of the war—but far more so when the question specifically supplied that option (table 267) than when it didn't (table 268). Half the population at that time was unable to recall how their representative or senator had voted on the war, and of those who could remember, the overwhelming majority recalled a vote in favor of war (table 271A, 271B).

In an election campaign Republican candidates could be expected to remind (or inform) voters how their Democratic incumbent had voted, and various polls conducted in the wake of the war suggest it would be to their comparative advantage to do so (tables 269, 270, 271C, 271D, 272). But even polls conducted shortly after the war suggest that this impact might not be all that great. The question in table 272 furnishes the respondent with quite a bit of information and seems, in apparent consequence, to polarize the results. In the other cases, however, even in the immediate aftermath of victory, half the people said that the Congressional war vote wouldn't have much impact on their choice, and only a quarter of those who did said it would be "one of the biggest factors" affecting their vote (table 269). A comparable question asked in late June (table 273) generates proportions that are quite similar to those which had been found in March (tables 269, 270, 271C).

Table 274 and 275 supply data from several different questions asked during and shortly after the war that ask about voter intentions for Congress in light of the Gulf War experience. In various ways, they seem to suggest further that the war might not be a major albatross for the Democrats. In one, most people say that the way a candidate voted on the war should not even be a matter of political debate (table 275D), a finding that might be taken to indicate that a campaign to make a major issue of the war could backfire. On the other hand, table 276, displaying results from early in the 1992 election year, suggests that it would be to the advantage of Republicans to make the war vote an issue.

Table 277 furnishes data suggesting that, at least for presidential candidates, the war had become more problematic for war opponents between March and July 1991 and that it stayed that way into 1992. The
question from 1992 in table 279 does not include an explicit "wouldn't
matter one way or the other" option and thus is not comparable to the
questions in tables 277 and 278. But, like those tables, it could be taken
to suggest that a pro-war president enjoyed better than a two-to-one
advantage on the issue, all other things being equal. Similarly, table 280,
from early 1992, finds 44 percent going so far as to say they would
"definitely not vote" for a candidate who had opposed the war.

As for broader political considerations, party identification levels do
not seem to have been notably changed by the war: Gallup's Personal
Omnibus ballots found the Republican/Democratic balance to be 33/
40 in 1989, 32/40 in 1990, 30/39 in 1991, and 29/38 in the first
half of 1992.[2] And when a set of questions dealing with the parties'
comparative ability to handle various jobs was asked in the immediate
aftermath of the war in March 1991 (table 287), it found little change
from a year earlier when hardly anybody had heard of Saddam Hussein.[3]

SOME HISTORICAL COMPARISONS

Before focusing more directly on the 1992 election campaign, it might
be useful to look at some electoral history. In general, historical experience suggests that it is not common for foreign wars to affect election
decisions as the voters balance out the war's benefits and costs and as
they assess credit and blame. Rather, the most common lesson seems to
be that voters simply come to neglect the war entirely as they turn to
other, more immediate concerns, particularly domestic ones.

The Electoral Consequences of World Wars I and II

The Democrats have quite a bit of experience with wars and elections.
Under popular presidents, they led the country into two world wars,
both of which were exhilarating and patriotic displays of the American
can-do spirit and both of which concluded in decisive victory over evil
enemies. Nevertheless, in the elections of 1920 and 1946, held a year
or two after the fighting stopped, the Democrats were clobbered as the
public came to focus on things at home. In 1920 they lost the White
House, 59 seats in the House, and 10 in the Senate; in the congressional elections of 1946 they lost 55 House seats and 12 in the Senate.

An even more vivid example is supplied by the British election of
1945. The war against Germany had been won only a few months ear-

lier, and the ruling Conservatives were led by an extraordinarily popular leader, Winston Churchill. Yet the electorate had already begun to focus on domestic issues, and it turned the Conservatives, and Churchill, out.

The Electoral Consequences of the Korean War

The Korean War was by no means popular. It had begun under the Democrats and had helped to ruin Harry Truman's presidency. In the election of 1952, the Republicans nominated Dwight Eisenhower who, promising to do something (or other) about Korea, was swept into the presidency. The Republicans gained substantially in Congress as well, gaining 22 House seats and one Senate seat.

Upon winning the election, Eisenhower set about trying to do something about the war, and by the middle of 1953, it was over. Although the ending of the war probably had much more to do with the death of Joseph Stalin and with other changes in the enemy camp (see Bundy 1988, 238–43; Mueller 1989, 126–27), Eisenhower was given great credit for the achievement with the American public. From the standpoint of public opinion, in fact, ending the Korean War may well have been the most significant achievement turned in by any postwar president (Mueller 1973, 234; Mueller 1979). It was still remembered as a great accomplishment seven years later as Eisenhower was leaving office, and in the 1968 election, a full 15 years after the event, the Republicans found it useful to remind voters of the achievement to get them to vote for their candidate who had been Vice President under Eisenhower at the time and who was promising (equally vaguely) to do something similar with the then-current, and most painful, war in Vietnam.

Despite this great accomplishment (or apparent accomplishment) by their leader and standard-bearer, however, the Republicans did poorly in the 1954 elections for Congress, losing 18 seats in the House and one in the Senate. This example might be taken to suggest that if success in the Gulf War had come to be seen and remembered as a truly monumental presidential accomplishment, it would help Bush's 1992 election prospects. But the example also suggests that even if the war had had that sort of benefit for Bush, Republicans in general were unlikely to garner much additional electoral profit from the episode.

The Electoral Consequences of the Falklands War

In 1982 the British fought a brief war with Argentina over the Falkland Islands in which a total of only about eight hundred people died. (However, since the conflict was over a desolate piece of territory populated by less than two thousand souls—an Argentine writer[4] characterized the war as "two bald men fighting over a comb"—the costs, proportionate to the value of the stakes, could be considered to be among the most horrific in history.) Like the Gulf War for the Americans, the Falklands War was mesmerizing to the British public and they were elated when their side won handily and at very little cost.

When the ten-week war began, the popularity of Prime Minister Margaret Thatcher and of her Conservative party soared. "In the space of three months," a British commentator concluded, "public opinion and party politics have been transformed" (quoted by Sanders, Ward, and Marsh 1987, 281). In the election of 1983, twelve months after the end of the war, the Conservatives gained substantially.

One group of analysts (Sanders, Ward, and Marsh 1987) has strongly challenged the notion that the Falklands War was responsible for these Conservative gains. They point out that the popularity of the Government was going up *before* the war begin and that in 1982–83 the country enjoyed substantial economic improvement. Thus, they argue, Conservative gains in the 1983 election were likely anyway, and they conclude that the Falklands effect faded away in a few weeks and had no visible impact at the time of the election a year later. Others have, in turn, challenged this conclusion and the methodology used to reach it (see Clarke, Mishler, and Whiteley 1990; but also Sanders, Marsh, and Ward 1990). And other analyses have concluded that, while the Falklands effect did fade, the residual effect of the war by the time of the election still boosted Conservative support by about 6 percentage points, even taking the economic recovery into account (Norpoth 1987a, 1987b).

Basically, that could be taken to be good news for the Republicans for 1992: there are at least some studies which suggest that quick, cheap, successful wars can lead to notable, if not necessarily overwhelming, electoral gains. There is, however, an important difference: the wars differ greatly in their aftermaths.

When the British won in the Falklands, the issue was settled, and the Argentines helpfully deposed the government that had led them into the pointless and humiliating war and replaced it with a reasonably responsive democracy. After the Gulf War, by contrast, there continued to be very substantial bloodshed and turmoil. Similarly, while the human costs to the Argentines in the Falklands War were almost as low as those of the British, the deaths dealt out to the Iraqis directly and indirectly by the American war machine in the Gulf proved to be very substantial.

As noted in the previous chapter, it is by no means clear that such concerns move the American electorate, though it does seem that few felt much animosity toward the Iraqi people. Nevertheless, there was something of a souring effect in the war's aftermath.

Most important in this respect, of course, is the fact that Saddam Hussein remained irritably in control in Iraq: reports heard shortly after the war of his imminent demise proved to be greatly exaggerated. As observed in the previous chapter, substantial numbers of Americans did not consider the war won as long as he continued to reign and to thumb his nose at the putative victors. Any positive electoral benefits of the war, accordingly, could be undercut as long as Hussein continued to hold sway in Iraq.

The Electoral Consequences of the Vietnam War

Another comparison may be instructive. Unlike the Gulf War, the Vietnam War came to an end in utter debacle. Although many, including John Kennedy and Lyndon Johnson, had greatly feared that a loss in Vietnam would lead to political turmoil in the United States, Vietnam played scarcely any role at all in the Presidential election held a year and a half later.[5]

Far from engendering a debate over "who lost Vietnam," the 1975 debacle in Indochina, amazingly enough, was actually used by the man who presided over it, Gerald Ford, as a point in his *favor* in his re-election campaign of 1976. When he came into office, he observed, "we were still deeply involved in the problems of Vietnam"; but now "we are at peace. Not a single young American is fighting or dying on any foreign soil" (Kraus 1979, 538–39). His challenger, Jimmy Carter, seems to have concluded that it was politically disadvantageous to point out the essential absurdity of Ford's remarkable argument.

Actually, foreign policy was the great non-issue of the 1976 campaign, which was dominated by domestic—particularly economic—considerations. Asked what was the most important problem facing the country in October 1976, less than 5 percent mentioned a foreign policy issue (Smith 1985, 273). Two polls in 1976 gave respondents lists of twenty or thirty issues and asked them to select those most important to them. The international item that did best on one poll ("The budget for national defense") came in tenth; the comparable item on the other ("Keeping our military and defense forces strong") scored eleventh (Mueller 1977, 328; on this issue, see also Mueller 1984b; Mueller 1989, 189–90; Niemi, Mueller, and Smith 1989, 44; Aldrich, Sullivan, and Borgida 1989).

THE ELECTIONS OF 1992

Thus, the experiences of Vietnam as well as of the elections of 1920, 1946, and perhaps 1954 suggest that Americans, like the British in 1945, are capable of turning from foreign to domestic preoccupations with a truly impressive alacrity. The Gulf War experience seems to have followed this pattern. As domestic concerns rose in comparative importance, the war faded into memory and succumbed to the American public's remarkable capacity for inattention—a phenomenon considered more fully in chapter 9. Thus, despite Bush's claims, promises, and prophecies, the Gulf War, at least in that special sense, did become "another Vietnam."

The Gulf War and the Presidential Campaign

The decline of interest certainly did not occur for a want of effort on Bush's part. In the early months of the postwar period, he gained political benefit as several prominent potential opponents in the Democratic party—including some who had voted for authorizing him to go to war—announced that, for various reasons, they had decided to sit out the 1992 campaign.

Bush sought repeatedly to wrap himself in the Gulf War mantle. When a soap opera–like television movie, "The Heroes of Desert Storm," was produced about the war, he was happy to introduce it, presumably hoping to cash in on the triumphal afterglow (Goodman 1991). At commemorations during the fiftieth anniversary of Pearl Harbor on December 7, 1991, he sought to draw parallels between that historic event and his later, rather smaller, war. And in his State of the Union message in January 1992, billed by the administration as the "defining moment of his presidency," he inappropriately, even preposterously, tried to apply the kind of macho rhetoric he had used in the Gulf War episode ("This will not stand!" and "Those who would stop us had better step aside!") to such distinctly non-macho issues as the budget and "hard times."[6]

Then, as the campaign of 1992 developed, Bush repeatedly tried to gain political capital and to compensate for his difficulties in domestic policy by bringing up the Gulf War. In a visit to New Hampshire he flailed out at "mournful pundits," "egghead academicians," "smart-aleck columnists," and "jacklegs jumping up demanding equal time with some screwy scheme," and contrasted the ease of the Gulf War with the trials of domestic policy. "When I moved those forces," he said, "I didn't have to ask Senator Kennedy or some liberal Democrat whether we were going to do it. We just did it"—rather ignoring the fact that he *had* asked for the approval of Congress before beginning the war (Dowd 1992). In the end, exit polls in the New Hampshire primary found that only 7 percent of Republican voters cited the Gulf War as an influential factor in their vote (Page 1992).

Moreover, despite Bush's rhetoric, the quixotic Patrick Buchanan, a syndicated columnist who had strongly opposed going to war, began to do rather well against Bush in the Republican primaries. The Bush strategists, who had hoped to "save" the Gulf War issue for the campaign against the Democrats in the fall, decided to spring it instead on Buchanan in the important Georgia primary. But despite that onslaught, Buchanan did better in Georgia than in almost any other primary (Congressional Quarterly 1992, 63). One study looked at likely Republican voters in Georgia who had seen the pro-war, anti-Buchanan television ad, and found that 28 percent said it made them more likely to vote for Bush, 7 percent said it made them more likely to vote for Buchanan, and 61 percent said it made no difference. However, Republicans who were less likely to vote said the ad made them more likely to support *Buchanan*—by 24 to 10—with 63 percent saying it made no difference. More relevant, however, the study found no significant differences in the reported vote of those who had seen the ad and those who had not (Hugick 1992).

At around the same time, Bush appeared before the staunchly supportive National-American Wholesale Grocers' Association, and before he came on, the audience was shown a film filled with pictures of the President reviewing and honoring American troops. The film met with utter silence (Sciolino and Wines 1992).

As the campaign really began to heat up in the spring and summer of 1992, Bush found himself opposed not only by the war-opposing and previously demoralized Democrats, who now began to sense victory in his rapidly declining poll ratings (see table 1, fig. 5) and in the growing concerns about the shape of the economy, but also by a maverick billionaire, Ross Perot, who not only had opposed the war but attacked Bush in the most scathing terms over it, arguing that Bush had sent Americans off to die in an unnecessary war in order to prove his manhood. By July 1992, Bush was given to angry, even pathetic, protests that he was "sick and tired" of not getting more credit for his triumph in the Gulf War—or Desert Storm, as he usually called it (Rosenthal 1992).

As discussed in chapter 5, Americans' retrospective views of the war had soured somewhat. A major burr, of course, was the defiant and unrepentant Saddam Hussein, an opponent Bush had billed not as a troublesome local thug but as a major menace, who was still alive and well and in control in Iraq, variously thumbing his nose at Bush, at UN nuclear weapons inspectors, and at the victorious allies. Although Bush insisted that the war had not been started as a device to remove Saddam Hussein from the scene, for the public it became one; and as long as he reigned in Iraq the war would remain unfinished, something of a frustration, and, in important respects, a nonvictory (tables 151–171, 193, 195, 196, and fig. 4). There was also some disillusionment because of the continuing instability in the Middle East (table 256–259, fig. 4) after Bush's hyperbolic promises of a New World Order, and there was some (limited) increase in the feeling not so much that the war was a bad idea (table 31), but that the area somehow wasn't worth going to war over (tables 40, 41, 43, fig. 4). Table 281 suggests—though it is hardly conclusive—that by early 1992 the Gulf War may have become only marginally beneficial to Bush: in that poll, 27 percent said the war made them more likely to support Bush, while 21 percent said it made them less likely to do so.

In addition, Bush's political opponents were able to seize upon evidence suggesting that his policy toward Hussein before the war had been one of considerable support—coddling, they often called it. Tables 283 and 284 suggest the issue was quite a punishing one for Bush.

For his part, Bush was given to making bold claims about how the war had kept Hussein from attaining nuclear weapons and control over world oil prices—claims examined more thoroughly in chapter 8. In his acceptance speech at the Republican nominating convention on August 20, 1992, Bush put it this way:

> The Mideast might have become a nuclear powder keg, our emergency supplies held hostage. So we did what was right and what was necessary. We destroyed a threat, freed a people and locked a tyrant in the prison of his own country.

And he went out of his way to ridicule the position his Democratic opponent, Arkansas governor Bill Clinton, had taken on the war:

> While I bit the bullet, he bit his nails. Two days after Congress voted to follow my lead, my opponent said this, and I quote, "I guess I would have voted with the majority if it was a close vote. But I agree with the arguments the minority made." Sounds to me like his policy can be summed up by a road sign he's probably seen on his bus tour, "Slippery When Wet."[7]

But all in all, Bush and the Republicans found that raising the issue simply reminded voters that Saddam Hussein still reigned, that Kuwait was still far from a democracy, that the administration's policy had been pro-Iraq before the invasion, and that Bush was focusing on foreign affairs to the detriment of domestic ones, which, as tables 45, 288, and 289 demonstrate, had now come to preoccupy the voters (Page 1992).

In some respects, the Gulf War issue was not truly met in the 1992 Presidential campaign because the Democrats nominated an opponent who had supported the war, at least in the rather curious and selective sense Bush highlighted in his acceptance speech. Moreover, Clinton selected as his running mate a man, Al Gore, who was one of the handful of Democrats to vote for the war in the Senate. But even if the Democrats had nominated an active and vocal war opponent, the selectee, like Perot (who ended up with 19 percent of the vote and who, unlike Clinton, *had* opposed the war), could have countered with criticisms about Bush's handling of Hussein both before and after the war. Or, the candidate could simply have given Bush his due on the war, admitted error on that policy, and turned to domestic issues and particularly to the economy, the issues that came to dominate the concerns and attention of the electorate in the aftermath of the war.

In some important respects the military success in the Gulf worked to Bush's tactical disadvantage. Understandably impressed by his high poll ratings at the end of the war and by the conventional wisdom that the 1992 election would be a walkover, he allowed himself to wallow in overconfidence, and he turned his attention to the re-election campaign only belatedly, even reluctantly (Toner 1991a; Goldman and Mathews 1992). Overconfidence was also inspired, it seems, by an anticipation that the economy would be in full recovery in 1992. On the day the war began, a White House spokesman came out with a confident prediction: "We in the Administration feel that the recession will be relatively short-lived, but nevertheless we are going to be in for a significant slowdown for number of months."[8] When the "slowdown" persisted well into the election year (quite possibly because of Bush's war policies, it is argued in chap. 8), Bush was caught unawares and unprepared, and the voters noticed. Notably, there was a surge in consumer confidence when Bush lost the election in November 1992 (tables 202, 203).

Although many voters claimed during the campaign that Bush's handling of the Gulf War would be an important factor in their vote decision (table 282), in the end, it seems, Bush's accomplishment in the Gulf turned out to be one of the nonissues of the 1992 campaign (tables 288, 289). Indeed, it played almost as limited a role as did his wars in Panama and on drugs, issues which had preoccupied him and the country in the early part of his administration. It was observed in chapter 3 that Bush was successful in keeping the Gulf crisis high on the public's agenda in the approach to war period. But he accomplished this more by actions than by words (see also Krauthammer 1991). In 1992, the time for action was over. Indeed, by the summer some polls were suggesting that even a military venture into Iraq that successfully forced the country to comply with UN resolutions would work *against* Bush unless Saddam Hussein were removed from power in the process. Moreover, even if Hussein were ousted, 79 percent said it would not affect their vote one way or the other (tables 285, 286).[9] Accordingly, Bush could only rely on his rhetoric—never his strong suit.[10]

Overall, it seems reasonable to suggest that the Gulf War helped Bush's vote—that is, he would have done even worse without the Gulf War success. But, judging from the shape of the campaign and from its results, the impact of the war on the election was small. It even seems reasonable to suggest that if the war had been a success in driving Hussein from office, it still would not have been of great moment in the election since the voters were using other criteria to judge the candidates. One indicator of this, perhaps, is that among the postelection post mortems there were few, if any, columns devoted to the remarkably small impact the Gulf War, so fascinating and obsessing in its time, had had on the subsequent election efforts of its once-lauded architect and champion. The war that had once so dominated the press had become such a distant memory that commentators were unable to remember it well enough to remark upon how little people remembered it.

The War's Impact on the Vote for Congress

It is impressive as well that the war had such a small impact on the congressional elections of 1992. With great fanfare and media attention, the members of Congress had solemnly debated the war authorization vote and then stood up to be counted on one side of the issue or the other. By the standards of most Americans, the war-opposers turned out to have been wrong, and it was not at all unreasonable to expect, as Gingrich and Muravchik had, that they would be punished at the polls for their error. That, after all, is what democracy is all about, by some reckonings.

But to their great surprise and relief, Democratic war opponents repeatedly found that the issue scarcely arose in their campaigns. For example, in urging the defeat of one prominent Democrat, Bush cited the Democrat's opposition to the Gulf War, to a balanced budget amendment, and to a line item veto. After Bush's speech the Democrat, who had expected his war vote to be a big problem in campaign, was interviewed by one of the top local television reporters. The reporter queried him about his opposition to the balanced budget amendment, but not about his vote on the war. Although the campaign was one of the closest and most hotly contested elections of the year, the Gulf War and the Democrat's vote on it scarcely ever came up in the campaign and in debates with his opponent.[11]

The Gulf War probably faded as a cutting issue—or indeed as much of an issue at all—in congressional contests for several reasons. First, as with the presidential campaign, the war had an unpleasant aftertaste and, because of its inconclusive nature in the minds of many voters, it could potentially be turned back on the candidate. Second, the evidence arrayed earlier in this chapter suggests that, since the Democrats went all out to support the war once it had begun, the electorate was not in a mood to punish them for their pre-war votes. Third and most important, the issue was simply not something the voters cared much about any more: they wanted to focus on current pains—the domestic economy—not on old, and somewhat tarnished, glories.

COMPARISONS WITH THE WAR OF 1812

The special experience of the War of 1812, one of the most dazzlingly incoherent conflicts in history,[12] may be most instructive for what it suggests about what could have happened if the Gulf War had gone awry. It indicates that the Democrats would have benefited at the polls in the short run if the war had gone badly, but not necessarily in the long run.

An important element of comparison is that, like the Gulf War, the War of 1812 was a partisan one. President James Madison and his Republican party were anxious to go to war with Britain for a number of reasons, and the opposition Federalists, a minority in Congress, strongly opposed such a venture. When Congress voted to declare war on June 18, 1812 after an extensive debate on the issue, the vote was largely split along partisan lines. Moreover, as with the Gulf War, the country went to war without the impetus of a specific and dramatic precipitating event of the sort that triggered World Wars I and II, the Spanish–American War, and the Korean War.

Unlike the Gulf War, however, the War of 1812 was anything but a walkover, and the Federalists, though persecuted by war-supporting mobs in a few areas (especially Baltimore), became extremely critical of the war's value, cost, and prosecution, making it the central issue of the campaign. This proved to be good politics, at least in the short run, because, although the Federalist party had been in decline, it did quite well in the elections in the fall of 1812, doubling its seats in the House of Representatives and coming within one (large) state of taking the presidency (Livermore 1962, 11; Risjord 1971, 249, 272; Turner 1971, 299; Hickey 1989, 100).

The War of 1812 dragged on, fitfully and inconclusively, for another two years, becoming in the process almost certainly the most unpopular war in American history as whole areas of the country, particularly New England, opposed and even obstructed the war effort. The costs of the war steadily increased. By the time it was over, some twenty thousand men had died in battle or from disease (Hickey 1989, 304–5), and the banking system had been pushed to the brink of collapse. Meanwhile, the federal government nearly went bankrupt and its debt almost tripled. Financially, as Thomas Jefferson put it in 1814, the war "arrested the course of the most remarkable tide of prosperity any nation ever experienced" (Hickey 1989, 303, 305).

Not surprisingly, the Republicans paid at the ballot box. "Although they counted on the war to enhance their popularity and silence the Federalists," observes Donald Hickey, "the effort of the conflict was just the opposite. In New England especially, the war served as a catalyst for a Federalist revival. As a result, Federalists achieved a more commanding position in this region than at any time since the 1790s" (1989, 232; see also Turner 1971, 299–300).

Nonetheless, despite the war's escalating costs, despite the steady barrage of criticism from the opposition and from elements within his own party, and despite declining electoral fortunes, the President and his party were able to continue what came to be called "Mr. Madison's War"[13] until peace talks brought it to an end late in 1814. The boys at the front continued to be supported.

The Building of Postwar Myths

The War of 1812 ended inconclusively, even pathetically, with an agreement to return to the territorial *status quo ante bellum* and with few notable concessions by either side. And its most memorable battle, at New Orleans, had preposterously taken place after the war was over. However, while the Federalists seem to have been right in predicting that the war would become a costly and pointless exercise in futility, they discovered that "opposition to the war was popular during the conflict but not afterwards" (Hickey 1989, 308).

In the war the young country had at least stood up to mighty England (which, however, was largely preoccupied at the time with a far more important war in Europe with Napoleon), and the Americans had pulled off several notable victories, especially the one at New Orleans. From such material, the Republicans were able to fashion a helpful and appealing myth. As Hickey concludes,

> As the years slipped by, most people forgot the causes of the war. They forgot the defeats on land and sea and lost sight of how close the nation had come to military and financial collapse. According to the emerging myth, the United States had won the war as well as the peace. Thus the War of 1812 passed into history not as a futile and costly struggle in which the United States had barely escaped dismemberment and disunion, but as a glorious triumph in which the nation had single-handedly defeated the conqueror of Napoleon and the Mistress of the Seas. (1989, 309)

The Federalists became the scapegoat for this new myth, and they were often successfully stigmatized as unpatriotic—even treasonous— obstructionists who had prolonged the war and undercut the gallant American fighting forces (Livermore 1962, 11–14; Hickey 1989, 308). They found, in Shaw Livermore's words, "that the Republican themes of honor and patriotism went deep into the hearts of American searching for self-respect and solace after the tremors of war." People "wanted to believe their efforts had been noble and effective," and they preferred the "soothing words" of the Republicans to the "continued carping of the Federalists." The Federalists had been briefly buoyed from decline by the failures of the war, but their long-range hopes for revival dissolved in their "pigheaded and spiteful" conduct during the war (1962, 14, 264).

Accordingly, by the time of the elections of 1816, they were again in very pronounced decline, and countless offices were won over the years by people who had participated in the misrepresented and misremembered war, including James Monroe, John Quincy Adams, Andrew Jackson, and William Henry Harrison, all of whom ascended to the presidency. Thus, "the most conspicuous casualty of the War of 1812," observes Lynn Turner, "was a noncombatant—the Federalist party" (1971, 299).

Relevance to the Gulf War

Unlike the Federalists of the 1810s, the Democrats of the 1990s are hardly a party in notable decline. And the experience of the War of 1812 does suggest that they might have gained substantially if the Gulf War had gone badly, quite probably destroying the presidency and the political career of George Bush in the process.

But the experience of the War of 1812 also suggests that political support for the war, even if it became thoroughly unpopular, could well have continued—as happened as well in Vietnam a century and a half later. Moreover, like the Federalists nearly two centuries earlier, the Democrats would have found it difficult as war critics to avoid appearing to undercut a great, if misguided, patriotic effort, and postwar Republican mythmakers, working with a willing clientele, might have been able to turn that to their advantage.

The Political Aftermath of Vietnam

In some respects the Vietnam postwar experience also supports this conclusion. That war ended in outright fiasco and, unlike the War of 1812, no one seriously challenged the notion that it was a failure, nor did anyone construct attractive myths to justify the sacrifices of Americans. After the war, the portion of the public holding the war to have been a mistake continued to climb, nearly reaching the 80 percentage mark by 1990 (Stanley and Niemi 1992, 352). Accordingly, in this case it would have been natural to find great virtue in those who had opposed it.

Yet, while the war's failure didn't hurt the political fortunes of war opponents (as the putative success of the War of 1812 had hurt *its* opponents), it didn't help them much either: that is, no one gave them credit for having been right. What mainly happened is that the American people largely put the humiliating events behind them, and no one seems notably either to have benefited or lost because of it: indeed, as noted above, it became the great nonissue of the postwar election of 1976.

In the 1980s, Ronald Reagan declared the war to have been a "noble cause," but this somewhat remarkable characterization seems to have neither helped nor hurt him. Similarly, antiwar (and pro-war) people were elected to various offices, but their success seems to have stemmed from other concerns, not from their record on the war. Then, in 1992, the Democrats nominated a strong and unabashed Vietnam War opponent, Bill Clinton, as their standard-bearer in the election against the principal author of the Gulf War, George Bush. Although Clinton made no secret of his views on the Vietnam War and although Bush tried in various ways to gain votes from Clinton's youthful antiwar activism, it seems to have affected Clinton's support little one way or the other.

Thus, if the Gulf War had become a fiasco like Vietnam, the Democrats might have used the experience and their apparently prescient war opposition to bring down George Bush. But, even if the Republicans hadn't been able eventually to spin attractive myths about the war (unlike their counterparts in the War of 1812), the long-range benefit to the Democrats might have been minimal.

Part Four

Conclusions, Implications, and Speculations

POLICY AND OPINION IN
THE GULF WAR

Several aspects of the relationship between policy and public opinion during the Gulf crisis, war, and aftermath are assessed in this chapter.

The first section deals with the relation between the public opinion polls and American policy in the Gulf. It considers how opinion affected planning for the war, the arguments in the debate about the war, and the decision to halt the war, and it critiques the commonly accepted belief that the public by January 1991 had turned favorable toward Bush's policies and toward war. It also discusses the curious assumption within the administration that, despite poll data and despite such dramatic precedents as Pearl Harbor, an Iraqi attack on American troops in Saudi Arabia would disable—rather than vastly intensify—the war effort.

The second section discusses the relation between public opinion and American casualties. It outlines strategies the Iraqis, however outnumbered and outclassed, might have used to increase American casualties, and it considers what the Democrats might have done if the war had gone awry.

The third assesses the role in the Gulf episode of the media, which occupy the information space between the events and leaders that make the news and its customers, the public, which consumes it. In this case, it seems to me, the desires and demands of media consumers and the force of events themselves primarily dictated the media coverage and set the agenda. It also appears that visuals—pictures and such—were not particularly important in this war. Also discussed is the media's characteristic of failing to follow up stories while rushing off to the next issue.

The chapter concludes with some brief reflections on war and democracy.

THE IMPACT OF POLLS ON POLICY

Public opinion polls seem to have importantly influenced Bush's decision-making in several notable respects. In concluding from the polls that the public was losing patience with sanctions or that it was turning favorable to war, the decision makers (and many postwar analysts) seem to have misread the data. In concluding that the nuclear and hostage issues were potent arguments or that the public would punish Bush for a costly war, however, they seem to have gotten it right. On the other hand, they neglected other data which suggest that an attack by the Iraqis on American troops stationed in Saudi Arabia would have a Pearl Harbor effect on the American public.

The October Slide and the Prospects for Long-Term Support for Sanctions

By October 1990 the Bush administration had become concerned about stopping a "downward slide" in the President's popularity and in the public's approval of his handling of the Gulf situation, a decline which it expected to get worse (U.S. News 1992, 174–75; Woodward 1991a, 316). This concern seems to have forced, or reinforced, Bush's conclusion in October about the policy of containment and sanctions: "I don't think there's time politically for that strategy" (Woodward 1991a, 42).

Poll results suggest that the Bush analysts were right about the downward slide, but that their fears of a further decline were probably not justified. As discussed in chapter 2, as happens after any rally event, there was a decline in support for Bush's Gulf measures between August and October. However, most of the data suggest that the decline had bottomed out in October, well before Bush's November 8 escalation announcement (see tables 20, 34, 36, 8, 12). During the same period the President's approval rating had plunged, but this was due not only to a natural post-rally decline but also to his acrimonious jostling with Congress in the budget fight that took place in October. This decline, too, seems to have bottomed out—at least for the time being—in October (table 1). Similarly, the limited data available do indicate that there was a marked decline between August and October in the percentage thinking that sanctions would work to make Iraq withdraw from Kuwait—but this, too, may have reached its low in October (see tables 67, 68).

Thus, insofar as concern about public support impelled the administration's sense of urgency about its Gulf policy, that concern does not seem to have been justified. There is no way to be certain about this, of course: we cannot know what would have happened if Bush had refrained from his escalation, and it is conceivable that his escalation prevented a decline in support that might have come about later. But the apparent bottoming out in October suggests that fair-weather supporters had already dropped off. A policy of patience—putting the issue on the back burner to concentrate on other pressing matters while waiting for sanctions to have their effect—would likely have generated continued support from the public, particularly if Hussein had returned the hostages and if no American troops were being killed (see table 75).

After all, the public had had no trouble supporting the stationing of American troops in Europe, Japan, and Korea for decades on end. A similar acceptance of troops in Saudi Arabia (particularly if the Saudis paid much of the upkeep) could surely be anticipated (see Mueller 1990c). The administration does seem to have been concerned that the Democrats would somehow exploit the issue to their benefit (U.S. News 1992, 175), and there were sobering memories of the lingering Iranian hostage crisis of 1979 and 1980 that had negatively affected President Jimmy Carter's re-election prospects. However, since the Democratic leadership had strongly supported Bush's sanctions policy in the Gulf and was extremely wary of war, it is not at all clear how it could have generated partisan gain from the situation.

With respect to the public's continuing support for sanctions against Iraq, the evidence, it seems, is now in. After the war, the administration and the United Nations decided to keep the sanctions pressure on until Saddam Hussein's administration agreed to a set of disarmament and inspection measures—and, according to Bush, until Hussein was ousted one way or another. Since Hussein dragged his feet on some of these demands (especially the one that seemed to require him to cease to exist), the sanctions remained in force, and the American public had no difficulty supporting their continuation. Indeed, as table 184 shows, it strongly supported Bush's policy of continuing them as long as Saddam still reigned in Iraq. Nor did the public notably object—as long as U.S. casualties were low—to maintain a military occupation force in the area to protect the rebelling Kurds in the north of Iraq and to enforce a no-fly zone in the south.

The Arguments in Support of Policy

The administration seems to have used the polls to good advantage in fashioning arguments to support its policies in the Gulf.

At the time of what it held to be the October slide, the administration, according to Bob Woodward, became concerned that its arguments about "the plight of the Emir of Kuwait, his people, aggression and oil were not selling to the American people." Accordingly, responding to poll figures like those in tables 122, 123, 131, and 136, it made a conscious effort to stress the plight of the American hostages, and by the end of the month Secretary of State Baker was making speeches about how the hostages were "forced to sleep on vermin-ridden concrete floors," were "kept in the dark during the day," and "had their meals cut to two a day." Calling this situation "simply unconscionable," he added that "we will not rule out a possible use of force if Iraq continues to occupy Kuwait" (Woodward 1991a, 316; see also Duffy and Goodgame 1992a, 154).

The hostage argument, while effective, had a disadvantage in that Hussein could obviate it by simply releasing the hostages—which, of course, he eventually did. In the meantime, however, Bush's pollster, Robert Teeter, had come up with a less transitory argument. Using results like those in tables 122, 131, 133, and 134, he urged that Hussein's nuclear potential could be a real "hot-button" issue with the public. So alerted, the administration responded and was soon arguing that, contrary to earlier reports that the Iraqis were five to ten years away from a nuclear bomb, they might be able to build one within a year (U.S. News 1992, 179; Albright and Hibbs 1991; Sciolino 1991, 235; Safire 1992).

For many waverers on the war, the nuclear argument may have been a decisive consideration. However, if the argument had an effect, it was to keep support for war from dropping lower; it did not notably increase overall support during the debate period.

The January "Turn-around"

Bush and others in his administration were apparently convinced that the "polls had finally turned around" by January, with clear public support for his Gulf policy and for the use of force (U.S. News 1992, 202).

Similarly, many postwar analysts have concluded that Bush managed to win over a growing portion of the public in the approach to war. Thus Bobby Inman, Joseph Nye, William Perry, and Roger Smith conclude that Bush "was able to lead, mobilize, and shape public opinion to support his actions; at every turn he was able to garner international support and then turn and use it to mobilize approval from Congress and from the general public" (Inman et al. 1992a, 70–71; 1992b, 287–88). Ronald Hinckley argues that from lows in November 1990, "Bush's approval rating for handling the Gulf crisis steadily increased until he launched the air war" the following January (Hinckley 1992, 113), and Bruce Jentleson comes to a similar conclusion (1992, 66). David Gergen writes about "how successful Bush was in generating grass roots support through a series of bold, unilateral actions at key points along the way" (1992, 181). Lawrence Freedman and Efraim Karsh observe that by January Bush "had reason to feel more confident that public opinion was moving in his direction" (1993, 291). *Time*'s Michael Duffy and Dan Goodgame, no great fans of Bush, nevertheless wax appreciative over the way "he encountered public resistance at half a dozen turns in the crisis and overcame it, not with soaring rhetoric, but with bold actions, each of which shifted public opinion toward support of his policy" (1992b, 41). And war opponent Anthony Lewis observes, "Even those critical of him know that in the Persian Gulf crisis he brilliantly marshalled American opinion, Congress and foreign governments for intervention against Saddam Hussein" (1992a; see also J. Smith 1992, 162; Ladd 1991b; Towle 1991, 40; Summers 1992, 19).

Thus the notion of the January "turn-around" seems to have become widely accepted. It is based in part on the facile (but not unreasonable) conclusion that, since Bush successfully started the war and since opinion rallied to him after it started, he must have convinced the public of its wisdom before he began it. And it also derives from some limited public opinion data assessments, often relying on results published shortly before the war by the *Washington Post*. These reports included selected points from several time series and give the impression of increasing support. By contrast, an assessment of the complete series leads to a different conclusion.

As demonstrated in chapter 2, there were poll results that could be used to suggest that a majority of the public favored war, but there were also ones to indicate that a majority was opposed to war. It all depended, of course, on how the question was phrased. Moreover, as also demonstrated in that chapter, for the most part there was precious little movement between November and January in various war support measures. An analysis of the full array of available data suggests, then, that, far from leading, mobilizing, or shaping public opinion, Bush was at best able to keep it from slipping away from him. And, of course, despite all his maneuverings and "international support," he barely won a congressional vote on the war.[1]

The notion that there had been a turnaround seems to stem in part from a January 8, 1991, article in the *Washington Post*. This report presents the December 14–18 and January 4–6 numbers from the question in table 63—a question that by its wording generates high amounts of war support since it rather blandly asks about going to war "at some point" after the UN deadline if Iraq refuses to withdraw from Kuwait. It concludes from this selection that "a growing majority believes force should be used to drive Iraq out of Kuwait" (Morin 1991a). Similarly, the *Post*'s January 11 report selectively prints the points from November 30–December 2, from December 14–18, from January 4–6, and from the instant poll of January 9, an array which also suggests increasing support for war (Morin 1991b). As can be seen in table 63, and as is discussed at length in chapter 2, a conclusion that support for war was growing is simply not justified by the full array of data in that table.

Hinckley's conclusion that Bush was able steadily to increase his rating for handling the crisis in the Gulf between November 1990 and the beginning of the war in January is based on a chart supplying only the November 14–15, December 9, and January 9 data from the ABC/ *Washington Post* data in table 12, a configuration that suggests Bush's numbers rose monotonically from 59 to 62 to 69 (Hinckley 1992, 111; see also Ladd 1991b). Similarly, Jentleson uses the November 30– December 2, the January 4–8, and the January 9 data from that table to conclude that a rise in "public support for Desert Shield" occurred (1992, 65). An examination of the full table demonstrates at once that the picture is more complicated and that no such general increase took place. In addition, as with the *Post*'s January 11 report, the *coup de grâce* number in these two analyses comes from the overnight poll of January 9, a survey that achieved an unreliably high hawkish response, as pointed out in chapter 2, and one that is not found in multi-day surveys carried out at the same time.

Freedman and Karsh rely on data in the January 8 *Washington Post* report (Morin 1991a) and conclude that "the President's approval rating for his handling of the crisis had picked up from its low point in December (from 61 percent to 67 percent), and readiness to go to war was up from 55 percent to 63 percent" (1993, 291). The report they use supplies the November 30–December 2, 1990 and the January 4–6, 1991 data from table 12 and, as noted above, the December 14–18 and January 4–6 data from table 63. Again, the full data from those tables do not support the notion that there were genuine increases in those measures.

Similarly, Gergen points to the 75 percent response from the January 9 ABC/ *Washington Post* poll to the question about using force in the Gulf in table 52, argues that it was "up some 10 points from the previous month," and then concludes that "public willingness to go to war rose sharply in late December and early January" (1992, 181–82). In this case the analysis is distorted not only by the hawkish inflation of the January 9 poll, but by his decision to compare it to the December 9 poll, which garnered the lowest number ever achieved by this question. By contrast, if one takes the multi-day January 4–8 poll as the comparison, war support had scarcely risen at all and was actually lower than it had been in August, September, October, or early November before Bush escalated.[2]

This exercise may help to illustrate the value of dealing comprehensively with poll data and of applying a range of information from a variety of sources.

The End of the War: Concern about U.S. (and Iraqi) Casualties

One of Bush's key decisions was to end the war when Iraqi forces had been defeated in the Kuwait theater but while Saddam Hussein was still in control in Iraq, and it was one that was to haunt him in later months and in his re-election campaign in 1992.

The decision to stop the war seems to have been influenced by a number of considerations—among them, the aesthetic appeal of being able to say that the ground war that routed what was billed as the world's fourth largest army had lasted exactly one hundred hours (U.S. News 1992, 397). As General Schwarzkopf says of White House decision-makers, a bit derisively perhaps, "I had to hand it to them: they really knew how to package an historic event" (1992, 471). If the war had gone as long as originally planned, it would have been more like a "five-day war," as Schwarzkopf pointed out to Colin Powell at the time. Since the Israelis had won a six-day (144-hour) war against the Arabs in 1967, the White House was perhaps looking for a label that seemed substantially, not marginally, shorter than the Israeli effort.

But the decision was partly influenced by a reading of public opinion as well. One of the January *Post* poll reports pointed out that "it may be difficult to sustain public support for the war effort if the conflict results in even modest casualties" (Morin 1991a; see also Mueller 1991a, 1991b), and the analysis in chapter 4 (and considered more fully below) suggests this conclusion is basically sound. Impelled by such reasoning, Bush was determined to minimize U.S. casualties. As he put it before the war, "I don't think that support would last if it were a long, drawn-out conflagration. I think support would erode, as it did in the Vietnam conflict" (Idelson 1991, 16).

Thus, Bush by no means wished to countenance the prospect of significant U.S. losses in a quagmire-like war inside Iraq as the military—which had not planned for such an extension of its mission—slogged around looking for Saddam Hussein. Moreover, he could reliably predict that Democratic doves, temporarily defanged by the amazing (100-hour) success of the war, would move quickly to criticize him if casualties began to mount in a foray into Iraq, pointing out as they did so that his lips had promised a short, low-cost war.

However, Bush may have underestimated the public's tolerance levels in this respect. By any reasonable standard, U.S. casualties in the Gulf War were so low they could hardly be said even to have risen to a level that could be called "modest." While thousands of deaths might have caused Bush enormous problems, the public, once its blood was up, would probably have been willing to tolerate the five hundred to one thousand battle deaths people like Congressman Les Aspin had predicted before the war—numbers that by the standards of Korea or Vietnam would be extremely low—if that venture would result in the permanent and deft removal from the scene of hostage-holding, atrocity-fomenting, environment-polluting, prisoner-torturing, near-nuclear, arch-demon Saddam Hussein (see table 163).

The White House also seems to have been overly concerned about public relations problems that might have been caused by excessive Iraqi deaths. Some members of the administration felt that the bombing of the Iraqi shelter was "a potentially devastating blow to the American public's support for the war" (U.S. News 1992, 272). In this, ironically, the administration was subscribing to the beliefs of Saddam Hussein, who had apparently been of the opinion that a couple of well-publicized and suitably destructive air raids on Baghdad would cause American popular support for the war to crumble in revulsion (Simpson 1991, 273, 281–82, 348). Moreover, the administration also seems to have been affected by stories coming out at the end of the war about the "highway of death" in which panicky Iraqis were being depicted as being casually slaughtered as they sought to flee Kuwait. A year after the war, White House press secretary Marlin Fitzwater pointed to "media criticism" as one reason the administration decided not to push into Iraq: "Right after the war they were blasting us for the 'Highway of Death.' If we had gone on, it would have been 10 times worse" (Murray 1992). As Schwarzkopf puts it disgustedly, "Washington was ready to overreact, as usual, to the slightest ripple in public opinion" (1992, 468; see also Simpson 1991, 7).

Schwarzkopf may be correct, but the data suggest that no such ripple existed. As noted in chapter 4, the public's view of Iraqi civilian deaths and its unalarmed reaction to the bombing of the Baghdad air raid shelter during the war (tables 250–255) indicate that the American people were quite insensitive to Iraqi casualties, even though they appear to have harbored little ill will toward the Iraqi people. Also relevant is the public's bland reaction to early estimates suggesting that a hundred thousand or more Iraqis had died in the war (as is discussed more fully in the next chapter, this number was probably very substantially exaggerated, as was the death toll on the "highway of death"). These grim statistics hardly dented the victory euphoria in the United States.

The Neglect of the Pearl Harbor Effect

The administration also seems to have neglected poll indications in another respect. When troops were first sent to the Middle East in August 1990, American leaders were intensely concerned that Iraq might attack American forces in Saudi Arabia when the Americans were greatly outnumbered (Woodward 1991a, 274, 304; Schwarzkopf 1991a; see also Simpson 1991, 197; Record 1993, 95–96). Public opinion data (see tables 126 and 136) strongly confirm the common sense that seems to have eluded the administration and some postwar analysts, but probably was grasped by the Iraqi leadership: any attack on American forces would almost certainly have had a Pearl Harbor impact on the American public and would, therefore, have been singularly unwise.

Indeed, the American public seems, if anything, to have been *more* willing to fight the Iraqis than it was to fight the Japanese if provoked. In table 126 it was found that upward of 90 percent said they were willing to "engage in combat" if the Iraqis attacked U.S. forces, while in a survey conducted six months before Pearl Harbor only 74 percent said they thought the United States should "declare war on Japan" if that country attacked Hawaii (Cantril and Strunk 1951, 1077), though the wording of the action option ("declare war" vs. "engage in combat") may account for this difference.

The image in the backs of the minds of administration decision-makers in August 1990 may have been of Lebanon in 1983 when a suicidal terrorist attack that killed hundreds of peace-keeping American marines eventually led the United States to withdraw from the country. But in Lebanon there was no clear enemy against whom to respond. An Iraqi invasion of Saudi Arabia would have been an outraging act of aggression against American forces by a hated and dangerous regime, and it would surely have provoked a reaction much more similar to the one inspired by the Pearl Harbor attack than to the one inspired by the lone terrorist in Lebanon.

CASUALTIES, POPULAR SUPPORT, IRAQI STRATEGIES, AND THE DEMOCRATS

Some analysts argue that, contrary to the discussion in chapter 4, the Gulf War experience demonstrates that the American public is not sensitive to U.S. casualty rates. For example, Norman Friedman argues, "Even though critics of the war predicted casualty rates in excess of [the] Vietnam experience, the public was generally willing to support President Bush" (1991, 255–56). Similarly, Bobby Inman and his colleagues argue that

> The U.S. public will support a war for a just cause, even one that may promise high casualties, as the Gulf War conceivably did in the autumn and early winter of 1990. They will withdraw their support when there does not appear to be any end in sight. (1992b, 288)

And Lawrence Freedman and Efraim Karsh argue that discontent in Vietnam "had not been so much stimulated by the absolute level of casualties . . . but by a faulty strategy. . . . The public and the politicians became disillusioned because casualties were being sustained *to little evident point*" (1993, 285; emphasis in the original; see also Record, 136–38).

In assessing these arguments, it should first be pointed out that American casualties in Vietnam numbered some 350,000, and no Gulf War "critics" were coming up with numbers of remotely that magnitude. Two well-publicized estimates were those of Joshua Epstein, who anticipated 3,344 to 16,059 U.S. casualties, and the antiwar Center for Defense Information, which predicted 45,000 U.S. casualties in the war that included an overland drive to Baghdad (Achenbach 1991; see also Muravchik 1991b, 18–19). Military analyst Trevor Dupuy, who boasted after the war that "fortunately, everything's turning out exactly as I said it would" (Achenbach 1991), had predicted U.S. casualties of around ten thousand with his various strategies (1991, 122).[3] And as noted earlier, the official worst case casualty estimate was ten to twenty thousand (Schwarzkopf 1991b, 349), again hardly comparable to Vietnam. Nor were war critics anticipating a war that would be nearly as long as Vietnam. In arguing against war, Senator Sam Nunn exclaimed, "What guarantee do we have that the war will be brief, that American casualties will be light? No one can say whether war will last five days, five weeks, or five months" (Apple 1991). For the United States the Vietnam War lasted not five months, but more like seven years.

Moreover, it is questionable whether it is useful to say the public "supported" the Gulf War before it began, since it all depended on how the question was asked. Indeed, it could be argued that Bush did not actually lead the American people to war, but rather, taking advantage of a somewhat permissive, and fatalistic, consensus, he simply started war while the public (and Congress) watched. As this study has shown, the poll evidence suggests that Bush was unable really to persuade an increasing number of Americans that war was either desirable or necessary—though he did perhaps keep the percentage favoring war from declining notably. And it is worth stressing that if the pre-war vote in Congress is taken to reflect public opinion, the United States entered the Vietnam War with wide support while it entered the Gulf War with support deeply divided.

It is no surprise that there was a substantial rally-round-the-flag boost once the war began. But the public was anticipating (and was promised) casualty rates that were quite low, certainly far lower than in Vietnam, and support would likely have declined if casualties mounted (see tables 92–95). And this would in all probability have happened even if the war was militarily successful—even if, in Inman's words, there appeared to be an "end in sight" or, in the words of Freedman and Karsh, there was an "evident point" to the war.

Iraqi Strategies

However, to inspire a substantial decline of popular support, the Iraqis needed to fight well enough to cause American casualty rates to rise. Because of the abysmal state of their morale and their leadership, this was probably never really in the cards—though no one could be really sure about this before the war began. The BBC's John Simpson puts it this way:

> It seems to me the Allies owe a great debt to the Iraqi people. If they had supported their leader, if they had felt the slightest enthusiasm for his posturings, if they had shared his hostility towards the West or his exaggerated notions of national honour and dignity, then they would have made Iraq a formidable opponent. Thousands of Arab, Islamic and Western soldiers would have died. (1991, xv)

Actually, even with a generally low state of morale, there were Iraqi strategies that could have inflicted substantial casualties on the Americans. After the war, Schwarzkopf was "happy as hell," he recalls, that "the politicians and military experts who had warned that dire things would happen if we went to war were eating their words." But he also points out that he "could conjure up a dozen scenarios in which the Iraqis would make victory extremely costly" (1992, 439, 467). It is to the great fortune of the United States, therefore, that Iraq did not have Schwarzkopf, or someone like him, commanding its side.

As it transpired, there is little evidence that the Iraqi leadership, such as it was, gave much coherent thought to how they might devise an effective strategy. But one possibility that was at least technically within Iraq's means would have been to make an Alamo-like fortress of populated (and therefore hostage-filled) areas like Kuwait City and to take a stand there, perhaps with only a few thousand, or even a few hundred, dedicated troops. This would have required the United States to destroy the city in order to save it, at a considerable cost. Indeed, the American military was deeply concerned that something like this might come about (see U.S. News 1992, 69; Moore 1993, 287; Friedman 1991, 215–16; Woodward 1991a, 280; Beeston 1991; Department of Defense 1992, 516; Freedman and Karsh 1993, 398). *Some* Iraqi troops, after all, *did* stand and fight. If these few stalwarts had been stationed in Kuwait City rather than in the desert, where they were hopelessly outclassed militarily, they could have raised the stakes considerably (see also Mueller 1991b).

Instead, the Iraqis played to American strengths by mindlessly putting their faith in set-piece defensive battles in the desert, a strategy that was destined to fail even if the Iraqi troops fought bravely (see Record 1993, 76–77). As discussed more fully in the next chapter, Iraqi forces were decidedly inferior in numbers—something the Iraqis were obviously in a position to appreciate if they had bothered to count their forces and to compare that number with the size of the enemy force conveniently and repeatedly published in newspapers and magazines, and on international television. Moreover, it should have been easy for them to determine that Iraqi equipment was vastly inferior to that of the opposing forces. For example, the best Iraqi tanks had a firing range of perhaps 1500 meters—something they were obviously in a good position to know—while U.S. tanks had a well-publicized range of better than 2000 meters.[4] Simple arithmetic, however, does not seem to be Saddam Hussein's strong suit.

Nor, it seems, did he or his commanders trouble themselves to think very hard about what their opponents might do. They apparently expected to be attacked only along or near the Kuwait–Saudi border or from the sea (U.S. News 1992, 290). However, their position in Kuwait left their right flank wide open for hundreds of miles and, as any number of armchair strategists in the West continually pointed out in the press and on television, a sensible strategy for coalition forces would be to sweep around that flank—exactly what happened.

For example, a book published and widely available before the war candidly discussed several possible strategies, most of them involving air strikes followed by enveloping movements around the Iraqis' right flank (Dupuy 1991). In an article published in the *New York Times* on February 6, 1991, two and a half weeks before the ground attack (and reprinted a few days later in the *International Herald Tribune*), columnist Leslie Gelb wondered aloud about how "everyone seems to know that the likely scenario calls for American and British forces to wheel around Kuwait and cut across the southern part of Iraq toward Basra." Meanwhile other newspapers were simply declaring "it is now no longer a secret" that mechanized forces "are to by-pass virtually all Iraqi fortifications on their way to the Basra area, thus slicing Kuwait from Iraq" (Taylor 1992, 234). Or, further, on page 24 of its February 11, 1991 issue, *Newsweek* magazine published a map "almost exactly depicting our flanking plan," as Schwarzkopf recalls. His reaction at the time, he says, was "This stinks! *Newsweek* has printed our entire battle plan. Now the Iraqis could put chemical weapons in that area and completely reorient their defenses" (1992, 440). Or as he put it in testimony after the war,

> I am quite concerned at the fact that some people went into a great deal of analysis . . . as to exactly what it was we could do, and then ended up publishing this in several well-known periodicals. . . . Had the Iraqis been a little bit smarter in the way they went about doing their business, they could have picked up on some of these things and used them very much to their advantage. (1991b, 341)[5]

But Iraq scarcely needed the amateurs. Weeks before the war, Chairman of the Joint Chiefs Powell had publicly telegraphed the essence of American strategy: "First we are going to cut [the army] off and then we are going to kill it" (Sciolino 1991, 257).

Nevertheless, as Norman Friedman observes, the Iraqis, "unbelievably, left their western flank entirely unprotected. . . . General Schwarzkopf could not believe that the Iraqis had not seen the same opportunity he had" (1991, 220, 224; see also Schwarzkopf 1992, 408, 439).

As it turned out, then, the Americans faced an opponent who was militarily incompetent to an almost monumental degree (see also

Mueller 1993b; Record 1993). In Schwarzkopf's contemptuous, but apt, assessment:

> As far as Saddam Hussein being a great military strategist, he is neither a strategist, nor is he schooled in the operational arts, nor is he a tactician, nor is he a general, nor is he a soldier. Other than that, he's a great military man. I want you to know that. (1991a)

But it was nonetheless entirely possible that, had the Iraqis been competently led, they could have inflicted substantial casualties on American forces.

The Democrats and the Potential for Declining Support

If that had happened, public support for the war—Bush's war, it would surely have been called—would have swiftly eroded. This decline would have been enhanced by a political element that was not found in Korea or in the early years of Vietnam. The opposition party had mostly voted against war in the Gulf, and if the war had begun to become costly in American lives, its leaders were certain, like their predecessors in the War of 1812, to become highly critical of Bush (but not, of course, of our gallant fighting forces) and to point out that they had advocated a viable nonviolent option, an option the trigger-happy Bush had rejected. If Bush found his promise of no new taxes to be political trouble, his strong assertions that a war against Iraq would be won quickly and decisively—a promise Lyndon Johnson had never made about Vietnam—would have been brought back to haunt him to a far greater degree.

In addition, a large antiwar movement had already been mobilized at the time of the war's outbreak. It largely fizzled as the United States met success in the war, but if U.S. casualties had mounted, the movement would surely have been rejuvenated, and, led by responsible Democrats and other notable war opponents, it might have had an impact if it could have kept its message from being smothered by the occasional flag-burners in its midst.[6]

This decline, of course, never happened, since the war was such a walkover: the United States suffered a total of only a few hundred casualties. However, as observed in chapter 4, on some measures there was some erosion of popular support during the Gulf War even with its exceptionally low casualties and even though the Democrats and other war opponents kept very quiet. Moreover, as demonstrated in chapter 5, there was some retrospective decline in support for the war even though it had fulfilled its declared "evident point" of pushing Iraq out of Kuwait and at very low cost. If the same thing had been accomplished at considerable cost, this decline would no doubt have been greater. Or, put another way, if there was disillusionment with the war because it failed to remove Saddam Hussein (not its stated "evident point"), it is reasonable to anticipate that the disillusion would have been far greater had this failure been accompanied by substantial casualties.

The Effect of Declining Support on the War Effort

Contrary to Saddam Hussein's ardent hopes, however, a drop in public support would not necessarily have led to effective demands to get out of the war. Once troops are engaged in combat, as has been discovered in such unpopular armed conflicts as the War of 1812 and Vietnam, it is difficult to generate the political will to back away. Indeed, although the Tet offensive of 1968 is often held to be the point at which the American public turned against the war in Vietnam,[7] direct American participation continued for another five years, and significant Congressional restrictions on the war effort were passed only after American troops were withdrawn from combat and American prisoners were returned.[8]

But a loss of support could have forced the President to compromise embarrassingly and, as happened to his predecessors in Korea and Vietnam, it could have ruined his presidency even if the war had eventually been won. And Bush, it seems, was well aware of this.

THE ROLE OF THE MEDIA

Characteristically, only a relatively few people actually fight in wars; the vast majority experience them through reports from others. Although this rather elemental observation has always been true, the Gulf War seems to have been special in the degree to which post mortems have been preoccupied with the role played by those assigned the job of reporting the events that took place (see, for example, H. Smith 1992; Fialka 1991; MacArthur 1992b; Taylor 1992; LaMay, FitzSimon, and Sahadi 1991).

Agenda Setting: The Message, the Messenger, and the Customer

The role of the media in influencing thought is often considered to be enormous. Most research on this issue, however, concludes that, in the main, media reports simply reinforce or strengthen beliefs already held by their readers and viewers (Kinder and Sears 1985, 705–14).[9]

However, some researchers, such as Shanto Iyengar and Donald Kinder, have concluded that the media—television in particular—are important not so much because of the way they influence opinion one way or the other, but because of the important independent role they play in framing issues and in setting the agenda for public discussion. "Americans' views of their society and nation are powerfully shaped by the stories that appear on the evening news," they argue, and they find that

> people who were shown network broadcasts edited to draw atten-
> tion to a particular problem . . . cared more about it, believed that
> government should do more about it, reported stronger feelings
> about it, and were much more likely to identify it as one of the
> country's most important problems. (1987, 112; see also Brody
> 1991, 111; Russett 1990, chap. 4; Page and Shapiro 1992,
> 339–48; Zaller 1992, chap. 12)[10]

In some important respects, however, the Gulf War experience seems to call into question, or at least to delimit, the notion that the media have a great independent impact in agenda-setting. The media, after all, lie in the middle between the events they report and the customers they serve. In a free, market-driven society, they must, of necessity, be sensitive to both, transmitting the actions of those who make the news and satisfying the demands of those who consume it. In the Gulf case, events, event-makers, and—particularly during and after the war itself—media consumers substantially called the shots (in all senses). The media, it seems, mostly followed, transmitting events more than shaping them. As Gladys and Kurt Lang observe in their study of press coverage of Watergate, "The main contribution of the media to moving opinion along was their extensive and full coverage of critical events" (1983, 304).[11]

Columnist Anthony Lewis may exaggerate somewhat when he argues that "Americans were not greatly exercised about Iraq's occupation of Kuwait . . . until George Bush skillfully used all his powers as President to bring the country into the Persian Gulf War" (1992b), but the data in tables 8 and 9 (see also fig. 2) do suggest a certain wariness and confusion on the part of the public immediately after the August 2 invasion. This evaporated by August 9 after Bush announced troops would be sent to Saudi Arabia (see also Zaller 1992, 269.). In general, it seems, the contest in the Gulf was put at the top of the agenda far more by the actions and statements of Bush and Hussein than by anything the media did. The media dutifully reported what was being said and done, of course, and they commented extensively on it in columns and editorials, but it was the message that dominated the media, not the other way around. Moreover, as noted in connection with the discussion of table 45, when the attention of the public and the media was diverted in October 1990 to the budget fight between the (newsmaking) President and Congress, it was the President, not the media, who brought the Gulf crisis back onto the agenda by his actions in escalating the troop commitment threateningly, and it was the ongoing debate between the President and his political opponents (and Hussein) that kept it there.

Once war began, as observed in chapter 4, the media found that their consumers had a nearly insatiable appetite for news—especially for supportive news—and that demand was assiduously serviced. Then, after the war, the media sensed correctly that their customers' interest had shifted—without being led or probed or manipulated by much of anyone, it might be noted. Accordingly, the media followed to focus on other issues—particularly the troubling state of the economy. A few months after the war, the main television network anchormen found themselves observing in a panel discussion on C-SPAN that, although they personally considered foreign affairs to be of major and increasing importance to the country, they were cutting their coverage of foreign events because their customers wanted them to concentrate on domestic issues. It was quite clear who was setting the agenda.

While the Gulf events demonstrate in some important ways the President's ability to lead and to set the public agenda, the postwar experience suggests that even he is far from all-powerful in this respect. It was clearly to Bush's electoral advantage to keep the war and foreign policy as lively political issues during the campaign and, as observed in chapter 6, he certainly tried to do that. But despite the advantage of his enormous postwar popularity (see Page and Shapiro 1992, 348–50), he found himself unable to divert attention to topics more congenial to him. The public had shifted its agenda and wanted now to focus on the sagging economy—something very much to the advantage of his challenger, Bill Clinton. Realizing this, the Democratic campaign doggedly sought to keep the attention on domestic issues: the campaign director's office was decorated with the slogan, "It's the economy, stupid." Only occasionally did Clinton bring up foreign affairs issues—and when he did, his remarks often received little play in the media. In general, instead of criticizing Bush's foreign policy, he substantially abdicated the area to the President under the apparently correct assumption that the voters didn't care much about it anyway (see tables 288 and 289).

Political campaigning often has far less to do with resolving issues than with encouraging the public to focus on issues that by their very nature will benefit the campaigner.[12] As Bush and the Republicans discovered in 1992, this is no easy task.

In sum, agenda setting during the period went something like this:

August–October 1990. The President focuses attention on Iraq's invasion of Kuwait and leads in putting the issue high on the public's agenda. The entire political elite strongly supports his policy. Actions by Saddam Hussein, especially in holding hostages, help to impel public support for Bush's policies. Nevertheless, on some important measures the public's support for the policy declines, probably bottoming out in October, as some of those who responded to the rally event fall from approval. In October, the public also allows the issue to fade from its agenda as it focuses, with considerable outrage, on the budget fight between the President and the Democratic Congress. The media dutifully report all this.

November 1990–January 16, 1991. The President escalates the troop commitment and leads the country toward war. His actions forcefully bring the issue back to the top of the public agenda and inspire a national debate. Most Democrats oppose his policy shift and vote against it in Congress. The debate leads to a polarization of support along party lines, but it is generally a stalemate with the public: support for going to war does not change notably one way or the other. There is, however, growing fatalism about the likelihood of war. The media dutifully report all this and variously comment on it.

January 16–March 1, 1991. The President launches war, which proves to be militarily successful beyond all expectation. There is a tremendous rally-round-the-flag effect and the issue dominates the public's agenda. Democrats cease criticism and vanish from sight, appearing in public only to wave the occasional flag in support of the troops. The media dutifully respond to Bush's event and also to the public's overwhelming desire for news about the war and for boosterism for the military effort. Despite the shrill unanimity of signals and the amazingly low American casualties, support for the war declines a bit—but then revives as victory is achieved. Bush becomes a popular paragon.

March 1991–November 1992. Almost immediately after the extremely successful war, the public, without cues from anybody, shifts its focus to the economy and comes to judge Bush not on his successful war, but on his apparently unsuccessful handling of the economy. The continued existence of Hussein in Iraq and the postwar turmoil in the area lead to some disillusionment with the war, but mainly the public simply ceases to think much about it one way or the other. The Democrats, peeking out from the shadows, gradually realize this and venture out to encourage the public to continue to focus on the economy. Bush, belatedly getting the message, forays out in his reelection campaign and tries very hard to shift the agenda focus from the troubling economy to the glorious war, but his efforts simply do not take, and he loses the election. The media dutifully report all this while complaining that its customers' demands are keeping it from spending as much time as it would like on foreign policy.

One view of the role of the media in all this would be to see them as purveyors or entrepreneurs of tantalizing information. They report on a wide variety of topics and they are constantly seeking to turn people on—and, consequently, to boost sales. For example, the editors of *Time* or *Newsweek* would be quite happy if every one of their cover stories proved to be a hot-button issue. Not all, however, do. If extensive promotion of a product could guarantee acceptance, we'd all be driving Edsels.

Like any other entrepreneur, the media are susceptible to the market. If they give an issue big play, it may arrest attention for a while, as found in the Iyengar and Kinder experiments, but this is no guarantee the issue will take. Like any business enterprise, they follow up on those menu items which stimulate their customers' interest. In that very important sense, the media do not set the agenda; ultimately the public does.

A useful case in point is the Ethiopian famine that received such big play and was so affecting in the mid-1980s. This is often taken to have been a media-generated issue since it was only after it received prominent play in the media that the issue—hardly a novel one—entered the public's agenda. But Christopher Bosso's study (1989) of the phenomenon suggests a different interpretation. At first the media were reluctant to cover the issue because they saw African famine as a dog-bites-man story. Moreover, the story had previously received some play, and it had stirred little response, thus suggesting that the customers were not interested. However, going against the consensus, NBC television decided to do a three-day sequence on the story in October 1984. This inspired a huge public response, whereupon NBC gave it extensive follow-up coverage and its television and print competitors scrambled to get on the bandwagon, deluging their customers with information that, to their surprise, was in demand. There is a sense, of course, in which it could be said that NBC put the issue on the public's agenda. But the network is *constantly* doing three-day stories, and this one just happened to catch on. It seems more accurate to say NBC put the issue out on the shelf—alongside a great many others—and that it was the public that put it on the agenda.

In the case of the Gulf War, similarly, the agenda does seem to have been set far more by the public (and by the dramatic events themselves) than by the media. Journalists and editors reported what was going on, and they correctly doped out that their public wanted more news about events in the Gulf. So instructed, they supplied that need, but they did not invent it; nor did they invent the issues that, for a while, so engrossed the public. Then, when the customers tired of the issue in the wake of the successful war, the media dutifully shifted their attention, despite the strenuous efforts of the previously influential President to keep the war euphoria and glow alive. In the Gulf crisis, it seems, the message and the customer dominated, even intimidated, the medium.

The Special Impact, If Any, of Visual Information

The Gulf War experience also suggests that the role of pictures—and therefore of television—in influencing public response has been exaggerated.

To insist on the importance of pictures is to suggest that people are so unimaginative that they only react when they see something visualized. Yet, Americans were outraged at the Pearl Harbor attack weeks—or even months—before they saw pictures of the event (see Mueller 1991/92). Visual stimuli were hardly required. Moreover, the Vietnam War was not noticeably more unpopular than the Korean War for the period in which the wars were comparable in American casualties, despite the fact that the later war is often seen to be a "television war" while the earlier was fought during the medium's infancy (Mueller 1973, 167; Mueller 1984b, 1991b; Mandelbaum 1981; Lichty 1984; Hallin 1986).[13] Similarly, as discussed in chapter 2, there was great sympathy for tortured and murdered Kuwaitis, even though there were no pictures of the atrocities.

It is not clear, in fact, that pictures were especially notable in influencing American support for the war at all. Pictures of oil fires, of birds caught in oil slicks, and of paraded American prisoners may have been vivid and outraging, but popular support for the war was already very high by then, and the public hardly needed additional visual assistance.[14]

During the war, one reporter observed that "you can be certain that if saturation bombing of the Iraqi capital becomes an American tactic, stomach-churning footage of bombed-out schools and hospitals will find their way on to American screens" (Taylor 1992, 11). The implication is that such pictures by themselves would cause war support to plummet—and, as noted earlier, Saddam Hussein seems to have been counting on such an effect. But the immunity the American public showed to the images of the extensively covered "highway of death" and bombed air raid shelter in Baghdad suggests there would have been little effect. As discussed above, the pictures of the "highway of death" may have influenced American policy by inspiring concerns in the administration about how the visuals would affect opinion. But, as also discussed, these concerns were not justified. In fact, war reportage (including information propagated by the American command) seems greatly to have exaggerated the actual extent of Iraqi military death. Yet, the public was scarcely moved by these reports.[15]

Moreover, if the most vivid overall perspective on the war is that it visited massive military slaughter upon the Iraqis, this impression was formed with only limited benefit from pictures. Except for the case of the "highway of death" (the bomb shelter raid in Baghdad mainly caused civilian, not military, deaths), the war generated few pictures that could be considered to suggest vast slaughter of Iraqi soldiers—for the simple reason that, as discussed in the next chapter, no such slaughter seems ever to have taken place.

The impression of slaughter, therefore, was conveyed more by words than by pictures. Many of these were issued by the military, particularly in briefings by Schwarzkopf. The rest came from the media which, for sensible journalistic reasons, generally find death and destruction more vivid and notable than their absence. For example, the front-page description of the "highway of death" in the *Washington Post* begins with these colorful words: "As far as the eye can see along this road to Iraq lies a tangled sea of scorched, twisted metal littered with bodies of Iraqi soldiers." Later in the report, the reporters estimate how far their eye can, in fact, see, noting that the "tangled sea" of metal and bodies occupies only one mile of this "road to Iraq." And they incidentally record that, so far, only 46 bodies had been found "littered" along the "scorched, twisted metal" (Claiborne and Murphy 1991). It would have been possible to place the story in a wider frame. Despite the appearance of massive destruction, the story might stress, the array of vehicles occupies only a one-mile stretch of road and the attack appears to have caused remarkably few Iraqi casualties. Similarly, a *Los Angeles Times* report discusses another road on which "Iraqi military units sit in gruesome repose, scorched skeletons of vehicles and men alike, black and awful under the sun." The report goes on to note, essentially, that there were only one or two vehicles per mile along this particular road and that the number of "scorched skeletons" numbered in the "scores" (Drogin 1991). Again, vividness is stressed over proportion or context.

This hardly seems to be a new phenomenon in war reporting. The destruction inflicted by the Japanese attack on Pearl Harbor was really quite limited, and it scarcely affected the pace of the ensuing war. Moreover, unlike the Gulf situation, official reports about the Pearl Harbor attack, including those by the President, tried to downplay the damage, claiming quite accurately that the Japanese had, for the most part, merely "temporarily disabled" ships and aircraft there, and that these had been quickly repaired or replaced. But despite such early, authoritative, and basically accurate debunking, words like "catastrophe" and "disaster" continue to be applied even in works that provide extensive information detailing how limited the damage was, how quickly it was repaired, and how irrelevant it was to the later war effort. It seems that writers simply find their fingers tapping out the words, "Disaster at Pearl Harbor," because the more nearly accurate "Inconvenience at Pearl Harbor" simply does not get the juices flowing (see Mueller 1991/92). In a similar manner, analysts after the Gulf War were casually referring to the destruction on the "highway of death" as a "classic slaughter" (Tsouras and Wright 1991, 115).

The Lack of Follow-Up

An enormous controversy has been generated since the war concerning the restrictions placed on the press by the U.S. military. Much of this has revolved around the "pool" system which supposedly kept reporters docile and under control at the time of the war (see, for example, H. Smith 1992, 1–220; Moore 1993, 319; Fialka 1991).

It seems to me, however, that a more serious concern comes from the media requirement to focus on the *now* and from its chronic need, mainly stimulated by the demands of its consumers, to move on to the next issue. Thus, there were very few stories retrospectively examining the war in a careful way or even seeking to explain why the Iraqis, previously so highly rated, committed such an astounding debacle. When the war came to an end, it became possible to find out what had happened by interviewing the troops and perhaps some of their many Iraqi prisoners. By that time, however, most reporters on the scene had rushed off to Kuwait City to document its rather predictable liberation, leaving the war behind for the historians, nostalgists, and mythmakers (Fialka 1991, 6).

In a book analyzing coverage of the Tet offensive in Vietnam, Peter Braestrup takes the press to task—with some notable exceptions—not so much for misreporting the offensive itself as for failing to follow up, for neglecting to reassess the event in its aftermath when more and fuller information became available. Instead, the press simply let its often erroneous first impressions become the established story (1983, chap. 13).

Something similar can probably be said for the Gulf War. As is discussed more fully in the next chapter, as the media dashed off to new issues they allowed the impression to linger that the Iraqi army had been massive and that it had been systematically demoralized and slaughtered by precise American firepower. And, although the media fragmentarily documented the depths of Iraqi morale—a key issue in assessing the war—they never really assessed when it was that this morale was shattered: Was it during the bombing, after it, or before the bombing ever took place? As the BBC's John Simpson pointed out a few months after the war was over, "Not many people seem interested in finding out what really happened" (1991, xiv). And a book published a full year after the war observes, "The complete story of why and how [the war] happened has gone largely untold" (U.S. News 1992, vii). It's a considerable indictment.

WAR AND DEMOCRACY

In *Perpetual Peace,* published almost 200 years before the Gulf War, the philosopher Immanuel Kant argued that democracies are inherently peaceful because

> if the consent of the citizens is required in order to decide that war should be declared . . . , nothing is more natural than that they would be very cautious in commencing such a poor game, decreeing for themselves all the calamities of war.

By contrast, in nondemocracies,

> a declaration of war is the easiest thing in the world to decide upon, because war does not require of the ruler . . . the least sacrifice of the pleasures of his table, the chase, his country houses, his court functions, and the like. (1957, 12–13)

In some respects, the Gulf experience of 1990–91 may supply support for Kant's argument. The Iraqis went to war almost at the whim of their dictatorial leader—though they seem to have had no intention of fighting very hard for that whim, and in deciding to go to war Hussein did face a considerable danger of substantial, even terminal, personal sacrifice. And the American democracy went to war only after a great deal of agonizing debate over the matter in which a great many people expressed a strong aversion to war. (Some people, like James Reston, suggest the President "snookered the country into war in the Gulf" [1991], and journalists Michael Duffy and Dan Goodgame argue that "crucial to Bush's success in winning support at home and abroad was his well-practiced and ruthless use of deception" [1992b, 41]. Others put the blame more on an ingenious and highly paid Kuwait lobby [MacArthur 1992a, 1992b]. But to the degree that these arguments suggest the American public didn't know what it was getting into when George Bush launched war in January 1991, they underestimate, it seems to me, the breadth and depth both of the public debate and of the ability of the public to assess what was going on.)

The Gulf experience, however, does suggest some weaknesses in Kant's argument. Bush was able to get the country into the war without increasingly bringing the public or Congress around to his view that war was necessary to resolve the conflict. And he carried the venture off in major part through unilateral Presidential actions that committed the country to a course of action that in turn increasingly caused people to become fatalistic about it. It is also important to recall that, whereas the United States entered wars like Korea, Vietnam, or World War II in the belief that only war could achieve the desired policy, the country went to war in the Gulf even though there existed a viable alternative for dealing with the problem presented by Iraq's aggression. Moreover, once Bush launched the war, the public (and Congress and the media) were catapulted into cheering, uncritical support that resembled bloodlust to some horrified observers. A true pacifism, it might seem, should be made of sterner—or of entirely different—stuff.

Policy Debates

Even more than other historical events, wars tend to be the subject of revisionist thinking, and in their aftermath it is common for myths—and countermyths—to be built about them. Often these become more real than the enterprise itself. As discussed in chapter 6, even though the inconclusive, even pathetic, War of 1812 brought the United States close to economic and military collapse, mythmakers afterward were still able to convince a willing public that the country had accomplished a glorious triumph. The Civil War became accepted as a noble crusade to end slavery, an issue that was essentially peripheral to its initiation. And the myths about Vietnam seem to be endless.

This chapter deals, rather speculatively, with the longer range impact (if any) of the Gulf War, and it reflects on how it might be remembered and evaluated in the future. At work, it seems, are two forces. On the one hand, there are the postwar efforts of George Bush and others to give the war a congenial and politically helpful spin, something that was of particular potential value, of course, during the election campaign of 1992. On the other, there are the efforts of various revisionists—many of them from the camp that opposed the war—to undercut the impression that the war was a major success, or indeed that it was a wise policy at all.[1]

Most active initially, not surprisingly, was the war's chief author, George Bush, who envisioned the war as his greatest moment and hoped to capitalize on it. As he found, however, there were problems: the war hardly delivered all the benefits he had variously seemed to promise in his successful campaign to lead the country into war.

139

THE DILEMMA OF SADDAM HUSSEIN

In the aftermath of the war, the most problematic concern for Bush, of course, was the continued tenure in office of Saddam Hussein. This dilemma developed from Bush's understandable reticence to extend the war into Iraq to bring down Hussein's regime. The public had followed him in major part because it accepted, or fully agreed with, his vision of Hussein as a singularly bad and dangerous character. Yet, in part because of the belief that the public had a low tolerance for casualties, an invasion of Iraq to remove Hussein was not built into Bush's war plan.[2] Thus when, contrary to ardent hopes, Hussein managed to linger on uncooperatively after the war, committing yet more outrages, the whole enterprise was soured. As Lawrence Freedman and Efraim Karsh observe, "Because so many people assumed, from the body language if not from the official statements, that the objective of the war was to remove Saddam, his continued presence served as a standing rebuke" (1993, 425). Or, as David Gergen notes, "It can be argued that Bush set himself up with the frequent Hitler analogy: if Saddam Hussein is Adolf Hitler, why did Bush leave him in power?" (1992, 183; see also Record 1993, 157).

As a result of all this, Hussein emerged from the war in the rather exquisite, if dicey, position of being able to inflict maximum psychic pain on his arch-nemesis, G. Bush, by simply remaining alive and in power—something he would want to do anyway. It presumably gave him great pleasure at the time of Bush's 1992 electoral defeat to organize huge celebrations in Baghdad (see Fineman 1992).

Because of Hussein's continued persistence in office, postwar criticism came from two perspectives. One was to suggest that the war was simply not thought through. Military analyst David Hackworth (1992), for example, argues that "the survival of Saddam Hussein at the head of a still-formidable Army means that the gulf war proved nothing. . . . For all the expense and sacrifice in Iraq, there was no strategic victory." And he quotes a returning solder who observed, "When we first got back to the United States, everyone was patting us on the back. And now they say: why didn't you finish the job?"

Hackworth, who favored a sanctions policy in the conflict, goes on, more grandly, to argue that "halfway measures don't work in war," that "once launched, war must be total," and that

it is time for America to learn that it must not go to war unless it intends to win on the battlefield. Bush and his generals were haunted by visions of casualties. . . . But if you fight to win, a lot of people are going to get hurt. The generals should have been willing to tell him not to risk any lives unless total victory was attainable.

Of course, if Hussein had been obligingly ousted after the Gulf War the way the Argentine militarists had been toppled after the Falklands conflict of 1982, the "halfway" war in the Gulf would have attained exactly the sort of "strategic victory" Hackworth calls for. But without that achievement, Bush can and will be criticized for failing to plan for what many people had come to think was the central problem.

The other area of criticism concerns Bush's policy toward Iraq before the crisis. Because Saddam Hussein came to be seen as a demon, Bush left himself peculiarly open to problems on this score. His precrisis policy toward Iraq had sought to placate Hussein, a policy Bush eventually admitted had been a mistake. But if people came to accept Hussein not merely as an irritating minor thug (like Panama's Manuel Noriega) but a world class criminal—the image Bush helped him to develop in the approach to war—the administration's inability to comprehend his full villainy before the crisis left it open to very substantial criticism. It took a year, but the Democrats and other Bush opponents finally began to zero in on this, and they sought to demonstrate that the administration had strongly tilted toward Iraq in the years before the crisis, helping Hussein to build up the military force which he eventually used to invade Kuwait and to confront Americans. As independent presidential candidate H. Ross Perot put it, Bush's preinvasion policy was to "burp, diaper and pamper" Hussein (Sciolino and Wines 1992; see Record 1993; 25–32; for counterargument, see Telhami 1992; Viorst 1992).

PEACE IN THE MIDDLE EAST

In the aftermath of the war, Bush and his secretary of state made strenuous efforts to bring the Israelis and the Arabs to the peace table, an accomplishment some, like political scientist Daniel S. Papp, credit as a notable gain for the war (Sciolino and Wines 1992). These talks made only limited progress, however. But then, in June 1992, an election in Israel brought in a government more agreeable to compromise with the Arabs and thus more congenial to American policy. This development can perhaps be credited in part to the Bush administration's tough policy on granting Israel some loan guarantees (a form of economic sanctions), but it would be difficult to argue that the election was notably influenced by the war which had ended fifteen months earlier. Israel and the Palestine Liberation Organization reached some agreement in 1993 (after Bush's defeat) in part because the PLO foolishly took Iraq's side in the Gulf crisis (and subsequent war) and became desperately impoverished when rich Arab states then stopped funding it.

Elsewhere in the Middle East, the Gulf War was followed not by a new tranquility to accompany Bush's highly touted New World Order, but by bloody rebellions by Kurds and Shiites within Iraq. The administration at first watched from the sidelines until badgered into humanitarian assistance by outraged pressures from within the United States.[3] In the meantime, however, Hussein's troops put down the rebellions with great loss of life and forced many Kurds into contentious exile, an unsettled condition that persisted throughout the 1992 election campaign season. Unlike the Falklands conflict, the Gulf War had a very messy and inconclusive aftermath—indeed, as suggested below, it appears that far more people died in the aftermath than in the war itself.

NUCLEAR WEAPONS

One of the arguments that was most potent with public opinion in the approach to war was the notion that Saddam Hussein must be stopped before he acquired nuclear weapons. It is not particularly clear that Hussein would have been able to do much with a nuclear bomb or two. After all, he was confronted by an enveloping coalition that possessed tens of thousands of those weapons, and these presumably could have been used to deter any use or threat of use. Thus, unless he and the people under him became utterly deranged, his bomb would probably have been of little consequence, though it might have helped to deter a military attack upon Iraq itself (see also Tucker and Hendrickson 1992, 114–19).

Nonetheless, Iraq's nuclear potential was something that was of deep concern to the American public (see tables 131–135), and it remained so after the war (tables 178, 180, 182). Thus the notion that the war had stopped the nuclear weapons program of this "near-nuclear dictator," in the words of columnist William Safire (1991), had substantial resonance. In fact, preventing Iraq from becoming a nuclear power, according to Safire, "was what the war was about" (1992).

Initially, there seemed to be great substance in this concern because postwar reports by inspectors in Iraq suggested the country had a vast nuclear weapons program and had been close to a bomb in 1990 (see, for example, Wines 1991; Milhollin 1992). Later analysis, however, concluded that Iraq was a long way from a bomb: it would have taken several years to make enough enriched uranium for a single bomb, and the design of its enrichment plant was fundamentally flawed (P. Lewis 1992b). Nevertheless, Bush was able to proclaim in one of the presidential campaign debates in 1992 without refutation from his opponents that "if it hadn't been for us, Saddam Hussein would . . . have nuclear weapons."[4] The nuclear issue may not fully realize its once-considerable potential, but it may continue to resonate.

LIBERTY

After the war, if not before, Bush was given to arguing that the war, after all, was about "liberty." Speaking in early 1992 before the Annual Convention of National Religious Broadcasters (whom he thanked "for helping America, as Christ ordained, to be 'a light unto the world,'"), he declared that "the finest soldiers, the finest sailors, marines, airmen, and coastguardsmen that any nation has every known" had fought a "struggle to protect what is right and true. . . . We fought for good versus evil. It was that clear to me: right versus wrong, dignity versus oppression. And America stood fast so that liberty could stand tall."[5]

General Schwarzkopf apparently reached a similar view. Before the war he had observed, "War is a profanity because, let's face it, you've got two opposing sides trying to settle their differences by killing as many of each other as they can" (Woodward 1991a, 313). And he had told an interviewer, "In a lot of ways I am a pacifist, though that may be too strong a term for it" (Simpson 1991, 206). After the war, explaining why, as a self-professed man of peace, he felt war was sometimes necessary, Schwarzkopf remarked, "There are certain things out there worth fighting for: . . . family, . . . liberty, freedom" (Frost 1991b). Since he ordered hundreds of thousands of troops into war in the Gulf, one of these, logic suggests, must have been at stake there.

It would not be difficult to argue that there was more liberty in Kuwait than in Iraq—either before or after the war—but the retrospective notion that the war was fought for that illusive, if valued, commodity is difficult to sustain. Nonetheless, the appeal of this claim may last. As with the War of 1812, Americans will want to believe the war was fought for something of value—as noted in chapter 5 and as can be seen in table 113, the war caused many people to shift to conclude that the Gulf conflict was mainly about moral principle. And *standing fast* so that liberty can *stand tall* does have a certain seductive swing to it.

THE LIBERATION OF KUWAIT

Bush and his supporters could also argue with pride and credibility that the war liberated little Kuwait—whatever its state of liberty. As indicated in chapter 2, there was comparatively little sympathy for Kuwait's monarchical government, and reports of its continued hostility to democratic reform in the postwar era did not enhance that condition. However, it does seem that Americans shared much of Bush's outrage over the atrocities committed in Kuwait by the invading Iraqis.

Revisionists can point out, of course, that pushing Iraq from Kuwait eventually brought about the deaths of a hundred or two hundred times more people than were killed by the Iraqis in their invasion and conquest, and they can suggest that perhaps war was not the best way to remedy the problem. And from a moral perspective they can wonder over the administration's remarkable insensitivity to the atrocities committed by Iraq against the Kurds and other Iraqis in the aftermath of the war (Tucker and Hendrickson 1992, 79, 100). And some will point out that the atrocity reports had been substantially exaggerated by paid agents of the Kuwait government (MacArthur 1992a, 1992b).

Administration defenders can argue that Bush's initial inattention to the conditions in postwar Iraq was justified on the grounds that undoing international military aggression does not necessarily commit a country to rooting out all injustice in the world, particularly where it is internal. On the other hand, the postwar horrors in Iraq were, of course, not random domestic events, but were in substantial degree the result of the war itself and of Bush's calls for uprisings against Hussein, who then brutally suppressed the revolts while the American administration watched from afar.

COUNTERING AGGRESSION AND MAINTAINING THE FLOW OF OIL

Bush and his supporters can also make use of the sound and appealing argument that the war threw back and punished "brutal aggression," as Bush usually put it. Moreover, the war did preserve the oil supplies so vital to Western economic development.

Sometimes Bush became positively hyperbolic on the oil issue, asserting to a campaign audience for example that, but for the war, "you'd be paying $20 a gallon for gas" (Dowd 1992). With somewhat more restraint, columnist William Safire claimed that the war stopped the dictator "before he could take over the world's oil supply and dictate our inflation and interest rates" (1991). And Daniel Papp argues, "Had we left Saddam there, he would have had control of something like 38 percent of the world's known oil reserves and he would have been sitting there menacing Saudi Arabia" (Sciolino and Wines 1992).

There are, however, other ways to look at these two key achievements and to question whether war was either necessary or wise to obtain them.

Aggression

It is possible to argue, for example, that to a considerable degree aggression had already been confronted and its rewards quashed before the war ever took place. Saddam's adventure was apparently stimulated primarily by perceived—if perhaps ill-considered—economic needs. It triggered a debilitating economic boycott in which he was unable to sell either the oil in his own country or the oil in captured Kuwait. Therefore aggression proved to be remarkably unrewarding. Although Bush and others are fond of invoking the Munich analogy of the 1930s, if the forces hostile to land-grabbing Hitler at the time had been able immediately to surround him with an alliance possessing infinitely greater force—tens of thousands of nuclear weapons to his zero, for starters—and been able, further, to fabricate an economic embargo which destroyed the German economy in a matter of weeks, he would have been stopped in his tracks, and world war in Europe would not have come about.

Thus if the point was to teach that aggression of this sort doesn't pay, the message was substantially conveyed without war.

Oil

Something similar can be said about the oil argument: any oil problems caused by Saddam Hussein's invasion of Kuwait were essentially solved long before the war began. There was, to begin with, a strong military force in place in Saudi Arabia effectively deterring an invasion of that country and undermining Hussein's ability consequentially to intimidate it. There is little or no evidence Hussein ever intended to attack Saudi Arabia (U.S. News 1992, 98; Hiro 1992, 120–22; Simpson 1991, 197; Record 1993, 95), and there are certainly no signs he contemplated doing so if it meant taking on the large international force encamped there which was backed by virtually every country (and every nuclear weapon) on earth.

In addition, Saudi Arabia and other countries were happily boosting their oil output to compensate for the supplies lost from Iraq and Kuwait—which together held some 20 percent of the world's proven oil reserves, not 38 percent, and only 8 percent of the world's oil production (Kuntz 1991, 22; see also Carpenter 1992, 192–94; Horwich 1992). Moreover, the excess profits the Saudis were garnering from expanded oil sales were enough, alone, to pay the costs of the deterring and protecting army implanted in their desert.

Interestingly, the fear of sanctions, so devastating to Iraq's economy, could be far more impressive to a future aggressor than the fear of aggression-punishing war (see Mueller forthcoming). The threat that the big countries of the world will gang up to attack a small-time aggressor is not inherently very credible because of the risks and costs they would bear in carrying out the war. Because of their post–Cold War unity, however, they can very credibly threaten massive economic punishment for aggression. After all, Iraq was a fairly significant country because of its oil trade; yet, the big countries showed that they could pulverize its economy at very little cost to themselves—that they could live quite well without it.

Alternate Strategies

Reflecting such a point of view, revisionists are led to suggest that there were viable alternatives to war to resolve the crisis. Robert W. Tucker and David C. Hendrickson argue that the United States should have applied a patient strategy of "punitive containment" which would extend security guarantees to Saudi Arabia and other Gulf states while lacing Iraq into economic sanctions until "it withdrew from Kuwait and gave satisfactory guarantees of good behavior in the future" (1992, 95; see also Brzezinski 1990; Mueller 1990a).

This policy differs from that pursued by Bush in its rejection of war, and it also suggests that the crisis was not nearly of the overwhelming importance Bush attached to it, at least as long as oil supplies would continue to be plentiful. Those advocating punitive containment would be prepared to continue the sanctions "indefinitely," and they would not require, even by implication, the removal of Saddam Hussein. One might have to wait for that desirable event to take place before the issue could be resolved if, as John Simpson concludes, "it is probably true than no measure short of war would have got him out of Kuwait" (1991, 218)—though it is worth noting that Hussein had agreed to punishing (but not suicidal) deals with Iran in 1975 and again in 1990 when his back was to the wall. Moreover, very much unlike Bush, advocates of this policy would be willing to make concessions over disputed territory and oil fields on the Kuwait–Iraq border.

THE WAR IN RETROSPECT: POLICY DEBATES

It could be argued that the huge anti-Iraq coalition had three central goals before the war: to free Kuwait, to make Iraq incapable of repeating its aggression, and to demonstrate to other potential aggressors that such aggression does not pay. As long as these goals were achieved, the coalition could make concessions. Appeasement is a bad idea only if it encourages further aggression—as the classic interpretation of Munich would have it. If the overall package of a deal is sound, concessions to an aggressor need not inspire repetition or emulation.

In the view of many, including Efraim Karsh and Inari Rautsi, the comparison of Hussein with Hitler is "largely misconceived." Unlike Hitler, Hussein carried "no ideological baggage." His "one and only goal" was "to reach the country's top position and to stay there for as long as he can"—one of the few things, it appears, he is good at. More-over, "he had not occupied Kuwait for reasons of power-seeking or po-litical aggrandizement. . . . Rather, the invasion had been a desperate attempt to shore up his regime in the face of dire economic straits." However, "public humiliation was his worst possible scenario," because he led a society where "loss of face is the gravest dishonor" and because "the public admission of a mistake as devastating as the Kuwait invasion could not but pose a mortal threat to Saddam's survival" (1991, 267–68, 239, 263; see also Dannreuther 1991/92, 45; Record 1993, 34–42). Or as Hussein put it to a Soviet negotiator, "The Iraqi people will not forgive me for unconditional withdrawal from Kuwait" (Freedman and Karsh 1993, 431).[6]

Hussein's estimate of his own survival possibilities seems to have been overly gloomy since, like Egypt's Nasser after defeat by Israel in the Six-Day War of 1967, he lived through a humiliating military debacle and was still able to hold on to his position. But the analysis of Karsh and Rautsi strongly suggests that he meant it when he said before the crisis,

> Do not push us to the point where we find war to be the sole avenue to a life of dignity for us and happiness for those of us who survive. . . . We are determined either to live in dignity or all die together. (Sciolino 1991, 277)

As one of those who survived, Hussein presumably has found a de-gree of "happiness" and "dignity." But as a result of his mindset, war was inevitable if the United States insisted, as it did, "that nothing less than an unambiguous humiliation for Saddam Hussein would consti-tute a policy success in the crisis," in the words of Tucker and Hendrick-son (1992, 86; see also Record 1993; Hoffman 1991). On the other hand, if he was not another Hitler, a deal would not necessarily have led him into other ventures elsewhere.

Revisionists might suggest that, in addition to lifting the embargo, the coalition could have given Saddam Hussein some of the things he had been lusting after: control over, or dignified and efficient access to, some disputed border territory and port facilities in Kuwait. The Kuwaitis had already suggested that they might be willing to work out something along these lines to get their country back. Moreover, Iraq could have received a no-invasion pledge from the United States and the rest of the coalition—something that effectively had already been granted by then-current policy. And there could have been agreement to hold a general Mideast conference to discuss, among other things, Israel's control of occupied territories. Israel had opposed such a conference, but just about everyone else, including the United States, had already endorsed such a meeting at least in general terms.

To obtain these concessions, a deal might have Iraq withdrawing from Kuwait and agreeing to reduce its armed forces to levels consistent with defense, but not with effective offense, thereby reducing its ability to repeat its aggression. As part of this, it would continue to accept repeated inspections to assure that it was not producing nuclear weapons. As an enforcement mechanism, Iraq might not be allowed to occupy militarily any areas of Kuwait that were ceded to it; these areas could therefore have been made hostage by setting them up so that the anti-Iraq forces could physically recover them should Iraq go back on the arms agreement. And of course the coalition could credibly threaten to boycott Iraq again if there were violations, since the world had shown by then that it could live quite well without Iraqi oil.

In the wake of an Iraqi withdrawal from Kuwait, it seems extremely likely that Iraq's neighbors—particularly the wealthy countries on the Persian Gulf—would develop protective military coalitions with the United States or other strong countries. People who live next door to a thug, even a reformed one, tend to be careful about locking their doors. Thus, in the future Hussein would have had no easy prey on his borders, and he would reign, until death or deposition, in a world of richly deserved distrust and hostility. To that degree, the notion that a substantial concession would leave Hussein with the ability to "cow the Arab Gulf states into subservience with his future wishes" (Karsh and Rautsi 1991, 239) would have been alleviated.

Moreover, after the crisis was over and Hussein was allowed to sell his oil on world markets, he was very likely to find, since other countries were still pumping, that the price was remarkably low—lower than it had been before the invasion and far lower than the price he had wanted the Organization of Petroleum-Exporting Countries (OPEC) cartel to demand before the crisis. Economically, therefore, the consequences of Iraq's aggression would have been severely punishing: the loss of all revenue during the embargo and the institution of an oil price lower than Hussein could have received if he had not invaded. And, as long as Hussein remained in control, international businesses, lending agencies, and other countries would surely approach Iraq with substantial distrust. Simply put, dealing with him had proved to be a risky business. He might still be able to cut deals, but the price would have been much higher than it would have been if he had kept the troops at home.

In all, therefore, under this sort of scenario there would have been little in Hussein's adventure to encourage other aggressors. Although he would have emerged with his "dignity" intact and although he would doubtless have done a lot of crowing about that, his expansion would have been stalemated, and he and Iraq would have suffered very substantially for his aggression. And Kuwait would have been liberated without a war that eventually brought about the deaths of tens—possibly hundreds—of thousands. Of course, no one would have had the pleasure of "kicking butt," but, as indicated in chapters 2 and 3, the public would in all probability have accepted a deal along these lines if Bush had led them to it.

The Defects of Punitive Containment

Whether this sort of abstruse reasoning about appeasement and aggression will weaken the popularity of the notion that war was necessary to push Iraq out of Kuwait is doubtful. Moreover, the punitive containment approach has its problems as policy.

For one thing, the despoilment of Kuwait would have continued during the lengthy sanctions period. The number of Kuwaitis killed during the occupation was probably only a few hundred (Cockburn 1991), but over time most would have been uprooted. Something like a third of the seven hundred thousand or so Kuwaitis were out of the country on vacation when Iraq invaded, and another third left during the occupation (Viorst 1991b, 42). No doubt most of the rest would have left, or been forced out, in fairly short order, creating a new diaspora (Ghabra 1991, 124–25). It would have been a rather well heeled diaspora— most Kuwaiti money, in fact, resided in accessible banks outside the country, not in oil reserves under it (Simpson 1991, 76). But it would have been a diaspora nonetheless. Moreover, as Stanley Hoffmann points out, the punitive containment policy essentially accedes to the (at least temporary) dismemberment of an accepted member of the United Nations (1992, 56; see also Simpson 1991, 213). Revisionists could stress, however, that the war that prevented this diaspora cost many lives, and they could argue therefore that the war was, on balance, significantly unwise policy.

The punitive containment strategy also would substantially leave intact Hussein's military power, leaving him technically free, after a time of recovery, to repeat his aggression. The policy does provide for reductions in Iraqi military strength and some restraint on its nuclear program. But to prevent future adventures, it relies primarily on deterrence—the ringing of Iraq with a hostile military opposition. Some may find this an inadequate safeguard and would hold that war and the forced inspections afterward were a far better guarantee, despite the huge loss of life entailed.

Another problem with the patient sanctions approach arises from concerns that the strategy simply wouldn't work because the anti-Iraq coalition would eventually fail, leaving Hussein not only with gains from aggression but also with threatening control over huge oil reserves. "If we had not liberated Kuwait and defeated Iraq's invading army," Bush argued in the 1992 campaign, "we would by now be facing the economic consequences, not of a mild recession, but of a deep depression brought on by Saddam Hussein's control over the majority of the world's oil." He was "absolutely certain," he said, that "if we had not moved against Saddam, the coalition would have fallen apart, he would be in Saudi Arabia, and we would be facing agony like we've never faced before in the history of our country." [7]

This justification for war may become accepted, but it relies on the questionable and minimally examined assumption that the coalition was somehow slated to fall apart. It is reasonable to expect that there would have been some leakage of the blockade, but by far the most important economic element—Hussein's inability to sell substantial quantities of oil abroad—could have been enforced forever by the only coalition component that mattered in this respect, the U.S. Navy.

Moreover, the postwar experience indicates that, in fact, the coalition *wasn't* weak. Because of Hussein's unwillingness to accept all the conditions of the postwar peace, the sanctions were continued and, although there were some leaks here and there, the essential elements in the coalition continued to hold, and Iraq remained unable to sell its oil. [8]

And to imply that neighboring countries like Turkey or the Soviet Union—desperate to curry good relations with Western Europe and the United States—would cut significant deals with the pathetic and increasingly impoverished thug in Baghdad seems an insult to their intelligence. Finally, this defense of the war ultimately relies on a rather fantastic notion that the Saudis and other oil-rich sheikdoms in the area would soon have become so terrified of the unreliable aggressor next door that they would order the protecting and deterring U.S. forces away, and then supinely give themselves over to the aggressor's dominance.

THE ECONOMIC EFFECTS OF THE GULF CRISIS AND WAR

In fact, far from bringing economic benefit, as Bush and others claim, it may be possible to argue that the drive toward war in the Gulf substantially caused or aggravated the recession that began in the fall of 1990. As documented in chapter 2, there was a precipitous drop in various measures of popular confidence in the country and in the economy in the aftermath of Iraq's invasion of Kuwait and during the fight in October 1990 between Congress and the President over the budget. These low ratings held until the outbreak of war in January (see tables 202 and 203 and fig. 7).

In discussing the economy in late November 1990, Federal Reserve Board Chairman Alan Greenspan allowed that the country had by then gotten into what he called "a meaningful downturn." He attributed this to three factors. One of these, the tightening of credit standards by banks, presumably had little to do with the Gulf situation. The other two, however, did. One of these, according to Greenspan, was the uncertainty about how the Persian Gulf situation would be resolved. The other was rising oil prices.[9] These rises, however, were not due to any objective factors of supply and demand: although Kuwaiti and Iraqi oil was no longer being sold on world markets, increased pumping, particularly by Saudi Arabia, had substantially compensated for the loss. Indeed, by early November, world oil prices were in a very substantial decline, a pattern that was arrested by Bush's announcement on November 8 that he was planning to prepare for war in the Gulf (Kuntz 1991, 25).

What was causing the high prices was fear of war: as Greenspan observed, "At the current apparent balance of supply and demand for crude oil, spot prices might have been expected to be substantially lower were it not for the uncertainties associated with the situation in the Gulf" (Murray 1990). Much of this uncertainty arose because Saddam Hussein had promised that he would destroy Saudi and other Middle

East oil fields (Greenberger and Sieb 1990). (When the war began, and this threat proved empty, oil prices actually dropped.) Realistically, however, although Hussein was creating uncertainty in the region, he was not threatening war in the fall of 1990; Bush was.

Thus to a substantial degree, the recession that became notable in the fall of 1990 was caused by Bush's drive toward war in the Gulf: as economic writer Leonard Silk observes, "the gulf crisis either triggered or aggravated the American recession."[10] Writing in the summer of 1991, five months after the war, he observed that the chairman of the President's Council of Economic Advisers was then arguing that "as the gulf crisis tipped the economy into recession, its end helped stop the recession and start the recovery" (1991). This prediction, however, proved optimistic—the recession, or at any rate its economic pain, lingered long into the 1992 election year. In its 1992 economic report, the Council of Economic Advisers noted that

> oil prices surged following Iraq's invasion of Kuwait and consumer and business confidence plummeted as the immediate outlook for growth weakened and uncertainty increased about the worldwide consequences of the crisis. . . . The Nation entered 1991 in the midst of the ninth recession since the end of World War II. (1992, 21–22)

Had Bush pursued and maintained a policy of patience and calm, of implanting troops in Saudi Arabia at deterrent, but not offensive, levels, and had he endeavored to put the whole issue firmly on the back burner while waiting for sanctions to work, it seems likely that the negative economic consequences of the Gulf episode would have been far less.

In a related manner, economist George Horwich (1992) has faulted Bush's refusal to follow the advice of his energy secretary and draw down the strategic petroleum reserve in the fall of 1990 to help dampen the bloated gasoline prices, a failure Horwich estimates caused a loss in gross national product of some $50 to $100 billion—a figure which exceeds "the entire cost to the coalition of the war against Iraq." Because the explanations from the White House for its policy were "bizarre"—assertions that there was no oil "shortage" and that a drawdown would amount to "price control"—Horwich speculates that the administration may have chosen "to allow fuel prices to remain high as long as possible to help persuade American and world opinion of the menace of Saddam Hussein to world peace and stability."

At the time of the crisis, Bush told aides "that he has no intention of allowing the Kuwait issue to linger, unresolved. If sanctions dragged on for twelve to eighteen months, Bush would lose face, popularity, and re-electability" (Barnes 1991b). Bush's successful war may have boosted his re-election prospects but, as it was to develop, the lingering economic malaise caused or aggravated by the war and by his drive to bring it about may have caused much greater harm to his postwar popularity and re-electability.

KICKING BUTT: THE ATTENUATED TRIUMPH OF THE AMERICAN MILITARY

Although the polls never seem to have asked about it with any specificity, one appeal of the war for some Americans was the sheer aesthetic pleasure they received from being on the side that thoroughly, elegantly, and cheaply kicked the contemptible enemy's butt. And, although the single most important physical butt, that of Saddam Hussein himself, was not fully, or at least not terminally, kicked, the war could still stand as a dazzling triumph for invincible American military skill and enterprise. As the victorious troops returned, they were met by exultant crowds proud of the way their forces had whipped what had been repeatedly billed as "the world's fourth largest army" at such amazingly little cost.

Bush's political opponents at first showed little interest in deflating this vision—that might require criticizing our heroic men and women in the military, after all—choosing instead to criticize his policies before and after the war. Thus Bush was left free to continue to wrap himself in the success of the U.S. military, and the impression of effortless triumph of craft and wizardry accordingly may linger and become built into folklore. Some revisionists, on the other hand, in part using the U.S. military's own data, eventually did come to argue that the war, far from an elegant exercise in kicking butt, was "arguably more slaughter than war," as journalists Peter Goldman and Tom Mathews characterized it a year and a half after its completion (1992, 22; see also Clark 1992).[11]

Because of first impressions, the image of the Tet offensive in Vietnam remains, despite the work of a generation of debunkers, one of Communist military success. In a similar manner it may be that, because of vivid first impressions left both by the media and by the military, the image that will last of the Gulf War will be, depending on one's perspective, that it was either one of overwhelming devastation caused by craft and wizardry or that it was one of mindless slaughter. But it may also be that, as the war becomes better studied, it will begin to take on more modest dimensions, suggesting that neither the wizardry nor the slaughter theorists had it right.

Increasingly, it seems that the enemy was far from being as large and as effective as feared and as touted. Not only was it ill led, as discussed in chapter 7, but it was mainly a pathetic, disorganized rabble, far smaller in numbers than pre-war (and postwar) estimates suggested. It was this circumstance more than any other, it seems, that led to the "miraculously" low U.S. casualty figures that so impressed General Norman Schwarzkopf. And it was this which caused the war to develop in such a surprising manner: as he put it, "We certainly didn't expect it to go this way" (1991a).

To begin with, evidence strongly suggests that Iraqi troop levels were greatly overestimated. Pre-war calculations by the military concluded that the Iraqi forces stood at 540,000 or even higher, and even well after the war Schwarzkopf continued to claim his forces were "outnumbered" (1991b, 336).[12] Subsequent, more thorough analysis suggests there were fewer than 250,000 Iraqi troops in the area when the ground war began (U.S. News 1992, 405–7; Freedman and Karsh 1993, 390), and another comes up with 183,000 while suggesting that the "number could easily be lower" (Aspin and Dickinson 1992, 33–34; see also Anderson and Binstein 1992; Mueller 1993b; Moore 1993, 233, 216).

Quite apart from troop strength, however, the unexpected outcome of the war was chiefly determined by the abysmally low state of Iraqi morale.[13] Thus, to evaluate the military prosecution of the war requires an estimation of when it was that their morale broke. It has been commonly concluded that "superior U.S. technology allowed the coalition to attack Iraqi forces and facilities with such precision that it broke their will" (Inman et al. 1992b, 184; see also Simpson 1991, 335; Hallion 1992, 232; Department of Defense 1992, 144; Freedman and Karsh 1993, 390). However, it seems more likely that the Iraqi will to fight, if any, had been substantially broken before a shot was fired or a bomb dropped.

The BBC's John Simpson frequently reported from Iraq both before and during the war, and it is his firm belief that "the population of Iraq as a whole had no interest in Saddam's holy war and simply wanted to be left alone to get on with their lives in peace." Most people, he concludes, "wanted to say exactly the same thing: how they hated the system in Iraq and the man who had created it, how wrong they felt the invasion of Kuwait had been, how crazy they thought the decision to oppose the West was." During the nearly five months he spent in Baghdad, "not a single Iraqi had defended Saddam Hussein to me in private, with the exception of two or three ministers and officials whose fate was closely bound up with Saddam's own." Simpson sums up, Hussein took "an almost entirely unwilling country into war" (1991, 182, 210, 267, 270, also 5).

Despite Simpson's impressions, there may have been some degree of enthusiasm for taking over Kuwait. The Kuwaitis are considered arrogant and contemptible by many other Arabs: when the Saudi ambassador was out with friends and needed to visit the washroom, he would say, "I've got to go to the Kuwait" (Woodward 1991a, 214). And many Iraqis may have bought the notion that Kuwait should be a province of Iraq. But that does not mean they were willing to *fight* for it. One senior U.S. official who debriefed Iraqi prisoners of war summarized their attitudes this way:

> While there was a feeling that it was worth occupying Kuwait, there was a widespread feeling that it was not worth fighting for. [The Iraqi military] felt Saddam would avoid a war and even up to the end there was a feeling he would find some way to pull out and save face.

Consequently they were not really preparing for war, just going through the motions: "There was no strategic design in the Iraqi troop development and the military debriefed say they thought they would go in, dig in and then withdraw if the coalition was serious about war." Not surprisingly, the troops became "plagued by a sense of defeatism as soon as the bombardment began" (Woodward 1991b). And a reporter who interviewed fifteen Iraqi prisoners said they

> sketched a picture . . . of soldiers demoralized and war-weary long before the Jan. 17 start of the allied bombing campaign and impatient for the ground offensive to begin so that during the confusion of battle they might run to the nearest U.S. outpost and surrender. (Claiborne 1991)

As one U.S. general put it, "Their heart just wasn't in this fight" (Moore 1993, 280; see also Record 1993, 100–101).

Many officers, it seems, abandoned their troops early (Cordesman 1993, 443; Dunnigan and Bay 1992, 75; Sciolino 1991, 259), leaving their pathetic charges to fend for themselves. However, since the Iraqi leadership, as noted in chapter 7, had no feasible strategy for dealing with its opponent, this was probably best for all involved.

After the war, Schwarzkopf was willing to credit America's great success in the war to weapons, modern technology, excellent training, high troop quality, and "fantastic host nation support" (1991b, 354). Another senior U.S. commander closed an important omission in this little list when he suggested that "Desert Storm was the perfect war" in part because U.S. troops were confronted with "the perfect enemy" (Aspin and Dickinson 1992, 3). To a considerable degree, then, wizardry was hardly required.

There have been efforts to ferret out rare examples of actual combat in the Gulf War and to build legends around them. But the real achievement for U.S. combat forces, contrary to the images projected both by the wizardry and by the slaughter theorists, may well be their humanity in routing their pathetic and terrified, but heavily armed, enemies without killing many of them. The United States and its allies had the Iraqis outnumbered, outtrained, outled, outclassed, outplanned, and, above all, outmotivated. However, they went into battle expecting the enemy to be numerous, dedicated, duplicitous, well-armed, and tenacious on the defense. Given such a perspective, they were entirely entitled to be edgy and trigger-happy. Moreover much of the war was fought at night and in the midst of ferocious weather and in dense smoke caused by oil fires, further confusing things. Yet, despite all this, massive firepower was kept in check and, while a great deal of Iraqi equipment was destroyed, there was a conscious, and apparently quite successful, effort to avoid the unnecessary killing of enemy troops.

Many of the initial estimates of enemy deaths seem to have been wildly high. Some allied intelligence officials speculated that as many as two hundred thousand Iraqis might have been killed in the war, another put the toll at 100,000, and a few weeks after it was all over, Schwarzkopf reportedly estimated that "as many as 150,000" might have died (Hiro 1992, 396; see also *New Statesman and Society*, June 21, 1991, p. 26; Heidenrich 1993, 109; Murphy 1991). These estimates arose in large part, it seems, from the colossal overestimate of enemy troop strength: if there were around 86,000 prisoners (Department of Defense 1992, 411) with perhaps a few hundred thousand escapees, and if Iraqi troop strength had stood at 540,000, it followed that, as Schwarzkopf put it in his famous briefing at the end of the war, there must be "a very, very large number of dead in some of these units—a very, very large number of dead" (1991a).

More careful assessments observe that Iraqi troops generally got the point that lingering in or near equipment like tanks meant certain death, and they stayed away from such obvious targets.[14] Accordingly, the famous "highway of death," which was actually only a few miles long, was more appropriately a road of destruction: most Iraqis "had jumped out of their vehicles and run away," recalls Schwarzkopf (1992, 468), and a journalist who inspected the sight estimated there were no more than four hundred deaths there (Simpson 1991, 350; see also U.S. News 1992, 409; Cordesman 1991, 66; Freedman and Karsh 1993, 408). Less than one thousand Iraqis were buried by the United States, and there were remarkably few wounded; in all, it seems quite possible that only a few thousand Iraqi troops died in the entire war (Heidenrich 1993; Mueller 1993b; see also U.S. News 1992, 406–9; Murphy 1991). And civilian deaths from the campaign of bombing Iraq itself—which also sought to avoid casualties—have been carefully estimated to be around three thousand at most (Middle East Watch 1991a, 19; Daponte 1993; see also U.S. News 1992, 409–10; Heidenrich 1993, 117–19; Simpson 1991, 5).

Militarily, the chief lesson of the Gulf war may be, in John Heidenrich's words, that "military effectiveness is not synonymous with human slaughter" (1993, 124). Yet the U.S. military seems remarkably unwilling to draw this lesson and to take pride in the remarkable way they managed handily to win the war without killing many of the (admittedly pathetic) enemy.

Ironically, as observed in chapter 7, it was the vast overestimate of the numbers of Iraqi troops, and the concomitant conclusion that the United States must have been killing huge numbers of them, that helped to inspire what is usually taken to have been the chief mistake in the prosecution of the war. Convinced that further warfare would simply be senseless death, the war was halted before it wreaked maximum damage on Hussein's army. In addition, as Norman Friedman points out, such overestimates in other circumstances "would have made offensive operations impossible, because too many forces would have been diverted against what turned out to be non-threats" (1991, 9).

In addition, the overestimate of Iraqi capabilities helped to bring about the major loss of life in the war. Erring on the safe side, the destruction of Iraq's communications and logistics capabilities became central to the American war effort even though it now seems clear that Iraq's problems as a military force were far more fundamental: when an army has no will to fight, an incompetent and uncaring leadership, and an almost complete absence of anything that could credibly be called either strategy or tactics, it is hardly necessary to devastate such capabilities to prevail militarily. But it was the destruction of these capabilities that seems to have helped to cause the greatest loss of life: not directly, but in the crippling of health and sanitation facilities.

Although Iraqi deaths in the Gulf War itself were probably not nearly so high as it first seemed, the war did lead to tens, possibly hundreds, of thousands of deaths (see the chart that follows). This mainly occurred in Iraq in the postwar uprisings and in the sanitation and health service breakdowns caused by the bombing, by Hussein's obstructionism, and by the persistence of postwar sanctions (see Ascherio et al. 1992; Daponte 1993; Tyler 1991; Murphy 1991; Simpson 1991, 6)—the part of the conflict the American military was never asked to plan for or to think about.

DEATHS IN THE GULF WAR

Kuwaiti citizens and residents killed by Iraqis in their invasion and occupation	500–700
Americans who died in Desert Shield and Desert Storm from accidents	108
American battle deaths	148[a]
Non-American coalition battle deaths	63
Iraqi battle deaths in Gulf War	Probably a few thousand
Iraqi civilians killed by bombing of Iraq	Some 3,000
Kuwaiti citizens and residents killed or executed by Kuwaitis in vengeance in the aftermath of the war	Several hundred
Iraqis killed in Kurdish and Shiite uprisings triggered by the war or dead as the result of breakdowns in sanitation and health facilities in the aftermath of the war	Tens of thousands, perhaps over 100,000

[a]Of these, 35 were killed by friendly fire, 11 by unexploded allied munitions, 18 by unexploded Iraqi munitions, 28 by a Scud strike on barracks in Dhahran, leaving a maximum of 56 killed directly by the Iraqi defenders.

9 THE DECLINE OF THE WAR AS A
MEMORABLE EVENT

The previous chapter speculates on how the Gulf War will be remembered in history. From the standpoint of American public opinion, however, the single most interesting, even amazing, aspect of the war is not *how* the Gulf War would be remembered—that is, whether the public would come to think ill or well of it. Rather, the question is whether the war, which boosted George Bush's ratings so spectacularly and which seemed so important and so tumultuous to so many Americans at the time, will be remembered at all. The war may have been the mother of all media events and the mother of all polling events, but it often seems that its only really lasting impact on American life will be the jocular addition to colloquial conversation of the phrase, "the mother of all . . ."

For some people it seems likely that the war will live on as a sort of glowing legend of manly achievement and American can-do prowess. But for most it seems hardly to have continued to resonate at all. The Gulf War experience, in fact, may say quite a bit not only about the impact of notable events on public opinion, but perhaps also about the nature of war itself.

WAR IN MEMORY

It is not uncommon for memorable events to exercise little long-range impact, particularly in elections: a very old political joke, after all, has as its punch line, "Yeah, but what have you done for me *lately?*" But the Gulf War at the time appeared to be no ordinary achievement. The five-month approach to the impending war was often tense and dramatic, and when it came about it seemed all-consumingly important: as one reporter told a friend, "This is the biggest story of my life" (Drew 1991, 90). As table 47 demonstrates, on the eve of the war, half of the people

159

claimed they thought about the crisis in the Gulf at least once an hour. Even as George Bush was asserting that the war would "chart the future of the world for the next 100 years" (1991b, 314), R. W. Apple of the *New York Times* was speculating that the war "could change the face of domestic politics, the map of the Middle East, the realities of big-power relationships and the world economy for years or decades to come" (1991). And the venture resulted in a colossal, almost storybook-like, victory.

The Vietnam War, as noted in chapter 6, was the great nonissue of the election campaign that was conducted a year after it was over. But in 1976, Americans didn't *want* to think about a costly and unpleasant failure like Vietnam. One would have thought in 1992, at a time when there were plenty of domestic and economic problems, that they would want to revel—at least a bit—in their recent and impressive Gulf success.

There may be special problems with remembering the Gulf War. Six months after it was over, there occurred in the Soviet Union a distracting development of potentially enormous historical significance as that country fell apart and Communism collapsed in the wake of a failed conservative coup. Moreover, because the Gulf War was such a walkover, it was difficult to generate memorable and attention-arresting tales of dash and derring-do.

But it also takes time to see how an event will play out in the public consciousness. Wars may often lack impact in subsequent elections, as suggested in chapter 6, but this doesn't mean they have been lost to all recall. The most memorable event in U.S. history was undoubtedly its Civil War. Yet for years after that conflict, there was a considerable desire to forget it. The building of myths—and of memorials and monuments—really began only some twenty years later (see Linderman 1987). Similarly, the Vietnam War was neglected not only in the election of 1976, but in most memory for several years. Americans, it seemed, scarcely even wanted to think about it—in part, perhaps, because they didn't want to have to consider doing something about the Khmer Rouge genocide then going on in Cambodia, a catastrophe that garnered a total of less than 29 minutes of coverage on all three networks at the time (see Adams and Joblove 1982; Mueller 1989, 190–91). Yet Vietnam eventually became a fabled and memorable event, even a haunting one, in the American consciousness.

On the other hand, wars can have an immediate impact but then fade from view. The Korean War may well have been the most important event since World War II in that it essentially crystallized the Cold War (see Gaddis 1974; Jervis 1980; May 1984; Mueller 1989, chap. 6), and there is quite a bit of evidence to suggest it was a major factor affecting public perceptions throughout the 1950s (see Mueller 1979, 314–15). And, as discussed in chapter 6, the impact of the War of 1812 also lingered for quite a while and importantly influenced several elections. But both of these wars eventually sagged from the public consciousness, and both, interestingly enough, have inspired books with titles proclaiming them to be "forgotten" conflicts (Hickey 1989, Blair 1987).

It seems important to take all that into account in seeking to explain the Gulf War phenomenon. Nevertheless, it is hard to escape the conclusion that, from the standpoint of American public opinion, as well as of world history perhaps, the war was really quite a minor event. It happened in a corner of the world far removed from the perspectives of most Americans, and it dealt with a second-rate dictator whose impact was not remotely comparable to that of Adolf Hitler, the figure he was often preposterously compared with. Moreover, however devastating the war and its aftermath may have been to Iraq, its costs in American lives made it comparable to the invasions of Panama and Grenada, and, as suggested in chapter 5, it seems so far to have had a somewhat similar impact on American consciousness.

Or perhaps it was America's Falklands. That little war, like the Gulf War, did lead to a "renewed national pride and self-confidence" for the victorious British (Hastings and Jenkins 1983, 340). And, arguably, it may have had at least some impact on the subsequent British election, although this may be attributable to the fact that, unlike the Gulf War, it had no unpleasant aftertaste (see chap. 6). In the long run, however, that almost comic-opera caper proved, not surprisingly, to be at best a footnote in British history.[1] A similar fate may await George Bush's "struggle to protect what is right and true."

WAR AS SPECTATOR SPORT

Another comparison may be useful. During the war, commentators were often swept away by analogies and metaphors from sports, particularly from American football. General Norman Schwarzkopf led the charge. He likened one of his most important military maneuvers to football's "Hail Mary" play (though it could probably more appropriately be compared to an end run). And discussing the enemy he noted, perhaps with some disappointment,

> You know, a football game can be over very quickly if the other team decides not to play. And that's what you had in this case.

When the kickoff came, okay, our team was there to play. Our team came to play ball. And they were not willing to fight. (Frost 1991b)

Or, as Major General Barry R. McCaffrey of the 24th Infantry Division put it, the war resembled "an eighth grade team playing a pro football team" (1991, 113; see also U.S. News 1992, 321). When explaining the American decision to halt the war when it did, Presidential Special Assistant Richard Haass also used a football analogy: "we didn't want to be accused of piling on once the whistle had blown" (Freedman and Karsh 1993, 405). And CBS anchor Dan Rather observed after the first day of war, "In sports page language—this is not a sport, it's war—but, so far, it's been a blowout" (Lichter 1992, 227).

As one writer put it a year after the conflict,

The Gulf War more resembled a Gulf Bowl. It was the biggest spectator sport of the year, and as euphoric as any playoff—a groundswell of giddy enthusiasm for Team America, like a homecoming game, with Stormin' Norman as Big Man on Campus. (Farwell 1992; see also Halberstam 1992, 139)

The analogy shouldn't be pushed too far, but there are quite a few similarities. Football, or at any rate tackle football, is indeed a spectator sport in the sense that, unlike other team sports, it is not commonly played in sandlots. Thus, like war, viewers mainly experience it vicariously—only a few actually participate. In both war and football, teamwork, team morale, and a sense of comradeship are extremely important. And in both cases the fans cheer for their team to win and to be Number One, experience a sort of catharsis when the event is over, and tend to overlook the longer range costs to the participants.[2] As a spectator event, war does have one notable advantage over sports: victory and defeat are not objective, but lie in the eye of the beholder. Consequently the fans for *both* sides can sometimes revel in what they take to be victory.[3]

For present purposes, the analogy with spectator sports carries with it one parallel that seems particularly instructive. At the time of breathless anticipation and then finally of violent consummation, the Big Game becomes thunderously, all-consumingly important. But once it is over, even the most ardent of fans, after perhaps a few hours or days of residual exhilaration and celebration (or depression and gloom), move on to other concerns and leave it all behind.

One last poll result might be instructive in this regard. In December

1984, CBS Sports conducted a poll in which people who said they were football fans were asked a series of memory-jogging questions about favorite players and teams. Then they were asked to name the team which had won the Super Bowl the previous January. Only 39 percent were able to recall.[4]

Something like this may be happening with the Gulf War. Those affected physically or personally by the event may never be able to forget it, but those affected only psychically are often able to do so quite easily. Few of the war's many American fans will forget who won, at least in the strict military sense. But like the Big Game, which at the time seems of such monumental importance and generates such overwhelming fascination, the Gulf War soon faded, it seems, as a notable and motivating event. From the standpoint of public opinion, that curious and rather unexpected quality appears to be its most striking—and in a sense memorable—legacy.

Part Five..

Tables

LIST OF TABLES ···

64. Should Congress endorse UN resolution?
65. Approve Congress voting to allow Bush to go to war
66. Begin to withdraw, continue presence, increase troop levels
67. Will the economic boycott make Iraq withdraw?
68. Can U.S. achieve its objectives solely through sanctions?
69. How long should U.S. wait for sanctions to work?
70. Favor waiting two years for sanctions to work
71. Would sanctions eventually have forced Iraqis from Kuwait?
72. Should Bush quickly begin military action, or wait?
73. Should Bush begin military action soon after January 15?
74. Should U.S. use military force in three months?
75. Should U.S. keep forces in Saudi Arabia until Iraq withdraws?
76. Withdraw, continue sanctions, initiate war
77. Should U.S. continue sanctions no matter how long it takes and not resort to war?
78. Have sanctions been given enough time?
79. Should sanctions be given more time, or should stronger action be taken?
80. Should U.S. start military actions after January 15 or wait longer?
81. Did U.S. do the right thing starting military actions?
82. Should U.S. attack Iraq after January 15 or give sanctions more time?
83. After January 15, should U.S. continue to wait or take military action?
84. Should U.S. go to war after January 15 or give sanctions more time?
85. Should U.S. go to war after January 15 or give sanctions more time?
86. Attack Iraq after January 15 or continue sanctions and diplomacy.
87. Should U.S. attack immediately after January 15, extend the deadline, or rely on sanctions?
88. Did Bush give sanctions enough time?
89. Favor going to war if Iraq does not withdraw by January 15
90. Pull out, diplomacy, tighten embargo, tougher military action
91. What should U.S. do concerning the situation? (open ended)
92. Attack if 1,000–30,000 troops are killed
93. Should U.S. go to war after January 15 if 1,000–10,000 troops are killed?
94. Should U.S. go to war after January 15 if 1,000–10,000 troops are killed? (experiment)
95. Consider war a success if 0–20,000 troops died
96. Is U.S. action in the Mideast morally justified?
97. Always opposed the war, agreed once it was on, always supported it

Negotiations

98. Has Bush tried hard diplomatically or been too quick to use military?

136. Conditions under which U.S. should take military action
137. Is liberation of Kuwait worth fighting for?
138. Conditions under which U.S. might withdraw troops
139. Seen media coverage of Hussein meeting with hostages
140. If hostages are released, are you more or less willing to support military action?
141. Is hostage release a sign Iraq is willing to pull out?
142. Is hostage release an effort for peace or a public relations gesture?
143. Troops should defend Saudi Arabia, regain Kuwait, invade Iraq and overthrow Hussein
144. Goal to force Iraq out, remove Hussein, destroy Iraq's nuclear capacity
145. Purposes for which military forces might be used
146. Approve attacking Iraqi troops in Kuwait, air strikes inside Iraq, assassinating Hussein
147. Support for covert assassination of Hussein to end crisis
148. Should U.S. assassinate Hussein?
149. Should U.S. attempt to kill Hussein?
150. If Iraq withdraws, should U.S. eliminate Hussein's war capability, or Hussein himself?
151. If war breaks out, should we fight for Kuwait or continue to remove Hussein?
152. Is it enough to drive Iraq from Kuwait or should U.S. see Hussein removed from power?
153. Should U.S. continue fighting to force Hussein from power if Iraq withdraws?
154. What must happen for U.S. to be successful in the war?
155. Should final objective be forcing Iraq from Kuwait or forcing Hussein from power?
156. End war only if Hussein leaves power?
157. Stop war after taking Kuwait or take control of Iraq too?
158. Should U.S. troops keep fighting until Iraq leaves Kuwait, its military is destroyed, or Hussein is removed?
159. Disappointed if Hussein is alive when the war ends
160. Disappointed in Bush if Hussein is still in power after the war
161. Did Bush make correct decision to stop the fighting or should he have continued until Hussein removed?
162. Should U.S. continue action until Iraq withdraws, or go beyond UN resolutions and fight until Hussein is removed?
163. Given UN limited authorization, should U.S. stop fighting when Iraq leave Kuwait, or continue until Hussein is removed?
164. Should U.S. have continued until Hussein was removed?
165. U.S. should not have ended the war with Hussein still in power
166. U.S. ended the war too soon
167. Cease-fire order too soon, before Hussein toppled
168. Was it correct to stop the fighting or should we have fought longer?

169. Should U.S. have stopped fighting or continued until Hussein was removed?
170. Did U.S. end the war too soon?
171. Should U.S. have continued fighting to force Hussein from power?
172. Should U.S. resume military action to force Hussein from power?
173. Steps U.S. should take to remove Hussein
174. Should U.S. try to remove Hussein?
175. Take military action against Iraq at this time
176. Use military force to remove Hussein
177. If Iraq uses chemical weapons against his own people, favor restarting military action
178. Resume military action if Iraq refuses to remove nuclear capability
179. Objective of resumption of military action should be to destroy Iraq's nuclear capability or remove Hussein
180. Use military means to remove Iraq's nuclear capabilities
181. If Iraq is not complying with cease fire terms, should U.S. bomb Iraq?
182. Should U.S. resume military action if Hussein continues to develop nuclear weapons?
183. If Hussein refuses to comply with cease fire terms, should U.S. take military action including removing Hussein?
184. Lift sanctions while Hussein remains in power
185. Most important reason it was worth going to war

Evaluations of Victory

186. What would a victory for the U.S. be?
187. How successful was the war?
188. How successful was the U.S. military effort?
189. How successful was the U.S. military effort?
190. Victory if Iraq leaves Kuwait but Hussein remains in power
191. Victory if Hussein leaves most of Kuwait but keeps an oilfield
192. Can U.S. claim victory if Hussein remains in power?
193. Victory with Hussein out of Kuwait but in power
194. Did U.S. win total, partial, or no victory?
195. With Hussein in power, was it a victory?
196. Was the war a success?

Satisfaction with, Confidence in, the Country

197. Satisfaction with the way things going in U.S.
198. Are things going in the right direction or pretty seriously off on the wrong track?

NOTE ON CONVENTIONS USED IN TABLES ....

The tables used in this study follow, and make use of the following conventions.

A *heavy bar* separates poll questions asked before Iraq's August 2, 1990 invasion of Kuwait from those asked after it.

Shaded entries in the tables indicate poll questions that were asked during the Gulf War (that is, between January 16 and February 28, 1991). Where a question was asked both before and after the war, but not during it, the table usually includes a blank shaded row to indicate when it was that the war took place relative to the other questions in the series.

In many cases there is a number to the right of the "Don't know" column, headed *n*. This indicates the sample size for the poll in question where that number was available. That number was usually obtained from materials at the Roper Center, a repository of survey results. When the number was obtained from other materials—chiefly press releases or other publications by the polling agencies—it is italicized. When any information in a table was obtained from a source other than the Roper Center, that source is indicated at the end of the table.

Responses that were *volunteered* by respondents are labeled "(vol)" in the table headings.

An asterisk (*) in a cell indicates a nonzero response below 0.5 percent.

Each table includes an indication of the sponsor of the survey—generally a newspaper, television network, or magazine—or of the survey agency which conducted the poll—Gallup Poll, Roper Organization, Gordon S. Black Corporation, etc.

APPROVAL OF, AND EVALUATIONS OF, GEORGE BUSH AND HIS DECISIONS ....

Do you approve or disapprove of the way George Bush is handling his job as president? (Gallup, Gallup/*Newsweek*, Gallup/*USA Today*/CNN)

	Approve Bush	Disapprove	Don't know
1989 Jan 24–26	51	6	43
1989 Feb 28–Mar 2	63	13	24
1989 Mar 10–13	56	16	28
1989 Apr 10–16	58	16	26
1989 May 4–7	56	22	22
1989 Jun 8–11	70	14	16
1989 Jul 6–9	66	19	15
1989 Aug 10–13	69	19	12
1989 Sep 7–10	70	17	13
1989 Oct 5–8	68	20	12
1989 Nov 2–5	70	17	13
1989 Dec 7–10	71	20	9
1990 Jan 4–7	80	11	9
1990 Feb 8–11	73	16	11
1990 Feb 15–18	73	16	11
1990 Mar 8–11	68	18	14
1990 Mar 15–18	74	15	11
1990 Apr 5–8	68	16	16
1990 Apr 19–22	67	17	16
1990 May 17–20	65	20	15
1990 Jun 7–10	67	18	15
1990 Jun 15–17	69	17	14

Table 1 continued

	Approve Bush	Disapprove	Don't know
1990 Jul 6–8	63	24	13
1990 Jul 19–22	60	25	15
1990 Aug 9–12	74	16	10
1990 Aug 16–19	75	16	9
1990 Aug 23–26	76	16	8
1990 Aug 30–Sep 2	74	17	9
1990 Sep 10–11	76	16	8
1990 Sep 14–16	73	17	10
1990 Sep 27–30	67	20	13
1990 Oct 3–4	66	25	9
1990 Oct 11–14	56	33	11
1990 Oct 18–21	53	37	10
1990 Oct 25–28	54	36	10
1990 Nov 1–4	58	32	10
1990 Nov 8–11	58	34	8
1990 Nov 15–18	54	33	13
1990 Nov 29–Dec 2	61	29	10
1990 Dec 6–9	58	33	9
1990 Dec 13–16	63	30	7
1991 Jan 3–6	58	31	11
1991 Jan 11–13	64	25	11
1991 Jan 17–20	82	12	6
1991 Jan 19–22	80	14	6
1991 Jan 23–26	83	13	4
1991 Jan 30–Feb 2	82	15	3
1991 Feb 7–10	79	18	3
1991 Feb 14–17	80	14	6
1991 Feb 21–24	80	13	7
1991 Feb 28–Mar 3	89	8	3
1991 Mar 7–10	87	8	5
1991 Mar 14–17	86	9	5
1991 Mar 21–24	84	10	6
1991 Mar 28–30	82	11	7
1991 Apr 4–6	83	12	5
1991 Apr 11–14	77	13	10

Table 1 continued

	Approve Bush	Disapprove	Don't know
1991 Apr 25–28	76	15	9
1991 May 2–5	74	19	7
1991 May 16–19	77	15	8
1991 May 23–26	76	16	8
1991 May 30–Jun 2	74	17	9
1991 Jun 13–16	71	22	6
1991 Jun 27–30	72	22	6
1991 Jul 11–14	72	21	7
1991 Jul 18–21	70	21	9
1991 Jul 25–28	71	21	8
1991 Aug 8–11	71	22	7
1991 Aug 23–25	74	18	8
1991 Aug 29–Sep 3	69	22	9
1991 Sep 5–8	70	21	9
1991 Sep 13–15	68	22	10
1991 Sep 26–29	66	25	9
1991 Oct 3–6	66	25	9
1991 Oct 10–13	66	28	6
1991 Oct 17–20	66	26	8
1991 Oct 24–27	62	29	9
1991 Oct 31–Nov 3	59	33	8
1991 Nov 7–10	56	36	8
1991 Nov 14–17	56	36	8
1991 Nov 21–24	52	39	9
1991 Dec 5–8	52	42	6
1991 Dec 12–15	50	41	9
1992 Jan 3–6	46	47	7
1992 Jan 16–19	46	48	6
1992 Jan 31–Feb 2	47	48	5
1992 Feb 6–9	44	48	8
1992 Feb 19–20	39	47	14
1992 Feb 28–Mar 1	41	53	6
1992 Mar 11–12	41	47	12
1992 Mar 20–22	41	49	10
1992 Mar 26–29	42	51	7

Table 1 continued

	Approve Bush	Disapprove	Don't know
1992 Apr 9–12	39	54	7
1992 Apr 20–22	42	48	10
1992 May 7–10	40	53	7
1992 May 18–20	41	52	7
1992 Jun 4–8	37	56	7
1992 Jun 12–14	37	55	8
1992 Jun 26–29	38	55	7
1992 Jul 24–26	32	59	9
1992 Jul 31–Aug 1	29	60	11
1992 Aug 8–10	35	58	7
1992 Aug 21–22	40	54	6
1992 Aug 31–Sep 2	39	54	7
1992 Sep 11–15	39	55	6
1992 Sep 17–20	36	54	10
1992 Oct 1–3	33	58	9
1992 Oct 12–14	34	56	10
1992 Nov 20–22	43	46	11
1992 Dec 4–6	49	47	4
1992 Dec 18–20	49	41	10

Gallup Poll Monthly, December 1992.

2   Please tell me which word or phrase better describes your impression of George Bush. If you feel neither phrase describes Bush, please say so. (Gallup)

A	Sincere	Insincere	Don't know	*n*
1988 Aug 5–7	59	26	15	
1988 Aug 18–19	74	15	11	1000
1990 Feb 8–11	85	9	6	1228
1990 Jul 6–8	75	18	7	1240
1990 Nov 8–11	74	19	7	1008
1991 Mar 7–10	87	7	6	1018

B	Steady	Undependable	Don't know	
1988 Aug 5–7	59	27	14	
1988 Aug 18–19	73	19	8	1000

182

Table 2 continued

B	Steady	Undependable	Don't know	
1990 Feb 8–11	83	8	9	1228
1990 Jul 6–8	72	19	9	1240
1990 Nov 8–11	67	23	10	1008
1991 Mar 7–10	88	6	6	1018

C	Intelligent	Average	Don't know	
1988 Aug 5–7	61	33	6	
1988 Aug 18–19	70	27	3	1000
1990 Feb 8–11	72	25	3	1228
1990 Jul 6–8	66	31	3	1240
1990 Nov 8–11	65	33	2	1008
1991 Mar 7–10	83	15	2	1018

D	Confident	Insecure	Don't know	
1988 Aug 5–7	56	32	12	
1988 Aug 18–19	67	25	8	1000
1990 Feb 8–11	82	12	6	1228
1990 Jul 6–8	76	18	6	1240
1990 Nov 8–11	72	22	6	1008
1991 Mar 7–10	91	6	3	1018

E	Warm, friendly	Cold, unfriendly	Don't know	
1988 Aug 5–7	49	28	23	
1988 Aug 18–19	65	18	17	1000
1990 Feb 8–11	86	5	9	1228
1990 Jul 6–8	84	7	9	1240
1990 Nov 8–11	80	11	9	1008
1991 Mar 7–10	89	4	7	1018

F	Strong	Weak	Don't know	
1988 Aug 5–7	42	39	19	
1988 Aug 18–19	57	28	15	1000

Table 2 continued

F	Strong	Weak	Don't know	
1990 Feb 8–11	73	14	13	1228
1990 Jul 6–8	63	21	16	1240
1990 Nov 8–11	62	22	16	1008
1991 Mar 7–10	88	5	7	1018

G	Leader	Follower	Don't know	
1988 Aug 5–7	37	52	11	
1988 Aug 18–19	50	39	11	1000
1990 Feb 8–11	75	18	7	1228
1990 Jul 6–8	67	24	8	1240
1990 Nov 8–11	68	20	12	1008
1991 Mar 7–10	88	7	5	1018

H	Active	Passive	Don't know	
1990 Jul 6–8	70	22	8	1240
1990 Nov 8–11	71	21	8	1008
1991 Mar 7–10	91	6	3	1018

1988 Aug 5–7 poll: registered voters only. *Gallup Poll Monthly,* March 1991, pp. 10–11

3 Now let me ask you about some specific problems facing the country. As I read off each one, would you tell me whether you approve or disapprove of the way President Bush is handling that problem? (Gallup)

	Approve	Disapprove	Don't know	*n*
A Foreign policy				
1989 Mar 10–13	62	15	23	
1989 Nov 9–12	65	21	14	1230
1990 Jul 6–8	62	26	12	1240
1990 Oct 11–14	61	29	10	1009
1991 Feb 28–Mar 3	84			
1991 Mar 7–10[a]	79	11	10	1018
1991 Jun 26–29	64	28	8	1000
1991 Jul 18–21	71	19	10	1002

Table 3 continued

	Approve	Disapprove	Don't know	*n*
1991 Aug 8–11	68	25	7	1013
1991 Aug 23–25[a]	74	20	6	1018
1991 Sep 13–15	70	21	9	1216
1991 Oct 3–6	70	25	5	1003
1991 Oct 24–27	68	26	6	1003
1991 Dec 5–8	64	29	7	1004
1992 Jan 3–6	64			
1992 Jan 31–Feb 2	65			
1992 Feb 28–Mar 1	55	40	5	1001
1992 Mar 20–22[b]	60	37	3	1301
1992 Apr 20–22[b]	60	35	5	1273

B Economic conditions in this country				
1989 Mar 10–13	52	27	21	
1989 Nov 9–12	40	51	9	1230
1990 Jul 6–8	40	53	7	1240
1990 Oct 11–14	30	65	5	1009
1991 Feb 28–Mar 3	51			
1991 Mar 7–10[a]	37	56	7	1018
1991 Jun 26–29	36	58	6	1000
1991 Jul 18–21	34	59	7	1002
1991 Aug 8–11	33	61	6	1013
1991 Aug 23–25[a]	36	59	5	1018
1991 Sep 13–15	32	60	8	1216
1991 Oct 3–6	29	64	7	1003
1991 Oct 3–6	28	64	7	1003
1991 Oct 24–27	28	67	5	1003
1991 Dec 5–8	22	73	5	1004
1992 Jan 3–6	24			
1992 Jan 31–Feb 2	22			
1992 Feb 28–Mar 1	21	76	3	1001
1992 Mar 20–22[b]	17	80	12	1301

Table 3 continued

	Approve	Disapprove	Don't know	*n*
C The situation in Central America				
1989 Mar	37	33	30	
1989 Nov 9–12	40	39	21	1230
1990 Jan 4–7	66	21	13	1226
1990 Jul 6–8	42	39	19	1240
1991 Mar 7–10[a]	52	21	27	1018
D The situation in Eastern Europe				
1989 Nov 9–12	63	16	21	1230
1990 Jan 4–7	73	13	14	1226
1990 Jul 6–8	63	20	17	1240
1991 Mar 7–10[a]	70	12	18	1018
E Relations with the Soviet Union				
1989 Mar	70	10	20	
1989 Nov 9–12	81	11	8	1230
1990 Jul 6–8	82	12	6	1248
1990 Oct 11–14	84	11	5	1009
1991 Mar 7–10[a]	86	10	4	1018
1991 Jul 18–21	80	12	8	1002
F The situation in the Middle East				
1989 Mar	62	15	23	
1991 Mar 7–10[a]	90	8	2	1018
1991 Jul 18–21	69	26	5	1002
1991 Aug 8–11	70	25	5	1013
1991 Sep 26–29[c]	64	30	6	1005
G The drug problem				
1989 Sep	72	18	10	
1989 Nov 9–12	53	41	6	1230
1990 Jan	69	24	7	
1990 Jul 6–8	46	48	6	1240

Table 3 continued

	Approve	Disapprove	Don't know	*n*
1991 Mar 7–10[a]	50	44	6	1018
1991 Jul 18–21	46	47	7	1002

H The abortion issue				
1989 Jul	43	35	22	
1989 Nov 9–12	38	45	17	1230
1990 Jul 6–8	36	44	20	1240
1991 Mar 7–10[a]	46	33	21	1018
1991 Jul 18–21	37	44	19	1002

I The savings and loan crisis				
1990 Jul 6–8	22	58	20	1240
1991 Mar 7–10[a]	28	56	16	1018

J Handling race relations				
1991 Mar 7–10[a]	63	26	11	1018
1991 Jul 18–21	58	29	13	1002

K Crime				
1991 Mar 7–10[a]	47	44	9	1018
1991 Jul 18–21	42	48	10	1002

L Health care policy				
1991 Mar 7–10[a,d]	34	57	9	1018
1991 Jul 18–21	27	60	13	1002
1991 Dec 5–8	28	63	9	1004
1991 Apr 20–22[b]	24	69	7	1273

M The energy situation in this country				
1991 Mar 7–10[a]	47	42	11	1018
1991 Jul 18–21	40	46	14	1002

187

Table 3 continued

	Approve	Disapprove	Don't know	n
N The federal budget deficit				
1989 Mar	40	36	24	
1989 Nov 9–12	32	53	15	1230
1990 Jul 6–8	26	64	10	1240
1990 Oct 11–14	25	68	6	1009
1991 Mar 7–10[a]	31	59	10	1018
O Environmental issues				
1989 Nov 9–12	46	40	14	1230
1990 Jul 6–8	42	46	12	1240
1990 Oct 11–14	45	45	10	1009
1991 Mar 7–10[a]	52	38	10	1018
1991 Jul 18–21	49	40	11	1002
P Poverty and homelessness				
1989 Nov 9–12	30	59	11	1230
1990 Jul 6–8	30	62	8	1240
1991 Mar 7–10[a]	27	65	8	1018
1991 Jul 18–21	26	67	7	1002
Q Education policy				
1989 Nov 9–12	53	35	12	1230
1990 Jul 6–8	46	41	13	1240
1991 Mar 7–10[a]	53	40	7	1018
1991 Jul 18–21	42	49	9	1002
1992 Apr 20–22[b,e]	36	57	7	1273

Gallup Poll Monthly, March 1991, p. 7; August 1991, p. 33; March 1992, p. 44
[a]Rotated
[b]Registered voters
[c]The situation in Iraq
[d]Availability of health care
[e]Education

How would you rate President George Bush's performance on each of the fol- **4**
lowing? Would you say his performance on . . . has been excellent, good, only
fair, or poor? (Gallup)

	Excellent	Good	Only fair	Poor	Don't know
A Making good appointments to cabinet and other positions					
1990 Feb	7	42	32	6	13
1990 Jul	5	40	36	7	12
1990 Nov	8	37	38	11	7
1991 Mar	18	47	22	5	8

	Excellent	Good	Only fair	Poor	Don't know
B Being an efficient manager of government					
1990 Feb	10	52	28	5	5
1990 Jul	7	45	33	11	4
1990 Nov	7	40	37	13	2
1991 Mar	22	52	20	4	2

	Excellent	Good	Only fair	Poor	Don't know
C Developing programs to address the pressing problems America faces					
1990 Feb	8	39	35	13	5
1990 Jul	4	31	42	19	4
1990 Nov	5	29	40	23	3
1991 Mar	8	41	35	13	3

	Excellent	Good	Only fair	Poor	Don't know
D Communicating his ideas to the American public					
1990 Feb	16	49	26	7	2
1990 Jul	9	46	30	13	2
1990 Nov	12	41	33	13	1
1991 Mar	35	44	15	5	1

	Excellent	Good	Only fair	Poor	Don't know
E Following through on his ideas and initiatives					
1990 Feb	10	45	32	7	6
1990 Jul	4	36	38	18	4
1990 Nov	5	34	38	20	3
1991 Mar	23	51	19	5	2

Table 4 continued

	Excellent	Good	Only fair	Poor	Don't know
F Working effectively with Congress					
1990 Feb	7	46	34	6	7
1990 Jul	5	46	35	7	7
1990 Nov	5	31	39	22	3
1991 Mar	18	51	23	4	4

	Excellent	Good	Only fair	Poor	Don't know
G Being a good representative or symbol of the United States					
1990 Feb	24	52	18	4	2
1990 Jul	22	49	22	6	1
1990 Nov	19	44	27	9	1
1991 Mar	45	42	9	3	1

	Excellent	Good	Only fair	Poor	Don't know
H Being an inspirational leader to the American people					
1990 Feb	17	47	27	8	1
1990 Jul	10	45	30	13	2
1990 Nov	10	37	32	20	1
1991 Mar	44	40	11	4	1

Gallup Poll Monthly, March 1991, p. 8

5   Here is a list of some problems and responsibilities facing the President and his administration. Do you think George Bush is making progress or is not making progress on handling each of these different problems? (rotated) (Gallup)

	Making progress	Not making progress	Don't know
A Keeping the nation out of war			
1990 Feb	77	17	6
1990 Nov	37	55	8
1991 Mar	64	31	5

	Making progress	Not making progress	Don't know
B Keeping America prosperous			
1990 Feb	59	33	8
1990 Nov	41	54	5
1991 Mar	60	35	5

190

Table 5 continued

	Making progress	Not making progress	Don't know
C Increasing respect for the United States abroad			
1990 Feb	73	21	6
1990 Nov	62	32	6
1990 Mar	87	8	5
D Improving educational standards			
1990 Feb	48	44	8
1990 Nov	42	48	10
1991 Mar	52	41	7
E Improving the quality of the environment			
1990 Feb	46	45	9
1990 Nov	50	43	7
1991 Mar	54	38	8
F Improving the lot of minorities and the poor			
1990 Feb	35	54	12
1990 Nov	28	62	10
1991 Mar	38	53	9
G Reducing the crime rate in the United States			
1990 Feb	37	54	9
1990 Nov	27	65	8
1991 Mar	41	52	7
H Reducing the federal budget deficit			
1990 Feb	30	58	12
1990 Nov	24	70	6
1991 Mar	28	63	9

	Making progress	Not making progress	Don't know
I Getting the drug crisis under control			
1990 Feb	57	39	4
1990 Nov	47	49	4
1991 Mar	50	46	5

	Making progress	Not making progress	Don't know
J Avoiding raising taxes			
1990 Feb	54	36	10
1990 Nov	21	74	5
1991 Mar	43	51	6

Gallup Poll Monthly, March 1991, p. 9

6   Generally speaking, do you trust President Bush and his advisors to make the right decision in the Mideast about whether we should go to war, or not? (*Los Angeles Times*)

	Trust Bush and advisors on going to war	Do not trust	Don't know	*n*
1990 Nov 14	62	32	6	1031
1991 Jan 8-12	67	27	6	2434

7   Generally speaking, do you trust President Bush and his advisors to make the right decision in the handling of the war in the Mideast, or not? (*Los Angeles Times*)

	Trust Bush and advisors on handling the war	Do not trust	Don't know	*n*
1991 Jan 17–18	87	10	3	1406

Do you approve or disapprove of the way George Bush is handling this current **8** situation in the Middle East involving Iraq and Kuwait?
After January 15: Do you approve or disapprove of the way George Bush is handling the situation in the Persian Gulf region? (Gallup)

	Approve Bush on Middle East/ Persian Gulf	Disapprove	Don't know	n
1990 Aug 3–4	52	16	32	810
1990 Aug 9–10[a]	77	13	10	770
1990 Aug 9–12	80	12	8	1227
1990 Aug 16–19	79	14	7	1241
1990 Aug 23–24[a]	75	18	7	767
1990 Aug 23–26	76	17	7	1010
1990 Aug 30–Sep 2	74	18	8	1007
1990 Sep 10–11	77	16	7	1031
1990 Sep 14–16	75	16	10	1024
1990 Sep 27–30	71	22	7	1000
1990 Oct 3–4	69	24	6	1010
1990 Oct 11–12[a]	64	29	7	757
1990 Oct 11–14	65	29	7	1009
1990 Oct 18–19[a]	61	29	10	755
1990 Oct 18–21	61	29	10	1002
1990 Oct 25–28	61	31	8	1012
1990 Nov 1–4	61	29	10	
1990 Nov 8–11	61	34	6	1008
1990 Nov 15–16[a]	57	35	8	754
1990 Nov 15–18	54	35	11	1018
1990 Nov 29–Dec 2	58	33	9	
1990 Dec 6–7[a]	60	32	8	769
1990 Dec 6–9	57	36	7	
1990 Dec 13–16	63	30	7	
1991 Jan 3–6	60	34	6	
1991 Jan 11-13	62	28	10	
1991 Jan 16	81	12	7	
1991 Jan 17–20	86	9	5	
1991 Jan 23–26	84	12	4	
1991 Jan 30–Feb 2	85	13	2	

Table 8 continued

	Approve Bush on Middle East/ Persian Gulf	Disapprove	Don't know	n
1991 Feb 7–10	79	17	4	
1991 Feb 15	84	10	6	
1991 Feb 14–17	82	14	4	
1991 Feb 22	84	10	6	
1991 Feb 24	86	10	4	
1991 Feb 28–Mar 3	92	6	2	
1991 Apr 4–6	78	18	4	
1991 Jul 11–14[b]	63	30	7	
1991 Sep 26–29	64	30	6	

Gallup Poll Monthly, December 1990, p. 7; February 1991, p. 16; April 1991, p. 4; July 1991, p. 33; October 1991, p. 5

[a]Do you approve or disapprove of the way President Bush is handling the current situation involving Iraq and Kuwait?

[b]Do you approve or disapprove of the way George Bush has handled the situation in Iraq since the war in the Persian Gulf ended?

9 Do you approve or disapprove of the way George Bush is handling Iraq's invasion of Kuwait? Would you say you approve/disapprove strongly or somewhat? (CBS/*New York Times*, CBS)

	Approve strongly		Approve somewhat	Disapprove somewhat	Disapprove strongly	Don't know	n
1990 Aug 7–8			64	18		18	733
1990 Aug 9–10[a]	48	(84)	26	9 (15)	6	2	670
1990 Aug 16–19	50	(76)	26	6 (14)	8	10	1422
1990 Sep 10			71	19		10	699
1990 Oct 8–10			57	34		9	960
1990 Oct 28–31			59	32		9	1445
1990 Nov 13–15			50	41		9	1370
1990 Dec 9–11			57	35		8	1044
1991 Jan 5–7			58	34		8	*1348*
1991 Jan 11–13			58	33		8	*1512*
1991 Jan 17–20			82	13		5	
1991 Jan			78	18		4	
1991 Feb 12–13			80	14		6	*1060*

194

Table 9 continued

	Approve strongly	Approve somewhat	Disapprove somewhat	Disapprove strongly	Don't know	*n*
1991 Feb 24		85	10		4	*687*
1991 Feb 25		84	10		5	*517*
1991 Feb 28		86	9		5	*528*

New York Times releases
ᵃ... of the way George Bush is dealing with ...

Do you think President Bush is doing a good or poor job handling this (the) **10** crisis with Iraq? (*Time*/CNN)

	Bush doing good job in crisis with Iraq	Bush doing poor job	Don't know	*n*
1990 Aug 9	83	12	4	500
1990 Aug 23	76	17	7	500
1990 Sep 13	75	19	6	500
1990 Oct 3	65	24	11	500
1990 Oct 10	65	27	8	500
1990 Oct 15–17	59	31	10	1000
1990 Nov 14	53	36	11	500
1990 Nov 27–28	54	37	9	1000

Do you approve or disapprove of the way George Bush is handling the Iraq **11** situation? (Black)

	Approve the way Bush is handling the Iraq situation	Disapprove	Don't know	*n*
1990 Aug 20–21	83	13	4	802
1990 Nov 12	51	40	9	615
1990 Dec 1–2	58	30	12	704
1990 Dec 29–30	58	33	9	1008

12 Do you approve or disapprove of the way George Bush is handling the situation caused by Iraq's invasion of Kuwait? Is that approve/disapprove strongly or approve/disapprove not strongly? (ABC/*Washington Post*, ABC)

	Approve strongly	Approve not strongly	Disapprove not strongly	Disapprove strongly	Don't know	*n*
1990 Sep 6–9	60 (78)	18	6 (19)	13	4	1011
1990 Oct 10–14	42 (64)	22	12 (31)	19	4	1006
1990 Nov 2–4[a]	41 (65)	24	12 (33)	21	2	1015
1990 Nov 6[a]		68	29		3	1212
1990 Nov 14–15		59	36[c]		5	515
1990 Nov 30–Dec 2	40 (61)	21	11[c] (36)	25[c]	4	758
1990 Dec 9		62	32		6	518
1991 Jan 2		66	29		5	352
1991 Jan 2–6		61	30		9	1007
1991 Jan 4–6		67	30		4	1057
1991 Jan 4–8		65	28		8	1003
1991 Jan 9[b]		69	29		2	511
1991 Jan 9–13		60	31		10	1009
1991 Jan 13		68	27		5	781
1991 Jan 11–15		61	29		11	1007

[a]Likely voters only

[b]Question preceded by: As you may know, U.S. Secretary of State James Baker held talks today with Iraqi Foreign Minister Tariq Aziz. They reported no progress in resolving the Persian Gulf situation. No further talks were scheduled.

[c]These then asked: Is that because you think he's moving too quickly against Iraq, or because you think he's moving too slowly against Iraq?

	Bush moving too quickly	Moving too slowly	Shouldn't move against Iraq (vol)	Other reason (vol)	Don't know
1990 Nov 14–15	37	44	6	9	5
1990 Nov 30–Dec 2	44	33	6	16	—

196

Do you approve or disapprove of the way George Bush is handling the Iraq situation in the Mideast? Is that approve/disapprove strongly or approve/disapprove somewhat? (*Los Angeles Times*) **13**

	Approve strongly	Approve somewhat	Disapprove somewhat	Disapprove strongly	Don't know	*n*
1990 Aug 29	48	25	9	13	4	1206
1990 Nov 14	29	25	16	24	6	1031
1990 Dec 8–12	32	30	15	18	5	2205
1991 Jan 8–12	39	25	12	19	5	2434
1991 Jan 17–18	67	21	3	7	2	1406
1991 Feb 15–17	68	17	6	7	2	1822

Do you approve or disapprove of the way Bush is handling the situation in the Persian Gulf? (ABC) **14**

	Approve Bush on Persian Gulf	Disapprove	Don't know
1991 Mar	94	6	—
1991 Jun	79	20	1
1991 Jul	69	28	3
1991 Sep 18–19	69	23	8

The Polling Report, September 30, 1991, p. 1

Do you approve or disapprove of George Bush's decision to send U.S. troops to Saudi Arabia? (CBS) **15**

	Approve Bush decision to send troops to Saudi Arabia	Disapprove	Don't know	*n*
1990 Aug 7–8	63	28	9	773

Do you approve or disapprove of President Bush's decision to send troops to help defend Saudi Arabia? (Black) **16**

	Approve Bush's decision to send troops to help defend Saudi Arabia	Disapprove	Don't know	*n*
1990 Aug 8	81	13	6	610
1990 Aug 20–21	86	11	3	802

17 Do you approve or disapprove of the United States sending troops to Saudi Arabia to protect Saudi Arabia from Iraq? (*New York Times*)

	Approve U.S. sending troops to Saudi Arabia to protect it from Iraq	Disapprove	Don't know	n
1990 Aug 9–10	66	28	6	670

18 Overall, do you approve or disapprove of the United States' sending military forces to Saudi Arabia and the Persian Gulf? (NBC/*Wall Street Journal*)

	Approve sending military forces to Saudi Arabia and the Gulf	Disapprove	Don't know	n
1990 Sep 4–5	76	20	5	800

Registered voters

19 All in all, do you approve of the United States (U.S.) sending troops to the Persian Gulf, or do you think we should have stayed out? (ABC, ABC/*Washington Post*)

	Approve sending troops to the Persian Gulf	We should have stayed out	Don't know	n
1990 Nov 2–4[a]	66	31	2	1015
1990 Nov 30–Dec 2	66	31	2	758

[a]Likely voters only

20 Do you approve or disapprove of the United States' decision to send U.S. troops to Saudi Arabia as a defense against Iraq? (Gallup)

	Approve U.S. decision to send troops to Saudi Arabia as a defense against Iraq	Disapprove	Don't know	n
1990 Aug 9–12	78	17	6	1227
1990 Aug 16–19	76	19	5	1241

Table 20 continued

	Approve U.S. decision to send troops to Saudi Arabia as a defense against Iraq	Disapprove	Don't know	n
1990 Aug 23–26	80	16	4	1010
1990 Aug 30–Sep 2	74	20	6	1007
1990 Sep 10–11	72	22	6	1031
1990 Sep 14–16	73	18	9	1024
1990 Sep 27–30	73	21	7	1000
1990 Oct 3–4	72	23	5	1010
1990 Oct 11–14	70	27	3	1009
1990 Oct 18–21	66	27	7	1002
1990 Oct 25–28	71	23	7	1012
1990 Nov 1–4	67	27	6	
1990 Nov 8–11	67	28	5	1008
1990 Nov 15–18	65	30	5	1018
1990 Nov 29–Dec 2	65	30	5	
1990 Dec 6–9	63	33	4	
1990 Dec 13–16	68	27	5	
1991 Jan 3–6	64	30	6	
1991 Jan 11–13	65	29	6	

Gallup Poll Monthly, December 1990, p. 15; January 1991, p. 11

Generally speaking, do you approve or disapprove of the decision to send American military troops to the Persian Gulf or not? Is that (approve/disapprove) strongly, or somewhat? (*Los Angeles Times*) **21**

	Strongly approve decision to send troops to Gulf	Approve somewhat	Disapprove somewhat	Disapprove strongly	Don't know	n
1990 Nov 14	36	25	12	22	5	1031
1991 Jan 17–18[a]	59	23	7	9	2	1406

[a]... do you now approve ...

199

22 Do you think George Bush has explained the situation in the Middle East well enough so that you feel you understand why the United States is sending troops to Saudi Arabia, or hasn't he? (CBS/*New York Times*)

	Bush has explained Middle East situation well enough	Has not	Don't know	*n*
1990 Aug 16–19	60	34	6	1422
1990 Nov 13–15	41	51	8	1370
1990 Dec 9–11	52	44	4	1044

23 Do you think President Bush has done an excellent job explaining why he sent American troops to the Persian Gulf, or do you think he has done a good job, or only a fair job, or do you think he has done a poor job explaining why he sent American troops to the Persian Gulf? (*Los Angeles Times*)

	Bush has done excellent job explaining why he sent troops	Has done good job	Has done fair job	Has done poor job	Don't know	*n*
1990 Nov 14	8	31	33	26	2	1031
1991 Jan 8–12	12	38	28	20	2	2434

24 Regardless of whether you agree with the way President Bush has handled the crisis with Iraq, do you think that he has done a good job or a poor job telling the American people why our troops are in the Middle East? (*Time/CNN*)

	Bush has done good job telling why troops are there	Has done poor job	Don't know	*n*
1990 Nov 14	49	45	6	500

As far as you are concerned, did President Bush do a good job of explaining **25**
why we are in the Persian Gulf? (Gallup)

	Bush did good job of explaining why we are there	Did not	Don't know
1991 Jan 30–31	82	14	4

Do you support or oppose President Bush's decision to attack (Iraq)? (Black) **26**

	Support Bush's decision to attack	Oppose	Don't know	n
1991 Jan 16	75	18	7	604
1991 Jan 20	76	16	8	641

Do you support President Bush's decision to go to war at this time, or not? (*Los* **27**
Angeles Times)

	Support Bush's decision to go to war at this time	Do not support	Don't know	n
1991 Jan 17–18	81	16	3	1406

Do you support or oppose President Bush's decision to start the war (with Iraq) **28**
last month? (Black)

	Support Bush's decision to start war	Do not support	Don't know	n
1991 Feb 14	81	15	4	601

29 Do you approve or disapprove of the United States having gone to war with Iraq? (Is that approve/disapprove strongly or approve/disapprove somewhat?) (*Washington Post*)

	Approve strongly of U.S. having gone to war with Iraq	Approve somewhat	Disapprove somewhat	Disapprove strongly	Don't know	n
1991 Jan 16	53	23	7	15	2	545
1991 Jan 20	52	24	9	14	2	532
1991 Jan 23–27	75		23		2	1015
1991 Feb 1–5	59	18	8	8	6	1008
1991 Feb 6–10	52	23	8	12	5	1012
1991 Feb 8–12	58	20	7	10	5	1011
1991 Feb 14	59	18	7	11	4	722
1991 Feb 22	59	21	9	9	2	520
1991 Feb 24	65	20	7	8	1	514
1991 Mar 1–5	82		11		7	1006

30 Do you approve or disapprove of the United States decision to start the ground war against the Iraqis in Kuwait? (Gallup)

	Approve of U.S. decision to start the ground war	Disapprove	Don't know	n
1991 Feb 24	84	12	5	783

Do you approve or disapprove of George Bush's decision to go to war with Iraq **31**
on (this past) January 16 (1991)? (Associated Press)

	Approve Bush's decision to go to war in January	Disapprove	Don't know	n
1991 Jan 23–24	74	24	2	1015
1991 Jul 17–21	73	19	9	1002
1992 Jan 2–5	65	25	11	1004

It's been almost a year since Iraq invaded Kuwait. Based on what you know **32**
now, do you think the U.S. (United States) attack on Iraqi forces was right or
wrong? (Black)

	U.S. attack on Iraqis was right	U.S. attack was wrong	Don't know	n
1991 Jul 23–24	79	16	5	610

    A. From what you have heard or read, do you approve or disapprove of the **33**
way George Bush is handling the situation in the Persian Gulf? (initially: Bush's
decision to send U.S. troops to the Persian Gulf?) (Percent approve)
    B. What do you think about the actions the U.S. has taken so far in the Per-
sian Gulf? Do you think U.S. actions have been too tough, not tough enough,
or just about right? (Percent not tough enough)
    C. The death of American soldiers in a fight with Iraq is too high a price to
pay in this Persian Gulf conflict. (Percent agree)
    D. Given everything that has happened, the U.S. is justified in launching an
attack against Iraq to drive them out of Kuwait. (Percent agree)
    E. What would you say is the single most important problem facing the
United States today, that is, the one you yourself are most concerned about?
(Percent saying the Mideast)
    F. Same. (Percent saying the economy)
    G. Now, I would like to get your feeling toward several individuals and coun-
tries that you may or may not be familiar with. I'm going to read you some
names and I'd like you to rate each one on a scale from 0 to 100, where a rating
of 0 means you feel not at all favorable toward that person or country, while a
rating of 100 means you feel extremely favorable toward the person or country.
Most people, of course, would be rated somewhere in between those two ex-
tremes. If you are not familiar with any of the names that I read, please let me
know and we will go on to the next one. Remember we just want to know your
opinion, with 0 being not at all favorable and 100 being extremely favorable.
(Mean value for George Bush)

Table 33 continued

H. Same. (Mean value for Saddam Hussein)

I. Did you happen to speak with anyone today about events in the Persian Gulf? (Percent saying yes)

	A	B	C	D	E	F	G	H	I
1990 Aug 22–29	80	66	56	67	27	23	72	8	
1990 Aug 30–Sep 8	80	65	64	67	22	22	70	8	
1990 Sep 9–15	83	61	60	70	15	17	72	7	24
1990 Sep 16–22	78	58	60	69			71	8	20
1990 Sep 23–Oct 1	78	56	66	64	12	19	71	7	26
1990 Oct 2–9	75	56	65	63	4	12	66	6	16
1990 Oct 10–18	68	53	66	62	17	38	63	6	16
1990 Oct 19–27	64	50	67	61	15	39	62	7	16
1990 Oct 28–Nov 5	63	50	69	62	19	35	62	8	16
1990 Nov 6–11	66	46	66	69	21	34	61	7	17
1990 Nov 12–19	60	48	70	63	26	28	62	6	17
1990 Nov 20–28	65	48	70	66	27	27	63	6	22
1990 Nov 29–Dec 6	68	51	69	70	28	28	64	6	26
1990 Dec 7–13	65	49	69	68	25	27	65	6	23
1990 Dec 14–21	65	53	72	70	25	26	66	9	15
1990 Dec 22–30	70	50	67	78	30	26	68	6	

Extrapolated from figures in Wilcox, Ferrarra, and Allsop 1991

VALUE OF COMMITMENT, OF WAR IN THE GULF

In view of the developments since we first sent our troops to Saudi Arabia, do you think the United States made a mistake in sending troops to Saudi Arabia, or not? (Gallup)

34

	U.S. made a mistake	U.S. did not make a mistake	Don't know	*n*
1990 Aug 16–19	17	75	8	1241
1990 Aug 23–26	18	76	6	1010
1990 Aug 30–Sep 2	16	76	8	1007
1990 Sep 10–11	19	76	5	1031
1990 Sep 14–16	18	73	9	1024
1990 Sep 27–30	20	73	7	1000
1990 Oct 3–4	21	71	8	1010
1990 Oct 11–14	27	68	6	1009
1990 Oct 18–21	26	67	7	1002
1990 Oct 25–28	24	71	5	1012
1990 Nov 2–4	25	67	8	1021
1990 Nov 8–11	27	68	5	1008
1990 Nov 15 18	27	65	8	1018
1990 Nov 29–Dec 2	29	66	5	
1990 Dec 6–9	28	66	6	
1991 Jan 3–6	31	61	8	
1991 Jan 11–13	29	65	6	
1991 Jan 17–20[a]	16	80	4	
1991 Jan 23–26[a]	18	77	5	1011
1991 Jan 30–Feb 2[a]	18	80	2	1005

Table 34 continued

	U.S. made a mistake	U.S. did not make a mistake	Don't know	*n*
1991 Feb 7–10[a]	21	76	3	1013
1991 Feb 28–Mar 3[a]	10	87	3	1012
1991 Jul 18–21[a]	15	82	3	1002

Gallup Poll Monthly, January 1991, p. 34; December 1990, p. 15; February 1991, p. 6
[a]"the Persian Gulf region" rather than "Saudi Arabia"

35 Do you think the United States did the right thing in sending troops to Saudi Arabia? (CBS/*New York Times*)

	U.S. did right thing sending troops to Saudi Arabia	Did not	Don't know	*n*
1990 Aug 16–19	77	18	5	1422
1990 Sep 10	76	15	9	699

36 Do you think the United States did the right thing in sending troops to Saudi Arabia, or should we have stayed out? (CBS/*New York Times*)

	U.S. did right thing sending troops to Saudi Arabia	U.S. should have stayed out	Don't know	*n*
1990 Oct 8–10	61	32	7	960
1990 Oct 28–31	66	27	8	1445
1990 Nov 13–15	61	30	8	1370
1990 Dec 9–11	62	30	8	1044
1991 Jan 5–7	61	32	7	*1348*
1991 Jan 11–13	59	31	10	*1512*

Overall do you think that the United States was right or wrong to have become **37**
involved in this conflict with Iraq? (*Time*/CNN)

	U.S. was right to have become involved in the conflict with Iraq	U.S. was wrong	Don't know	*n*
1990 Sep 13	75	18	7	500
1990 Nov 14	60	30	10	500
1991 Jun 4–5	76	16	8	1000

New York Times/CBS News Poll, January 11–13, 1991, p. 1

Do you think the United States made a mistake getting involved in the war **38**
against Iraq or not? (*New York Times*/CBS)

	Mistake getting involved in the war against Iraq	War not a mistake	Don't know	*n*
1991 Jan 17	17	78	5	
1991 Jan 18	14	77	9	
1991 Jan 19	18	75	7	908
1991 Jan 20	15	80	5	
1991 Feb early	22	71	7	
1991 Feb 24[a]	13	85	3	514
1991 Feb 28[b]	13	80	7	528
1991 Jun 3–6	22	72	6	1424
1991 Oct 5–7	22	74	4	1280

New York Times Ground War Tracking Poll, Feb 24–Mar 1, 1991, p. 2; *New York Times*/CBS
News Poll, June 3–6, 1991, p. 6; *New York Times*, October 11, 1991, p. A8; CBS/*New York Times*
release, October 10, 1991, p. 6
[a]In view of the developments since the start of the war in the Persian Gulf, do you think the
United States made a mistake sending armed forces to fight in the Persian Gulf or not? (ABC/*Washington Post*)
[b]Or Feb 24—Mar 1

39 Do you think the United States made a mistake sending troops to fight against Iraq? (*Los Angeles Times*)

	Mistake sending troops to fight against Iraq	Not a mistake	Don't know	*n*
1991 Feb 15–17	16	80	4	1822
1991 Mar 9–11	12	87	1	1836
1991 Jun 28–30[a]	17	78	5	1439

[a]"or not" added to question

40 All in all, is the current situation in the Mideast worth going to war over, or not? (Gallup)

	Situation worth going to war over	Not worth going to war	Don't know	*n*
1990 Aug 23–26	49	41	10	1010
1990 Aug 30–Sep 2	45	44	11	1007
1990 Sep 27–30	49	41	10	1000
1990 Nov 15–18	46	45	9	1018
1990 Nov 29–Dec 2	51	41	8	
1990 Dec 6–9	47	45	8	
1990 Dec 13–16	49	44	7	
1991 Jan 3–6	47	44	9	
1991 Jan 11–13	46	44	10	
1991 Jan 30–Feb 2	71	24	5	1005
1991 Feb 28–Mar 3[a]	80	15	5	1012
1991 Apr 4–6[a]	72	22	7	1002
1991 Apr 25–28[b]	70	24	6	
1991 May 23–26[b]	72	23	5	1003
1991 Jul 11–14[b]	66	28	6	1217
1992 Jan 6–9[c]	59	38	3	1421
1992 Feb 6–9[c]	66	32	2	1002

Gallup Poll Monthly, December 1990, p. 16; January 1991, p. 12; June 1991, p. 50

[a]. . . was the situation in the Mideast involving Iraq and Kuwait ...

[b]. . . was the current situation in the Mideast ...

[c]All in all, do you think the situation in the Persian Gulf region was worth going to war over, or not?

Given the loss of life and the other costs of the war in the Persian Gulf, do you **41** think the war to defeat Iraq is likely to be (after Feb 25: was) worth the cost or not? (*New York Times*/CBS)

	War worth the loss of life and other costs	War not worth the cost	Don't know	n
1991 Jan 17	63	23	14	
1991 Jan 18	58	25	16	
1991 Jan 19	55	27	18	908
1991 Jan 20	61	23	17	
1991 Jan 20 (CBS)	59	29	12	
1991 Feb early	60	26	14	
1991 Feb 24	65	24	11	*687*
1991 Feb 25	65	22	13	*517*
1991 Feb 28[a]	72	17	11	528
1991 Jun 3–6	66	30	4	1424
1991 Oct 5–7	61	33	6	1280
1992 Jan 22–25	59	36	5	1281
1992 Dec 7–9	58	37	5	1333

New York Times Ground War Tracking Poll, Feb 24–Mar 1, 1991, p. 2; *New York Times*/CBS
News Poll, June 3–6, 1991, p. 3; *New York Times*, October 11, 1991, p. A8
[a]Or Feb 24–Mar 1

Do you think winning the war with Iraq has been worth the costs or not? **42** (*Time*/CNN)

	Winning the war has been worth the costs	Winning has not been worth the costs	Don't know	n
1991 Mar 7	77	17	6	1000

43 All in all, considering the costs to the United States versus the benefits to the United States, do you think the Persian Gulf war was worth fighting, or not? (ABC/*Washington Post*)

	Considering the costs and benefits, the war was worth fighting	The war was not worth fighting	Don't know	n
1991 Mar 1–4[a]	86	13	1	1215
1991 May 30–Jun 2	70	26	3	1511
1991 Jul 25–28	67	30	3	1205
1992 Jan 30–Feb 2	66	32	2	1512

[a]. . . do you think this war (in the Persian Gulf) was worth fighting, or not?

44 Thinking about the current situation in the Persian Gulf, do you think the war with Iraq was worth it? (NBC/*Wall Street Journal*)

	The war with Iraq was worth it	War was not worth it	In between (vol)	Don't know	n
1991 May 10	74	19	4	3	1508

IMPORTANCE OF, ATTENTION PAID TO, UNDER-STANDING OF THE ISSUE..............................

What do you think is the most important problem facing this country today? **45**
(Gallup, *Los Angeles Times*, CBS/*New York Times*, ABC/*Washington Post*, *Time*/CNN, *Washington Post*)

	Gulf crisis	Fear of war	Federal deficit, spending	Drugs	Poverty	Economy	Un-employment	Infla-tion	n
1980 Jul 11–14		2	3				15	56	
1980 Sep 12–15		3	3				16	61	
1981 Jan 30–Feb 2		2	1				8	73	
1981 May 8–11		3	4				15	59	
1981 Oct 2–5		4	4				19	52	
1982 Jan 8–11		5	3				28	49	
1982 Jun 11–14[a]		10	5			11	38	26	
1982 Aug 13–16		6	5			16	45	23	
1982 Oct 15–18		3	4			11	61	18	
1983 Apr 15–18		11	5			8	53	18	
1983 Nov		37	5		*	3	32	11	
1984 Feb		28	12		*	5	28	10	
1984 Aug		22	16		3	8	23	18	
1985 Jan 25–28		27	18		6	6	20	11	
1985 May		23	6	6	6	8	21	11	
1985 Oct		20	16	3	3	4	24	7	
1986 Jan		30	11	2	7	4	18	8	
1986 Jul		22	13	8	6	7	23	4	

Table 45 continued

	Gulf crisis	Fear of war	Federal deficit, spending	Drugs	Poverty	Economy	Unemployment	Inflation	*n*
1987 Jan		23	10	10	6	8	16	6	
1987 Apr 10–13		23	11	11	5	10	13	5	
1988 Sep 9–11		9	12	11	7	12	9	2	1003
1989 May 4–7		2	7	27	10	8	6	3	1239
1989 Jun–Jul		4	6	27	8	7	2	3	1005
1989 Jul 18–21		2	6	27	8	7	2	3	1247
1989 Sep 7–10		2	5	63	5	4	2	1	1238
1989 Nov 9–12		1	7	38	10	7	3	2	1230
1990 Mar 22–26		1	8	34	11	4	4	1	1016
1990 Apr		1	6	30	11	7	3	1	
1990 May 1–31		1	11	36	11	5	7	3	3004
1990 Jul		1	21	18	7	7	3	1	
1990 Aug 16–19	21	2	8	10	4	10	5	3	1422
1990 Sep 6–9	22	2	6	16	4	9	3	1	1011
1990 Oct 11–14	10	5	16	10	5	10	3	1	1009
1990 Oct 28–31	15		14	10		12	3	2	1445
1990 Nov	17	3	11	8	6	11	3	2	
1990 Nov 27–28[b]	21	5	5	7	3	19	4	2	
1991 Jan (3–6?)	25	4	4	9	6	15	4	2	
1991 Jan 30–Feb 2	37	3	6	5	6	16	5	1	1005
1991 Mar 1–4	13	2	8	11	9	12	7	4	1215
1991 Mar 4–6	2		7	10	5	23	10		1252
1991 Mar 7[b]	2		8	20	7	25	9	1	1000
1991 Mar 7–10	4	2	8	11	10	24	8	2	1018
1991 Apr 1–3	3		4	11	9	20	12		1283
1991 Apr 24–29[b]	1	*	2	17	5	30	9	1	1008
1991 Apr 25–28	3	1	6	10	13	20	8	2	1005
1991 May 6	2		6	16	7	19	9	1	589
1991 May 23–26	2	1	6	10	12	21	9	2	1003
1991 Jun 3–6			5	8	13	16	12		1424
1991 Jun 4–5[b]		*	7	18	8	17	9	1	1000
1991 Jun 28–30	1		7	10	12	18	7	1	1439
1991 Nov 21–24			4	10	16	32	23		

Table 45 continued

	Gulf crisis	Fear of war	Federal deficit, spending	Drugs	Poverty	Economy	Unemployment	Inflation	*n*
1992 Mar 26–29[c]			8	8	15	42	25		
1992 Aug 28–Sep 2[d]	2	1	9	6	13	37	27	2	

Gallup Poll Monthly, March 1982, p. 27; June 1983, p. 5; March 1985, pp. 20–21; September 1986, p. 29; May 1987, p. 7; October 1988, pp. 6–7; January 1991, p. 4; May 1991, p. 35; June 1991, p. 47; April 1992, p. 30; September 1992, p. 11.

Note: Other problems were cited in each poll. The table includes all problems that were mentioned by at least 10 percent. Multiple responses were accepted.

[a]10% also mentioned high interest rates.
[b]. . . main problem facing the country today?
[c]12% also mentioned health care.
[d]12% also mentioned health care and 10% mentioned education.

How closely have you followed news about the situation involving the invasion **46** of Kuwait by Iraq and the sending of U.S. troops to Saudi Arabia? Would you say you have followed it very closely, fairly closely, not too closely, or not at all closely? (Gallup, CBS)

	Follow Gulf news very closely	Fairly closely	Not too closely	Not at all closely	Don't know	*n*
1990 Aug 3–4[a]	18	39	25	18	*	810
1990 Aug 7–8[a,b]	28	44	21	7	1	773
1990 Aug 9–12[a]	40	43	12	5	*	1227
1990 Aug 16–19[a,b]	38	46	14	2	—	1422
1990 Aug 16–19[a]	45	42	11	2	*	1241
1990 Aug 23–26	44	42	12	2	*	1010
1990 Aug 30–Sep 2	43	43	11	2	1	
1990 Sep 10–11	36	48	12	4	*	1031
1990 Sep 14–16	42	43	12	2	*	1024
1990 Sep 27–30	36	49	12	3	*	1000
1990 Oct 3–4	35	50	13	3	*	1010
1990 Oct 8–10[c]	29	55	13	3	—	960
1990 Oct 11–14	35	50	12	3	*	
1990 Oct 18–21	38	46	13	3	*	1002
1990 Oct 25–28	40	48	10	2	1	1012
1990 Nov 1–4	37	49	12	2	*	
1990 Nov 8–11	35	52	11	2	1	1008

Table 46 continued

	Follow Gulf news very closely	Fairly closely	Not too closely	Not at all closely	Don't know	n
1990 Nov 15–18	33	45	17	5	*	1018
1990 Nov 29–Dec 2	40	49	10	1	*	
1990 Dec 6–9	43	46	9	2	*	
1990 Dec 13–16	44	45	10	1	*	
1991 Jan 3–6	41	47	10	2	*	
1991 Jan 11–13	50	41	8	1	*	
1991 Jan 17–20[d]	70	27	3	0	*	
1991 Jan 23–26[d]	59	34	6	1	0	1011
1991 Feb 7–9[d]	55	38	6	1	*	1013

Gallup Poll Monthly, January 1991, p. 32; February 1991, p. 6
[a] Did not include "and the sending of U.S. troops to Saudi Arabia"
[b] . . . have you been following . . . (CBS)
[c] . . . are you following news about the situation in the Persian Gulf? (CBS)
[d] . . . about the situation in the Persian Gulf region?

47   How often do you think about the crisis in the Mideast: every few minutes, at least once an hour, a few times a day, or once a day or less? (Black)

	Think about crisis every few minutes	At least once an hour	A few times a day	Once a day or less	Don't know	n
1991 Jan 14	22	27	41	10	—	600

48   Index of News Coverage

	Persian Gulf crisis	Other major issue
1990 Aug 6–19	56.1	6.1
1990 Aug 20–Sep 2	68.3	4.9
1990 Sep 3–17	39.8	8.0
1990 Sep 17–30	34.1	12.9
1990 Oct 1–14	13.1	22.8[a]
1990 Oct 15–28	14.1	14.8[b]
1990 Oct 29–Nov 11	24.0	22.7[c]
1990 Nov 12–25	28.4	6.3

Table 48 continued

	Persian Gulf crisis	Other major issue
1990 Nov 26–Dec 9	31.6	8.3
1991 Jan 21–Feb 3	92.9	5.3
1991 Feb 4–17	72.4	6.4
1991 Feb 18–Mar 3	104.3	3.4

LaMay 1991, p. 46

Note: The index tracks the content of the three networks' nightly broadcasts, five major newspapers, and *Time, Newsweek,* and *U.S. News and World Report.* These items are then weighted according to where Americans with at least a high school diploma get information on national issues. No data are reported for the period between December 9, 1990 and January 21, 1991.

[a]Federal deficit
[b]Federal budget
[c]Campaign 1990

Do you feel that you have a clear idea or not a clear idea why President Bush **49** (George Bush) has sent U.S. (United States) military forces to Saudi Arabia and the Persian Gulf? (*Washington Post*, ABC/*Washington Post*)

	Have clear idea why Bush sent troops to Gulf	Do not have clear idea	Don't know	*n*
1990 Aug 24–28[a]	70	28	2	1001
1990 Sep 6–9[b]	77	22	*	1011
1990 Nov. 14–15	69	30	1	515
1990 Nov 30–Dec 2	68	31	1	758

[a]Did not include the phrase "or not a clear idea"
[b]"sent" rather than "has sent"

50 Do you feel you have a clear idea of what the United States military involvement in the Iraqi situation is all about—that is, why our troops are in Saudi Arabia? (Gallup)

	Have clear idea why U.S. troops are in Saudi Arabia	Do not have clear idea	Don't know	n
1990 Aug 16–19	74	24	2	1241
1990 Aug 23–26	70	28	2	1010
1990 Aug 30–Sep 2	76	23	1	1007
1990 Sep 27–30	75	23	2	1000
1990 Nov 15–18	69	29	2	1018
1990 Nov 29–Dec 2	73	26	1	
1990 Dec 13–16	74	24	2	
1991 Jul 18–21	81	18	1	1002

Gallup Poll Monthly, July 1991, p. 36

51 What's the first thing you did when you learned that the United States had gone to war with Iraq? (ABC/ *Washington Post*)

1991 Jan 20		*n* = 532
First response (percent):	33	Turned on television/radio
	22	Prayed
	8	Got choked up/emotional
	4	Cried
	3	Telephoned a relative/friend
	3	Was numb
	2	Cheered
	1	Hugged a friend/relative
	1	Shouted, yelled, screamed
	21	Other, not specified
	1	Don't know

Do you agree or disagree that the United States should take all action necessary, **52**
including the use of military force, to make sure that Iraq withdraws its forces
from Kuwait? (ABC, ABC/*Washington Post*)

	Agree, use force	Disagree	Don't know	n
1990 Aug 8	66	33	1	769
1990 Aug 17–20	76	20	4	815
1990 Sep 6–9	75	22	4	1011
1990 Oct 10–14	70	27	3	1006
1990 Nov 2–4[a]	70	27	3	1015
1990 Nov 6[a]	66	29	5	1212
1990 Nov 5–6[b]	68	27	5	1028
1990 Nov 14–15	65	26	8	515
1990 Nov 30–Dec 2	67	29	4	758
1990 Dec 9	65	31	3	518
1991 Jan 2	71	26	3	352
1991 Jan 2–6	68	28	4	1007
1991 Jan 4–6	68	28	3	1057
1991 Jan 4–8	69	27	4	1003
1991 Jan 9	75	23	2	511
1991 Jan 13	74	24	3	781

[a]Likely voters only
[b]Non-voters

53 Overall, taking into consideration everything you heard or read about the Mideast crisis, do you think the United States should go to war against Iraq, or not? (*Los Angeles Times*)

	Go to war	Do not go to war	Don't know	*n*
1990 Nov 14	38	53	9	1031

54 All in all, which of these courses of action do you agree with:

The U.S. should keep troops, planes, and ships in and around Saudi Arabia as long as is necessary to prevent Iraq from invading Saudi Arabia, but without initiating a war;

The U.S. should initiate a war against Iraq in order to drive Iraq out of Kuwait and bring the situation to a close. (Gallup)

	Initiate war	No war	Don't know	*n*
1990 Nov 15–18	28	65	7	1018

55 If Iraq does not withdraw from Kuwait, should the United States go to war with Iraq to force it out of Kuwait at some point after January 15th, or not? (ABC/ *Washington Post*)

	U.S. should go to war at some point after Jan 15 if Iraq does not withdraw from Kuwait	U.S. should not go to war	Don't know	*n*
1990 Nov 30–Dec 2	63	32	4	758

56 Here are some reasons that President Bush has given for our presence in the Middle East. For each, please tell me if it is something worth going to war over or not? . . . To force Iraq to withdraw from Kuwait. (*Time*/CNN)

	Worth going to war to force Iraq from Kuwait	Not worth going to war	Don't know	*n*
1990 Nov 14	45	49	6	500

218

57

If the current situation in the Middle East involving Iraq and Kuwait does not change by January (January 15th), would you favor or oppose the U.S. going to war with Iraq in order to drive the Iraqis out of Kuwait? (Gallup)

	Favor going to war with Iraq in January	Oppose going to war with Iraq	Don't know	n
1990 Nov 15–18	37	51	12	1018
1990 Nov 29–Dec 2	52	40	7	1013
1990 Dec 6–9	53	40	7	1007
1990 Dec 13–16	48	43	9	1019
1991 Jan 3–6	52	39	9	1006
1991 Jan 11–13	55	38	7	1004

Gallup Poll Monthly, December 1990, p. 7; January 1991, pp. 8, 14

58

Recently, the United Nations Security Council passed a resolution that allows Iraq one final opportunity to pull out of Kuwait by January 15th or else face possible military action. If Iraq lets this deadline pass, would you favor the U.S. and its allies going to war with Iraq in order to drive the Iraqis out of Kuwait, or not? (Gallup)

	Favor going to war with Iraq in January	Oppose going to war with Iraq	Don't know
1990 Nov 29–Dec 2	64	31	5
1990 Dec 6–9	61	33	6
1990 Dec 13–16	59	34	7
1991 Jan 3–6	62	32	6
1991 Jan 11–13	63	33	4

Gallup Poll Monthly, January 1991, p. 8

Do you approve or disapprove of the United States' decision to go to war with Iraq in order to drive the Iraqis out of Kuwait? (Gallup)

	Approve U.S. decision to go to war with Iraq	Disapprove	Don't know	n
1991 Jan 16[a]	79	15	6	
1991 Jan 17–20	80	15	5	
1991 Jan 19–22	79	18	3	
1991 Jan 23–26	81	15	4	1011

Table 59 continued

	Approve U.S. decision to go to war with Iraq	Disapprove	Don't know	n
1991 Jan 30–Feb 2	80	18	2	1005
1991 Feb 14–17	79	17	4	1009
1991 Jul 18–21ᵇ	78	21	1	1002

Gallup Poll Monthly, January 1991, pp. 17, 34

ᵃ. . . of the U.S. decision today to go to war . . .

ᵇLooking back, do you approve or disapprove of the U.S. (United States) decision last January (1991) to go to war with Iraq in order to drive the Iraqis out of Kuwait?

60 If the economic embargo of Iraq does not make Iraq withdraw from Kuwait, should the United States attack militarily to force it out of Kuwait, or not? (ABC/*Washington Post*)

	Attack militarily if embargo fails	Do not attack if embargo fails	Don't know	n
1990 Oct 10–14	46ᵃ	48	6	1006
1990 Nov 2–4ᵇ	51	44	5	1015
1990 Nov 6ᵇ	53	39	8	1212
1990 Nov 5–6ᶜ	52	38	10	1028

ᵃThese then asked: How long should the United States wait to see if the economic embargo (to force Iraq to withdraw from Kuwait) works before attacking Iraq militarily:

44%	Less than 3 months
39	Up to 6 months
13	Up to a year
3	Longer than that
1	Don't know
100	

ᵇLikely voters only

ᶜNon-voters

61 Most of the world's countries are participating in an economic embargo of Iraq. If the economic embargo does not make Iraq withdraw from Kuwait, should the United States attack militarily to force it out of Kuwait, or not? (ABC/*Washington Post*)

	Attack militarily if embargo fails	Do not attack if embargo fails	Don't know	n
1990 Nov 14–15	54	36	10	515

220

As you may know, the United Nations Security Council has authorized the use **62** of force against Iraq if it doesn't withdraw from Kuwait by January 15th. Do you approve or disapprove of that resolution? (ABC/*Washington Post*)

	Approve UN resolution authorizing force after January 15 if Iraq doesn't withdraw from Kuwait	Disapprove UN resolution	Don't know	*n*
1990 Nov 30–Dec 2	69	26	5	758

As you may know, the United Nations Security Council has authorized the use **63** of force against Iraq if it doesn't withdraw from Kuwait by January 15th (1991). If Iraq does not withdraw from Kuwait, should the United States go to war with Iraq to force it out of Kuwait at some point after January 15th, or not? (ABC, ABC/*Washington Post*, *Washington Post*)

	Go to war at some point after January 15 if Iraq doesn't withdraw from Kuwait	Do not go to war	Don't know	*n*
1990 Nov 30–Dec 2[a]	63	32	4	758
1990 Dec 9	58	38	4	518
1990 Dec 14–18	55[e]	30	16	1000
1991 Jan 2	65[e]	29	6	352
1991 Jan 2–6	62[e]	33	5	1007
1991 Jan 4–6	63[e]	32	6	1057
1991 Jan 4–8	62[e]	31	6	1003
1991 Jan 9	68[e]	29	2	511
1991 Jan 9–13[b]	61[e]	32	7	1009
1991 Jan 13	69[e]	26	4	781
1991 Jan 11–15[c]	60	33	7	1007
1991 Jan 16–20[d]	70	26	5	1004

[a]First sentence not included in question, but substance conveyed in earlier questions in the survey
[b]Asked of one-half of sample
[c]Asked of one-third of sample
[d]As you may know, the United Nations Security Council authorized the use of force against Iraq if it did not withdraw from Kuwait by January 15th (1991). The deadline has expired. Do you think the United States should go to war with Iraq at some point to force it out of Kuwait, or not?
[e]These then asked: How long after January 15th (1991) should the United States wait for Iraq to withdraw from Kuwait before going to war to force it out? (see next page)

221

Table 63 continued

How long after January 15th (1991) should the United States wait for Iraq to withdraw from Kuwait before going to war to force it out? (Asked of those who favored going to war in the question on the previous page)

	Immediately, right away	Less than 1 month	1–3 months	4–6 months	Longer	Don't know
Dec 14–18	28	51	2	2	2	6
Jan 2	25	57	9	*	1	7
Jan 2–6	23	52	15	2	1	9
Jan 4–6	29	49	13	2	—	7
Jan 4–8	30	48	12	2	1	6
Jan 9	39	43	12	2	—	4
Jan 9–13	30	45	14	3	2	7
Jan 13	54	30	9	1	1	5

64 Should the Congress endorse the United Nations resolution or not? (ABC/ *Washington Post*)

	Congress should endorse UN resolution	Should not	Don't know	*n*
1990 Nov 30–Dec 2	74	19	7	758
1991 Jan 9	77	17	6	511

65 As you may know, Congress voted this weekend to allow President Bush to go to war against Iraq if Iraq is not out of Kuwait by January 15th (1991). Do you approve or disapprove of Congress having voted to allow Bush to go to war? (ABC/ *Washington Post*)

	Approve of Congress voting to allow Bush to go to war	Disapprove	Don't know	*n*
1991 Jan 13	76	22	1	781

66

Just from what you have heard, read, or seen, which of these statements comes closer to how you, yourself, feel about the United States presence in the Mideast?

The United States should begin to withdraw its troops

The United States should continue its present level of troop presence

The United States should increase the level of its troops to force Iraq to leave Kuwait. (Gallup)

	Begin to withdraw	Continue at present level	Increase troops to force Iraq out	Don't know	n
1990 Aug 16–19	12	49	35	4	1241
1990 Aug 23–26[a]	11	51	34	4	1010
1990 Aug 30–Sep 2	12	51	31	6	1007
1990 Sep 27–30[a]	14	44	35	7	1000
1990 Nov 1–4	20	41	32	7	

Gallup Poll Monthly, November 1990, p. 29
[a]Items rotated

67

Most of the world's countries are participating in an economic boycott of Iraq. The boycott is designed to put economic pressure on Iraq so that it will withdraw from Kuwait. Just your best guess. Do you think the economic boycott will make Iraq withdraw from Kuwait, or not? (ABC/*Washington Post*)

	Boycott will make Iraq withdraw	Boycott won't make Iraq withdraw	Don't know	n
1990 Aug 17–20[a]	53	44	3	815
1990 Sep 6–9	51	46	3	1011
1990 Oct 10–14	38	58	4	1006
1990 Nov 30–Dec 2	30	66	4	758
1990 Dec 9	38	59	3	518

[a]Question did not include first three sentences.

68 Do you feel that the United States can or cannot achieve its objectives solely through economic sanctions and the blockade? (NBC/*Wall Street Journal*)

	U.S. can achieve its objectives solely through sanctions and blockade	Cannot	Depends (vol)	Don't know	
1990 Aug 18–19	43	37	7	13	805
1990 Sep 4–5	45	40	4	10	800
1990 Oct 19–21	38	45	6	11	1019
1990 Dec 8–11	36	48	7	9	1002

Registered voters only

69 How long should the U.S. be prepared to wait for sanctions against Iraq to work? (NBC/*Wall Street Journal*)

	Until Jan 15, 1991	For another six months or less	For six months to a year	For one to two years	For more than two years	We've waited too long already	Don't know	n
1990 Dec 8–11	27	23	11	5	5	13	16	1002

Registered voters only

70 Suppose it takes up to two years for the economic sanctions against Iraq to work. Would you favor or oppose keeping 200,000 troops in Saudi Arabia while we were waiting for the sanctions to work? (NBC/*Wall Street Journal*)

	Favor waiting up to two years for sanctions to work with 200,000 troops in Saudi Arabia	Do not favor waiting	Don't know	n
1990 Dec 8–11	24	72	4	1002

Registered voters only

Do you think the Iraqis would eventually have been forced to leave Kuwait if the U.S. (United States) and its allies had relied only on economic sanctions and diplomacy, or would military force have eventually been necessary in any case? (Gallup)

	Sanctions and diplomacy would eventually have forced Iraq from Kuwait	Military force would have eventually been necessary	Don't know	n
1991 Feb 28–Mar 3	8	87	5	1012

71

Some people feel that President Bush should quickly begin military action against Iraq. Others say he should wait to see if economic and diplomatic sanctions are effective. Which comes closer to your view? (Gallup)

72

	Quickly begin military action	Wait for sanctions	Don't know	n
1990 Aug 23–24[a]	17	80	3	767
1990 Oct 18–19	21	73	6	755
1990 Nov 15–16	24	70[b]	6	754
1990 Nov 15–18	23	70	6	1018

[a]Should (President) Bush quickly begin military action against Iraq, or should he wait to see if economic and diplomatic sanctions are effective? (Gallup)
[b]These were then asked: How long should the U.S. wait to see if economic and diplomatic sanctions are effective before taking military action against Iraq? Do you think the U.S. should wait . . .

12%	Another month
32	Two to three months
26	Up to six months
8	Up to one year
11	More than one year
11	Don't know/refused
100	

73

Some people feel that President Bush should begin military action against Iraq soon after the January 15th United Nations deadline if Iraq has not withdrawn from Kuwait by then. Others say he should wait longer to see if economic and diplomatic sanctions are effective. Which comes closer to your view? (Gallup)

	Begin military action after Jan 15	Wait longer for sanctions	Don't know	n
1990 Dec 6–7	41	53	6	769

74 If after three months the economic sanctions against Iraq do not work, should the United States use military force to get the Iraqis out of Kuwait, or not? (NBC/*Wall Street Journal*)

	U.S. should use military force after three months	U.S. should not	Don't know	n
1990 Sep 15–18	56	31	13	1508
1990 Oct 19–21	47	42	11	1019

Registered voters

75 Should the United States keep military forces in Saudi Arabia and the Persian Gulf until Iraq withdraws its troops from Kuwait, even if it means keeping American forces there for many months or even years? (ABC/*Washington Post*, ABC)

	Keep U.S. forces there for years	Do not keep U.S. forces there	Don't know	n
1990 Aug 8	63	33	4	769
1990 Sep 6–9	75	23	3	1011
1990 Oct 10–14	60	38	2	1006
1990 Nov 2–4	64	32	3	1015

76 Which of the following three statements comes closest to your opinion?

The United States should withdraw its troops from Saudi Arabia

The United States should continue to enforce sanctions and seek some form of peaceful solution to the crisis, no matter how long it takes, without initiating a war to drive Iraq out of Kuwait

The United States should initiate a war to drive Iraq out of Kuwait if Iraq does not change its position within the next several months, in order to draw matters to a close. (Gallup)

	Withdraw troops	Continue sanctions	Initiate war	Don't know
1990 Nov 29–Dec 2	9	46	42	3
1990 Dec 6–9	10	41	46	3
1990 Dec 13–16	9	44	43	4
1991 Jan 3–6	8	43	45	4
1991 Jan 11–13	9	36	50	5

Gallup Poll Monthly, December 1990, p. 17; January 1991, p. 12

Do you agree or disagree with the following statement . . . The U.S. should continue to enforce economic sanctions, no matter how long it takes, and not resort to war . . . (*Los Angeles Times*)

	Strongly agree	Agree somewhat	Disagree somewhat	Strongly disagree	Don't know	n
1990 Nov 14	35	22	15	23	5	1031
1990 Dec 8–12	37	22	16	19	6	2205
1991 Jan 8–12	22	17	23	32	6	2434

Do you think that economic sanctions against Iraq have been given enough time or not? (Yankelovich)

	Sanctions have been given enough time	Have not	Don't know	n
1990 Nov 14	43	49	8	500
1990 Nov 27–28	50	43	7	1000

Some people feel the sanctions imposed by the international community against Iraq should be given more time to work. Other people feel that it is time to take stronger action against Saddam Hussein, including the use of armed force. Which one of these views comes closer to how you feel? (Gallup)

	Give sanctions more time to work	Time to use armed force against Saddam	Don't know
1990 Nov 29–Dec 2	46	48	6
1990 Dec 6–9	47	46	7
1991 Jan 3–6	36	57	7

Gallup Poll Monthly, January 1991, p. 2

80 The United Nations has passed a resolution authorizing the use of military force against Iraq if they do not withdraw their troops from Kuwait by January 15 (1991). If Iraq does not withdraw from Kuwait by then, do you think the United States should start military actions against Iraq, or should the United States wait longer to see if the trade embargo and other economic sanctions work? (*New York Times*/CBS)

	Start military actions after Jan 15	Wait longer to see if sanctions work	Don't know	*n*
1990 Dec 9–11	45	48[a]	7	1044
1991 Jan 5–7	46	47	7	
1991 Jan 9–13[b]	48	46	5	1009
1991 Jan 11–13	47	46	6	*1512*

New York Times, January 9, 1991, p. A6; New York Times/CBS Poll Jan 11–13, 1991, p. 2; New York Times/CBS Poll, Tracking, Feb 24–Mar 1, 1991, p. 2

[a]These then asked: How long do you think the United States should wait to see if the trade embargo works. . .

24%	3 months
10	6 months
4	a year
4	longer
6	Don't know
48	

[b]*Washington Post*, asked of half of sample

81 Do you think the United States did the right thing in starting military actions against Iraq, or should the United States have waited longer to see if the trade embargo and other economic sanctions worked? (*New York Times*/CBS)

	U.S. was right in starting military actions	U.S. should have waited longer to see if sanctions worked	Don't know	*n*
1991 Jan 17–20	75	20	5	
1991 Feb 28[a]	82	14	4	528

New York Times/CBS News Poll, Tracking, Feb 24–Mar 1, 1991, p. 2
[a]Or Feb 24–Mar 1

Last week, the United Nations authorized the use of force against Iraq if Iraq doesn't leave Kuwait by January 15 (1991). If the January 15 deadline elapses without Iraq leaving Kuwait, should the United States attack Iraq or should we give economic sanctions more time to work? (Black) **82**

	Attack after Jan 15	Give sanctions more time	Don't know	n
1990 Dec 1–2	44	48	9	704

Which statement do you agree with more: **83**

   Statement A: After the UN (United Nations) deadline of January 15, the United States should continue to wait for economic sanctions to force Iraq out of Kuwait, or

   Statement B: After the UN deadline of January 15, the United States should take military action to force Iraq out of Kuwait?
(rotated) (NBC/ *Wall Street Journal*)

	Take military action after Jan 15	Continue to wait for sanctions	Both or neither (vol)	Don't know	n
1990 Dec 8–11	46	44	5	5	1002
1991 Mar 15–19[a]	76	21	2	1	1505

   Registered voters
   [a]Thinking back to how you felt before the war started, which of the following statements came closer to your point of view last January?

As you may know, the United Nations set a January 15 (1991) deadline for Iraq **84** to get out of Kuwait. If Saddam Hussein does not comply by the deadline, should the United States go to war (with Iraq), or should the U.S. give economic sanctions more time to work? (AP)

	Go to war after Jan 15	Give sanctions more time to work	Don't know	n
1991 Jan 4–8	44	50	6	1004

85 As you may know, the United Nations passed a resolution authorizing force against Iraq if it doesn't remove its troops by the January 15 (1991) deadline. overall, taking into consideration everything you heard or read about the Mideast crisis, do you think the United States should go to war against Iraq if the United Nations deadline of January 15th is not met, or do you think we should give economic sanctions more time to work? (*Los Angeles Times*)

	Go to war after Jan 15	Give sanctions more time to work	Don't know	*n*
1991 Jan 8–12	47	46	7	2434

86 If Iraq doesn't withdraw from Kuwait by January 15 (1991), which of the following options would you most prefer? Attack Iraq to force them to withdraw or continue economic sanctions and diplomacy? (Black)

	Attack after Jan 15	Continue sanctions	Don't know	*n*
1991 Jan 9	49	46	5	800

87 If Iraq doesn't withdraw from Kuwait by January 15 (1991), should the United States attack immediately, extend the deadline a few weeks, or set no deadlines but rely on diplomacy and economic sanctions? (Black)

	Attack after Jan 15	Extend deadline a few weeks	Rely on sanctions	Don't know	*n*
1991 Jan 14	48	15	27	10	600

88 Generally speaking, do you think President Bush gave economic sanctions enough time to work, or do you think economic sanctions were not given enough time to work? (*Los Angeles Times*)

	Bush gave sanctions enough time to work	Sanctions not given enough time to work	Don't know	*n*
1991 Jan 17–18	72	24	4	1406

As you may know, the United Nations recently passed a resolution that permits **89** the use of force against Iraq if it does not withdraw from Kuwait. Would you favor or oppose the U.S. going to war against Iraq if Iraq does not withdraw its troops from Kuwait by the United Naitons' deadline of January 15? (NBC/ *Wall Street Journal*)

	Favor going to war after Jan 15	Oppose going to war	Depends (vol)	Don't know	*n*
1990 Dec 8–11	54	34	7	5	1002

Registered voters

Which of the following do you think we should do now in the Persian Gulf: **90** pull out U.S. forces entirely; try harder to find a diplomatic solution; tighten the economic embargo; or take tougher military action? (National Election Study)

	Pull out U.S. forces entirely	Try harder to find a diplo- matic solution	Tighten the economic embargo	Take tougher military ation	Other (vol)	Don't know	*n*
1990 Nov 7–1991 Jan 26	10	50	25	27	1	4	*2000*

Multiple answers possible; percentages sum to 117. 97% of interviews completed before January 6, 1991, 92% before December 23, 1990.

In your opinion, what, if anything, should the United States do concerning the **91** current situation involving Iraq and Kuwait? (Gallup)

	1990 Aug 3–4	1990 Aug 9–12	1990 Aug 23–26	1990 Aug 30–Sep 2	1991 Jan 3–6
Take action quickly/get it over with	—	—	1	4	13
Send in troops to actively fight against Iraq	6	6	4	3	7
Bomb/airplane strikes	2	3	4	2	6
Do whatever it takes	—	—	3	2	3
Get the Iraqis out of Kuwait	—	—	1	1	1
Bomb Iraq's oil pipelines thru Turkey and Saudi Arabia	—	*	*	1	*

Table 91 continued

	1990 Aug 3–4	1990 Aug 9–12	1990 Aug 23–26	1990 Aug 30–Sep 2		1991 Jan 3–6
Send U.S. troops/ships to the area but don't use them	3	5	2	1		*
Impose a naval blockade on Iraq's imports and exports	—	1	1	*		*
Stay strong/show our force/be firm	—	—	10	6		7
Get American civilians out/ protect them	—	—	6	3		*
Assassinate Hussein	—	—	2	2		1
Impose economic sanctions/embar- goes/boycotts/ freeze assets	9	4	4	2		2
Wait & see, wait for further develop- ments	13	15	10	9		6
Do all we can to prevent war	—	—	3	2		3
Talk/negotiate/ use diplomatic process or the UN	—	—	6	8		13
Keep things as they are now	—	—	10	7		7
Do nothing	14	8	3	4		2
Pull out, don't get involved/stay neutral/let Arabs do it	—	—	5	6		10
Other	19	32	6	20		4
No opinion	36	27	25	24		18

Gallup Poll Monthly, January 1991, p. 5

If Iraq doesn't withdraw from Kuwait by January 15th (1991), which of the following options do you support the most? (A) Withdrawing United States forces from Saudi Arabia, (B) U.S. forces attacking Iraq through the air, (C) U.S. forces attacking Iraq using combined power of the air force, naval bombardments, including ground troops, (D) giving the sanctions time to work. (Black)

	Withdraw U.S. from Saudi Arabia	U.S. air attack	U.S. air, sea, and ground attack	Give sanctions time to work	Don't know	n
1990 Dec 29–30	5	19[a]	38[a]	36[b]	2	1008

[a]These (57% of sample) then asked: Would you support military action (after January 15, 1991) under the following circumstances?

. . . If 1,000 United States soldiers killed and wounded
44% Support
56 Don't support/Don't know

. . . If 10,000 United States soldiers killed and wounded
30% Support
70 Don't support/Don't know

. . . If 30,000 United States soldiers killed and wounded
23% Support
77 Don't support/Don't know

. . . If 100,000 or more Iraqi military/civilians killed, wounded
36% Support
64 Don't support/Don't know

[b]These then asked: If Iraq is not out of Kuwait at the end of six months, which of the following options would you support:

25%	Giving the sanctions another 6 months to work
24%	air war against Iraq by United States forces
25	full-scale war against Iraq by the combined U.S. forces including ground troops
20	scaling down the U.S. presence in Saudi Arabia by withdrawing troops
6	Don't know
100	

93 As you may know, the United Nations Security Council has authorized the use of force against Iraq if it doesn't withdraw from Kuwait by January 15th (1991). If Iraq does not withdraw from Kuwait, should the United States go to war with Iraq to force it out of Kuwait at some point after January 15th, or not? (ABC/ *Washington Post*)

	Go to war at some point after Jan 15 if Iraq doesn't withdraw Kuwait	Do not go to war	Don't know	*n*
1991 Jan 4–6	63[a]	32	6	1057
1991 Jan 4–8	62[b]	31	6	1003

[a]These then asked: Would you favor or oppose going to war with Iraq at some point after the January 15 deadline if it means 1,000 American troops would be killed in the fighting?

70% Favor war   24% Oppose   5% Don't know

Would you favor or oppose going to war with Iraq at some point after the January 15 deadline if it means 10,000 American troops would be killed in the fighting?

55% Favor war   37% Oppose   7% Don't know

[b] These then asked: Would you favor or oppose going to war with Iraq at some point after the January 15th (1991) deadline if it meant 10,000 American troops would be killed in the fighting?

61% Favor war   32% Oppose   7% Don't know

94 As you may know, the United Nations Security Council has authorized the use of force against Iraq if it doesn't withdraw from Kuwait by January 15th (1991). If Iraq does not withdraw from Kuwait, should the United States go to war with Iraq to force it out of Kuwait at some point after January 15th, or not? (*Washington Post*)

	Go to war at some point after Jan 15 if Iraq doesn't withdraw from Kuwait	Do not go to war	Don't know	*n*
1991 Jan 11–15[a]	60	33	7	1007

[a]Asked of one-third of sample

As you may know, the United Nations Security Council has authorized the use of force against Iraq if it doesn't withdraw from Kuwait by January 15th (1991). Would you favor or oppose going to war with Iraq at some point after the January 15th deadline if it meant 1,000 American troops would be killed in the fighting? (*Washington Post*)

234

Table 94 continued

	Favor war at some point after Jan 15 if it meant 1,000 American troops would be killed	Oppose war if 1,000 American troops would be killed	Don't know	*n*
1991 Jan 11–15ᵃ	52	43	5	1007

ᵃAsked of one-third of sample

As you may know, the United Nations Security Council has authorized the use of force against Iraq if it doesn't withdraw from Kuwait by January 15th (1991). Would you favor or oppose going to war with Iraq at some point after the January 15th deadline if it meant 10,000 American troops would be killed in the fighting? (*Washington Post*)

	Favor war at some point after Jan 15 if it meant 10,000 American troops would be killed	Oppose war if 10,000 American troops would be killed	Don't know	*n*
1991 Jan 11–15ᵃ	37	56	7	1007

ᵃAsked of one-third of sample

Assuming Iraq leaves Kuwait, would you consider the war with Iraq a success if 500 American troops died, or not? (IF YES) Would you consider it a success if 1,000 American troops died, or not? (IF YES) Would you consider the war with Iraq a success if 5,000 American troops died, or not? (IF YES) And would you consider the war with Iraq a success if 10,000 American troops died, or not? (IF YES) And would you consider the war with Iraq a success if 20,000 American troops died, or not? (accept "considers no American troops died as a success" as a volunteered response) (*Los Angeles Times*)

95

1991 Jan 17–18	Consider war with Iraq a success if Iraq leaves Kuwait and	
n = 1406	no American troops die	80%
	500 American troops die	50%
	1,000 American troops die	37%
	5,000 American troops die	27%
	10,000 American troops die	20%
	20,000 American troops die	16%
	Don't know	13%
	Refused	7%

96 Do you think the U.S. (United States) action in the Mideast is morally justified, or not? (*Los Angeles Times*)

	U.S. action is morally justified	U.S. action is not morally justified	Don't know	*n*
1990 Aug 29	66	23	11	1206
1990 Nov 14	63	29	8	1031
1991 Jan 17–18	75	17	8	1406
1990 Feb 15–17	74	19	7	1822

97 Which of the following best describes your attitude about the war (with Iraq). I always opposed the war, I did not want to go to war January 16 (1991) but agreed with the decision after the war had ended, I always supported the war. (Black)

	I always opposed the war	Did not want to go to war, but agreed after the war ended	I always supported the war	None (Vol)	Don't know	*n*
1991 Apr 4	14	28	53	3	2	612

NEGOTIATIONS ....

In its dealings with the Middle East, do you think the Bush administration has **98** tried hard enough to reach diplomatic solutions, or has it been too quick to get American military forces involved? (*New York Times*/CBS)

	Bush has tried hard enough for diplomatic solutions	Bush too quick to get military forces involved	Don't know	*n*
1990 Aug 9–10	48	40	12	670
1990 Aug 16–19	51	38	11	1422
1990 Nov 13–15	38	47	15	1370
1990 Dec 9–11	44	43	13	1044
1991 Jan 5–7	47	42	10	*1348*

New York Times/CBS News Poll, January 5–7, 1991, p. 2

Do you think the United States has done enough to seek a diplomatic solution **99** to the Persian Gulf situation, or not? (ABC/*Washington Post*)

	U.S. has done enough for diplomatic solution	U.S. has not	Don't know	*n*
1991 Jan 9	71	27	2	511
1991 Jan 13	66	30	4	781

100 Do you think the United States should hold additional talks with Iraq before the January 15th (1991) deadline, or not? (ABC/*Washington Post*)

	U.S. should hold additional talks before Jan 15	U.S. should not	Don't know	*n*
1991 Jan 9	79	21	0	511
1991 Jan 13	64	35	1	781

101 Do you think the United States should hold additional talks with Iraq after the January 15th (1991) deadline, or not? (ABC/*Washington Post*)

	U.S. should hold additional talks after Jan 15	U.S. should not	Don't know	*n*
1991 Jan 9	53	45	1	511
1991 Jan 13	57	42	1	781

102 Please tell me if you agree or disagree with this statement: George Bush is too eager to wage war (with Iraq) and not willing enough to negotiate. (ABC/*Washington Post*)

	Bush too eager to wage war and not willing enough to negotiate	Disagree	Don't know	*n*
1990 Feb 22	27	72	1	520

103 Suppose that eventually we have to choose between compromise with Saddam Hussein or starting a war. Which would you choose: compromise or war? (I.C.R. Survey Research Group)

	Compromise with Saddam Hussein	Start a war	Don't know	*n*
1990 Nov 9–13	58	34	7	1020

If Iraq agreed to withdraw from most of Kuwait but not all of it, do you think **104**
the United States should accept that or not? (ABC/*Washington Post*)

	Accept agreement giving Iraq part of Kuwait	Do not accept agreement	Don't know	n
1990 Nov 30–Dec 2	30	66	4	758
1990 Dec 9	35	59	6	518
1991 Jan 4–6	36	58	6	1057
1991 Jan 4–8	35	58	7	1003
1991 Jan 9	35	63	2	511
1991 Jan 13	31	65	4	781

Do you think the United States should be willing to negotiate a compromise **105**
with Saddam Hussein about how to solve the situation in the Persian Gulf, or
do you think the U.S. should stick to its original demand that Iraq leave Kuwait
entirely? (CBS/*New York Times*)

	Negotiate with Saddam	Stick to original demand that Iraq leave entirely	Don't know	n
1990 Dec 9–11	29	62	9	1044

Which statement do you agree with more? **106**
   Statement A: The U.S. should accept an agreement with Iraq in which Iraq
releases all of the hostages and withdraws from Kuwait, with some concessions
being made to Iraq on the control of disputed oil fields; or
   Statement B: The U.S. should not accept an agreement with concessions,
and that after the UN (United Nations) deadline of January 15th, the U.S.
should use military force to get Iraq to release the hostages and to withdraw
from Kuwait? (rotated) (NBC/*Wall Street Journal*)

	Accept agreement with some concessions	Refuse agreement and use military force	Both or neither (vol)	Don't know	n
1990 Dec 8–11	51	39	5	5	1002

Registered voters

107 Israel occupied the West Bank and the Gaza Strip after its Arab neighbors attacked Israel in 1967. As you know, Iraq invaded and took over Kuwait this summer. Would you approve of a deal in which Iraq gave up Kuwait and Israel gave up the West Bank and the Gaza Strip, or don't you think these issues should be linked? (ABC, ABC/*Washington Post*)

	Approve deal linking Kuwait and West Bank	Issues should not be linked	Don't know	n
1990 Dec 9	19	73	8	518
1991 Jan 4–6	23	65	13	1057
1991 Jan 4–8	25	63	12	1003
1991 Jan 9	25	68	8	511

108 Suppose the government of Kuwait offers to trade a piece of its territory in return for Iraq's withdrawal from the rest of Kuwait. If the government of Kuwait did that, would that be acceptable or not acceptable to you as a way of ending the crisis? (New York Times/CBS)

	Trading land for withdrawal would be acceptable	Would not be acceptable	Don't know	n
1991 Jan 11–13	47	37	16	*1512*

New York Times/CBS News Poll, January 11–13, 1991, p. 2

109 The Bush administration opposes making any concession to Iraq to get it to withdraw from Kuwait, including an international conference on Arab–Israeli problems. Some people say such a conference would be a concession that would reward Iraqi aggression by linking the Arab–Israeli dispute with Iraq's invasion of Kuwait. Other people say such an agreement would be worth it if it got Iraq to withdraw from Kuwait without a war. Do you think the United States should agree to an Arab–Israeli conference if Iraq agreed to withdraw from Kuwait, or not? (ABC/*Washington Post*)

	U.S. should agree to Arab-Israeli conference	Should not agree	Don't know	n
1991 Jan 9	66	30	3	511
1991 Jan 13	67	29	4	781

240

Do you think talks between the United States and Iraq would produce a diplo- **110**
matic solution to the Persian Gulf situation or not? (ABC/*Washington Post*)

	Talks between U.S. and Iraq would produce diplomatic solution	Talks would not	Don't know	*n*
1991 Jan 2	43	50	6	352
1991 Jan 2–6	48	45	7	1007
1991 Jan 4–6[a]	49	44	7	1057
1991 Jan 4–8	50	44	6	1003
1991 Jan 9[b]	35	58	7	511
1991 Jan 13[b]	35	59	6	781

[a]"will" instead of "would"
[b]Do you think additional talks . . .

111   What do you think is the main reason why American troops have been sent to
the Mideast? (*Los Angeles Times*)

1990 Aug 29	$n = 1206$
50%	Do you think it's because we want to protect our oil supplies,
13	or is it to defend Saudi Arabia,
28	or is it to protect the lives of American hostages in Kuwait and Iraq,
11	or is it to help restore the legitimate government of Kuwait,
45	or is because we want to show that countries cannot get away with aggression, or what?
4	Other
7	Don't know
168	

112   Of the following two alternatives, which do you feel is the most important reason for establishing an international force in the Gulf? (Gallup)

	The restoration of independence to Kuwait	The protection of oil supplies to Western countries	Both equally important	Neither	Don't know	n
1990 Nov 8–11	46	36	11	4	4	1008

242

Which of these two views best describes yours: A. The United States has sent **113** troops to the Middle East (Persian Gulf) because of the (a) moral principle that we cannot allow Iraq or any other country to invade another, or B. The United States has sent troops to the Middle East (Persian Gulf) because of the economic reality that we cannot let Iraq or any other country gain too much control over the flow and price of Middle Eastern oil? (ABC/*Washington Post*)

	U.S. sent troops because of moral principle	Because of economic reality	Both	Neither	Don't know	n
1990 Nov 30–Dec 2	41	48	7	2	2	758
1991 Jan 20	54	35	6	3	2	532
1991 Mar 1–4	56	34	9	1	1	1215

Why do you think we are involved in the Iraqi situation and why are our troops **114** in Saudi Arabia? (Gallup)
1 Defend oil/interests
2 We should be/have to defend other countries
3 Stop Iraqi aggression
4 Defend Saudi Arabia
5 Protect U.S. citizens
6 Get Iraq out of Kuwait

	1	2	3	4	5	6	Other	None	Don't know
1990 Aug 16–19	49	17	11	6	4	1	6	1	5
1990 Nov 15–18	39	9	23	5	4	5	10	*	5
1990 Nov 29–Dec 2	43	7	19	5	5	6	10	*	5

Gallup Poll Monthly, December 1990, p. 12

Do you think the U.S. sent military troops to the Middle East mainly because **115** the U.S. has a duty to protect its friends, or mainly because the price of oil will increase too much if we let the Iraqis control oil fields in the Middle East? (CBS/*New York Times*)

	U.S. has a duty to protect its friends	Oil price will increase too much if Iraqis control	Both equal	Don't know	n
1990 Nov 13–15	26	43	17	14	1370

116 Do you think the United States sent military troops to the Middle East mainly to stop an Iraqi invasion of Saudi Arabia, or mainly to protect the supply of oil to the U.S.? (CBS, CBS/*New York Times*)

	Troops sent mainly to stop Iraqi invasion of Saudi Arabia	Troops sent mainly to protect U.S. oil supply	Both (vol)	Neither (vol)	Don't know	*n*
1990 Sep 10	20	44	26	2	8	699
1990 Oct 8–10	20	55	18	1	6	960

117 I'm going to read you three reasons why some people think U.S. troops are in Saudi Arabia. Please tell me which one you think is the single most important reason why U.S. troops are there. (NBC/*Wall Street Journal*)

	To protect the world's oil supply	To force Iraq to withdraw from Kuwait	To overthrow Saddam Hussein	Don't know	*n*
1990 Sep 4–5	50	39	9	2	800
1990 Oct 30–31[a]	35	46	13	6	670

Registered voters
[a]Items rotated

118 I'm going to read you six reasons why some people think U.S. troops are in the Persian Gulf and Saudi Arabia. Please tell me which one you think is the single most important reason why U.S. troops are there. (NBC/*Wall Street Journal*)
  A. To protect the world's oil supply
  B. To force Iraq to withdraw from Kuwait
  C. To overthrow Saddam Hussein
  D. To free the hostages
  E. To protect Saudi Arabia and other Persian Gulf nations
  F. To prevent Iraq from developing nuclear weapons
  G. All equally (vol)
  H. None of these (vol)

	A	B	C	D	E	F	G	H	Don't know	*n*
1990 Dec 8–11	33	18	10	6	10	10	9	2	2	1002

Registered voters

244

The United States has stationed hundreds of thousands of troops in the Middle **119**
East. Which of the following reasons best explains why we are there?
(Greenberg/Lake)

	Liberating Kuwait from Iraqi occupation	Secure Middle East oil supplies for the U.S. and its allies	Neutralize Iraq's growing chemical and nuclear weapons capability	Don't know	*n*
1990 Dec 8–11	28	50	14	8	1200

Of these three reasons, which do you think is the *main* reason U.S. military **120**
forces are in the Persian Gulf? (CBS/*New York Times*)

	To protect the supply of oil to the United States	To restore the government of Kuwait	To stop Iraq from attacking Saudi Arabia and other Middle Eastern countries	More than one, other	Don't know	*n*
1991 Jan 11–13	29[a]	11[a]	42[a]	14[a]	4	*1512*

New York Times/CBS News Poll January 11–13, 1991, p. 4
[a]These then asked: Do you think that is a good enogh reason to go to war, or not?
45% Good enough reason   46% Not good enough reason   5% Don't know (total:96%)

Please tell me if each of the following are good reasons or poor reasons for **121**
getting involved in this (Middle East) conflict . . . (*Time*/CNN)

	Good reason for involvement	Poor reason for involvement	Don't know	*n*
A . . .To deter further aggression by Iraq				
1990 Aug 23	78	14	8	500

	Good reason for involvement	Poor reason for involvement	Don't know	*n*
B . . .To protect the oil supply in the Middle East				
1990 Aug 23	78	18	4	500

	Good reason for involvement	Poor reason for involvement	Don't know	*n*
C . . .To force Iraq to remove its troops from Kuwait				
1990 Aug 23	73	20	7	500

	Good reason for involvement	Poor reason for involvement	Don't know	*n*
D . . .To protect Saudi Arabia from Iraq				
1990 Aug 23	67	25	8	500

Table 121 continued

	Good reason for involvement	Poor reason for involvement	Don't know	*n*
E ...To remove Saddam Hussein from power				
1990 Aug 23	63	28	9	500

122 Which of the following should be among the goals for U.S. forces (in the Middle East crisis) and which should not? (Gallup)

	Should be a U.S. goal	Should not	Don't know	*n*
A ...Rescuing as many hostages as possible				
1990 Aug 23–24	92	7	1	767
B ...Forcing Iraq to leave Kuwait				
1990 Aug 23–24	84	10	6	767
C ...Restoring the former government of Kuwait				
1990 Aug 23–24	70	20	10	767
D ...Destroying Iraq's nuclear and chemical weapons and military capabilities				
1990 Aug 23–24	78	17	5	767
E ...Removing Saddam Hussein's government from power in Iraq				
1990 Aug 23–24	73	19	8	767

123 In the crisis (with Iraq), which of the following is the most important goal? (Black)

	Protecting and freeing United States hostages	Protecting Saudi Arabia from an Iraqi invasion	Getting Iraq out of Kuwait	Ensuring a sufficient supply of oil to the U.S. and other countries	Don't know	*n*
1990 Aug 20–21	52	8	18	14	9	802
1990 Nov 12	50	12	22	9	7	615

246

Here are some things the U.S. might try to achieve in its confrontation with Iraq. For each one, please tell me if you think that objective is: extremely important, very important, somewhat important, or not very important? (Americans Talk Security)

	Extremely important	Very important	Somewhat important	Not very important/not a goal	Don't know	n
A . . . Defending Saudi Arabia from an invasion by Iraq						
1990 Sep 21–26	33	42	18	6	1	1000
B . . . Making sure oil from the Middle East flows freely to the world						
1990 Sep 21–26	41	36	17	6	1	1000
C . . . Making Iraq withdraw from Kuwait						
1990 Sep 21–26	47	37	11	4	1	1000
D . . . Eliminating the ability of Iraq to wage aggressive wars						
1990 Sep 21–26	37	36	19	7	2	1000
E . . . Removing the President of Iraq, Saddam Hussein, from power						
1990 Sep 21–26	46	29	13	11	1	1000
F . . . Keeping war from breaking out in the Middle East						
1990 Sep 21–26	46	36	11	6	1	1000
G . . . Producing a lasting peace in the Middle East						
1990 Sep 21–26	50	37	9	4	1	1000
H . . . Promoting democracy in the Middle East						
1990 Sep 21–26	28	29	28	15	1	1000
I . . . Returning the Kuwaiti royal family to govern Kuwait						
1990 Sep 21–26	16	27	30	21	5	1000
J . . . Punishing Iraq for invading Kuwait						
1990 Sep 21–26	21	23	30	25	2	1000
K . . . Establishing the principle that aggression by one country against another will no longer be tolerated						
1990 Sep 21–26	49	34	11	5	1	1000

125   Which one of the 11 objectives I just read do you think should be the number one goal of the U.S. in its confrontation with Iraq?

Which one of the 11 objectives I just read do you think is the number one goal of President Bush in the confrontation with Iraq? (Americans Talk Security)

1990 Sep 21–26 N = 1000	Should be number one goal of the U.S.	Is number one goal of Bush
Defending Saudi Arabia from an invasion by Iraq	3	4
Making sure oil from the Middle East flows freely to the world	12	26
Making Iraq withdraw from Kuwait	11	13
Eliminating the ability of Iraq to wage aggressive wars	4	4
Removing the President of Iraq, Saddam Hussein, from power	20	10
Keeping war from breaking out in the Middle East	12	7
Producing a lasting peace in the Middle East	22	13
Promoting democracy in the Middle East	2	3
Returning the Kuwaiti royal family to govern Kuwait	2	3
Punishing Iraq for invading Kuwait	1	1
Establishing the principle that aggression by one country against another will no longer be tolerated	9	8

248

Now that the U.S. (United States) forces have been sent to Saudi Arabia and **126** other areas of the Middle East, do you think they should engage in combat if Iraq . . . (Gallup)

	Engage in combat	Do not engage in combat	Don't know	*n*
A ...invades Saudi Arabia?				
1990 Aug 9–10	67	23	10	770
1990 Oct 18–19ª	68	19	13	755
B ...refuses to leave Kuwait and restore its former government?				
1990 Aug 9–10	42	40	18	770
1990 Oct 18–19ª	45	37	18	755
1990 Nov 15–16ª	46	40	14	754
1990 Dec 6–7	56	33	11	769
1991 Jan 3–4	61	29	10	759
1991 Jan 10–11	62	32	6	751
C ...continues to hold U.S. civilians hostage?				
1990 Aug 9–10ᵇ	61	30	9	770
1990 Oct 18–19ª	57	32	11	755
1990 Nov 15–16ª	55	34	11	754
D ...kills American civilians in Kuwait and Iraq?				
1990 Aug 9–10	79	14	7	770
E ...begins to control or cut off oil?				
1990 Aug 9–10	58	31	11	770
F ...attacks U.S. forces?				
1990 Aug 9–10	94	4	2	770
1990 Oct 18–19ª	93	3	4	755
1990 Nov 15–16ª	91	6	3	754

ªresponse items rotated
ᵇholds American civilians hostage?

127 Do you think it's worth risking the lives of American soldiers (in the Middle East) in order to protect our oil supplies, or not? (*Los Angeles Times*)

	Worth risking lives of American soldiers to protect oil supplies	Not worth risking lives of American soldiers	Don't know	n
1990 Aug 29	29	61	10	1206
1990 Nov 14	29	65	6	1031

128 Do you think it's worth risking the lives of American soldiers (in the Middle East) in order to keep down gasoline prices, or not? (*Los Angeles Times*)

	Worth risking lives of Ame.ican soldiers to keep gasoline prices down	Not worth risking lives of American soldiers	Don't know	n
1990 Aug 29	5	91	4	1206

129 Do you think it's worth risking the lives of American soldiers (in the Middle East) in order to demonstrate that countries should not get away with aggression, or not? (*Los Angeles Times*)

	Worth risking lives of American soldiers to show aggressors they can't get away with it	Not worth risking lives of American soldiers	Don't know	n
1990 Aug 29	53	37	10	1206
1990 Nov 14	48	44	8	1031

There are times when it is worth the country making sacrifices in blood and **130**
money to achieve a more important return. Do you feel it is worth the loss of
American lives and billions of dollars in this present (Mideast) crisis to

	Worth it	Not worth it	Don't know	*n*
A ... make sure American oil supplies in the Middle East are not cut off by a military power such as Iraq ... or not?				
1990 Aug 17–21	44	52	4	1255
B ... serve notice on Iraq and other aggressor nations that they cannot militarily invade and take over other nations and get away with it ... or not? (Harris)				
1990 Aug 17–21	62	35	3	1255

I am going to mention several reasons that have been offered to explain why the **131**
United States should be involved in the Mideast crisis. For each of the following
reasons, would you please tell me whether you think it justifies a major war, a
limited military involvement but not a major war, or does it not justify U.S.
military involvement at all? (*Los Angeles Times*)

A ... Do you think the U.S. is justified in getting involved in a major war to protect
our oil supplies in the Persian Gulf, or does it justify a limited military involvement but
not a major war, or protecting our oil supplies in the Persian Gulf does not justify a U.S.
military involvement at all?

	Protecting oil justifies a major war	Justifies limited military involvement	Does not justify military involvement at all	Don't know	*n*
1990 Nov 14	16	50	28	6	1031

B ... What about defending Saudi Arabia from attack by Iraq? Does this justify the U.S.
getting involved in a major war, or does it justify a limited military involvement but not a
major war, or defending Saudi Arabia from attack by Iraq does not justify a U.S. military
involvement at all?

	Defending Saudi Arabia from Iraq attack justifies a major war	Justifies limited military involvement	Does not justify military involvement at all	Don't know	*n*
1990 Nov 14	24	47	25	4	1031

Table 131 continued

C . . . What about protecting the lives of American hostages in Kuwait and Iraq? Does this justify the U.S. getting involved in a major war, or does it justify a limited military involvement but not a major war, or protecting the lives of American hostages in Kuwait and Iraq does not justify a U.S. military involvement at all?

	Protecting the lives of American hostages justifies a major war	Justifies limited military involvement	Does not justify military involvement at all	Don't know	n
1990 Nov 14	32	45	18	5	1031

D . . . What about helping to restore the previous government of Kuwait? Does this justify the U.S. getting involved in a major war, or does it justify a limited military involvement but not a major war, or helping to restore the previous government of Kuwait does not justify a U.S. military involvement at all?

	Helping restore Kuwait government justifies a major war	Justifies limited military involvement	Does not justify military involvement at all	Don't know	n
1990 Nov 14	13	46	36	5	1031

E . . . What about the removal of Saddam Hussein from power? Does this justify the U.S. getting involved in a major war, or does it justify a limited military involvement but not a major war, or the removal of Saddam Hussein from power does not justify a U.S. military involvement at all?

	Removal of Saddam Hussein from power justifies a major war	Justifies limited military involvement	Does not justify military involvement at all	Don't know	n
1990 Nov 14	30	35	29	6	1031

F . . . Do you think the U.S. is justified in getting involved in a major war in order to neutralize Iraq's army, or does it justify a limited military involvement but not a major war, or wanting to neutralize Iraq's army does not justify a U.S. military involvement at all?

	To neutralize Iraq's army justifies a major war	Justifies limited military involvement	Does not justify military involvement at all	Don't know	n
1990 Nov 14	22	41	30	7	1031

252

Table 131 continued
G . . . Do you think the U.S. is justified in getting involved in a major war in order to destroy Iraq's nuclear and chemical facilities, or does it justify a limited military involvement but not a major war, or wanting to destroy Iraq's nuclear and chemical weapons faciliites does not justify a U.S. military involvement at all?

	To destroy Iraq's nuclear and chemical weapons facilities justifies a major war	Justifies limited military involvement	Does not justify military involvement at all	Don't know	*n*
1990 Nov 14	34	36	24	6	1031

A. Do you think the United States is justified in getting involved in a major war in order **132** to get Iraq out of Kuwait and restore the previous Kuwaiti government, or not? (*Los Angeles Times*)

	To get Iraq out of Kuwait and restore Kuwaiti government justifies a major war	Does not justify a major war	Don't know	*n*
1990 Jan 8–12	54	36	10	2434

B. Do you think the United States is justified in getting involved in a major war in order to destroy Iraq's nuclear and chemical weapons, or not? (Los Angeles Times)

	To destroy Iraq's nuclear and chemical weapons justifies a major war	Does not justify a major war	Don't know	*n*
1990 Jan 8–12	54	36	10	2434

133 I'm going to read to you some reasons people give for going to war against Iraq. Please tell me whether you think each is a good reason for the U.S. to go to war against Iraq or whether it is not a good reason to go to war? (rotated) (Gallup)

	Good reason to go to war	Not a good reason to go to war	Don't know	n
A ... To restore the former government of Kuwait back to power				
1990 Nov 15–16	53	38	9	754
1990 Dec 6–7	60	34	6	769
B ... to prevent Iraq from ultimately attacking Israel				
1990 Nov 15–16	53	39	8	754
1990 Dec 6–7	57	36	7	769
C ... to prevent Iraq from controlling a larger share of Mideast oil and threatening the U.S. economy				
1990 Nov 15–16	57	38	5	754
1990 Dec 6–7	60	36	4	769
D ... To prevent Saddam Hussein from threatening the area with chemical and biological weapons				
1990 Nov 15–16	76	21	3	754
1990 Dec 6–7	78	20	2	769
E ... To prevent Saddam Hussein from developing nuclear weapons				
1990 Nov 15–16	71	25	4	754
1990 Dec 6–7	70	26	4	769
F ... To lower oil prices				
1990 Nov 15–16	30	67	3	754
1990 Dec 6–7	31	66	3	769

A. Some people say the United States should attack Iraq in order to restore the government of Kuwait and defend Saudi Arabia against aggression. As far as you are concerned, is that a good enough reason for the United States to take military action against Iraq, or not? (CBS/*New York Times*)

	To restore the government of Kuwait and defend Saudis is good enough reason to take military action	Is not good enough reason to take military action	Don't know	*n*
1990 Nov 13–15	35	56	9	1370

B. Some people say the United States should take military action against Iraq in order to stop Saddam Hussein from developing nuclear weapons. As far as you are concerned, is that a good enough reason for the United States to take military action against Iraq, or not? (CBS/*New York Times*)

	To stop Saddam Hussein from developing nuclear weapons is good enough reason to take military action	Is not good enough reason to take military action	Don't know	*n*
1990 Nov 13–15	54	39	7	1370

C. Some people say the United States should take military action against Iraq in order to protect the source of much of the world's oil. As far as you are concerned, is that a good enough reason for the United States to take military action against Iraq, or not? (CBS/*New York Times*)

	To protect the source of much of the world's oil is good enough reason to take military action	Is not good enough reason to take military action	Don't know	*n*
1990 Nov 13–15	31	62	7	1370

135 A Is "To restore Kuwait's government" a good reason or not a good reason for the United States to go to war (with Iraq)? (How about . . . Was that a good reason or not a good reason for the United States to have gone to war against Iraq?) (Associated Press)

	To restore Kuwait's government is (was) a good reason to go to war	Not a good reason	Don't know	n
1991 Jan 4–8	59	38	3	1004
1991 Jul 17–21	69	26	5	1002

B Is "To prevent Iraqi troops from continuing to kill or mistreat the Kuwaiti people" a good reason or not a good reason for the United States to go to war (with Iraq)? (How about . . . Was that a good reason or not a good reason for the United States to have gone to war against Iraq?) (Associated Press)

	To prevent Iraqi troops from continuing to kill or mistreat the Kuwaiti people is (was) a good reason to go to war	Not a good reason	Don't know	n
1991 Jan 4–8	81	16	2	1004
1991 Jul 17–21	86	13	1	1002

C Is "To eliminate Saddam Hussein's war-making ability" (power) a good reason or not a good reason for the United States to go to war (with Iraq)? (How about . . . Was that a good reason or not a good reason for the United States to have gone to war against Iraq?) (Associated Press)

	To eliminate Saddam Hussein's war-making ability (power) is (was) a good reason to go to war	Not a good reason	Don't know	n
1991 Jan 4–8	71	25	4	1004
1991 Jul 17–21	85	12	2	1002

Table 135 continued

D Is 'To prevent Iraq from developing nuclear weapons" a good reason or not a good reason for the United states to go to war (with Iraq)? (How about . . . Was that a good reason or not a good reason for the United States to have gone to war against Iraq?) (Associated Press)

	To prevent Iraq from developing nuclear weapons is (was) a good reason to go to war	Not a good reason	Don't know	*n*
1991 Jan 4–8	74	24	3	1004
1991 Jul 17–21	86	12	1	1002

E Is "To prevent Iraq from having control of a major source of the world's oil" a good reason or not a good reason for the United States to go to war (with Iraq)? (How about . . . Was that a good reason or not a good reason for the United States to have gone to war against Iraq?) (Associated Press)

	To prevent Iraq from having control of a major source of the world's oil is (was) a good reason to go to war	Not a good reason	Don't know	*n*
1991 Jan 4–8	69	28	3	1004
1991 Jul 17–21	72	25	3	1002

I'm going to mention some things that may or may not happen in the Middle East and for each one, please tell me whether the U.S. should or should not take military action (Dec 8–11: should or should not go to war) in connection with it. (NBC/*Wall Street Journal*) **136**

A . . .If Iraq invades Saudi Arabia				
	U.S. should take military action	Should not take military action	Don't know	*n*
1990 Aug 18–19	74	18	8	805
1990 Sep 4–5	84	11	5	800

Table 136 continued

	U.S. should go to war	Should not go to war	Don't know	*n*
1990 Dec 8–11[a]	69	26	5	1002

B . . .If Iraq imprisons or mistreats Americans left in Kuwait

	U.S. should take military action	Should not take military action	Don't know	*n*
1990 Aug 18–19	70	18	12	805
1990 Sep 4–5	73	22	5	800

	U.S. should go to war	Should not go to war	Don't know	*n*
1990 Dec 8–11[a]	55	37	8	1002

C . . .If terrorists loyal to Iraq kill Americans anywhere

	U.S. should take military action	Should not take military action	Don't know	*n*
1990 Aug 18–19	67	21	12	805
1990 Sep 4–5	68	26	6	800

	U.S. should go to war	Should not go to war	Don't know	*n*
1990 Dec 8–11[a]	48	44	8	1002

D . . .If Iraq refuses to withdraw from Kuwait

	U.S. should take military action	Should not take military action	Don't know	*n*
1990 Aug 18–19	43	42	15	805
1990 Sep 4–5	56	36	8	800

E . . .If the U.S. develops a major shortage of oil that increases the price of gasoline to over $2 per gallon

	U.S. should take military action	Should not take military action	Don't know	*n*
1990 Aug 18–19	27	64	9	805
1990 Sep 4–5	24	71	5	800

	U.S. should go to war	Should not go to war	Don't know	*n*
1990 Dec 8–11[a]	19	77	4	1002

258

Table 136 continued

F . . .If the U.S. develops a major shortage of oil that threatens an economic recession and closes some of our factories

	U.S. should take military action	Should not take military action	Don't know	*n*
1990 Aug 18–19	39	50	11	805
1990 Sep 4–5	37	57	6	800
	U.S. should go to war	Should not go to war	Don't know	*n*
1990 Dec 8–11[a]	27	68	5	1002

G . . .If any of the hostages are harmed

	U.S. should take military action	Should not take military action	Don't know	*n*
1990 Sep 4–5	72	22	6	800
	U.S. should go to war	Should not go to war	Don't know	*n*
1990 Dec 8–11[a]	49	44	7	1002

H . . .To make sure that Iraq cannot use chemical or biological weapons

	U.S. should go to war	Should not go to war	Don't know	*n*
1990 Dec 8–11[a]	56	37	7	1002

I . . .If other nations refuse to commit significant military forces

	U.S. should go to war	Should not go to war	Don't know	*n*
1990 Dec 8–11[a]	34	58	8	1002

J . . .If Iraq attacks Israel

	U.S. should go to war	Should not go to war	Don't know	*n*
1990 Dec 8–11[a]	51	41	8	1002

K . . .If military experts estimate that 10,000 American troops could be killed

	U.S. should go to war	Should not go to war	Don't know	*n*
1990 Dec 8–11[a]	46	41	13	1002

Registered voters
[a]response items rotated

137 Do you think that the liberation of Kuwait is worth fighting for or not? (*Time*/CNN)

	Liberation of Kuwait is worth fighting for	Liberation of Kuwait is not worth fighting for	Don't know	n
1990 Nov 14	49	42	9	500
1990 Nov 27–28	59	31	10	1000
1991 Jan 10	59	32	9	1000

138 Here are some conditions under which the United States might consider withdrawing its troops from the Mideast. For each, please tell me if you favor or oppose the U.S. withdrawing its troops if that condition is met. (Gallup)

	Withdraw U.S. troops	Do not withdraw U.S. troops	Don't know	n
A ... If Iraq allows all U.S. and other foreign citizens to leave Kuwait but Iraqi troops remain in Kuwait and Saddam Hussein remains in power				
1990 Aug 30–Sep 2	21	72	7	1007
1990 Sep 27–30ᵃ	19	74	7	1000
B ... If Iraq pulls all of its troops out of Kuwait, but Saddam remains in power in Iraq				
1990 Aug 30–Sep 2	45	46	9	1007
1990 Sep 27-30ᵃ	42	49	9	1000
C ... If Iraq pulls all its troops out of Kuwait, and (but) Saddam Hussein is removed from power in Iraq				
1990 Aug 30–Sep 2	86	9	5	1007
1990 Sep 27–30ᵃ	86	8	6	1000

ᵃresponse items rotated

Have you seen any of the media coverage of Iraqi President Saddam Hussein's **139** recent meeting with hostages? (NBC/*Wall Street Journal*)

	Have seen media coverage of Hussein's meeting with hostages	Have not seen the coverage	Don't know	*n*
1990 Sep 4-5	73[a]	27	0	800

Registered voters

[a]These then asked: Do you think these meetings have helped or hurt President Hussein's image with the American people?

6%	Helped
86	Hurt
5	No difference (vol)
2	Don't know
99	

If Saddam Hussein follows through on his promise to release all U.S. hostages **140** soon, would that make you less willing to support U.S. military action against Iraq, more willing, or wouldn't it make much difference? (Gallup)

	Less willing to support military action if Hussein releases all US hostages	More willing	Wouldn't make much difference	Don't know	*n*
1990 Dec 6–7	18	18	60	4	769

Do you think Iraq's release of the hostages is a sign that Iraq is willing to pull **141** out of Kuwait, or not? (ABC)

	Hostage release is a sign Iraq is willing to pull out of Kuwait	Is not	Don't know	*n*
1990 Dec 9	34	61	5	518

142 You may also know that Saddam Hussein recently announced that Iraq will release all of its foreign hostages. Do you think this is a real and sincere effort to find a peaceful solution to the situation in the Persian Gulf, or do you think it is just a public relations gesture to put pressure on the United States not to attack Iraq? (NBC/*Wall Street Journal*)

	Hostage release is a real effort to find a peaceful solution	Release is just a public relations gesture	Don't know	n
1990 Dec 8–11	15	78	7	1002

Registered voters

143 Do you think the U.S. and ally troops should only defend Saudi Arabia; or should defend Saudi Arabia and regain control in Kuwait; or should defend Saudi Arabia, regain control in Kuwait, and invade Iraq to overthrow Saddam Hussein? (NBC/*Wall Street Journal*)

	Troops should only defend Saudi Arabia	Troops should defend Saudi Arabia and regain control in Kuwait	Troops should defend Saudi Arabia, regain control in Kuwait, and invade Iraq to overthrow Saddam Hussein	Don't know	n
1990 Sep 4–5	15	43	31	10	800

Registered voters

144 Which, if any, of these military goals in the Middle East do you favor? (*Time/CNN*)

	Forcing Iraq to remove its troops from Kuwait	Removing Iraq's leader Saddam Hussein from power	Destroying Iraq's capacity for making nuclear weapons	None of these (vol)	Don't know	n
1990 Sep 13	77	74	73	6	2	500

Multiple responses accepted

There are a number of different purposes for which military forces might be **145** used in the Gulf crisis. For each of the following please say whether you would support or oppose the use of military force. (Gallup)

	Favor use of military force	Oppose use of military force	Don't know	n
A ... The defense of Saudi Arabia and the Gulf states				
1990 Nov 8–11	76	19	6	1008

B ... To make Iraq withdraw from Kuwait				
1990 Nov 8–11	79	17	4	1008

C ... Toppling Saddam Hussein's regime in Iraq				
1990 Nov 8–11	70	24	6	1008

D ... The defense of Israel if attacked				
1990 Nov 8–11	67	25	8	1008

E ... Protecting the West's oil supplies				
1990 Nov 8–11	71	25	5	1008

F ... The release of hostages				
1990 Nov 8–11	84	14	2	1008

I'm going to mention some actions that Bush might take against Iraq. And for **146** each, I want you to tell whether you would approve or disapprove of this action. Would you approve or disapprove of . . . (ABC/*Washington Post*)

	Approve	Disapprove	Don't know	n
A ... U.S. forces attacking Iraqi troops near the Saudi Arabian border in an pre-emptive strike before Iraq has a chance to invade Saudi Arabia?				
1990 Aug 8	31	68	2	769

B ... U.S. military air strikes at military targets inside Iraq, even if Iraq hasn't yet invaded Saudi Arabia?				
1990 Aug 8	22	77	1	769

C ... doing whatever is necessary to topple the Iraqi government, even if it means assassinating Iraqi leader Saddam Hussein?				
1990 Aug 8	42	55	3	769

147 Some people would support a covert assassination of Iraqi leader Saddam Hussein as a way of quickly ending the current Middle East crisis. Others oppose such a plan as wrong even if it worked. Which comes closer to your view? (Gallup)

	Support covert assassination of Saddam	Oppose, wrong even if it worked	Don't know	n
1990 Aug 9–10	34	58	8	770
1990 Oct 18–19	37	54	9	755

148 Do you think that the United States should take extreme actions—such as assassination—to remove Saddam Hussein from power? (*Time*/CNN)

	U.S. should take extreme actions, like assassination of Saddam	Oppose	Don't know	n
1990 Aug 23	47	44	9	500

149 Do you think the United States should attempt to kill Saddam Husein (the President of Iraq), or not? (ABC/*Washington Post*)

	U.S. should attempt to kill Saddam	Should not	Don't know	n
1991 Jan 20	44[a]	52	4	532

[a]These then asked: How high a priority should that be for the United States military—the number one priority, one of several top priorities, or a lower level priority?

31%	Number one priority
48	One of several
20	Lower
1	Don't know
100	

150 Even if Iraq withdraws from Kuwait, should the United States take military action to eliminate Saddam Hussein's war-making capability, or Saddam himself, or both, or neither? (Gallup)

	Eliminate Saddam's war-making capability	Eliminate Saddam himself	Both	Neither	Don't know	n
1990 Oct 18–19	8	11	23	47	11	755
1990 Dec 6–7	9	9	21	53	8	769

264

If war breaks out, should we fight the war until Hussein agrees to withdraw from Kuwait or should we continue fighting to remove Hussein from power? (Black)

151

	Fight until Hussein withdraws from Kuwait	Continue fighting to remove Hussein	Don't know	n
1990 Dec 29–30	34	60	6	1008
1991 Jan 16[a]	25	59	16	604

[a]Should the war with Iraq continue until Saddam Hussein is removed from power, whether or not Iraq has withdrawn from Kuwait?

Is it enough for the United States to drive Saddam Hussein's troops out of Kuwait, or should the United States also see to it that Saddam Hussein is removed from power? (CBS/*New York Times*)

152

	Is enough to drive Saddam's troops out of Kuwait	U.S. should remove Saddam from power	Don't know	n
1991 Jan 19	12	82	6	908

If Iraq withdraws from Kuwait, should the United States continue fighting to force Saddam Hussein from power? (Associated Press)

153

	U.S. should continue to fight to force Saddam from power	U.S. should not continue to fight	Don't know	n
1991 Jan 23–24	59	38	3	1015

154 People have different ideas about what must happen in order for the United States to be successful in the war against Iraq. I'm going to read you some things that could happen relating to the war. For each, please tell me if you feel it is necessary or not necessary for this to happen in order for the U.S. to be successful in the war against Iraq. (*Los Angeles Times*)

	Necessary	Not necessary	Don't know	n
A ... In order for the U.S. to be successful, it is necessary or not necessary for the Iraqis to get out of Kuwait?				
1991 Feb 15–17	95	4	1	1822
B ... In order for the U.S. to be successful, it is necessary or not necessary for the Iraqi armed forces to be completely destroyed?				
1991 Feb 15–17	24	73	3	1822
C ... In order for the U.S. to be successful, it is necessary or not necessary for Saddam Hussein to be removed as President of Iraq?				
1991 Feb 15–17	84	15	1	1822
D ... In order for the U.S. to be successful, it is necessary or not necessary for Saddam Hussein to be tried as a war criminal?				
1991 Feb 15–17	70	25	5	1822

155 What do you think should be the final objective of the United States in this war: forcing Iraq out of Kuwait, or forcing Iraqi President Saddam Hussein out of power? (ABC/*Washington Post*)

	U.S. final objective is forcing Iraq out of Kuwait	U.S. final objective is forcing Saddam out of power	Don't know	n
1991 Jan 20	33	65	2	532
1991 Feb 22	28	71	1	520

156 Please tell me if you agree or disagree with this statement: the United States should end the war only if Iraqi President Saddam Hussein leaves power. (ABC/*Washington Post*)

	U.S. should end war only if Hussein leaves power	Disagree	Don't know	n
1991 Feb 22	61	37	3	520

266

Should the United States and its allies stop the war after taking control of Kuwait, or should they move on into Iraq and take control of Iraq too? (ABC/ *Washington Post*)

	U.S. should stop the war after taking control of Kuwait	U.S. should move into Iraq to take control there	Neither (vol)	Don't know	*n*
1991 Feb 24	46	44	4	6	514

Do you agree or disagree? (Black)

	Agree	Disagree	Don't know	*n*
A . . . United States troops should keep fighting until Iraq withdraws from Kuwait.				
1991 Feb 24	92	6	3	603

B . . . United States troops should keep fighting until Iraq's military capability is destroyed.				
1991 Feb 24	77	18	5	603

C . . . United States troops should keep fighting until Saddam Hussein is removed from power.				
1991 Feb 24	75	21	4	603

Will you be disappointed if Saddam Hussein is still alive when the war (with Iraq) ends? (Black)

	Will be disappointed if Hussein is still alive after the war	Will not be disappointed	Don't know	*n*
1991 Feb 24	53	40	7	603

Will you be disappointed in President Bush if Saddam Hussein is still in power after the war (with Iraq) ends? (Black)

	Disappointed in Bush if (because) Hussein is still in power	Not be disappointed	Don't know	*n*
1991 Feb 24	49	46	5	603
1991 Jul 25–28[a]	57	41	2	1205

[a]Are you disappointed in George Bush because the war (with Iraq) ended with (Iraqi President) Saddam Hussein still in power, or not? (ABC)

161 Looking back to the war with Iraq, do you think George Bush made the correct decision to stop the fighting when he did, or do you think Bush should have continued fighting until Saddam Hussein was removed from power? (*Time/CNN*)

	Bush made correct decision to stop fighting when he did	Should have continued to remove Hussein	Don't know	*n*
1992 Aug 19–20	30	64	6	1250

162 Some people think the United States should continue the military action against Iraq only until Iraq agrees to withdraw from Kuwait, in keeping with the United Nations Security Council resolutions. Others think the U.S. should go beyond the UN resolutions and continue fighting until Saddam Hussein is removed from power or his war-making capability is destroyed. Which comes closest to your view? (Gallup)

	Continue action only until Iraq withdraws from Kuwait	Go beyond UN and fight until Hussein is removed or his war-making capability is destroyed	Don't know	*n*
1991 Feb 7–10	34	62	4	1013
1991 Feb 24ª	24	72	4	783

ªSome people think that the United States and its allies should continue the military action against Iraq only until Iraq agrees to withdraw from Kuwait, in keeping with the Unitied Nations resolutions. Others feel that the U.S. and its allies should go beyond the UN resolutions and continue fighting until Saddam Hussein is removed from power or his war-making capability is destroyed. Which comes closer to your view?

163 The United Nations has authorized the use of force in the Persian Gulf only to remove Iraqi troops from Kuwait. What do you think the United States should do? Should the United States stop fighting when Iraqi troops leave Kuwait, or should the U.S. continue fighting Iraq until Saddam Hussein is removed from power? (*New York Times*)

	Stop fighting when Iraqis leave Kuwait	Continue fighting until Hussein is removed	Don't know	*n*
1991 Feb 24–Mar 1	39	55ª	6	528

ªThese then asked: Suppose removing Saddam Hussein from power would cost the lives of several thousand additional American troops. Do you think removing him from power would be worth that cost, or not?

53%	Worth the cost
35	Not worth the cost
13	Don't know
101	

Do you think that the U.S. (United States) and its allies should have continued **164** fighting until Saddam Hussein was removed from power, or not? (Gallup)

	U.S. should have continued fighting until Hussein removed from power	Disagree	Don't know	n
1991 Feb 28–Mar 3	46	48	5	1012
1991 Apr 4–6	56	36	8	1001
1991 Jul 18–21	76	20	4	1002

Please tell me if you agree or disagree with this statement: the United States **165** should not have ended the war with Iraqi President Saddam Hussein still in power. (ABC/*Washington Post*, ABC)

	U.S. should not have ended the war with Hussein still in power	Disagree	Don't know	n
1991 Apr 3	55	40	5	769
1991 May 30–Jun 2	63	34	3	1511
1991 Jul 25–28	73	24	2	1205

Agree or disagree: Based on what we know now, the U.S. (United States) ended **166** the war with Iraq too soon. (Black)

	U.S. ended the war too soon	Disagree	Don't know	n
1991 Apr 4	42[a]	45[b]	13	612
1991 Jul 23–24	60	33	7	610

[a] 23% strongly agree, 19% somewhat agree
[b] 22% strongly disagree, 23% somewhat disagree

167 Do you think the cease-fire in the Persian Gulf was ordered too soon, before Saddam Hussein was toppled from power in Iraq or not? (Gallup)

	Cease-fire ordered too soon, before Hussein toppled	Disagree	Don't know	*n*
1991 Apr 4–5	49	45	6	751
1991 Apr 18–22	57	37	6	761

168 Looking back to the war with Iraq, do you think we made the correct decision stopping the fighting when we did, or do you think we should have fought longer? (*Time*/CNN)

	We made correct decision stopping the fighting	We should have fought longer	Don't know	*n*
1991 Apr 10–11	58	35	7	1000

169 Should the United States have stopped fighting when Iraqi troops left Kuwait, or should the U.S. have continued fighting until President Saddam Hussein was removed from power? (CBS/*New York Times*)

	U.S. should have stopped fighting when Iraq left Kuwait	U.S. should have continued fighting until Hussein removed from power	Don't know	*n*
1991 May 7–8	31	63	6	909
1991 Jun 3–6	25	69	6	1424
1992 Mar 26–29	21	74	5	1638
1992 Jun 17–20	21	72	7	1315
1992 Aug 11–14	20	75	5	1434

Do you think the United States did or did not end the war with Iraq too soon? **170**
(NBC/ *Wall Street Journal*)

	U.S. ended the war too soon	U.S. did not end the war too soon	Don't know	*n*
1991 May 10–14	54	40	6	1508
1991 Jul 26–29	66	31	3	1004
1991 Dec 6–9	63	32	5	1004

Registered voters

Should the U.S. (United States) have continued fighting (Iraq) to force Saddam **171**
Hussein from power? (Associated Press)

	U.S. should have continued fighting to force Hussein from power	Disagree	Don't know	*n*
1991 Jul 17–21	70	22	8	1002
1992 Jan 2–5	67	23	10	1004

Would you support or oppose having U.S. (United States) forces resume mili- **172**
tary action against Iraq to force Saddam Hussein from power? (Gallup)

	Support resuming military action to force Hussein from power	Oppose resuming military action	Don't know	*n*
1991 Mar 14–15	57	38	5	763
1991 Apr 4–5	54	37	9	751
1991 Apr 10–11	58	34	8	1000
1991 Apr 18–22	51	43	6	761
1992 Feb 6–9	62	35	3	
1992 Jul 24–26[a]	67	28	5	
1992 Aug 6–7[b]	65	30	6	930
1992 Aug 21[b]	65	30	5	944

Gallup Poll Monthly, July 1992, p. 50
[a]Preceded by this question: Turning to the situation in the Middle East, if Iraq refuses to allow
United Nations inspectors access to Iraqi buildings—as specified by the terms of the U.S. resolutions
which ended the Gulf War—would you favor or oppose the use of military action, including air
strikes, against Iraq by the U.S. and its allies? 70% favored, 24% opposed.
[b]Registered voters

173 What steps, if any, do you think the U.S. (United States) should take to remove Saddam Hussein from power? Do you think the U.S. should . . . (Gallup)

	Support	Oppose	Don't know	*n*
A . . . continue economic sanctions against Iraq?				
1991 Apr 4–5	69	24	7	751
1991 Apr 18–22	70	20	10	761
B . . . capture Saddam and try him for war crimes?				
1991 Apr 4–5	71	25	4	751
1991 Apr 18–22	75	22	3	761
C . . . arrange a covert assassination of Hussein?				
1991 Apr 4–5	30	62	7	751
1991 Apr 18–22	36	57	7	761
D . . . agree not to capture and try him if he leaves power?				
1991 Apr 4–5	30	62	8	751
1991 Apr 18–22	27	65	8	761

174 Do you think that the United States should try to remove Saddam Hussein from power? (*Time*/CNN)

	U.S. should try to remove Hussein from power	U.S. should not	Don't know	*n*
1991 Jul 17–18	76	19	5	1000

175 Do you think the U.S. (United States) should take military action against Iraq at this time? (Black)

	U.S. should take military action against Iraq at this time	Should not	Don't know	*n*
1991 Jul 23–24	21	71	7	610

Do you favor or oppose using military force now to remove Saddam Hussein **176**
from power? (*Time/CNN*)

	Favor using force now to remove Hussein	Do not	Don't know	*n*
1992 Aug 19–20	56	32	12	1250

If the Iraqi army uses chemical weapons against its own people, would you favor **177**
or oppose the United States restarting military action against the Iraqi army?
(NBC/*Wall Street Journal*)

	Favor restarting military action against Iraq if it uses chemical weapons against own people	Oppose	Don't know	*n*
1991 Mar 15–19	69	25	6	1505

Registered voters

Would you favor or oppose the U.S. (United States) resuming military action **178**
against Iraq if the Iraqis refuse to observe the UN (United Nations) resolution
calling for destruction of their nuclear weapons capability? (Gallup)

	Favor resuming military action if Iraq refuses UN resolution to destroy its nuclear capability	Oppose	Don't know	*n*
1991 Jul 11–14	74	18	8	1217

If the U.S. (United States) does resume military action against Iraq, what should **179**
be our objective? (Gallup)

	To destroy Iraq's nuclear weapons capability	To remove Saddam Hussein from power	Both	Don't know	*n*
1991 Jul 11–14	6	14	77	3	1217

180 At the end of the recent war in the Persian Gulf, Iraq agreed to destroy all of its nuclear and chemical weapons. Now that Iraq has been found hiding nuclear weapons facilities and materials from United Nations inspectors, do you think we should use military means to remove Iraq's nuclear capabilities, or not? (*Time*/CNN)

	Should use military means to remove Iraq's nuclear capabilities since Iraq has been hiding them	Should not	Don't know	*n*
1991 Jul 17–18	74	20	6	1000

181 If the United States government believes Iraq is not complying with the terms of the cease fire that ended the Persian Gulf war, should the United States bomb Iraq, or not? (ABC)

	U.S. should bomb Iraq if it is not complying with cease fire terms	U.S. should not	Don't know	*n*
1991 Jul 25–28	50	43	7	1205
1991 Sep 18–19	47	40	12	608
1992 Aug 21–23	53	41	6	709

182 Would you favor or oppose the United States resuming military action against Iraq if Saddam Hussein continues to develop nuclear weapons? (NBC)

	Favor U.S. resuming military action if Hussein continues to develop nuclear weapons	Oppose	Depends on type of action taken (vol)	Don't know	*n*
1991 Jul 26–29	78	16	3	3	1004

If Saddam Hussein again fails to comply with United Nations ceasefire resolu- **183**
tions, do you think the U.S. (United States) should . . . take no military action
or, take military action to force Saddam to comply with the resolutions, or take
military action to force Saddam to comply with the resolutions and remove him
from power in Iraq? (Gallup)

	Take no military action to force Hussein to comply with UN	Take military action	Take military action and remove him from power	Don't know	n
1992 Jul 31– Aug 2	14	11	69	7	1001
1992 Aug 17ᵃ	14	13	62	11	895

ᵃRegistered voters

As you may know, United Nations economic sanctions are in place against Iraq. **184**
Some people say the economic sanctions should be lifted because they are preventing Iraq from taking care of its people. Others say Iraq can take care of its
people well enough and the sanctions should not be lifted while Saddam Hussein remains in power. What do you think—should the sanctions be lifted while
Saddam Hussein remains in power or should they be lifted only if he leaves
power? (ABC)

	Lift sanctions while Hussein is in power	Lift sanctions only if Hussein leaves power	Neither (vol)	Don't know	n
1992 Jul 25–28	10	84	2	4	1205

What do you think is the most important reason why the situation in the Middle **185**
East was worth going to war over? Asked of those who had previously said it
was worth going to war over—66% of the sample (see table 40) (Gallup)

1991 Jul 11–14	n = 1217
Keep peace/stability of world/Defend freedom/Can't have countries being overrun/Have to defend/stand up for what we believe/It was right	31%
Stop Hussein/Stop that madman/Another Hitler	32
For oil/To protect oil supply	12
Free Kuwait/its people/Stop the atrocities/mistreatment of Kuwaitis	12
To free American hostages	*
Other	7
None	*
Don't know	6
	100

EVALUATIONS OF VICTORY ....

186 In order for us to withdraw American troops, what would you consider a victory for the United States in the Middle East crisis? Would it be a victory for the U.S. if we prevent Saudi Arabia from being attacked, or if we force the Iraqis out of Kuwait, or if the Iraqis release all the American hostages unharmed, or would it be a victory if the government of Saddam Hussein is overthrown, or what? (*Los Angeles Times*)

	Would be victory if we prevent Saudi Arabia from being attacked	Victory if we force Iraqis out of Kuwait	Victory if the Iraqis release all American hostages unharmed	Victory if the gov't of Saddam Hussein is overthrown	All (vol)	Other (vol)	Don't know	*n*
1990 Aug 29	5	24	23	24	13	1	10	
1990 Nov 14	4	17	19	31	20	3	6	615

276

Given the current events in Iraq, do you think that the war with Iraq was totally **187** successful, largely successful, only partially successful, or not at all successful? (*Time*/CNN)

	Given current events in Iraq, the war was totally successful	Largely successful	Only partially successful	Not at all successful	Don't know	*n*
1991 Apr 10–11	19	33	40	5	3	1000
1991 May 8	13	32	46	7	2	500
1991 Jun 4–5	12	32	47	8	2	1000

Would you say the U.S. (United States) military effort in the Persian Gulf was **188** successful, partly successful, or not at all successful? (Associated Press)

	U.S. military effort in Gulf was successful	Partly successful	Not at all successful	Don't know	*n*
1991 Jun 12	57	39	3	2	1004

Would you say the U.S. (United States) military effort in the Persian Gulf was **189** completely successful, mostly successful, only somewhat successful, or not at all successful? (Associated Press)

	U.S. military effort in Gulf was completely successful	Mostly successful	Only somewhat successful	Not at all successful	Don't know	*n*
1991 Jul 17–21	12	48	34	5	1	1002
1991 Jan 2–5	16	36	36	9	4	

Polling Report, January 27, 1992, p. 8

190 What would you consider a victory from war with Iraq? Would you consider it victory if Iraq leaves all of Kuwiat, but Saddam Hussein remains in power in Iraq, or not? (*Los Angeles Times*)

	Is a victory if Saddam remains in power	Not a victory	Don't know	*n*
1991 Jan 17–18	30	63	7	1406

191 Would you consider it victory if Hussein leaves most of Kuwait, but keeps an oilfield and some of Kuwait, or not? (*Los Angeles Times*)

	Is a victory if Hussein keeps some of Kuwait	Not a victory	Don't know	*n*
1991 Jan 17–18	5	89	6	1406

192 Will the United States be able to claim victory in the war (with Iraq) if Saddam Hussein remains in power? (ABC/*Washington Post*)

	US able to claim victory if Hussein remains in power	US cannot claim victory	Nobody can claim victory; is partial victory (vol)	Don't know	*n*
1991 Mar 1–4	56	40	3	1	1215

193 Saddam Hussein has withdrawn from Kuwait but remains in power in Iraq. Do you think this is a victory for the U.S. and allied forces, or not? (Gallup)

	Is a victory if Saddam remains in power	Not a victory	Don't know	*n*
1991 Mar 1	55	38	7	
1991 Mar 14–15	50	43	7	763
1991 Apr 4–5	46	45	9	751
1991 Apr 18–22	36	55	9	761
1992 Jul 31–Aug 2[a]	25	69	6	1002

Gallup Poll Monthly, August 1992, p. 34

[a]Last year, Saddam Hussein withdrew from Kuwait but he remains in power in Iraq. Do you think this was a victory for U.S. and allied forces in the Persian Gulf region, or not?

Do you think the U.S. (United States) won a total victory in the war with Iraq, **194**
or do you think it won a partial victory, or do you think it didn't win a victory
at all? (Black)

	U.S. won a total victory	Won a partial victory	Didn't win a victory at all	Don't know	n
1991 Jul 23–24	16	67	15	2	610

Last year, Saddam Hussein withdrew from Kuwait but he remains in power in **195**
Iraq. Do you think this was a victory for U.S. (United States) and allied forces
in the Persian Gulf region, or not? (Gallup)

	Is victory with Hussein in	Is not a victory	Don't know	n
1992 Jul 31–Aug 2	25	69	6	1001

Would you say the Persian Gulf War was a success for the United States or not? **196**
(*Los Angeles Times*)

	Was a success for U.S.	Was not a success	Don't know	n
1992 Aug 12–14	42	50	8	1460

SATISFACTION WITH, CONFIDENCE IN, THE COUNTRY ....

197 In general, are you satisfied or dissatisfied with the way things are going in the United States at this time? (Gallup)

	Satisfied with U.S.	Dissatisfied	Don't know
1979 Feb	26	69	5
1979 Jul	12	84	4
1979 Nov	19	77	4
1981 Jan	17	78	5
1981 Jun	33	61	6
1981 Dec	27	67	6
1982 Apr	25	71	4
1982 Nov	24	72	4
1983 Aug	35	59	6
1984 Feb	50	46	4
1984 Sep	48	45	7
1984 Dec	52	40	8
1985 Nov	51	46	3
1986 Mar	66	30	4
1986 Sep	58	38	4
1986 Dec	47	49	4
1987 Aug	45	49	6
1988 Jan	39	55	
1988 May	41	54	5
1988 Sep	56	40	4
1989 Feb	45	50	5
1990 Feb	55	39	6

Table 197 continued

	Satisfied with U.S.	Dissatisfied	Don't know
1990 May	41	54	
1990 Jul	45	51	4
1990 Aug 9–12	43	51	6
1990 Aug 30–Sep 2	51	44	5
1990 Sep 27–30	37	58	5
1990 Oct 11–14	29	67	4
1990 Oct 25–28	31	66	3
1990 Nov 1–4	31	64	5
1990 Dec 13–16	33	64	3
1991 Jan 3–6	32	61	7
1991 Jan 17–20	62	33	5
1991 Feb 14–17	54	40	6
1991 Feb 28—Mar 3	66	31	3
1991 Mar 21–24	52	43	5
1991 May 23–26	49	49	2
1991 Aug	49	45	5
1991 Oct	39	57	4
1991 Nov	35	62	3
1991 Dec	37	60	3
1992 Jan 3–6[a]	24	74	2
1992 Jan 31–Feb 2[a]	24	75	1
1992 Feb 28–Mar 1	21	78	1
1992 Apr 20–22[a]	19	80	1
1992 May 7–10	20	77	3
1992 Jun 12–14	14	84	2
1992 Aug 28–Sep 2	22	73	5

Gallup Poll Monthly, January 1991, p. 22; March 1991, p. 19; June 1991, p. 48; March 1992, p. 48; June 1992, p. 18; September 1992, p. 3

[a]Registered voters only

1. Do you think things in this country are generally going in the right direction, or do you feel things have gotten pretty seriously off on the wrong track? (ABC/*Washington Post,* ABC, *Washington Post*)

2. Do you feel things in this country are going in the right direction, or do you feel things have pretty seriously gotten off on the wrong track? (*New York Times*/CBS)

3. Generally speaking, would you say things in this country are going in the right direction, or have they pretty seriously gotten off on the wrong track? (Wirthlin)

4. Do you feel things in this country are moving in the right direction, or do you feel things are pretty seriously off on the wrong track? (Americans Talk Security)

5. Do you feel (that) things in this country are generally going in the right direction, or do you feel that things have pretty seriously gotten off on the wrong track? (Roper, Opinion Research Center)

6. Do you feel things in this country are generally going in the right direction, or do you feel things have pretty seriously gotten off on the wrong track? (CBS, *New York Times*/CBS)

7. Do you think things in this country today are generally moving in the right direction, or do you feel things have pretty seriously gotten off on the wrong track? (ABC/*Washington Post*)

	Question	Things are generally going in the right direction	Things have gotten pretty seriously off on the wrong track	Don't know	*n*
1971 Aug 21–22	5	29	63	8	1002
1971 Sep 7–8	5	27	64	9	1031
1971 Oct 18–27[a]	5	26	63	11	1499
1973 Sep 28–Oct 6[a]	5	16	74	10	1263
1974 Sep 27–Oct 5[a]	5	15	75	11	1998
1975 Sep 27–Oct 4[a]	5	19	71	9	2007
1977 Feb 12–26[a]	5	41	44	14	2004
1978 Feb 11–25[a]	5	34	53	13	2002
1979 Feb 10–24[a]	5	20	65	15	2004
1980 Feb 9–23[a]	5	20	70	10	2001
1981 Feb 14–28[a]	5	32	54	14	2005
1982 Feb 12–27[a]	5	27	63	10	2000
1983 Feb 12–26[a]	5	34	58	8	2000
1983 Feb 25–Mar 2	7	43	53	3	1504
1983 Apr 8–12	7	41	54	4	1516

Table 198 continued

	Question	Things are generally going in the right direction	Things have gotten pretty seriously off on the wrong track	Don't know	n
1983 Sep 24–Oct 1[a]	5	32	58	10	2000
1983 Nov 3–7	1	51	44	5	1505
1983 Dec 8–13	1	43	51	6	1506
1984 May 16–22	1	47	48	5	1511
1985 Jan 11–16	1	59	36	4	1505
1985 Feb 4–23[a]	5	49	39	12	2000
1985 Jul 25–29	1	52	43	6	1506
1986 Jan 24–26	1	45	47	8	504
1986 Feb 8–22[a]	5	45	42	13	1993
1986 Sep 2–8	1	50	48	2	1507
1986 Oct	5	43	48	9	1654
1986 Dec 9–11	5	39	55	6	1003
1987 Jan 13–19	1	39	56	5	1505
1987 Feb 14–28[a]	5	31	57	12	1996
1987 Mar 5–9	1	38	58	4	1511
1987 Apr 9–13	1	37	60	3	1509
1987 Jun 25–29	1	35	62	3	1506
1987 Sep 17–23	1	43	54	4	2116
1987 Oct 15–19	4	42	48	10	1002
1987 Nov 30–Dec 2	1	35	61	4	1000
1987 Dec 11–13	1	49	47	4	1005
1987 Dec 14–16	5	41	51	8	1003
1988 Jan 7–14[b]	4	46	44	11	1000
1988 Jan 17–23	1	39	59	2	1505
1988 Feb 17–24[b]	4	37	48	15	1004
1988 Mar 22–27[b]	4	46	46	8	1004
1988 Apr 18–24[c]	4	41	50	9	1017
1988 Apr 25–May 1[b]	4	42	48	9	1000
1988 May 19–25	1	35	59	6	1500
1988 May 24–27[b]	4	41	47	12	1003
1988 Jun 15–19	1	41	54	3	1012

Table 198 continued

	Question	Things are generally going in the right direction	Things have gotten pretty seriously off on the wrong track	Don't know	*n*
1988 Jun 25–Jul 7[b]	4	39	43	18	1006
1988 Jul 6–13	1	40	56	4	1500
1988 Jul 31–Aug 7[b]	4	41	42	17	1005
1988 Sep 7–18[b]	4	46	44	10	1005
1988 Sep 14–19[b]	1	48	50	3	1506
1988 Sep 21–27[c]	1	48	44	8	1100
1988 Sep 21–25[c]	1	45	47	7	1003
1988 Sep 23–27[c]	1	49	42	9	1005
1988 Sep 21–Oct 10[b]	1	49	48	2	1200
1988 Sep 30–Oct 4[b]	4	45	41	14	1008
1988 Sep 28–Oct 4[c]	1	47	45	8	1196
1988 Sep 28–Oct 2[c]	1	49	43	8	1003
1988 Sep 30–Oct 4[c]	1	43	47	8	1010
1988 Oct 5–11[c]	1	48	44	8	1100
1988 Oct 5–9[c]	1	51	44	6	600
1988 Oct 12–18[c]	1	50	42	8	1195
1988 Oct 19–25[c]	1	49	46	6	1242
1988 Oct 26–30[c]	1	47	46	8	1010
1988 Oct 28–Nov 1[c]	1	46	47	7	1009
1988 Nov 4–7[b]	4	46	41	13	1006
1988 Dec 10–13[b]	4	53	37	9	1000
1989 Jan 12–16	1	51	46	3	1503
1989 Mar 3–7	1	50	44	7	1047
1989 May 12–16	1	44	46	9	1009
1989 May 19–23	1	42	55	3	1513
1989 Nov 30–Dec 4	1	43	52	4	1008
1990 Jan 11–16	1	48	49	3	1518
1990 Jan 21–23	3	45	44		
1990 Feb 1–4	1	49	48	3	1008
1990 Feb	3	48	43		
1990 Mar	3	43	48		

284

Table 198 continued

	Question	Things are generally going in the right direction	Things have gotten pretty seriously off on the wrong track	Don't know	*n*
1990 Mar 22–26	1	44	53	2	1016
1990 Apr	3	40	51		
1990 May	3	36	56		
1990 May 17–21	1	39	60	2	1526
1990 Jun	3	38	53		
1990 Jul	3	35	58		
1990 Jul 19–23	1	37	60	2	1500
1990 Aug	3	35	57		
1990 Sep 6–9	1	36	60	4	1011
1990 Sep	3	35	54		
1990 Sep 21–26	4	44	49	7	1000
1990 Oct 10–14	1	19	79	2	1006
1990 Oct	3	20	73		
1990 Nov 6[c]	1	21	75	14	1212
1990 Nov	3	25	64		
1990 Dec	3	26	64		
1991 Jan 17	2	63	25	12	544
1991 Jan 18	2	58	31	11	683
1991 Jan 19	2	55	33	12	908
1991 Jan 20	2	55	32	13	867
1991 Jan 21–23	3	58	32		
1991 Jan 23–27	1	49	48	4	1015
1991 Jan 27–28	6	51	39	10	1173
1991 Feb	3	47	43		
1991 Feb 22–26	1	58	39	3	1004
1991 Mar 4–6	6	51	42	7	1252
1991 Mar 19–24	4	56	36	9	1000
1991 Apr 5–9	1	42[d]	51	7	1000
1991 Apr 15–17	3	44	47		
1991 May 30–Jun 2	1	39	57	4	1511
1991 Jun 17–19	3	39	56	5	1000

Table 198 continued

	Question	Things are generally going in the right direction	Things have gotten pretty seriously off on the wrong track	Don't know	n
1991 Jun 23–Jul 1	4	40	53	8	1000
1991 Jul 25–28	1	30	67	3	1205
1991 Aug 5–7	3	35	57	8	1000
1991 Aug 23–27	1	31	60	9	1017
1991 Sep 3–5	3	34	59	7	1000
1991 Oct 1–3	3	32	58	10	1008
1991 Oct 15–18	6	33	60	7	1280
1991 Oct 24–29	1	26	71	3	1009
1991 Nov 4–7	3	23	70	7	1039
1991 Nov 5–10	1	24	72	4	1174
1991 Nov 25–Dec 2	4	24	68	8	1000
1991 Dec 19–22	3	17	75	8	1000
1992 Jan 6–9	3	20	72	8	1000
1992 Jan 13–15	1	19	78	3	810
1992 Jan 25–Feb 1[b]	5	18	72	10	1189
1992 Jan 29–30[c]	3	15	78	7	1000
1992 Feb 3–5	3	17	77	6	1021
1992 Mar 4–6	3	18	76	6	1008
1992 Mar 11	1	18	79	4	781
1992 Mar 28–Apr 1	6	19	72	8	1000
1992 Apr 8–9	1	16	81	3	1009
1992 Apr 7–9	3	20	75	4	1001
1992 May 4–6	3	14	83	3	1019
1992 Jun 3–7	1	14	83	3	1512
1992 Jun 3–5	3	12	81	7	1029
1992 Jul 8–10	3	15	79	4	1054

Public Opinion and Demographic Report, May/June 1991, p. 84

[a]Personal interviews

[b]Registered voters

[c]Likely voters

[d]These then asked, And is your feeling that things are going in the right direction mainly due to the outcome of the war with Iraq, or mainly due to other things?

42% Due to outcome of war   52% Due to other things   6% Don't know (1000)

286

All in all, do you think things in the nation are generally headed in the right **199** direction, or do you feel that things are off on the wrong track? (NBC/*Wall Street Journal*)

	Things are generally headed in the right direction	Things are off on the wrong track	Mixed (vol)	Don't know	*n*
1990 Jan 13–16[a]	49	29	17	5	1510
1990 Feb 26–Mar 1[b]	46	33	16	5	1494
1990 Mar 10–13	44	31	20	5	1003
1990 Apr 11–16	47	32	13	8	1001
1990 May 18–22	42	38	16	4	1007
1990 Jul 6–10	40	37	18	5	1555
1990 Sep 4–5	45	40	10	5	800
1990 Oct 19–21	22	59	14	5	1019
1990 Dec 8–11	28	51	15	6	1002
1991 Feb 26–27	65	22	9	4	811
1991 Mar 15–19	55	26	15	4	1505
1991 May 10–14	40	38	17	5	1508
1991 Jun 22–25	40	44	13	4	1006
1991 Jul 26–29	33	50	12	5	1004
1991 Aug 28	41	38	15	6	800
1991 Sep 20–24	33	49	14	4	1510
1991 Oct 25–29	25	57	13	5	1500
1991 Nov 20–21	19	64	13	4	726
1991 Dec 6–9	20	68	9	3	1004
1992 Jan 17–21	18	67	11	3	1502
1992 Feb 28–Mar 2	19	67	11	3	1000
1992 Apr 11–14	17	70	9	4	1001
1992 May 15–19	14	72	9	5	1118
1992 Jul 5–7	14	71	9	6	1105

Asked of registered voters only
[a]Question did not include "that"
[b]Different sponsor. Did not include "do you feel that"

200 We are interested in how people's financial situation may have changed. Would you say that you are financially better off now than you were a year ago, or are you financially worse off now? (Gallup)

	Better off now than a year ago	Same (vol)	Worse off	Don't know
1976 Sep	33	36	30	1
1976 Nov	32	32	34	2
1976 Dec	32	33	34	1
1977 Jan	35	32	32	1
1977 Feb	28	37	34	1
1977 Mar	35	30	34	1
1977 Apr	31	34	33	2
1977 May	30	37	32	1
1977 Jun	39	28	31	2
1977 Jul	36	30	33	1
1977 Aug	29	32	37	2
1977 Sep	37	31	31	1
1977 Oct	38	31	28	3
1977 Nov	31	36	31	2
1977 Dec	39	32	27	2
1978 Jan	35	34	29	2
1978 Feb	36	32	30	2
1978 Mar	26	37	35	2
1978 Apr	29	32	37	2
1978 May	32	34	33	1
1978 Jun	35	31	32	2
1978 Jul	33	31	34	2
1978 Aug	35	30	34	1
1978 Sep	35	34	30	1
1978 Oct	32	31	35	2
1978 Nov	35	31	33	1
1978 Dec	40	26	33	1
1979 Jan	36	29	33	2
1979 Feb	33	28	34	5
1979 Mar	35	31	31	3
1979 Apr	29	28	40	3
1979 May	32	31	36	1

Table 200 continued

	Better off now than a year ago	Same (vol)	Worse off	Don't know
1979 Jun	30	27	41	2
1979 Jul	25	28	46	1
1979 Aug	29	29	42	*
1979 Sep	36	27	35	2
1979 Oct	28	28	43	1
1979 Nov	28	28	42	2
1979 Dec	29	28	42	1
1980 Jan	30	26	43	1
1980 Feb	27	28	43	2
1980 Mar	30	24	45	1
1980 Oct	45	25	21	9
1981 Jun	33	30	35	2
1981 Oct	28	28	43	1
1982 Feb	28	24	47	1
1982 Apr	28	30	40	2
1982 Aug	25	26	46	3
1982 Nov	28	34	37	1
1983 Mar	25	28	46	1
1983 Jun	28	32	39	1
1984 Mar	36	37	26	1
1984 Jul	40	34	25	1
1984 Sep	39	34	26	1
1984 Nov–Dec	43	32	24	1
1985 Mar	48	26	25	1
1985 Jun	43	26	29	2
1985 Oct	38	34	27	1
1986 Jan	40	29	30	1
1986 Mar	46	24	30	*
1986 Jun	46	28	25	1
1986 Jul	39	35	25	1
1986 Sep	40	29	29	2
1987 Jan	39	33	28	*
1987 Mar	46	23	30	1
1987 Jun	43	24	32	1

Table 200 continued

	Better off now than a year ago	Same (vol)	Worse off	Don't know
1987 Aug–Sep	43	27	29	1
1988 Jan	41	29	28	2
1988 May	47	28	24	1
1988 Sep–Oct	53	23	23	1
1989 Jun	42	31	25	2
1990 Feb	49	26	24	1
1990 Jul	44	27	28	1
1990 Aug	43	29	27	1
1990 Sep	40	32	27	1
1990 Oct 11–14	32	26	41	1
1990 Oct 18–21	27	30	41	2
1990 Oct 25–28	38	26	35	1
1990 Dec 13–16	38	26	36	*
1991 Jan 3–6	35	32	32	1
1991 Jan 11–13	27	39	33	1
1991 Feb 14–17	37	35	28	*
1991 Feb 28–Mar 3	37	34	28	1
1991 Mar 21–24	30	32	37	1
1991 Apr 11–14	29	37	33	1
1991 May 16–19	32	33	32	3
1991 Jul 11–14	34	33	32	1
1991 Sep 5–8	34	37	28	1
1991 Oct	35	22	42	1
1991 Dec	33	26	40	1
1992 Jan	30	26	43	1
1992 Feb	34	19	46	1

Gallup Report No. 277 (October 1988), p. 30; *Gallup Poll Monthly,* April 1991, p. 26; July 1991, p. 3; September 1991, p. 17; February 1992, p. 19

290

Looking ahead, do you expect that at this time next year you will be financially better off than now or worse off than now? (Gallup)

	Will be better off a year from now	Same (vol)	Will be worse off	Don't know
1976 Sep	44	31	12	13
1976 Nov	47	25	17	11
1976 Dec	45	31	13	11
1977 Jan	50	27	12	11
1977 Feb	45	28	17	10
1977 Mar	48	26	15	11
1977 Apr	43	28	20	9
1977 May	40	30	22	8
1977 Jun	47	27	17	9
1977 Jul	45	29	17	9
1977 Aug	39	27	25	9
1977 Sep	43	31	15	11
1977 Oct	45	29	16	10
1977 Nov	42	30	19	9
1977 Dec	46	32	14	8
1978 Jan	43	28	17	12
1978 Feb	42	32	19	7
1978 Mar	41	29	19	11
1978 Apr	40	29	23	8
1978 May	41	28	22	9
1978 Jun	38	30	20	12
1978 Jul	41	27	23	9
1978 Aug	42	26	21	11
1978 Sep	43	28	18	11
1978 Oct	39	29	21	11
1978 Nov	40	29	23	8
1978 Dec	47	26	22	5
1979 Jan	39	28	24	9
1979 Feb	38	28	25	9
1979 Mar	39	28	22	11
1979 Apr	36	26	30	8
1979 May	35	28	29	8

Table 201 continued

	Will be better off a year from now	Same (vol)	Will be worse off	Don't know
1979 Jun	33	27	30	10
1979 Jul	30	25	37	8
1979 Aug	34	27	31	8
1979 Sep	41	26	25	8
1979 Oct	34	27	32	7
1979 Nov	38	25	27	10
1979 Dec	36	25	31	8
1980 Jan	37	26	29	8
1980 Feb	33	27	32	8
1980 Mar	36	24	31	9
1980 Jun	41	25	26	8
1980 Oct	45	25	21	9
1981 Jun	41	25	26	8
1981 Oct	41	25	26	8
1982 Feb	42	21	31	6
1982 Aug	37	24	29	10
1982 Nov	41	27	22	10
1983 Mar	45	24	22	9
1983 Jun	43	28	19	10
1984 Mar	54	28	11	7
1984 Jul	52	28	12	8
1984 Sep	53	28	9	10
1984 Nov–Dec	50	28	17	5
1985 Mar	57	26	12	5
1985 Jun	52	19	19	10
1985 Oct	49	32	12	7
1986 Jan	53	25	15	7
1986 Mar	61	16	18	5
1986 Jun	57	17	20	6
1986 Jul	51	28	15	6
1986 Sep	57	19	16	8
1987 Jan	51	26	16	7
1987 Mar	59	18	17	6

292

Table 201 continued

	Will be better off a year from now	Same (vol)	Will be worse off	Don't know
1987 Jun	57	18	17	8
1987 Aug–Sep	56	20	16	8
1988 Jan	58	18	14	10
1988 May	63	17	9	11
1988 Sep–Oct	67	17	9	7
1989 Jun	58	20	13	9
1990 Feb	65	16	13	6
1990 Jul	58	18	17	7
1990 Aug	57	20	16	7
1990 Sep	51	20	17	12
1990 Oct 11–14	48	13	30	9
1990 Oct 18–21	41	16	34	9
1990 Oct 25–28	50	15	27	8
1990 Dec 13–16	58	17	18	7
1991 Jan 3–6	52	20	18	10
1991 Jan 11–13	41	21	25	13
1991 Feb 14–17	57	20	15	8
1991 Feb 28–Mar 3	64	20	9	7
1991 Mar 21–24	56	20	18	6
1991 Apr 11–14	56	18	17	9
1991 May 16–19	57	19	16	8
1991 Jul 11–14	57	19	15	9
1991 Sep 5–8	53	22	19	6
1991 Oct	55	16	23	6
1991 Dec	54	17	21	8
1992 Jan	51	15	28	6
1992 Feb	54	14	28	6

Gallup Report No. 277 (October 1988), p. 32; *Gallup Poll Monthly,* April 1991, p. 26; July 1991, p. 4; September 1991, p. 17; February 1992, p. 19

1988 Feb	91.6
1988 Mar	94.6
1988 Apr	91.2
1988 May	94.8
1988 Jun	94.7
1988 Jul	93.4
1988 Aug	97.4
1988 Sep	97.3
1988 Oct	94.1
1988 Nov	93.0
1988 Dec	91.9
1989 Jan	97.9
1989 Feb	95.4
1989 Mar	94.3
1989 Apr	91.5
1989 May	90.7
1989 Jun	90.6
1989 Jul	92.0
1989 Aug	89.6
1989 Sep	95.8
1989 Oct	93.9
1989 Nov	90.9
1989 Dec	90.5
1990 Jan	93.0
1990 Feb	89.5
1990 Mar	91.3
1990 Apr	93.9
1990 May	90.6
1990 Jun	88.3
1990 Jul	88.2
1990 Aug	76.4
1990 Sep	72.8
1990 Oct	63.9
1990 Nov	66.0
1990 Dec	65.5
1991 Jan	66.8

Table 202 continued

1991 Feb	70.4
1991 Mar	87.7
1991 Apr	81.8
1991 May	78.3
1991 Jun	82.1
1991 Jul	82.9
1991 Aug	82.0
1991 Sep	83.0
1991 Oct	78.3
1991 Nov	69.1
1991 Dec	68.2
1992 Jan	67.5
1992 Feb	68.8
1992 Mar	76.0
1992 Apr	77.2
1992 May	79.2
1992 Jun	80.4
1992 Jul	76.6
1992 Aug	76.1
1992 Sep	75.6
1992 Oct	73.3
1992 Nov	85.3
1992 Dec	91.0

University of Michigan, *Surveys of Consumers*

Consumer Confidence, Conference Board (Index numbers, 1985 = 100)   **203**

	Consumer confidence index	Present situation	Expectations
1989 Jan	115.8	133.4	104.1
1989 Feb	120.7	139.2	108.3
1989 Mar	117.4	136.2	104.9
1989 Apr	116.6	138.9	101.8
1989 May	116.7	137.2	103.0
1989 Jun	117.2	135.5	105.1
1989 Jul	120.4	141.1	106.6
1989 Aug	115.4	133.0	103.7
1989 Sep	116.3	131.7	106.1

Table 203 continued

	Consumer confidence index	Present situation	Expectations
1989 Oct	117.0	133.0	106.4
1989 Nov	115.1	132.3	103.7
1989 Dec	113.0	125.9	104.4
1990 Jan	106.5	120.7	97.0
1990 Feb	106.7	126.3	93.7
1990 Mar	110.6	123.7	101.9
1990 Apr	107.3	119.4	99.2
1990 May	107.3	117.8	100.3
1990 Jun	102.4	111.1	96.6
1990 Jul	101.7	116.6	91.8
1990 Aug	84.7	100.4	74.2
1990 Sep	85.6	97.5	77.7
1990 Oct	62.6	73.2	55.6
1990 Nov	61.7	70.3	56.1
1990 Dec	61.2	63.3	59.8
1991 Jan	55.1	54.7	55.3
1991 Feb	59.4	53.1	63.6
1991 Mar	81.1	51.7	100.7
1991 Apr	79.4	48.9	99.7
1991 May	76.4	47.8	95.5
1991 Jun	78.0	43.7	100.9
1991 Jul	77.7	43.8	100.3
1991 Aug	76.1	45.1	96.8
1991 Sep	72.9	39.1	95.4
1991 Oct	60.1	31.0	79.5
1991 Nov	52.7	27.1	69.7
1991 Dec	52.5	22.5	72.6
1992 Jan	50.2	22.6	68.7
1992 Feb	47.3	23.0	63.5
1992 Mar	56.5	26.2	76.7
1992 Apr	65.1	28.0	89.7
1992 May	71.9	34.4	96.9
1992 Jun	72.6	37.7	95.9
1992 Jul	61.2	32.7	80.1

Table 203 continued

	Consumer confidence index	Present situation	Expectations
1992 Aug	59.0	30.1	78.3
1992 Sep	57.3	32.0	74.2
1992 Oct	54.6	30.5	70.7
1992 Nov	65.6	35.5	85.7
1992 Dec	78.1	39.3	103.9

Conference Board, *Consumer Confidence Survey*

Some people say the United States is in decline as a world power. Do you agree **204**
or disagree? If agree or disagree: Do you (agree/disagree) strongly, or only
somewhat? (*New York Times*/CBS)

	Strongly agree	Agree somewhat	Disagree somewhat	Strongly disagree	Don't know	n
1989 Feb	23	25	21	22	9	
1989 Jun	19	31	21	23	6	
1990 Aug 23–24[a]		37	55		8	767
1991 Mar 4–6	8	14	28	45	5	

New York Times/CBS News Poll, March 4–6, 1991, p. 7
[a]Gallup

In the next century, which country do you think will be the number one eco- **205**
nomic power in the world—the United States, Japan, or some other country?
(*New York Times*/CBS)

	United States	Japan	Germany[a] (vol)	Other	Don't know	n
1989 Jun	47	38	1	7	8	
1990 Jun	32	50	5	6	7	
1991 Mar 4–6	39	43	5	3	10	1252

New York Times/CBS News Poll, March 4–6, 1991, p. 6
[a]West Germany in 1989 poll

206 How proud are you to be an American? Very proud, quite proud, not very proud, not at all proud? (Gallup)

	Very proud to be an American	Quite proud	Not very proud	Not at all proud	Don't know
1981	80	16	2	1	1
1986	89	10	1	*	*
1991	77	19	3	*	1

Gallup Poll Monthly, July 1991, p. 39

207 How much confidence do you have in the ability of the United States to deal wisely with the present world problems—very great, considerable, little, or very little confidence? (Gallup)

	Very great confidence in ability of U.S. to deal wisely with world problems	Consider-able confidence	Little confidence	Very little confidence	None at all (vol)	Don't know
1980	14	39	22	19	2	1
1985	19	49	19	11	1	1
1991	22	62	10	5	*	1

Gallup Poll Monthly, July 1991, p. 40

208 Has your confidence in the ability of the United States to deal with world problems tended to go up lately, go down, or remain about the same? (Gallup)

	Confidence in ability of U.S. to deal with world problems has tended to go up lately	Confidence down	Confidence remain about the same	Don't know
1980	10	45	41	4
1985	16	22	60	2
1991	41	8	51	*

Gallup Poll Monthly, July 1991, p. 40

How much confidence do you have in the future of the United States: quite a **209**
lot, some, very little, or none at all? (Gallup)

	Quite a lot of confidence in future of U.S.	Some confidence	Very little confidence	None at all	Don't know
1974	68	19	10	2	1
1980	64	24	8	2	2
1986	76	19	4	*	1
1991	59	34	5	1	1

Gallup Poll Monthly, July 1991, p. 40

If you were free to do so, would you like to go and settle in another country? **210**
(Gallup)

	Would like to go and settle in another country	Would not	Don't know
1948	4	94	2
1959	6	92	2
1960	6	91	3
1971	12	85	3
1972	11	86	3
1972	13	87	*
1974	10	87	3
1976	9	89	2
1991	9	90	1

Gallup Poll Monthly, July 1991, p. 41

Do you display an American flag outside your home on national holidays or **211**
other days during the year? (Gallup)

	Display American flag on holidays	Do not display flag	Don't have a flag (vol)	No place to hang flag (vol)	Don't know
1986	43	47	7	3	—
1991	59	36	3	2	—

Gallup Poll Monthly, July 1991, p. 43

212   Suppose you were talking to a person, in a general way, about the United States and other countries. Which one of these statements best expresses your own point of view? (Gallup) (rotated)

	The United States is the greatest country in the world, better than all other countries in every possible way	The United States is a great country, but so are certain other countries	In many respects, certain other countries are better than the United States	None of these (vol)	Don't know
1955	66	31	1	1	1
1991	37	54	9	*	*

Gallup Poll Monthly, July 1991, p. 44

213   At the present time, do you think religion as a whole is increasing its influence on American life or losing its influence? (Gallup)

	Religion is increasing its influence on American life	Religion is losing its influence	Staying the same (vol)	Don't know	*n*
1957 Mar 15–20	69	14	10	6	1627
1962 Feb 8–13	45	32	17	7	1529
1965 Feb 19–24	33	45	13	8	1550
1967 Mar 9–14	23	57	14	6	2192
1968 Apr 4–9	19	67	8	7	1504
1969 May 1–6	14	71	11	5	1481
1970 Jan 15–20	14	75	7	4	1573
1974 Dec 6–9	31	56	8	5	1517
1975 Dec 12–15	39	51	7	3	1538
1976 Dec 10–13	44	45	8	3	1559
1977 Dec 9–12	37	45	10	9	1518
1978 Dec 8–11	37	48	10	5	1552
1980 Apr 11–14	35	46	11	8	1549
1981 Dec 11–14	38	47	10	6	1483
1982 Dec 10–13	41	45	9	5	1509
1983 Oct 21–24	44	42	9	5	1549
1984 Jul 27–30	42	39	14	6	1579

Table 213 continued

	Religion is increasing its influence on American life	Religion is losing its influence	Staying the same (vol)	Don't know	n
1985 Mar 8–11	48	39	10	3	1571
1985 Nov 11–18	45	41	14		1008
1986 Sep 13–17	48	38	6	7	978
1988 Mar 8–12	36	49	6	9	1003
1989 Apr 10–16	33	49	9	9	1007
1990 Jun 15–17	33	48	8	11	1236
1991 Mar 21–24	48	43	9		1010
1991 May 30–Jun 2	34	57		9	1012
1991 Nov 21–24	27	66	3	4	1005

How important would you say religion is in your own life—would you say it is **214**
very important, fairly important, or not very important? (Gallup)

	Religion is very important in own life	Fairly important	Not very important	Don't know	n
1965 Nov	70	22	7	1	2783
1978 Apr 14–17	52	32	14	2	1523
1980 Aug 1–4	55	31	13	1	1538
1980 Aug 15–18	57	29	13	*	1600
1980 Nov 21–24	56	31	12	1	1551
1980 Dec 5–8	53	31	15	1	1549
1981 May 8–11	55	28	16	*	1519
1981 Sep 18–21	58	29	12	1	1540
1981 Dec 11–14	54	30	15	1	1483
1982 Apr 23–26	54	32	14	1	1589
1982 Nov 5–8	56	29	14	*	1540
1982 Dec 10–13	56	31	12	1	1509
1983 May 13–16	53	29	16	2	1540
1983 Jun 24–27	55	33	11	1	1558
1983 Sep 9–12	57	30	12	1	1574

Table 214 continued

	Religion is very important in own life	Fairly important	Not very important	Don't know	n
1983 Sep 16–19	57	29	14	1	1533
1984 Mar 16–19	56	32	11	1	1514
1984 Jun 29–Jul 2	57	30	12	2	1516
1984 Aug 10–13	55	29	14	2	1585
1984 Sep 21–24	54	31	14	2	1518
1984 Oct 26–29	55	32	12	1	1520
1985 Aug 13–15	62	27	10	1	1009
1987 Dec 16–17	57	30	18	1	606
1988 Mar 11–20	54	31	14	1	2556
1989 Sep 7–10	57	29	13	1	1238
1990 Nov 15–18	52	32	16	1	1018
1991 Jan 17–20	61	26	12	2	1019
1991 Jan 23–26	60	27	12	1	1011
1991 Jan 30–Feb 2	63	28	9	*	1005
1991 Feb 7–10	60	29	11	1	1013
1991 Feb 21–24	55	31	14	*	1006
1991 Nov 21–24	55	29	15	1	1005
1992 Apr 9–12	61	30	9		1002

If the United States did get involved in a war with Iraq, who do you think would win? (ABC/*Washington Post*)   **215**

	United States would win	Iraq would win	Neither side	Don't know	*n*
1990 Aug 8	85	4	5	6	769
1990 Aug 17–20	89	2	4	6	815
1991 Jan 16ᵃ	89	1	8	2	545

ᵃWho do you think will win the war, Iraq or the United States?

How confident are you in the capabilities of the American military forces in the Persian Gulf winning a war against Iraq—are you very confident, somewhat confident, or not very confident, or not confident at all in the capabilities of the American military forces winning a war against Iraq? (*Los Angeles Times*)   **216**

	Very confident U.S. would win a war against Iraq	Somewhat confident	Not very confident	Not confident at all	Don't know	*n*
1990 Nov 14	58	26	9	3	4	1031
1991 Jan 8–12	61	29	5	2	3	2434

217   If the United States goes to war with Iraq, which of the following do you think is the most likely outcome? (*Time*/CNN)

	A quick war, with few casualties and a U.S. victory	A long war, with many casualties and a U.S. victory	Eventual U.S. withdrawal without victory	Don't know	*n*
1990 Nov 14	38	41	12	9	500

218   How likely do you think it is that the United States involvement in Saudi Arabia could turn into another situation like Vietnam—that is, that the United States could become more and more deeply involved as time goes on? Would you say this is very likely, fairly likely, fairly unlikely, or very unlikely? (Gallup)

	Another Vietnam very likely	Fairly likely	Fairly unlikely	Very unlikely	Don't know	*n*
1990 Aug 9–12	22	26	28	18	6	1227
1990 Aug 16–19	28	29	23	17	3	1241
1990 Aug 23–26	30	28	22	17	3	1010

219   Do you think it is likely or unlikely that U.S. involvement in the Middle East will result in a situation like Vietnam? (*Time*/CNN)

	U.S. involvement likely to result in a situation like Vietnam	Unlikely	Don't know	*n*
1990 Aug 23	38	57	3	500

220   From what you have seen or heard, do you think the crisis in the Middle East could bog down and become another Vietnam situation for this country? Would you say the chances of that are very likely, or somewhat likely, or somewhat unlikely, or very unlikely that the crisis in the Middle East could become another Vietnam situation? (*Los Angeles Times*)

	Another Vietnam very likely	Somewhat likely	Somewhat unlikely	Very unlikely	Don't know	*n*
1990 Aug 29	17	32	19	28	4	1206
1990 Nov 14	31	31	14	22	2	1031
1991 Jan 8–12	21	27	19	30	2	2434

Do you think the United States is heading for the same kind of involvement in **221**
the Middle East as it had in the Vietnam war, or do you think the United States
will avoid that kind of involvement this time? (ABC/*Washington Post*, ABC)

	U.S. heading for Vietnam kind of involvement	U.S. will avoid that kind of involvement	Don't know	*n*
1990 Aug 17–20	22	74	4	815
1990 Sep 6–9	18	78	4	1011
1990 Nov 14–15	26	69	5	515
1990 Nov 30–Dec 2	32	66	3	758
1991 Jan 20[a]	11	86	3	532
1991 Apr 3[a]	8	89	3	769

[a]"Persian Gulf" rather than "Middle East"

If fighting begins with Iraq, how likely is it to become another prolonged situa- **222**
tion like the Vietnam conflict? (Black)

	A prolonged Vietnam very likely	Somewhat likely	Somewhat unlikely	Very unlikely	Don't know	*n*
1990 Dec 1–2	20	20	23	30	7	704

Do you think a war between the United States and Iraq would be a relatively **223**
short war lasting a few weeks or months, or do you think such a war would last
for a long time, a year or more? (ABC/*Washington Post*, ABC)

	Expect a war to last a few weeks or months	Expect a war to last a year or more	Don't know	*n*
1990 Aug 17	61	35	4	815
1990 Sep 6–9	63	34	4	1011
1990 Oct 10–14	57	40	3	1006
1990 Nov 14–15	52	42	6	515
1990 Nov 30–Dec 2	56	40	4	758
1991 Jan 4–6	67	29	5	1057
1991 Jan 4–8	65	30	5	1003
1991 Jan 13	69	28	3	781
1991 Jan 16	82	13	5	545

224   If the U.S. takes (Now that the U.S. has taken) military action against Iraq, do you think the fighting will continue for just a few days, a matter of weeks, several months, a year or more? (Gallup)

	Fighting will take just a few days	Weeks	Several months	A year or more	Don't know	n
1990 Oct 18–19	10	19	35	28	8	755
1991 Jan 10–11	9	25	36	20	10	
1991 Jan 16	17	39	23	5	16	
1991 Jan 17–18	6	38	36	7	13	
1991 Jan 17–20	4	39	39	8	10	
1991 Jan 19–22	2	29	49	12	8	
1991 Jan 23–26	2	12	62	19	5	1011
1991 Jan 24–25	1	11	63	18	7	
1991 Feb 7–10	2	15	63	16	4	
1991 Feb 15	3	31	48	10	8	
1991 Feb 22	13	39	30	7	11	
1991 Feb 24	14	45	24	4	13	

Gallup Poll Monthly, February 1991, p. 18

225   Do you think the war with Iraq will be over in just a few weeks, or do you think it is more likely to continue for several months, or do you think it's likely to continue for a year or longer? (CBS/*New York Times*)

	War will be over in just a few weeks	Likely to continue for several months	Likely to continue for a year or more	Don't know	n
1991 Jan 19	22	55	14	9	908

226   If the U.S. takes (Now that the U.S. has taken) military action against Iraq, do you think that the number of Americans killed and injured will be . . . (Gallup)

	Less than 100	Several hundred	Up to a thousand	Several thousand	Tens of thousands	Don't know	n
1990 Oct 18–19	6	15	15	35	18	11	755
1991 Jan 10–11	4	11	13	44	18	10	
1991 Jan 17–18	12	21	14	28	4	21	
1991 Jan 17–20	12	24	16	29	4	15	
1991 Feb 7–10	6	21	17	39	8	9	

Table 226 continued

	Less than 100	Several hundred	Up to a thousand	Several thousand	Tens of thousands	Don't know	n
1991 Feb 22	10	22	20	28	5	15	
1991 Feb 24	10	31	20	20	3	16	

Gallup Poll Monthly, February 1991, p. 18

Just your best guess, do you think a war between the United States and Iraq **227** would result in a high number of deaths among American troops, a low number of deaths, or what? (ABC/*Washington Post*)

	War would result in a high number of American deaths	Low number	Somewhere in between (vol)	Don't know	n
1991 Jan 4–6	61	28	5	6	1057
1991 Jan 4–8	62	27	4	6	1003
1991 Jan 13	55	29	12	4	781
1991 Jan 16	29	59	7	5	545
1991 Feb 24	21	68	8	3	514

Just your best guess, how many American troops do you think would be killed? **228** (ABC/*Washington Post*)

	0 to 1,000	1,001 to 5,000	5,001 to 10,000	10,001 to 50,000	50,001 to 80,000	50,001 to 100,000	100,000 or more	Over 100,000	Don't know	n
1991 Jan 4–6	13	11	11	16		6		5	38	1057
1991 Jan 4–8	11	10	10	21	1		14		36	1003

229 How likely do you think it is that the U.S. forces in and around Saudi Arabia will become engaged in combat? (Gallup)

	Very likely U.S. forces will become engaged in combat	Somewhat likely	Not too likely	Not at all likely	Don't know	n
1990 Aug 9–10[a]	29	45	17	5	4	770
1990 Aug 23–24	35	45	12	3	5	
1990 Oct 18–19	29	43	16	7	5	755
1990 Nov 2–4	40	36	13	5	6	1021
1990 Nov 15–16	41	39	11	4	5	754
1990 Nov 15–18	41	36	13	5	6	1018
1990 Dec 6–7	31	42	16	6	5	769
1990 Dec 13–16	39	45	9	2	5	
1991 Jan 3–6	46	38	6	4	6	
1991 Jan 11–13	66	24	3	2	5	

[a]How likely do you think it is that the U.S. forces will become engaged in combat with Iraqi troops?

Gallup Poll Monthly, January 1991, p. 11

230 How likely are United States military forces to wind up in combat with Iraq as a result of the current crisis? (Black)

	U.S. military forces very likely to wind up in combat with Iraq	Somewhat likely	Somewhat unlikely	Very unlikely	Don't know	n
1990 Aug 20–21	48	38	6	5	3	802
1990 Nov 12	44	36	7	5	7	615
1990 Dec 1–2	46	36	6	5	7	704
1990 Dec 29–30	59	30	5	4	2	1008
1991 Jan 9	69	20	2	4	4	800

Just your best guess, do you think the United States is going to get involved in **231** a war with Iraq? (ABC/*Washington Post*, ABC)

	Think U.S. is going to get involved in a war with Iraq	Think U.S. will not	Don't know	n
1990 Aug 8	60	38	2	769
1990 Aug 17–20[a]	66	29	5	815
1990 Sep 6–9	65	32	3	1011
1990 Oct 10–14	69	28	3	1006
1990 Nov 2–4[b]	69	27	5	1015
1990 Nov 14–15	71	22	6	515
1990 Nov 30–Dec 2[c]	75	22	3	758
1990 Dec 9[c]	61	37	2	518
1991 Jan 2[c]	77	20	4	352
1991 Jan 2–6[c]	75	22	4	1007
1991 Jan 4–6[c]	72	23	5	1057
1991 Jan 4–8[c]	72	22	6	1003
1991 Jan 9[c]	86	12	1	511
1991 Jan 13[c]	86[d]	12	2	781

[a]Question did not include the phrase, "Just your best guess"
[b]Likely voters
[c]Question added "or not?" at the end
[d]These then asked: Would you say the chances are high, low, or somewhere in between?
(80% High, 1% Low, 19% Somewhere in between, * Don't know)

232 Do you expect the United States military to end up fighting against Iraq, or do you think the situation will be resolved without fighting? (CBS/*New York Times*, CBS, *New York Times*)

	Expect U.S. military to end up fighting Iraq	Think situation will be resolved without fighting	Don't know	*n*
1990 Aug 9–10	36	53	11	670
1990 Aug 16–19	39	51	10	1422
1990 Sep 10	27	64	5	699
1990 Oct 8–10	43	47	10	960
1990 Nov 13–15	51	36	13	1370
1990 Dec 9–11	44	44	12	1044
1991 Jan 5–7	57	31	12	*1348*
1991 Jan 11–13	66	26	7	*1512*

New York Times/CBS News Poll, January 11–13, 1991, p. 2

233 In your view, is war with Iraq inevitable, or is there likely to be a peaceful settlement? (*Time*/CNN)

	War with Iraq is inevitable	Likely to be a peaceful settlement	Don't know	*n*
1990 Oct 3	35	47	18	500
1990 Oct 15–17	35	53	12	1000
1990 Nov 14	46	41	13	500
1990 Nov 27–28	48	41	11	1000

Do you think that the likelihood of war with Iraq has increased, decreased, or stayed about the same during the past few weeks? (*Time*/CNN, *Los Angeles Times*)

	Likelihood of war with Iraq has increased in past few weeks	Has decreased	Has stayed about the same	Don't know	*n*
1990 Oct 15–17	26	11	60	4	1000
1990 Nov 14	54	7	36	3	500
1990 Nov 27–28	62	5	31	2	1000
1990 Dec 8–12	32	40	26	2	2205

Which of the following do you think will be the ultimate result of our actions in the Middle East: (NBC/*Wall Street Journal*)

	America will have to withdraw without meeting its objectives	America will achieve its objectives without a shooting war	America will end up in a war with Iraq	Don't know	*n*
1990 Aug 18–19	8	40	42	10	805
1990 Sep 4–5	8	52	36	4	800
1990 Oct 19–21	9	34	48	9	1019
1990 Dec 8–11	7	34	50	9	1002

Registered voters

WAR PROTESTERS ....

236 Generally speaking, do you think it is appropriate for Americans to continue to protest the war in Iraq now that the United States forces are in combat, or not? (*Los Angeles Times*)

	Appropriate to protest while U.S. forces are in combat	Not appropriate to protest	Don't know	n
1991 Jan 17–18	33	64	3	1406
1991 Feb 15–17	34	62	4	1822

237 Do you think Americans who oppose the war (with Iraq) should be able to hold protest marches and rallies or does that hurt the war effort? (CBS/*New York Times*)

	Protesters should be able to hold rallies	That hurts the war effort	Both (vol)	Don't know	n
1991 Jan 19	48	38	9	5	908

238 When you see the anti-war protests (against the U.S. being at war with Iraq), how do you feel: proud, angry, or somewhat in between? (Black)

	Feel proud about anti-war protest	Feel angry	Feel in between	Don't know	n
1991 Jan 20	7	50	38	5	641

312

Regardless of your own views, do you approve or disapprove of the anti-war **239** protests (against the war with Iraq) being held around the United States? Is that approve/disapprove strongly or approve/disapprove somewhat? (ABC/ *Washington Post*)

	Approve anti-war protest strongly	Approve somewhat	Neutral (vol)	Dis-approve somewhat	Dis-approve strongly	Don't know	n
1991 Jan 20	13	18	5	17	47	1	532

Would you agree or disagree with the following statement: if people who op- **240** pose the war (with Iraq) want to hold anti-war demonstrations, that's all right with me. (ABC/*Washington Post*)

	Agree it's all right to hold anti-war demonstrations	Disagree	Don't know	n
1991 Jan 20	62	35	3	532

Do you think anti-war protesters are undermining the war effort (with Iraq) or **241** not? (ABC/*Washington Post*)

	Anti-war protesters are undermining the war effort	Are not	Don't know	n
1991 Jan 20	43	54	3	532

Have you yourself attended any anti-war demonstrations, or have you attended **242** any pro-war demonstrations, since the war with Iraq began? (ABC/*Washington Post*)

	Have attended anti-war demonstration	Have attended pro-war demonstration	Have not attended any	n
1991 Jan 20	1	1	98	532

243 Which of the following statements better describes the way you personally feel about the anti-war demonstrations now taking place in the United States? (Gallup)

	It is a good thing that Americans who disagree with the government are speaking out on what they believe	It is a bad thing for Americans to be demonstrating against the war when U.S. troops are fighting overseas	Don't know	*n*
1991 Jan 23–26	34	63	3	1011

244 Would you favor or oppose a law to ban peace demonstrations while U.S. troops are fighting overseas? (Gallup)

	Favor ban on peace demonstrations while U.S. troops are fighting overseas	Oppose ban on demonstrations	Don't know	*n*
1991 Jan 23–26	31	65	4	*1011*

Gallup Poll Monthly, January 1991, p. 35

245 Do you agree or disagree with the following statement: It is possible to speak out and protest against the decision to go to war against Iraq and still be a patriotic American. Is that (agree/disagree) strongly or somewhat? (*Los Angeles Times*)

	Strongly agree it is possible to protest war decision and still be a patriotic American	Agree somewhat	Disagree somewhat	Strongly disagree	Don't know	*n*
1991 Feb 15–17	40	30	10	17	3	1822

314

Do you agree or disagree with the following statement: Speaking out and pro- **246**
testing against the war with Iraq hurts our troops there. Is that (agree/disagree)
strongly or somewhat? (*Los Angeles Times*)

	Strongly agree protest hurts our troops	Agree somewhat	Disagree somewhat	Strongly disagree	Don't know	*n*
1991 Feb 15–17	50	21	16	11	2	1822

247 Just your best guess, do you think the Iraqi people support or don't support the war with the United States and its allies? (ABC/*Washington Post*)

	Iraqi people support war with U.S.	Iraqi people don't support war with U.S.	Don't know	*n*
1991 Feb 14	43	49	9	722

248 Do you think the people of Iraq must share the blame for Saddam Hussein's policies in the Middle East or are they innocent of any blame for Hussein's policies? (*Los Angeles Times*)

	People of Iraq must share blame for Hussein's policies	People of Iraq are innocent of any blame for Hussein's policies	Don't know	*n*
1991 Feb 15–17	32	60	8	1822

249 How much do you think the people of Iraq are to blame for allowing Saddam Hussein to remain in power as a dictator—a great deal, somewhat, or not at all? (*New York Times*)

	Blame people of Iraq a great deal for allowing Hussein to remain as dictator	Blame them somewhat	Blame them not at all	Don't know	*n*
1991 Feb 24–Mar 1	36	38	17	9	528

Should American bombers attack all military targets in Iraq, including those in **250** heavily populated areas where civilians may be killed, or should American bombers attack only those military targets that are not in heavily populated areas? (CBS/*New York Times*)

	U.S. should attack all military targets including those in civilian areas	U.S. bombers should only attack military targets not in heavily populated areas	Don't know	*n*
1991 Jan 19	48	43	9	908

Do you think United States bombers should pass up some possible targets if **251** Iraq civilians might be killed in the attack or not? (ABC/*Washington Post*)

	U.S. bombers should pass up possible targets if civilians might be killed	Should not pass up targets	Don't know	*n*
1991 Jan 20	37	56	6	532
1991 Feb 14	34	60	5	772

Which of these three statements comes closer to your own view? (*Washington* **252** *Post*, ABC/*Washington Post*)

	The United States should be making a greater effort to avoid bombing civilian areas in Iraq	The United States is making enough of an effort to avoid bombing civilian areas in Iraq	The United States is making too much of an effort to avoid bombing civilian areas in Iraq	Don't know	*n*
1991 Feb 8–12	13	60	22	4	1011
1991 Feb 14	13	67	18	2	722

253 A. Iraq says hundreds of civilians were killed when the United States bombed an air raid shelter in Baghdad on Wednesday. The United States says the site was being used as a military command bunker. Have you heard or read about this? (92% Yes) Do you think the site was a legitimate military target or not? (ABC/*Washington Post*)

	Bombed shelter was a legitimate military target	Shelter was not a legitimate target	Don't know	*n*
1991 Feb 14	81	9	11	722

B. Who do you hold most responsible for the deaths at the bombing site? (ABC/*Washington Post*)

	Hold Saddam Hussein responsible for deaths at bombing site	Iraq	U.S. military	Bush	U.S.	Pilot/ crew	Other	Don't know	*n*
1991 Feb 14	67	12	3	2	2	*	6	8	722

C. Do you think the United States should stop bombing the city of Baghdad in order to avoid civilian deaths or not? (ABC/*Washington Post*)

	U.S. should stop bombing Baghdad in order to avoid civilian deaths	U.S. should not stop bombing Baghdad	Don't know	*n*
1991 Feb 14	20	75	5	722

254 A. Do you feel what the United States has accomplished in the war against Iraq so far has been worth the number of deaths and injuries suffered by American forces, or not? (*Los Angeles Times*)

	U.S. accomplishments worth the U.S. death and injury	Not worth it	Don't know	*n*
1991 Feb 15–17	63	29	8	1822

318

Table 254 continued

B.   Do you feel what the United States has accomplished in the war against Iraq so far has been worth the number of deaths and injuries suffered by civilians in the war zone, or not? (*Los Angeles Times*)

	U.S. accomplish-ments worth the civilian death and injury	Not worth it	Don't know	*n*
1991 Feb 15–17	52	37	11	1822

C.   Do you think the United States military is doing all it can to keep down the number of civilian casualties in the war against Iraq, or not? (*Los Angeles Times*)

	U.S. military doing all it can to keep down civilian casualties	Not doing all it can	Don't know	*n*
1991 Feb 15–17	52	37	11	1822

D.   As you may know, a few days ago the American Air Force bombed a major target in Iraq's capital of Baghdad, which Iraq claims was a bomb shelter for civilians and which the United States claims was an Iraqi military command center. Do you think the target the U.S. bombed was actually only a civilian bomb shelter, or was it only a military command center, or was it both a civilian bomb shelter and a military command center, or haven't you heard enough about the incident to say? (*Los Angeles Times*)

	Only a civilian shelter	Only a military center	Both	Not heard enough to say	Don't know	*n*
1991 Feb 15–17	3	23	59	10	5	1822

255

Some other countries say United States forces are inflicting (inflicted) excessive damage on Iraq. Do you think the U.S. is causing (caused) excessive damage to Iraq or is (was) the damage about what should be expected in wartime? (*New York Times, CBS/New York Times*)

	U.S. damage to Iraq excessive	Damage about what should be expected in wartime	Damage less than expected (vol)	Don't know	*n*
1991 Feb 28[a]	6	83	6	6	528
1991 Mar 4–6	6	83	8	3	1252
1991 Apr 1–3	3	80	11	6	1283

[a]Or Feb 24–Mar 1

319

256   Taking everything into consideration, in the long run, do you think the war against Iraq will end up (has ended up) making the Middle East a more stable and secure place, a less stable and secure place, or won't it have (hasn't it had) much effect one way or the other? (*Los Angeles Times*)

	War makes Middle East more stable and secure	Less stable and secure	Not much effect one way or the other	Don't know	*n*
1991 Feb 15–17	44	19	33	3	1822
1991 Mar 9–11	53	13	30	4	1836
1991 Jun 28–30ᵃ	35	23	38	4	1439

ᵃDid not include "in the long run"

257   As a result of the war (with Iraq), do you think the Middle East now will be more stable, less stable, or what? (ABC/*Washington Post*)

	Middle East will be more stable	Will be less stable	Neither (vol)	Both (vol)	Don't know	*n*
1991 Mar 1–4	63	22	10	2	3	1215

Now that the war with Iraq has ended, do you think that the political situation in the Middle East will become more stable, become less stable, or won't it make any difference? (*Time*/CNN)

258

	Middle East will become more stable	Will become less stable	Won't make any difference	Don't know	*n*
1991 Mar 7	44	20	29	7	1000

As a result of the Persian Gulf war, do you think ... the Middle East is a more stable region? (Gallup)

259

	Middle East is more stable as result of the war	Is not	Don't know	*n*
1991 Jul 18–21	34	59	7	1002

Should the United States try to change a dictatorship to a democracy where it can, or should the United States stay out of other countries' affairs? (*New York Times*/CBS)

260

	Try to change	Stay out		Don't know	*n*
1986 Apr	28	62		10	
1989 May	29	60		11	
	Try to change	Stay out	Depends (vol)	Don't know	
1990 Jan	26	51	18	5	
1991 Mar 4–6	17	60	19	4	*1252*
1991 Oct 5–7	21	59	16	4	*1280*

New York Times/CBS News Poll, March 4–6, 1991, p. 7; CBS/*New York Times* release, October 10, 1991, p. 7

261 Which of these, if any, do you think are the lessons from the war with Iraq? (*Time*/CNN)

	A lesson	Not a lesson	Don't know	*n*
A . . . The United States is still the greatest military power				
1991 Mar 7	86	11	3	1000

B . . . The United States must increase its efforts to end the unrest in the Middle East				
1991 Mar 7	65	28	7	1000

C . . . The United States should not hesitate to use military force to protect its interests around the world				
1991 Mar 7	58	34	8	1000

D . . . Only the United States can take the lead in protecting democracy in the world				
1991 Mar 7	43	50	7	1000

262 Are you concerned that the American success in the war with Iraq will encourage the United States to get involved in future foreign conflicts? (*Time*/CNN)

	Concerned success in Gulf will encourage U.S. to get involved in foreign conflicts	Not concerned	Don't know	*n*
1991 Mar 7	41	53	6	1000

263 As a result of the war with Iraq, do you think the United States is going to be more willing or less willing to use military force to resolve international disputes in a way favorable to the U.S.? (*Washington Post*)

	U.S. going to be more willing to use military force to resolve disputes favorably	U.S. going to be less willing to use force	No change	Don't know	*n*
1991 Mar 15–19	74	13	7	5	1015

Which of the following statements comes closer to your point of view? (NBC/ **264**
Wall Street Journal)

	The war with Iraq taught us that the United States should be more ready and willing to use its forces and superior weapons when American interests are threatened	The war with Iraq taught us that this was a special circumstance in which the United States had the support of many countries, and that the United States should use military force only as a last resort	Both or neither (vol)	Don't know	n
1991 Mar 15–19	15	80	3	2	1505

Some people feel that war is an outmoded way of settling differences between **265**
nations. Others feel that wars are sometimes necessary to settle differences. With
which point of view do you agree? (Gallup)

	War is outmoded	Wars are sometimes necessary	Don't know
1971	46	43	11
1975	45	46	9
1981	50	43	7
1990 Mar	48	49	3
1991 Feb 7–10	17	80	3

Gallup Poll Monthly, February 1991, p. 19

Do you think it will be best for the future of this country if we take an active **266**
part in world affairs, or if we stayed out of world affairs? (National Opinion
Research Center, Gallup, Survey Research Center, General Social Survey)

	Take active part in world affairs	Stay out of world affairs	Don't know	n
1945 Oct[a]	70	19	11	3074
1946 Feb[a]	75	20	5	3104
1946 Nov[a]	78	19	3	3194

Table 266 continued

	Take active part in world affairs	Stay out of world affairs	Don't know	*n*
1947 Aug[a]	65	26	9	2989
1947 Jun	66	26	8	1273
1947 Mar	68	25	7	537
1948 Mar	70	24	6	1289
1948 Jun	70	23	7	1301
1949 Sep	67	25	8	1273
1950 Nov	69	23	8	1340
1950 Jan	67	24	9	1284
1950 Dec	66	25	9	1258
1952 Oct	68	23	9	1306
1953 Feb	73	22	5	1293
1953 Sep	71	21	8	1262
1954 Apr	69	25	6	1207
1955 Mar	72	21	7	1225
1956 Nov	71	25	4	1286
1965 Jun	79	16	5	1464
1973 Mar	66	31	3	1495
1975 Mar	61	36	4	1484
1976 Mar	63	32	5	1496
1978 Mar	64	32	4	1530
1982 Oct	54	35	12	1547
1982 Mar	61	34	5	1501
1983 Mar	65	31	4	1592
1984 Mar	65	29	6	1449
1985 Mar	70	27	2	745
1986 Mar	65	32	4	1443
1988 Mar	65	32	4	982
1990	62	28	10	
1991 Sep	71	23	6	

Niemi, Mueller, and Smith, 1989, p. 52; *Gallup Poll Monthly,* October 1991, p. 6
[a] . . . would be best . . .

POLITICAL RAMIFICATIONS............................

During the war (with Iraq), do you think one political party supported the war more than the other, or do you think they were equal in their support of the war? (If one more than the other: Which party supported the war more? (CBS/ *New York Times*) **267**

	Republicans supported the war more	Democrats supported the war more	Parties equal in their support	Don't know	*n*
1991 Mar 4–6	18	1	73	8	1252

Which political party's politicians tended to support the war against Iraq more strongly, the Democrats, the Republicans, or did support not break down by political party? (*Los Angeles Times*) **268**

	Republicans tended to support the war more strongly	Democrats tended to support the war more strongly	War support did not break down by party	Don't know	*n*
1991 Mar 9–11	48	5	41	6	1836

269 If your representative in Congress or your United States senator voted against the resolution that authorized George Bush to start the Gulf War, would that make you more likely to vote to re-elect your representative or senator, less likely, or wouldn't it make much difference in your vote? (ABC/*Washington Post*)

	More likely to re-elect Representative or Senator who voted against Bush to start war	Less likely	Wouldn't make much difference	Don't know	n
1991 Mar 1–4	13[a]	35[a]	51	1	1215

[a]These then asked: Would that be one of the biggest factors in your vote, or one of many factors?

	More likely	Less likely
One of biggest factors	23%	26%
One of many factors	77	74
Don't know	1	
	101	100

270 If your congressman voted against giving President Bush the authority to use force in the Persian Gulf and instead favored continuing economic sanctions only, would that make any difference in how you vote when that person runs for re-election? (CBS/*New York Times*)

	Would make difference if congressman voted against giving Bush authority to use force, instead favoring sanctions	Wouldn't make any difference	Don't know	n
1991 Mar 4–5	52[a]	42	6	935

[a]These then asked: Would you be more likely or less likely to vote to re-elect him or her?

More likely	17%
Less likely	79
Don't know	4
	101

A. Do you happen to know if your congressman or congresswoman voted in favor or against the resolution allowing the President to use military force in the Persian Gulf? (Gallup)

	Congressman voted in favor of resolution allowing President to use military force in Gulf	Voted against	Don't know	n
1991 Mar 7–10	35	14	51	1018

B. Do you happen to know if your senator voted in favor or against the resolution allowing the President to use military force in the Persian Gulf? (Gallup)

	Senator voted in favor of resolution allowing President to use military force in Gulf	Voted against	Don't know	n
1991 Mar 7–10	40	12	48	1018

C. If you knew that your congressman/congresswoman voted against the resolution allowing the President to use military force in the Persian Gulf, would that make you more likely, or less likely to vote for his or her re-election, or wouldn't that have much effect on your vote? (Gallup)

	More likely to vote for Congressman who voted against resolution allowing President to use military force in Gulf	Less likely	Wouldn't have much effect on vote	Don't know	n
1991 Mar 7–10	8	30	56	6	1018

Table 271 continued

D.   If you knew that your senator voted against the resolution allowing the President to use military force in the Persian Gulf, would that make you more likely or less likely to vote for his or her re-election, or wouldn't that have much effect on your vote? (Gallup)

	More likely to vote for senator who voted against resolution allowing President to use military force in Gulf	Less likely	Wouldn't have much effect on vote	Don't know	*n*
1991 Mar 7–10	7	33	55	4	1018

272   If you learned that your representative in Congress voted against giving President Bush the authority to take military action against Iraq after the January 15 (1991) UN (United Nations) deadline and in favor of giving economic sanctions more time to get Iraq out of Kuwait, would you be more likely or less likely to support your representative for reelection next year, or would it not make much difference? (NBC/*Wall Street Journal*)

	More likely to vote for representative who voted against giving Bush authority to take military action, relying on sanctions	Less likely	Would not make much difference	Don't know	*n*
1991 Mar 15–19	18	41	36	5	1505

Registered voters

328

I'd like you to think back to January (1991), when Congress debated whether or not to authorize the war against Iraq. If you learned that your congressman had voted "no" to using force against Iraq after the January 15 deadline had expired—would it make you more likely or less likely to vote for his or her re-election, or wouldn't it affect you? (*Los Angeles Times*)

	More likely to vote for congressman who voted 'no' to using force against Iraq	Less likely	Wouldn't affect	Don't know	n
1991 Jun 28–30	13	30	53	4	1439
1991 Nov 21–24	10	42	44	4	1709

Many members of Congress voted against giving President Bush authority to use military force in the Persian Gulf. Does that make you feel more favorable toward them, less favorable toward them, or doesn't that make much difference? (CBS/*New York Times*)

	Feel more favorable toward Congress members who voted against giving Bush authority to use force in Gulf	Feel less favorable	Doesn't make much difference	Don't know	n
1991 Jan 19	18	22	56	4	908

A. As you may know, many politicians opposed the original decision to go to war against Iraq. Generally speaking, do you think those politicians are more patriotic than politicians who supported the decision to go to war, or are they less patriotic, or are they no more or less patriotic? (*Los Angeles Times*)

	Politicians opposed to the war are more patriotic	Are less patriotic	Are no more or less patriotic	Don't know	n
1991 Mar 9–11	5	10	80	5	1836

Table 275 continued

B.   Generally speaking, do you think those politicians who opposed the original decision
to go to war against Iraq showed good judgment, bad judgment, or isn't it possible to
say? (*Los Angeles Times*)

	Politicians opposed to the war showed good judgment	Showed bad judgment	Isn't possible to say	Don't know	*n*
1991 Mar 9–11	21	19	58	2	1836

C.   Regardless of your feelings about the war against Iraq, do you generally respect the
convictions of those politicians who opposed the original decision to go to war or not?
(*Los Angeles Times*)

	Respect convictions of politicians opposed to the war	Do not respect convictions	Don't know	*n*
1991 Mar 9–11	76	19	5	1836

D.   Do you think the record of the politicians who supported and opposed the decision
to go to war with Iraq should be discussed and debated as a political issue or not?

	Record of politicians for and opposed to the war should be debated as political issue	Should not be debated	Don't know	*n*
1991 Mar 9–11	26	71	3	1836

E.   Generally speaking, did the things that happened during the war against Iraq make
you more favorable to the Democratic party, less favorable to the Democratic party, or
didn't it change your opinion of the Democratic party much one way or the other? (*Los
Angeles Times*)

	During the war became more favorable to Democratic party	Became less favorable	Didn't change opinion of party much one way or other	Don't know	*n*
1991 Mar 9–11	3	11	85	1	1836

F.   Generally speaking, did the things that happened during the war against Iraq make
you more favorable to the Republican party, less favorable to the Republican party, or

Table 275 continued

didn't it change your opinion of the Republican party much one way or the other? (*Los Angeles Times*)

	During the war became more favorable to Republican party	Became less favorable	Didn't change opinion of party much one way or other	Don't know	*n*
1991 Mar 9–11	17	5	77	1	1836

Thinking back to last year's debate about using force in the Persian Gulf—if this coming November's election for Congress were held today, for whom would you vote if you learned the Republican candidate favored using military force in the Persian Gulf and the Democrat candidate opposed using military force in the Persian Gulf? (Public Opinion Strategies) **276**

	Vote for Republican favoring	Democrat opposed to force	Don't know	*n*
1991 Jan 29–30	65	24	10	1000

If you knew that a Democratic presidential candidate voted against the resolution allowing President Bush to use military force in the Persian Gulf War, would that make you more likely or less likely to vote for him—or would it not much affect your vote? (Gallup) **277**

	More likely to vote for a Democratic presidential nominee who voted against allowing Bush to use military force in Gulf War	Less likely	Would not much affect vote	Don't know	*n*
1991 Apr 25–28[a]	11	23	61	5	1005
1991 Jul 18–21	8	35	53	4	1002
1992 Jan 6–9[b]	13	31	53	3	1421
1992 Feb 6–9[b]	11	34	53	2	1002

[a]Registered voters only (81%)
[b]. . . or would it not make much difference?

278 Suppose a candidate for president opposed starting the war in the Persian Gulf—would that make you more likely to vote for him, less likely, or wouldn't it matter in deciding how you vote? (CBS/*New York times*)

	More likely to vote for a presidential candidate who opposed starting Gulf War	Less likely	Wouldn't matter	Don't know	*n*
1991 Oct 15–18	14	36	43	7	1280

279 Would you be more or less likely to vote for a candidate for president who ... (Gallup)

. . . Opposed U.S. military action against Iraq after it invaded Kuwait?

	More likely to vote for a Presidential candidate who opposed U.S. military action against Iraq	Less likely	Wouldn't affect vote (vol)	Don't know	*n*
1992 Apr 15–16	23	60	7	10	*754*

Registered voters
Polling Report, April 27, 1992, p. 2

280 What if a candidate for president had opposed the use of U.S. (United States) military force in last year's (1991) war against Iraq. Would you still consider voting for that candidate or would you definitely not vote for that candidate? (*Los Angeles Times*)

	Would consider voting for war opponent for president	Would definitely not vote for war opponent	Don't know	*n*
1992 Jan 31–Feb 3	46	44	10	1776

As a result of the Gulf War, are you now more likely to support Bush for a **281** second term as President, less likely to support him for a second term, or didn't the war change your feeling on that? (ABC/*Washington Post*)

	More likely to support Bush due to war	Less likely	War didn't change feelings	Don't know	*n*
1992 Jan 30–Feb 2	27	21	51	1	1512

I'm going to mention things that some people may consider in deciding which **282** presidential candidate to vote for in November (1992). For each one please tell me how important it will be in deciding your vote for President—will it be the single most important factor, very important, somewhat important, or not very important at all in your decision? . . . (George) Bush's handling of the Persian Gulf War (ABC/*Washington Post*)

	Bush's handling of war would be single most important factor in vote	Very important	Somewhat important	Not very important	Don't know	*n*
1992 Sep 16–20	3	28	38	29	1	1512

Likely voters

I will read you some recent events that might influence how you vote—and **283** whether you vote at all—in this fall's presidential election (1992). As I read each one, tell me if you think it will be a major influence, a minor influence, or not an influence on your presidential vote this year. . . . U.S. (United States) aid to Iraq before it invaded Kuwait. (Gallup)

	Aid to Iraq before invasion would be major influence on vote	Minor influence	Not an influence	Don't know	*n*
1992 Jul 9–10	38	36	24	2	1010

Registered voters

284 Have reports that the Bush administration supplied aid to Saddam Hussein's government in Iraq in the months and years prior to the Gulf War made you more likely to vote for Bush (for president 1992) in November, less likely to vote for Bush, or haven't they affected the way you might vote one way or the other? (*Los Angeles Times*)

	Aid to Hussein before war makes more likely to vote for Bush	Less likely	No effect on vote	Don't know	n
1992 Oct 24–26	3	47	48	2	1829

Registered voters

285 A. If George Bush orders military action (in Iraq) that results in Saddam Hussein being removed from power would you be . . . (asked of registered voters) (Gallup)

	More likely to vote for Bush	Less likely to vote for him	Would it not have much effect on your vote	Don't know	n
1992 Aug 17	12	6	79	3	700

B. If George Bush orders military action that forces Iraq to comply with UN resolutions, but does not result in Saddam Hussein being removed from power, would you be . . . (asked of registered voters) (Gallup)

	More likely to vote for Bush	Less likely to vote for him	Would it not have much effect on your vote	Don't know	n
1992 Aug 17	2	10	83	5	700

If George Bush took any further military action against Iraq between now and **286** the (1992 Presidential) election, would that make you more likely to vote for Bush, less likely, or wouldn't that have any effect on how you plan to vote? (*Time*/CNN)

	More likely to vote for Bush if he takes military action against Iraq before election	Less likely	No effect on vote	Don't know	*n*
1992 Aug 19–20	5	17	76	2	1250

Registered voters

Which political party, the Democrats or the Republicans, do you trust to do a **287** better job at . . . (ABC/*Washington Post*)

	Democrats	Republicans	Both/Neither/Don't know
A handling the nation's economy			
1990 Jan 11–16	33	52	15
1991 Mar 1–4	32	49	19
B controlling inflation			
1990 Jan 11–16	33	50	18
1991 Mar 1–4	34	49	18
C handling foreign affairs			
1990 Jan 11–16	29	55	16
1991 Mar 1–4	23	59	18
D maintaining a strong national defense			
1990 Jan 11–16	25	62	14
1991 Mar 1–4	17	68	14
E helping the middle class			
1990 Jan 11–16	53	32	16
1991 Mar 1–4	48	34	18
F protecting the environment			
1990 Jan 11–16	46	31	23
1991 Mar 1–4	40	35	25

Table 287 continued

	Democrats	Republicans	Both/Neither/ Don't know
G protecting the social security system			
1990 Jan 11–16	52	31	19
1991 Mar 1–4	52	29	16

	Democrats	Republicans	Both/Neither/ Don't know
H helping the poor			
1990 Jan 11–16	62	25	12
1991 Mar 1–4	64	22	14

The Ladd Report, 1991, pp. 8–9

288 Which of these is the main problem the candidates should be addressing? (*Time*/CNN)

	Eco-nomy	Health care	Educa-tion	Family values	Environ-ment	Foreign policy	Don't know	n
1992 Aug 25–27	60	13	11	5	3	2	6	836

Time, September 7, 1992, p. 31

289 What one issue do you wish the candidates would talk most about? (*New York Times*/CBS)

1992 Sep 9–13		n = 1006
	46%	Economy, unemployment
	8	Health care
	7	Education
	6	Federal deficit
	5	Taxes
	20	All other issues (less than 5% each)
	8	Don't know
	100	

New York Times, September 16, 1992, p. A17

NOTES ....

ONE: A Perspective on Public Opinion

1. For able, if unusual, journalistic discussions of this issue, see Morin 1991b, Brennan 1991. For a classic discussion, see Payne 1951. For a major scholarly treatment, see Schuman and Presser 1981. For a somewhat different perspective on "biased" questions, see Page and Shapiro 1992, 29.

2. Social science research on foreign policy attitudes has often found it useful to arrange people by the nature of their general perspective toward foreign affairs, grouping them, for example, as isolationists, internationalists, accomodationists, and hardliners (Wittkopf 1990), or as Cold War internationalists, post–Cold War internationalists, and semi-isolationists (Holsti and Rosenau 1984). The data in this study come overwhelmingly from polls that do not characteristically contain questions allowing one to create such groupings.

3. One oft-repeated error about public opinion on the Vietnam War relates to this set of questions. During the period, Gallup's war support question followed the form of the middle question: "Do you think the U.S. made a mistake in getting into the war?" As it happened, according to this question most people with opinions supported the war before the Tet offensive of 1968 and most opposed it after the offensive—a change of only a few percentage points. This has led to the observation, found in dozens of books and articles, that, because of Tet a "majority" of Americans came to oppose the war. But if Gallup's question had been of the form "Has the war been worthwhile?" the "majority" in opposition would have been reached much earlier. Or, if the question had been of the form "Did we do right to send troops to stop the Communists?", it would have taken longer for the "majority" to materialize.

TWO: The Approach to War: Data

1. See also J. Smith 1992. On the electoral effects of the Falklands War, see chapter 6.

2. For a different view, see Tucker and Hendrickson 1992, 90–91. See also Simpson 1991, 215–16.

3. As columnist Fred Barnes observed at the time, in the first fifteen minutes

of one television interview "Bush ruled out compromise nineteen separate times" (1991b, 8).

4. Although it appears to have been fabricated (Cockburn 1991; MacArthur 1992a; MacArthur 1992b, 53–77), one of the most dramatic atrocity stories held that occupying Iraqi troops had thrown babies out of incubators, a tale Bush had first heard directly from the newly exiled Emir of Kuwait on September 28 (Barnes 1991b; MacArthur 1992, 65). The Kuwait government in exile claimed that the Iraqis killed over one thousand people in Kuwait during and after the invasion (Department of Defense 1992, 27). Middle East Watch put the number at between five hundred and seven hundred (Cockburn 1991).

5. White House press secretary Marlin Fitzwater, however, insisted that this "wasn't macho talk" (Barnes 1991b, 9).

6. However, when the phrase, "or should we have stayed out," was added to the query (table 36 vs. table 34), measured support for sending the troops generally dropped a few percentage points, though a similar comparison in tables 19 and 20 shows no such effect.

7. The rise between the November 14 and December 8–12 figures in table 13 probably also reflect this, and shows the advantage of having multiple measures. One might argue from the data in tables 34 and 36 that the percentage holding involvement to have been a mistake increased a very few points after the announcement. But, if so, they merely went back to levels attained in early or mid-October. By contrast, Bush's mid-November support as measured by the questions in tables 8, 9, and 10 reached new lows. Moreover, there was no subsequent rebound in tables 34 and 36 after the UN vote.

8. The authors of the poll reports in *Public Opinion and Demographic Report* (March/April 1991, p. 77), whose writeups betray a notably hawkish orientation, report the first of these breakdowns, but not the second. They also neglect to report the 6 percent who volunteered that they felt the United States shouldn't move against Iraq. Similarly, Everett Carll Ladd uses the first of these breakdowns to demonstrate that "polls now show a growing segment wanting stronger US action" (1991a; see also Gergen 1991/92, 9; Gergen 1992, 179). How one can show from a single data point that sentiment is growing is not made clear. See also Idelson 1991, 16.

9. Something similar apparently happened with some *New York Times*/CBS News polls: "In late October, of the 32 percent who disapproved of Mr. Bush's approach, roughly half wanted stronger action and half did not." But in the November 13–15 poll, "of the 41 percent who disapproved of Mr. Bush's handling of the gulf situation, three-quarters preferred to take a wait-and-see approach rather than starting military action" (Dowd 1990).

10. As table 1 demonstrates, Bush's first approval rating after becoming president in 1989 was only 51 percent, but that is because of a very high "no opinion" percentage. Only 6 percent disapproved.

11. As table 2 shows, there had also been a big jump upward earlier, in August 1988 after the Republican convention nominated him for the presidency.

12. For an argument that lays considerable stress on these phenomena, see Hinckley 1992, 111–13.

13. For a valuable discussion of some of the problems in this issue, see Morin 1991c.

14. The comparison in January with table 52 uses the January 4–8 poll because of the problems, explained below, with the instant January 9 and 13 polls.

15. The December 14–18 survey in table 63 garners an exceptionally large "no opinion" percentage and thus finds comparatively low support both for going to war and for not going to war. The high "no opinion" result was probably caused by the fact that this rather complicated question was, in this case only, asked first in the survey.

16. The polls from January 13 and January 11–15 are separate and were conducted by different agencies. Information available at the Roper Center does not make it clear what the origins of the January 9 and January 9–13 polls are, and it is possible that the January 9 poll comprises those respondents from the January 9–13 poll who were interviewed on the evening of January 9. If that is the case, the impact of events on instant results would be seem to be even more marked. It is worth pointing out in addition that there are some problems with the ABC/*Washington Post* data from early January as reported in table 63 and elsewhere. The tables present the information as reported in the *Post* and as deposited at the Roper Center. However, it turns out that the polls from early January are not entirely independent. Specifically, there were actually two polls, not four, both conducted by the same agency: one was conducted between January 2 and 6, the other between January 4 and 8. The January 2 poll in question represents the results obtained from those respondents questioned on January 2 from the January 2–6 poll. The January 4–6 poll is a composite of those people interviewed between those dates by the January 2–6 and the January 4–8 polls.

17. The table presents all the data presently available from this series. The complete data have not yet been released.

18. As noted in chapter 1, although Gallup asked a number of questions which showed little or no change of opinion between December and January (tables 8, 20, 34, 40, 57, 58, 76, 126B), it was this series that was played up on the cover of the January 1991 issue of *The Gallup Poll Monthly*.

19. The question in table 89 was apparently asked first: it is numbered R19C, while the one in table 83 is numbered R24B in the Roper Center files.

20. Hinckley (1992, 122–23) criticizes the wording of this question. Observing that it begins by talking about "an international conference on Arab–Israeli problems" and ends by referring to "an Arab–Israeli conference," he argues that "it is fairly easy to see why Americans would agree to a question where Iraq would get out of Kuwait and Arabs and Israeli would have a conference and, by implication, U.S. forces would come home." That ease does not seem so apparent to me. The question does, after all, specifically point out that this would be a concession to aggression and that the Bush administration opposes it.

21. To mention one other category, in the demographic breakdowns published by Gallup, a group whose religion is designated as "none" seem consistently to be more dovish than Protestants and Catholics. Data do not permit sorting out a comparable group in earlier wars for comparison.

22. For a related discussion concerning findings from World War II, Korea, and Vietnam, see Mueller 1973, 62–63.

THREE: The Approach to War: Conclusions

1. After the war Luttwak claimed that he was intentionally exaggerating. "I was not going to give my real forecast of casualties," he explained. He was trying to argue for air power and against a ground attack, and "As an advocate, you only make forecasts when they are conducive to your advocacy" (Achenbach 1991).

2. For a discussion of the sense of fatalism about war that developed in Iraq, see Viorst 1991a, 67–68; Sciolino 1991, 31; Karsh and Rautsi 1991, 240–41; Freedman and Karsh 1991, 9 n. On war fatalism before World War I, see Joll 1984.

3. On Bush's lobbying efforts on the vote, see Seib 1991b; Freedman and Karsh 1993, 294.

4. For a critique of American entry into the Pacific War in reaction to Pearl Harbor, see Mueller 1991/92; Mueller forthcoming. In the cases of the Spanish–American War and World War I, American war involvement was also triggered by dramatic and enraging acts of war by the opponent (putatively in the former case)—the sinking of the battleship *Maine* and the beginning of unrestricted submarine warfare, respectively.

5. The wording of the 1941 question is, "If the question of the United States's going to war against Germany and Italy came up for a national vote within the next two or three weeks, would you vote to go into the war or stay out of the war?" Not surprisingly, less support for war was found when the question included a clause about sending troops abroad: "Do you think the United States should declare war on Germany and Italy and send our army and navy abroad to fight?" (Cantril 1967, 173).

6. Asked in the summer of 1941 what Hitler would do if he defeated Britain, 72 percent of the public picked this option: "Hitler won't be satisfied until he has tried to conquer everything including the Americas" (Cantril and Strunk 1951, 1111).

7. Gulf War supporter Stephen Solarz, who had opposed the Vietnam War in his youth, argued that, unlike the Gulf situation, "in Vietnam, no vital American interests were at stake" (1991, 18). Few saw it that way at the time; see Mueller 1989, 168–73.

FOUR: War

1. Unlike the other comparisons, the one in table 96 contrasts attitudes at the start of war with those measured in the previous November, not with ones tapped just before the initiation of hostilities.

2. Something similar ought to be said about Carter's approval, which stood at only 32 percent before the hostage seizure. He, like Truman, had plenty of room to move upward—compared to Bush and Roosevelt, whose pre-crisis ratings were in the 60s and 70s. Carter's total increase over a couple of polls was 29 percentage points.

3. This issue is one in which question wording is, if anything, even more important than usual: see Mueller 1973, 165 n.; 1988.

4. McGeorge Bundy's comment in 1968 is apt: "It is a miracle in a way, that our people have stayed with the war as long as they have" (Hallin 1986, 211). On this point, see also Ladd 1991a, 1991b; Freedman and Karsh 1993, 285. On the issue of American war strategy and calculations in Vietnam, see Mueller 1980; Mueller 1989, 168–83.

5. On Aspen's influential role, see Moore 1991a. For a suggestion of the impact of this argument, see the trend in table 223 and figure 4.

6. Jentleson (1992, 69) seems to underestimate the prewar hostility to Hussein and accordingly to exaggerate the war's effect in this regard.

FIVE: The War's Aftermath

1. As Bush put it a few weeks after the war, "With this much turmoil it seems to me that Saddam cannot survive . . . people are fed up with him. They see him for the brutal dictator he is" (Freedman and Karsh 1993, 417). Many Iraqis were to be equally disappointed: some of John Simpson's contacts there "openly welcomed the coming war as their only hope of getting rid of a régime they hated" (1991, 267). He reports that Hussein was said to have let it be known that "if anyone tried to overthrow him and failed, three entire layers of their extended family would be destroyed" (1991, 367).

2. When the UN, on American urging, finally voted to repeal its Zionism-is-racism resolution after the war, Kuwait went so far as to abstain. Saudi Arabia, however, voted against repeal.

3. It is possible that the differences in these results can be accounted for by differences in question wording. Comparing the responses at the end of the war when all three questions were asked, 86 percent found the war was worth it if asked to consider both costs and benefits (table 43), 80 percent did so if they were simply asked whether the war was worth it or not (table 40), and only 72 percent did so when the question specifically reminded the respondent about the loss of life (table 41). The first, and to a lesser extent, the second of these probably garnered more casual supporters than the third, and these people were more quickly disillusioned. By June and July, all three questions inspired about the same amount of support—66 or 67 percentage points. Thus in this case a question-wording effect appeared only when the basic question was comparatively popular; when its popularity declined, the effect did as well. However, there are some problems deriving from differences in "no opinion" responses, and the lesson may be different if one looks at the percentages finding the war *not* to be worth it. But these results may suggest that people are not uniformly manipulable by question effects: they are more susceptible when

the question is generating peak appeal. This may be a phenomenon worth exploring further.

SIX: Electoral Consequences of the War

1. For his extended critique of those who had predicted incorrectly that a war against Iraq would be costly, see Muravchik 1991b.

2. *Gallup Poll Monthly,* July 1992, p. 49.

3. For an early discussion presciently suggesting that the political impact of the war might be minimal, see Yang 1991.

4. Quoted in Norpoth 1987b, 957.

5. On Kennedy, see Rostow 1972. On Johnson, see Karnow 1991, 336, 499. This fear was based on a facile analogy: that the "loss" of China to Communism in 1949 caused McCarthyism to erupt in the United States. McCarthy was propelled far more by the Communist attack in Korea in 1950 than by the earlier events in China.

6. *Weekly Compilation of Presidential Documents,* February 3, 1992, p. 176.

7. *Los Angeles Times,* August 21, 1992, p. A8.

8. *New York Times,* January 16, 1991, p. D17.

9. For calls early in the year for military action against Iraq, with the attendant suggestion this would help Bush's reelection prospects, see Gelb 1992, Safire 1992. On this issue, see Omestad 1992/93, 78.

10. This conclusion shouldn't be pushed too far, however. In his campaign of 1988 and particularly during his first year as president, Bush had successfully moved drugs to the top of the public's agenda. In his Inaugural Address, he pledged that "this scourge will stop," and he made a major speech on the subject in September 1989. He was working with something the public was already concerned about, but, as the data in table 45 suggests, his speechifying and policy leadership did have an impact.

11. Curiously, a rare congressman who said the war cost him votes and contributed to his defeat (in a primary) was Democrat Stephen Solarz, a leading and highly vocal hawk on the war (Gurson 1992).

12. For a critique, see Small 1980, 29–73.

13. The epithet is probably inaccurate. While George Bush seems to have been the principal author of the Gulf War, Madison did not have the same relation to the War of 1812. The war "never bore his stamp," notes Hickey. "Cautious, shy, and circumspect, Madison was unable to supply the bold and vigorous leadership that was needed" (1989, 301). He did, however, show great and remarkable respect for the civil rights of his domestic opponents and critics during the trying experience.

SEVEN: Policy and Opinion in the Gulf War

1. For a critique of Bush's rather inept handling of Congress during the approach to war ("We screwed up," says one of the President's advisers), see Gergen 1992, 171–78.

2. On this issue, see also Mueller 1993a; Cooper, Higgott, and Nossal

1991. Gergen also uses the responses from the November 14–15 ABC/*Washington Post* poll in the lower section of table 12 to argue that those Bush's actions because he was moving too slowly on the Gulf outnumbered those disapproving because he was moving too quickly (1992, 178, 179; see also Ladd 1991a). As discussed in chapter 2 and as can be seen in the table, these numbers more than reversed themselves in two weeks.

3. His book also confidently proclaims, "It is most unlikely that Saddam Hussein's regime . . . will survive the war" (1991, 129).

4. These ranges are from a popular book available in U.S. bookstores well before the war: Chadwick 1991, 37, 56. However, American troops were told that the best Iraqi tank had a firing range of 2,800 meters and was "almost unbeatable" because it

> was built so close to the ground that it would be very hard to hit. When they were dug deep into the sand in a fighting position with only their guns poking out, they would be impossible to see until the Americans were well within their gun range. (U.S. News 1992, 364)

The probable kill range of the best American tanks is variously given as 3000 meters (U.S. News 1992, 364) or 4000 meters or more (Dunnigan and Bay 1992, 19). For an open discussion before the ground war of the vast qualitative U.S. superiority in tanks, see Mearsheimer 1991. On the inadequacy of Iraq's "mixed bag of equipment" which had been bought from "half-a-dozen suppliers," see Simpson 1991, 334, 337. Simpson also states that Iraq had fewer than half the forty-five hundred tanks U.S. intelligence estimated (1991, 343; for a similar conclusion, see U.S. News 1992, 412; Cordesman 1991, 68).

5. For a prediction that the United States would try the frontal assaults the Iraqis hoped for and would quickly win, suffering less than a thousand fatalities, see Mearsheimer 1991.

6. The media might have been of little help in this. In a book put together by the editors of *Time* shortly after the war, the one picture devoted to the antiwar cause depicts a demonstrator burning a flag (Friedrich 1991, 218).

7. For the observation that the offensive did not notably lower general support for the war as measured by a key indicator, see Mueller 1973, 57. See also chapter 1, n. 3.

8. Although it may not make a great deal of sense to continue a war costing thousands of lives to gain the return of a few hundred prisoners, it would be difficult to exaggerate the potency of the prisoner issue. In a May 1971 poll, 68 percent agreed that U.S. troops should be withdrawn from Vietnam by the end of the year. However, when asked if they would still favor withdrawal if that would mean a "communist takeover of South Vietnam," only 29 percent agreed. And when asked if they approved of withdrawal "even if it threatened [not *cost*] the lives or safety of United States POWs held by North Vietnam," support for withdrawal dropped to 11 percent (Mueller 1973, 97–98). The force of this attitude was fully felt by diplomats and politicians: negotiator Henry Kissinger recalls that "unilateral withdrawal . . . would not do the trick;

344 ·······························NOTES TO PAGES 129–32

it would leave our prisoners in Hanoi's hands," and "Vietnamization pursued to the end would not return our prisoners" (1979, 1011, 1039). Apparently the option of ending the war without the return of the prisoners was not even a hypothetical consideration. The emotional attachment to prisoners of war has often been a dominant theme in U.S. history. The issue was central to the lengthy and acrimonious peace talks in Korea, and outrage at the fate of American POWs on Bataan probably intensified hatred for the Japanese during World War II almost as much as the attack on Pearl Harbor. And the fate of American prisoners and of those missing in action has haunted postwar Vietnam discussions for decades. From the standpoint of influencing public opinion, Hussein's decision to parade captured American pilots on television early in the Gulf War ranks high among his many major blunders. Concerning the remarkable preoccupation by politicians and press with hostages held by Iran during the crisis of 1979–1981 to the virtual exclusion of issues and events likely to be of far greater importance historically, see Mueller 1984a, 1987.

9. Very often the media are given undue credit for the message. For example, although they review most effectively the extensive research which shows that the media have only minimal effects on opinion, Kinder and Sears suggest that the conclusion should not be pushed too far (1985, 712–14). They note that cumulative news stories about U.S. casualty counts during the Korean and Vietnam wars were associated with declining support for the wars. But, surely, it was the *fact* of the casualties that was motivating, not the method by which the fact was purveyed. It seems likely that the support of the Soviet people for their government's venture in Afghanistan declined as Soviet casualties mounted, even though this information came to them at least as much by word of mouth as by the controlled media. Kinder and Sears also point to "television's unique power" in the case of the Kennedy assassination and funeral and argue that television was a "full partner" in the "remarkable transformation" in which a not terribly popular president became something of a paragon in the popular mind. They observe that it is "impossible to separate the effects of the media coverage from those of the event itself," but it seems useful to note that the reputation of Abraham Lincoln underwent a similar transformation without benefit of TV.

10. Iyengar and Kinder's research stresses the importance of television news, and it reports a set of experimental results in which they have manipulated television news programs to see how viewers' responses are affected. However, although they emphasize the impact of television, they have no evidence that newspapers and other media might not have the same effects. Indeed, they base much of their discussion of agenda-setting on some propositions developed in the 1920s by Walter Lippmann concerning agenda-setting by the print press (1987, 2–3, 114).

11. See also Nacos 1990, 189; and the discussion about "audience effects" in Erbring, Goldenberg, and Miller 1980.

12. For example, in the campaign of 1952, the Republicans seem to have been notably successful at increasing the importance of the Korean War as an issue: see Harris 1954, 25.

13. The Korean War also differed from the Vietnam War in that there was no public protest movement as for Vietnam. Since the wars were about equally unpopular, this suggests not only that television had no peculiar effect but also that the Vietnam antiwar movement was also to that degree ineffective (see Mueller 1973, 164–65). People, it seems, need neither pictures of a war nor people screaming at them to determine that they don't like the costs very much. For the argument that the Vietnam antiwar movement's chief political impact was to help elect Richard Nixon, see Mueller 1984b.

14. As with Vietnam, the most influential pictures may have been stills as displayed in newspapers and magazines, not pictures in motion on television.

15. Similarly, during World War II an experiment was made to determine whether "realistic" war pictures would hurt morale. It found that those who were exposed to such pictures were not any more or less likely to support the war than an unexposed control group. Those exposed, however, did become more favorable to showing people realistic war pictures (National Opinion Research Center 1944). In general, efforts of the military to use propaganda films to indoctrinate new draftees were ineffective: see Kinder and Sears 1985, 706.

EIGHT: The War in Retrospect

1. There is also a possibility—a danger, from Bush's perspective—that media outrage over the way the press was handled (or manipulated) during the war could lead to some self-interested revisionism from them as well: people who think they were taken often seek to exact revenge later. Braestrup observes that resentment over the manipulative treatment of the press by the administration before the Tet offensive in Vietnam helped inspire its later reaction to the offensive that was so hostile to the administration (1983, xii, 510).

2. As observed in chapter 5, on some measures there seems to have been a drop at the end the war in the belief that taking Saddam's scalp was necessary for true victory (compare table 190 with tables 192 and 193). Quite quickly after the war, however, this changed (see the trend in table 193).

3. As one administration official said of Bush's State Department, "They respond to opinion makers to a degree you wouldn't believe" (Binder 1992).

4. *New York Times*, October 17, 1992, p. 12.

5. *Weekly Compilation of Presidential Documents*, February 3, 1992, p. 165.

6. Simpson concludes that "the survival of his régime was more important to him than the outcome of the war," and characterizes Hussein's condition as "malignant narcissism": "a paranoid approach to those around him; and almost total self-absorption; a lack of interest in or awareness of the suffering of others; the absence of anything that might be called conscience in the pursuit of his own drives and impulsions" (1991, 17, 20).

7. *Weekly Compilation of Presidential Documents*, March 16, 1992, p. 458; see also Friedrich 1991, 197. By the time of his Presidential debates in October, Bush had raised the portion of the world's oil controlled by Hussein under this scenario to three-fifths (*New York Times*, October 17, 1992, p. 12). As noted in chapters 2 and 3, the oil argument was the least popular with the public; thus from a political standpoint it was also the least likely to resonate effectively.

8. Compare Simpson's conclusion that "Iraq was not a suitable case for the imposition of sanctions" in part because "its oil was too valuable a commodity to have remained unsold for long" (1991, 214–15).

9. Moreover, concluded Greenspan, "The interaction of rising oil prices, Persian Gulf uncertainties and credit tightening is apparently creating a greater suppression of economic activity than the sum of the forces individually" (Cranford 1991).

10. A fear of terrorism at the time also massively reduced bookings on trans-Atlantic airplane flights. This, combined with high fuel prices, moved several major airlines, particularly international carriers, toward bankruptcy—and a few into it. There was a strong tendency among the American public to blame high gasoline price rises on gouging oil companies.

11. Early on, debunkers were able to dim some of the glow of the high-tech image. The best-known and best-remembered aspect of the war concerns American efforts to intercept Iraq's Scud missiles or to destroy them on the ground. Although these missiles were militarily insignificant, they had great potential for generating political mischief by drawing Israel into the war, something the Bush administration thought politically undesirable because it might split the Arabs off from the coalition. These efforts were initially branded a terrific success, with oft-replayed television pictures to prove it, but longer range analysis suggests Scud-busting may have been a substantial failure (see Postol 1991/92, Miller 1992, R. Stein 1992, Postol 1992).

It is often concluded that the Gulf War differed from the Vietnam War in that the military commanders were left free to fight the war as they saw fit (see, for example, U.S. News 1992, 400). This perspective is very likely to last, but it is far from sound. In Vietnam, the generals came up with an attrition strategy on the ground, and they were given great leeway to carry it out. There were political restrictions on the bombing, particularly of North Vietnam: civilian casualties were to be minimized, and bombing was not to get too close to China for fear of bringing that country into the war (as had happened in Korea). However, there were similar restrictions on bombing in the Gulf War (Evans 1991). There was a prohibition on attacking certain targets like mosques and monuments to Saddam Hussein (Simpson 1991, 38). Moreover, civilian casualties were to be kept to a minimum; the planes the Iraqis flew into Iran were not to be hit, since this might outrage the Iranians; and tremendous resources were diverted to getting the Scuds, even though they were, as Schwarzkopf points out (1992, 417), militarily insignificant, and even though the entrance into the war of Israel—with by far the best armed forces in the Mideast—would logically have been of great benefit from a strictly military standpoint. And, unlike Vietnam, the politicians in Washington put quite explicit limits on the numbers of American casualties that would be tolerated: no more than the equivalent of "three companies per Coalition brigade" or about 9000 (Department of Defense 1992, 70; Cushman 1992). See also Mueller 1993b.

12. The Pentagon's final report to Congress of April 1992 dutifully repeats the half-million estimate of Iraqi troop strength (Department of Defense 1992,

71, 85, 254), as does Schwarzkopf's autobiography (1992, 308). According to the press, the report had once included an indication that Iraqi troop strength was much smaller, but this was excised before it was sent to Congress (Anderson and Binstein 1992). See also Smith 1991.

13. Even as the unexpected outcome of the Vietnam War was chiefly determined by the astounding ability of the Communist side to maintain morale and fighting cohesion despite losses that, as a percentage of the population, were virtually unprecedented historically. See Mueller 1980. For commentaries that explain the American military success in the Gulf War with scarcely any attention to the state of Iraqi morale, see Summers 1992, Taylor and Blackwell 1991.

14. Millions of leaflets were dropped on the Iraqis. As a Defense Department spokesman observed after the war, "The leaflets in effect said in Arabic, 'Tonight we have dropped a leaflet, tomorrow it will be a bomb. Don't sleep in your tank.' They soon got the message as they saw the tanks destroyed night after night" (Woodward 1991b). For a discussion, see Mueller 1993b.

NINE: The Decline of the War as a Memorable Event

1. It was a rather costly one, however. In the aftermath of that war, the British felt it necessary to send over a large occupation force to protect the near-barren islands. The cost of the war and the additional cost of defending the islands through the 1980s alone came to over $3 million for every liberated Falklander (Freedman 1988, 116). "Far from proving that aggression does not pay," observed one American official, "Britain has only proved that resisting it can be ridiculously expensive" (Hastings and Jenkins 1983, 339).

2. The gladiators of professional football average only four and a half seasons. Each season 80 percent are injured, and virtually all suffer later from spinal compression. Among the million or so boys and men who play football at the high school, college, and professional level each year, there are nearly half a million injuries. Knee injuries account for 125,000 and 30,000 of these are severe enough to require surgery. There are no data for retired players, but a large percentage undergo multiple operations, and many are permanently disabled. See Else, Couturié, and Moore 1985.

3. Quite a few people have seen sport as a substitute for war. Writing in 1623, the French peace advocate Eméric Crucé argued that wars were undertaken "for honor, for profit, for righting some wrong, and for exercise." The last of these he thought was the most "difficult to remedy" and suggested it could be expatiated by sport—tournaments and mock battles—as well as by hunting, which he found "a noble and fitting exercise for warriors." He added that not only would wild beasts "serve as suitable opponents for working off this desire for violence," but also "savages that do not use reason" and "pirates and thieves who do nothing but steal" (1972, 8, 18, 22–23). More recently, Konrad Lorenz has proposed dealing with the war impetus by engineering devices for "discharging aggression in an innocuous manner" and has suggested sport could be such a "healthy safety valve" (1966, 269, 272). For a discussion, see Mueller 1991c.

4. Actually, in some respects this number is high. The winner of the previous Super Bowl had been the Los Angeles Raiders, but the poll accepted the erroneous response "Oakland Raiders" as correct even though the team had moved to Los Angeles three seasons earlier. The poll was based on a sample of 1,340 adults, of whom 744 were determined to be football fans.

REFERENCES ....

ABC News. 1991. "This Week with David Brinkley." January 13. (Cited from edited transcript.)

Achenbach, Joel. 1991. The experts in retreat: After-the-fact explanations for the gloomy predictions. *Washington Post*, February 28, D1.

Adams, William C., and Michael Joblove. 1982. The unnewsworthy holocaust: TV news and terror in Cambodia. Pp. 217–25 in *Television Coverage of International Affairs*, ed. William C. Adams. Norwood, N.J.: Ablex.

Albright, David, and Mark Hibbs. 1991. Hyping the Iraqi bomb. *Bulletin of the Atomic Scientists*, March, 26–28.

Aldrich, John H., John L. Sullivan, and Eugene Borgida. 1989. Foreign affairs and issue voting: Do presidential candidates "Waltz before a Blind Audience"? *American Political Science Review* 83, no. 1 (March): 123–41.

Alford, John R., and John R. Hibbing. 1992. The 1990 congressional election results and the fallacy that they embodied an anti-incumbent mood. *PS: Political Science & Politics* 25, no. 2 (June): 217–19.

Anderson, Jack, and Michael Binstein. 1992. Operation intelligence breakdown. *Washington Post*, February 13, B23.

Apple, R. W., Jr. 1991. Stake for Bush: Presidency and politics. *New York Times*, January 16, A1.

Ascherio, Alberto, Robert Chase, Tim Coté, Godelieve Dehaes, Eric Hoskins, Jalali Laaouej, Megan Passey, Saleh Qaderi, Saher Shuqaidef, Mary C. Smith, and Sarah Saidi. 1992. Effect of the Gulf War on infant and child mortality in Iraq. *New England Journal of Medicine* 327, no. 13 (September 24): 931–36.

Aspin, Les. 1990. *The Role of Sanctions in Securing U.S. Interests in the Persian Gulf*. Washington, D.C.: Committee on Armed Services, U.S. House of Representatives, December 21.

———. 1991. *The Military Option: The Conduct and Consequences of War in the Persian Gulf*. Washington, D.C.: Committee on Armed Services, U.S. House of Representatives, January 8.

Aspin, Les, and William Dickinson. 1992. *Defense for a New Era: Lessons of the Persian Gulf War*. Washington, D.C.: U.S. House of Representatives, Committee on Armed Services, U.S. Government Printing Office.

349

Atkins, James E. 1991. Hooray? The Gulf may not be calm for long. *New York Times*, March 3, sec. 4, p. 17.

Atkinson, Rick. 1991. "A defining moment in history": As midnight deadline approaches, stakes for U.S. are enormous. *Washington Post*, January 15, A1.

Barnes, Fred. 1991a. The wimp factor. *New Republic*, January 7 and 14, 10–11.

———. 1991b. The hawk factor. *New Republic*, January 28, 8–9.

———. 1991c. The unwimp. *New Republic*, March 18, 17–18.

Beeston, Richard. 1991. Bitter fight for city expected. *Times* (London), February 20, 3.

Binder, David. 1992. Why U.S. bears down on Belgrade. *New York Times* May 27, A6.

Blair, Clay. 1987. *The Forgotten War: America in Korea, 1950–1953*. New York: Times Books.

Bosso, Christopher. 1989. Setting the agenda: Mass media and the discovery of famine in Ethiopia. Pp. 153–74 in *Manipulating Public Opinion: Essays on Public Opinion as a Dependent Variable*, ed. Michael Margolis and Gary A. Mauser. Pacific Grove, Calif.: Brooks/Cole.

Braestrup, Peter. 1983. *Big Story: How the American Press and Television Reported and Interpreted the Crisis of Tet 1968 in Vietnam and Washington*. New Haven, Conn.: Yale University Press.

Brennan, John. 1991. Key words influence stands on minorities. *Los Angeles Times*, August 21, A5.

Brody, Richard A. 1991. *Assessing the President: The Media, Elite Opinion, and Public Support*. Stanford, Calif.: Stanford University Press.

Brzezinski, Zbigniew. 1990. Patience in the Persian Gulf, not war. *New York Times*, October 7, 4–19.

Bundy, McGeorge. 1988. *Danger and Survival: Choices about the Bomb in the First Fifty Years*. New York: Random House.

Bush, George. 1991a. Kuwait is liberated. Pp. 449–51 in *The Gulf War Reader: History, Documents, Opinions*, ed. Micah L. Sifry and Christopher Cerf. New York: Times Books/Random House. [Speech of February 27, 1991.]

———. 1991b. The liberation of Kuwait has begun. Pp. 311–14 in *The Gulf War Reader: History, Documents, Opinions*, ed. Micah L. Sifry and Christopher Cerf. New York: Times Books/Random House. [Speech of January 16, 1991.]

———. 1991c. *Public Papers of the Presidents of the United States: George Bush, 1990*. Washington, D.C.: Government Printing Office.

Cantril, Hadley. 1967. *The Human Dimension: Experiences in Policy Research*. New Brunswick, N.J.: Rutgers University Press.

Cantril, Hadley, and Mildred Strunk. 1951. *Public Opinion 1935–1946*. Princeton, N.J.: Princeton University Press.

Carpenter, Ted Galen. 1992. *A Search for Enemies: America's Alliances after the Cold War*. Washington, D.C.: Cato Institute.

CBS Sports/New York Times Poll. 1984. "The state of the NFL," press release. December.

Chadwick, Frank. 1991. *Desert Shield Fact Book*. Bloomington, Ill.: Game Designers' Workshop.

Claiborne, William. 1991. "We thought of nothing but escape." *Washington Post*, March 3, A35.

Claiborne, William, and Carlyle Murphy. 1991. Retreat down highway of doom: U.S. war planes turned Iraqis' escape route into deathtrap. *Washington Post*, March 2, A1.

Clark, Ramsey. 1992. *The Fire This Time*. New York: Thunder's Mouth Press.

Clarke, Harold D., William Mishler, and Paul Whiteley. 1990. Recapturing the Falklands: Models of Conservative popularity, 1979–83. *British Journal of Political Science* 20, no. 1 (January): 63–81.

Clarke, I. F. 1966. *Voices Prophesying War, 1763–1984*. London: Oxford University Press.

Cockburn, Alexander. 1991. Beat the Devil. *Nation*, February 4, 114–15.

Congressional Quarterly. 1992. *Guide to the 1992 Republican National Convention*. Washington, D.C.: Congressional Quarterly.

Cooper, Andrew Fenton, Richard A. Higgott, and Kim Richard Nossal. 1991. Bound to follow? Leadership and followership in the Gulf conflict. *Political Science Quarterly* 106, no. 3 (Fall): 391–410.

Cordesman, Anthony H. 1991. Rushing to judgment on the Gulf War. *Armed Forces Journal International*, June, 66–72.

———. 1993. *After the Storm: The Changing Military Balance in the Middle East*. Boulder, Colo.: Westview.

Council of Economic Advisers. 1992. *Economic Report of the President*. Washington, D.C.: Government Printing Office.

Cranford, John R. 1991. Hopes for quick end to recession entagled in Persian Gulf crisis. *Congressional Quarterly Weekly Report* 49, no. 1 (January 5): 18–20.

Crucé, Eméric. 1972. *The New Cineas*. New York: Garland. (Original work published 1623.)

Curran, Tim. 1991. Gingrich plan: Run Gulf vets vs. Dems. *Roll Call*, March 4, 1.

Cushman, John H. 1992. Pentagon report on the Persian Gulf War: A few surprises and some silences. *New York Times*, April 11, 1–4.

Dannreuther, Roland. 1991/92. The Gulf conflict: A political and strategic analysis. *Adelphi Papers* 264 (Winter). London.

Daponte, Beth Osborne. 1993. A case study in estimating Iraqi casualties from the Gulf War and its aftermath: The 1991 Persian Gulf War. *PSR Quarterly* 3, no. 2 (June): 57–66.

Delli Carpini, Michael X., and Scott Keeter. 1991. Stability and change in the U.S. public's knowledge of politics. *Public Opinion Quarterly* 55, no. 4 (Winter): 583–612.

Department of Defense. 1992. *Conduct of the Persian Gulf War: Final Report to Congress*. Washington, D.C.: Department of Defense, April.

Doherty, Carroll J. 1991. Congress faces grave choices as clock ticks toward war. *Congressional Quarterly Weekly Report* 49, no. 1 (January 5): 7–10.

Dowd, Maureen. 1990. Americans more wary of Gulf policy, poll finds. *New York Times,* November 20, A12.

———. 1991. Unable to out-hero Bush, Democrats just join him. *New York Times,* March 8, A1.

———. 1992. Immersing himself in nitty-gritty, Bush barnstorms New Hampshire. *New York Times,* January 16, A1.

Drew, Elizabeth. 1991. Letter from Washington. *New Yorker,* February 4, 82–90.

Drogin, Bob. 1991. On forgotten Kuwait road, 60 miles of wounds of war. *Los Angeles Times,* March 10, A1.

Duffy, Michael, and Dan Goodgame. 1992a. *Marching in Place: The Status Quo Presidency of George Bush.* New York: Simon and Schuster.

———. 1992b. Warrior for the Status Quo. *Time,* August 24, 32–45.

Dunnigan, James F., and Austin Bay. 1992. *From Shield to Storm: High-Tech Weapons, Military Strategy, and Coalition Warfare in the Persian Gulf.* New York: Morrow.

Dupuy, Trevor N. 1991. *How to Defeat Saddam Hussein: Scenarios and Strategies for the Gulf War.* New York: Warner Books.

Edwards, George C., III. 1990. *Presidential Approval: A Sourcebook.* Baltimore, Md.: Johns Hopkins University Press.

Elliott, Kimberly A., Gary C. Hufbauer, and Jeffrey Schott. 1990. The Big squeeze: Why the sanctions on Iraq will work. *Washington Post,* December 9.

Else, John, Bill Couturié, and Bob Moore (writers). 1985. *Disposable Heroes.* HBO. (Television program.)

Erbring, Lutz, Edie N. Goldenberg, and Arthur H. Miller. 1980. Front-page news and real-world cues: A new look at agenda-setting by the media. *American Journal of Political Science* 24, no. 1 (February): 16–49.

Evans, Michael. 1991. Civilian risks keep strategic sites off allied target list. *Times* (London), February 15, 11.

Farwell, Rebecca. 1992. Two Cents. *TDC* [The Discovery Channel magazine], January, 4.

Fialka, John J. 1991. *Hotel Warriors: Covering the Gulf War.* Washington, D.C.: Woodrow Wilson Center Press.

Fineman, Mark. 1992. Iraqis celebrate news of Bush's defeat. *Los Angeles Times,* November 5, A38.

FitzSimon, Martha. 1991. Public perception of war coverage: A survey analysis. Pp. 86–95 in *The Media at War: The Press and the Persian Gulf Conflict,* ed. Craig LaMay, Martha FitzSimon and Jeanne Sahadi. New York: Columbia University, Freedom Forum Media Studies Center.

Freedman, Lawrence. 1988. *Britain and the Falklands War.* Oxford: Basil Blackwell.

Freedman, Lawrence, and Efraim Karsh. 1991. How Kuwait was won: Strategy in the Gulf War. *International Security* 16, no. 2 (Fall): 5–41.

————. 1993. *The Gulf Conflict, 1990–1991: Diplomacy and War in the New World Order.* Princeton, N.J.: Princeton University Press.

Friedman, Norman. 1991. *Desert Victory: The War for Kuwait.* Annapolis, Md.: Naval Institute Press.

Friedrich, Otto, ed. 1991. *Desert Storm: The War in the Persian Gulf.* Boston: Little, Brown.

Frost, David (interviewer). 1991a. "Talking with David Frost: An Interview with President and Mrs. Bush." PBS, January 2. (Taped December 28, 1990; cited from edited transcript).

————. 1991b. "Talking with David Frost: General Norman Schwarzkopf." PBS, March 22. (Cited from videotape.)

Gaddis, John Lewis. 1974. Was the Truman Doctrine a real turning point? *Foreign Affairs* 52, no. 2 (January): 386–401.

Gelb, Leslie H. 1991. Gulf military questions. *New York Times,* February 6, A21.

————. 1992. Target Al Atheer. *New York Times,* March 23, A17.

Gergen, David R. 1991/92. America's missed opportunites. *Foreign Affairs: America and the World* 71(1):1–19.

————. 1992. The unfettered presidency. Pp. 169–93 in *After the Storm: Lessons from the Gulf War,* ed. Joseph S. Nye, Jr. and Roger K. Smith. Lanham, Md.: Madison Books.

Ghabra, Shafeeq. 1991. The Iraqi occupation of Kuwait: An eyewitness account. *Journal of Palestine Studies* 20, no. 2 (Winter): 112–25.

Goldman, Peter, and Tom Mathews. 1992. America changes the guard. *Newsweek* special issue, November/December, 20–23.

Goodman, Walter. 1991. Appropriating history to serve politics on TV. *New York Times,* October 7.

Greenberger, Robert S., and Gerald F. Sieb. 1990. Iraq threatens wide-scale war in Middle East. *Wall Street Journal,* November 24, A3.

Gurson, Lindsey. 1992. Rep. Solarz, in Defeat, looks back with pride. *New York Times,* October 7, B3.

Hackworth, David H. 1992. We didn't finish the job: Soldiers should be allowed to fight to win. *Newsweek,* January 20, 29.

Halberstam, David. 1965. *The Making of a Quagmire.* New York: Random House.

————. 1992. *The Next Century.* New York: Avon.

Hallin, Daniel C. 1986. *The "Uncensored War": The Media and Vietnam.* New York: Oxford University Press.

Hallion, Richard P. 1992. *Storm Over Iraq: Air Power and the Gulf War.* Washington, D.C.: Smithsonian Institution Press.

Harris, Louis. 1954. *Is There a Republican Majority? Political Trends, 1952–1956.* New York: Harper's.

Hastings, Max, and Simon Jenkins. 1983. *The Battle for the Falklands.* New York: Norton.

Heidenrich, John G. 1993. The Gulf War: How many Iraqis died? *Foreign Policy,* Spring, 108–25

Hickey, Donald R. 1989. *The War of 1812: A Forgotten Conflict.* Urbana and Chicago: University of Illinois Press.

Hinckley, Ronald H. 1992. *People, Polls, and Policymakers: American Public Opinion and National Security.* New York: Lexington Books.

Hiro, Dilip. 1992. *Desert Shield to Desert Storm: The Second Gulf War.* New York: Routledge.

Hoffman, David. 1991. In ocean of misunderstandings, diplomacy had little chance. *Washington Post,* January 17, A28.

Hoffmann, Stanley. 1992. Bush abroad. *New York Review of Books,* November 5.

Holsti, Ole R. 1992. Public opinion and foreign policy: Challenges to the Almond-Lippmann consensus. *International Studies Quarterly* 36, no. 4 (December): 439–66.

Holsti, Ole R., and James N. Rosenau. 1984. *American Leadership in World Affairs.* Boston: Allen and Unwin.

Horwich, George. 1992. Energy policy, oil markets, and the Middle East War: Did we learn the lessons of the 1970s? Pp. 25–39 in *International Issues in Energy Policy, Development, and Economics,* ed. James P. Dorian and Fereidun Fesharaki. Boulder, Colo.: Westview.

Hufbauer, Gary C., and Kimberly A. Elliott. 1991. Sanctions will bite—and soon. *New York Times,* January 14, A17.

Hufbauer, Gary C., Jeffrey J. Schott, and Kimberly Ann Elliott. 1990. *Economic Sanctions Reconsidered: History and Current Policy.* 2d ed. Washington, D.C.: Institute for International Economics.

Hugick, Larry. 1991. Bush approval slide continues. *Gallup Poll Monthly,* November, 13–15.

———. 1992. Georgia voters showed varied response to negative ads: Audience may not have been receptive. *Gallup Poll Monthly,* March, 32–39.

Hugick, Larry, and Alec M. Gallup. 1991. "Rally Events" and presidential approval. *Gallup Poll Monthly,* June, 15–27.

Ibrahim, Youssef M. 1992a. A peace that still can't recover from the war. *New York Times,* May 6, A4.

———. 1992b. Rulers of Kuwait on a spending spree, raising debt fears. *New York Times,* May 4, A1.

Idelson, Holly. 1991. National opinion ambivalent as winds of war stir Gulf. *Congressional Quarterly Weekly Report* 49, no. 1 (January 5): 14–17.

Inman, Bobby, Joseph S. Nye, Jr., William J. Perry, and Roger K. Smith. 1992a. Lessons from the Gulf War. *Washington Quarterly* 15, no. 1 (Winter): 57–74.

———. 1992b. U.S. strategy after the Storm. Pp. 267–92 in *After the Storm: Lessons from the Gulf War,* ed. Joseph S. Nye, Jr. and Roger K. Smith. Lanham, Md.: Madison Books.

Iyengar, Shanto, and Donald R. Kinder. 1987. *News That Matters: Television and American Opinion.* Chicago: University of Chicago Press.

James, William. 1911. *Memories and Studies.* New York: Longmans, Green.

Jentleson, Bruce W. 1992. The pretty prudent public: Post post-Vietnam American opinion on the use of military force. *International Studies Quarterly* 36, no. 1 (March): 49–74.

Jervis, Robert. 1980. The impact of the Korean War on the Cold War. *Journal of Conflict Resolution* 24, no. 4 (December): 563–92.

Joll, James. 1984. *The Origins of the First World War.* New York: Longman.

Kant, Immanuel. 1957. *Perpetual Peace.* Trans. Louis White Beck. Indianapolis: Bobbs-Merrill. (Original work published 1796.)

Karnow, Stanley. 1991. *Vietnam: A History.* Rev. ed. New York: Penguin.

Karsh, Efraim, and Inari Rautsi. 1991. *Saddam Hussein: A Political Biography.* New York: Free Press.

Kinder, Donald R., and David O. Sears. 1985. Public opinion and political action. Pp. 659–741 in *Handbook of Social Psychology,* vol. 3, ed. Gardner Lindzey and Elliot Aronson. New York: Random House.

Kissinger, Henry. 1979. *White House Years.* Boston: Little, Brown.

Kraus, Sidney. 1979. *The Great Debates: Carter vs. Ford, 1976.* Bloomington: Indiana University Press.

Krauthammer, Charles. 1991. Bush's march through Washington: How a president incapable of rhetoric could take a country to war. *Washington Post,* March 1, A15.

Kuntz, Phil. 1991. Unstable Mideast oil supply rocks the world market. *Congressional Quarterly Weekly Report,* 49, no. 1 (January 5): 21–25.

Ladd, Everett Carll. 1991a. Americans Don't Want War, But . . . *Christian Science Monitor,* December 7, 18.

———. 1991b. Iraq: Good policy is good politics. *Christian Science Monitor,* September 7, 18.

———. 1992a. Big swings in the national mood are a staple of contemporary politics. *Public Perspective,* January/February, 3–5.

———. 1992b. Public support for Gulf policy has remained quite steady. *Baltimore Sun,* January 27, 1C.

LaMay, Craig. 1991. By the numbers. Pp. 41–50 in *The Media at War,* ed. Craig LaMay, Martha FitzSimon, and Jeanne Sahadi. New York: Columbia University, Freedom Forum Media Studies Center.

LaMay, Craig, Martha FitzSimon, and Jeanne Sahadi, eds. 1991. *The Media at War: The Press and the Persian Gulf Conflict.* New York: Columbia University, Freedom Forum Foundation Media Center.

Lang, Gladys Engel, and Kurt Lang. 1983. *The Battle for Public Opinion: The President, the Press and the Polls During Watergate.* New York: Columbia University Press.

Lesch, Ann M. 1991. Palestinians in Kuwait. *Journal of Palestine Studies* 20, no. 4 (Summer): 42–54.

Lewis, Anthony. 1992a. Changing the rules. *New York Times,* December 4, A31.

———. 1992b. Yesterday's man. *New York Times,* August 3, A19.

Lewis, Paul. 1992a. Immovable object: Granite regime of Saddam Hussein seems little worn by political storm. *New York Times,* July 31, A6.

————. 1992b. U.N. experts now say Baghdad was far from making an A-bomb before the Gulf War. *New York Times,* May 20, A6.

————. 1993. U.S. and Britain softening emphasis on ousting Iraqi. *New York Times,* March 30, A3.

Lichter, Robert. 1992. The instant reply war. Pp. 224–30 in *The Media and the Gulf War: The Press and Democracy in Wartime,* ed. Hedrick Smith. Washington, D.C.: Seven Locks Press.

Lichty, Lawrence W. 1984. Comments on the influence of television on public opinion. Pp. 158–60 in *Vietnam as History,* ed. Peter Braestrup. Lanham, Md.: University Press of America.

Linderman, Gerald F. 1987. *Embattled Courage: The Experience of Combat in the Civil War.* New York: Free Press.

Livermore, Shaw, Jr. 1962. *The Twilight of Federalism: The Disintegration of the Federalist Party, 1815–1830.* Princeton, N.J.: Princeton University Press.

Lorenz, Konrad. 1966. *On Aggression.* New York: Bantam.

Luttwak, Edward N. 1990. Testimony. In *Crisis in the Persian Gulf: U.S. Policy Options and Implications. Hearings before the Committee on Armed Services, United States Senate,* 101st Cong., 2nd sess., November 29.

MacArthur, John R. 1992a. Remember Nayirah, witness for Kuwait? *New York Times,* January 6, A17.

————. 1992b. *Second Front: Censorship and Propaganda in the Gulf War.* New York: Hill & Wang.

Mandelbaum, Michael. 1981. Vietnam: The television war. *Daedalus,* Fall, 157–69.

May, Ernest R. 1984. The Cold War. Pp. 209–30 in *The Making of America's Soviet Policy,* ed. Joseph S. Nye, Jr. New Haven, Conn.: Yale University Press.

McCaffrey, Barry R. 1991. Testimony. Pp. 103–75 in *Operation Desert Shield/ Desert Storm. Hearings before the Committee on Armed Services, United States Senate,* 102nd Cong., 1st sess., May 9.

Mearsheimer, John. 1991. Liberation in less than a week. *New York Times,* February 8, A31.

Middle East Watch. 1991a. *Needless Deaths in the Gulf War: Civilian Casualties During the Air Campaign and Violations of the Laws of War.* New York: Human Rights Watch.

————. 1991b. *A Victory Turned Sour: Human Rights in Kuwait Since Liberation.* New York: Middle East Watch.

Milhollin, Gary. 1992. Building Saddam Hussein's bomb. *New York Times Magazine,* March 8, 30–36.

Miller, Mark Crispin. 1992. Operation Desert Sham. *New York Times,* June 24, A21.

Moore, Molly. 1991a. Aspin: War would start with air strikes, escalate to ground battles. *Washington Post,* January 9, A15.

————. 1991b. Porous minefields, dispirited troops and a dog named Pow. *Washington Post,* March 17, A1.

————. 1993. *A Woman of War: Storming Kuwait with the U.S. Marines.* New York: Scribner's.

Morin, Richard. 1991a. Gulf poll: Most Americans want Hill to back Bush. *Washington Post,* January 8, A12.

———. 1991b. Poll: Americans expect war but back peace conference. *Washington Post,* January 11, A1.

———. 1991c. Two ways of reading the public's lips on Gulf policy: Differently phrased questions seem at first glance to yield contradictory results. *Washington Post,* January 14, A9.

Morin, Richard, and E. J. Dionne, Jr. 1990. *Vox populi:* Winds of war and shifts of opinion. *Washington Post,* December 23, C1.

Morrison, David C. 1991. Weighing ground war in the Gulf. *National Journal,* February 2, 276–78.

Mueller, John. 1970. Presidential popularity from Truman to Johnson. *American Political Science Review* 64, no. 1 (March): 18–34.

———. 1973. *War, Presidents and Public Opinion.* New York: Wiley. (Reprinted 1985, Lanham, Md.: University Press of America.)

———. 1977. Changes in American public attitudes toward international involvement. Pp. 323–44 in *The Limits of Military Intervention,* ed. Ellen Stern. Beverly Hills, Calif.: Sage.

———. 1979. Public expectations of war during the Cold War. *American Journal of Political Science* 23, no. 2 (May): 301–29.

———. 1980. The search for the "Breaking Point" in Vietnam: The statistics of a deadly quarrel. *International Studies Quarterly* 24, no. 4 (December): 497–519.

———. 1984a. Lessons learned five years after the hostage nightmare. *Wall Street Journal,* November 6, 28.

———. 1984b. Reflections on the Vietnam protest movement and on the curious calm at the war's end. Pp.151–57 in *Vietnam as History,* ed. Peter Braestrup. Lanham, Md.: University Press of America.

———. 1987. Presidents and terrorists should not mix. *Wall Street Journal,* March 31, 36.

———. 1988. Trends in political tolerance. *Public Opinion Quarterly* 52, no. 1 (Spring): 1–25.

———. 1989. *Retreat from Doomsday: The Obsolescence of Major War.* New York: Basic Books.

———. 1990a. The art of a deal: No rewards for Iraqi aggression. *Arizona Republic,* December 16, C1.

———. 1990b. The lonely commander: President is threatening a war Americans don't want to fight. *Atlanta Journal/Constitution,* November 18, C1–C2.

———. 1990c. Will America stand a stalemate in Iraq? *New York Times,* August 27, A17.

———. 1991/92. Pearl Harbor: Military inconvenience, political disaster. *International Security* 16, no. 3 (Winter): 172–203.

———. 1991a. Korea, Vietnam and the Gulf. *The Polling Report* 7, no. 4 (February 18): 1, 7–8.

———. 1991b. A quick victory? It better be. *New York Times,* January 19, 31.

———. 1991c. War: Natural, but not necessary. Pp. 13–29 in *The Institution of War*, ed. Robert A. Hinde. London: Macmillan.

———. 1992a. Democracy and Ralph's Pretty Good Grocery: Elections, inequality, and the minimal human being. *American Journal of Political Science* 36, no. 4 (November): 983–1003.

———. 1992b. Theory and democracy: A reply to Michael Lienesch. *American Journal of Political Science* 36, no. 4 (November): 1015–22.

———. 1993a. American public opinion and the Gulf War: Some polling issues. *Public Opinion Quarterly* 57, no. 1 (Spring): 86–97.

———. 1993b. The Perfect Enemy: Assessing the Gulf War. Rochester, N.Y.: University of Rochester, Department of Political Science.

———. Forthcoming. *Quiet Cataclysm: Reflections on the Recent Transformation of World Politics*. (New York: HarperCollins).

Muller, Henry, and John Stacks. 1991. Interview: Determined to do what is right. *Time*, January 7, 32–33.

Muravchik, Joshua. 1991a. At last, Pax Americana. *New York Times*, January 24, A23.

———. 1991b. The end of the Vietnam paradigm? *Commentary*, May, 17–23.

Murphy, Caryle. 1991. Iraqi death toll remains clouded. *Washington Post*, June 23, A1.

Murray, Alan. 1990. Greenspan says GNP likely to fall. *Wall Street Journal*, November 29, A2.

Murray, Frank J. 1992. U.S. concedes public opinion tilted war aim. *Washington Times*, January 17, A1.

Nacos, Brigitte Lebens. 1990. *The Press, Presidents, and Crises*. New York: Columbia University Press.

National Opinion Research Center. 1944. *The Effect of Realistic War Pictures*. Report EW 20, March 13. Chicago: National Opinion Research Center.

Niemi, Richard G., John Mueller, and Tom W. Smith. 1989. *Trends in Public Opinion: A Compendium of Survey Data*. Westport, Conn.: Greenwood.

Norpoth, Helmut. 1987a. The Falklands War and government popularity in Britain: Rally without consequence or surge without decline? *Electoral Studies* 6(1):3–16.

———. 1987b. Guns and butter and government popularity in Britain. *American Political Science Review* 81, no. 3 (September): 949–59.

Omestad, Thomas. 1992/93. Why Bush lost. *Foreign Policy*, Winter, 70–81.

Page, Benjamin I., and Robert Y. Shapiro. 1992. *The Rational Public: Fifty Years of Trends in American Policy Preferences*. Chicago: University of Chicago Press.

Page, Susan. 1992. War a double-edged issue. *Newsday*, March 1, 6.

Payne, Stanley C. 1951. *The Art of Asking Questions*. Princeton, N.J.: Princeton University Press.

Pelletiere, Stephen C., and Douglas V. Johnson II. 1991. *Lessons Learned: The Iran-Iraq War*. Carlisle Barracks, Pa.: U.S. Army War College, Strategic Studies Institute.

Peters, Charles. 1991. Stop that blank check. *New York Times,* January 16, A23.

Popkin, Samuel L. 1991. *The Reasoning Voter: Communication and Persuasion in Presidential Campaigns.* Chicago: University of Chicago Press.

Postol, Theodore A. 1991/92. Lessons of the Gulf War experience with the Patriot. *International Security* 16, no. 3 (Winter): 119–71.

———. 1992. Correspondence: Patriot experience in the Gulf War. *International Security* 17, no. 1 (Summer): 225–40.

Quindlen, Anna. 1991. The microwave war. *New York Times,* March 3, 4–17.

Record, Jeffrey. 1993. *Hollow Victory: A Contrary View of the Gulf War.* Washington, D.C.: Brassey's (US).

Reston, James. 1991. The puzzling George Bushes. *New York Times,* September 20, A27.

Rich, Norman. 1973. *Hitler's War Aims: Ideology, the Nazi State, and the Course of Expansion.* New York: Norton.

Rielly, John E., ed. 1987. *American Public Opinion and U.S. Foreign Policy 1987.* Chicago: Chicago Council on Foreign Relations.

———. 1991. *American Public Opinion and U.S. Foreign Policy 1991.* Chicago: Chicago Council on Foreign Relations.

Risjord, Norman K. 1971. Election of 1812. Pp. 249–72 in *History of American Presidential Elections, 1789–1968,* ed. Arthur M. Schlesinger, Jr. New York: Chelsea House.

Rosenthal, Andrew. 1991a. Americans don't expect short war. *New York Times,* January 15, A11.

———. 1991b. U.S. Expecting Hussein to be out by year's end. *New York Times,* March 18, A8.

———. 1992. Taking heat at every turn, Bush shows a boiling point. *New York Times,* July 1, A1.

Rostow, Walt W. 1972. *The Diffusion of Power.* New York: Macmillan.

Rugg, Donald. 1941. Experiments in wording questions, II. *Public Opinion Quarterly* 5:91–92.

Russett, Bruce. 1990. *Controlling the Sword: The Democratic Governance of National Security.* Cambridge, Mass.: Harvard University Press.

Safire, William. 1991. Optimists are the realists. *New York Times,* December 26, A25.

———. 1992. The April surprise. *New York Times,* January 13, A15.

Sanders, David, Dave Marsh, and Hugh Ward. 1990. A reply to Clarke, Mishler and Whiteley. *British Journal of Political Science* 20, no. 1 (January): 83–90.

Sanders, David, Hugh Ward, and Dave Marsh. 1987. Government popularity and the Falklands War: A reassessment. *British Journal of Political Science* 17, no. 3 (July): 281–313.

Schmitt, Eric. 1991. U.S. battle plan: Massive air strikes. *New York Times,* January 10, A17.

Schneider, William. 1990. American's aren't ready to go to war. *National Journal,* November 24, 2894.

Schuman, Howard. 1992. Context effects: State of the past/state of the art.

Pp. 5–20 in *Context Effects in Social and Psychological Research,* ed. Norbert Schwarz and Seymour Sudman. New York: Springer-Verlag.

Schuman, Howard, and Stanley Presser. 1981. *Questions and Answers in Attitude Surveys.* New York: Academic Press.

Schwarzkopf, H. Norman. 1991a. Briefing. February 27. (Cited from videotape.)

———. 1991b. Testimony. Pp. 314–68 in *Operation Desert Shield/Desert Storm. Hearings before the Committee on Armed Services, United States Senate,* 102nd Cong., 1st sess., June 12.

———. 1992. *It Doesn't Take a Hero.* Written with Peter Petre. New York: Bantam.

Sciolino, Elaine. 1991. *The Outlaw State: Saddam Hussein's Quest for Power and the Gulf Crisis.* New York: Wiley.

Sciolino, Elaine, and Michael Wines. 1992. Bush's greatest glory fades as questions on Iraq persist. *New York Times,* June 27, 1.

Seib, Gerald F. 1991a. Bush stays calm, cool as Jan. 15 looms, fielding criticism with a deep resolve. *Wall Street Journal,* January 7, A10.

———. 1991b. How President Bush deftly orchestrated swift victory over Iraq. *Wall Street Journal,* March 1, A1.

Sheehan, Neil. 1964. Much is at stake in Southeast Asian struggle. *New York Times,* August 16, E4.

Silk, Leonard. 1991. Economic scene: The broad impact of the Gulf War. *New York Times,* August 16, D2.

Simpson, John. 1991. *From the House of War: John Simpson in the Gulf.* London: Arrow Books.

Small, Melvin. 1980. *Was War Necessary? National Security and U.S. Entry into War.* Beverly Hills, Calif.: Sage.

———. 1988. *Johnson, Nixon, and the Doves.* New Brunswick, N.J.: Rutgers University Press.

Smith, Hedrick, ed. 1992. *The Media and the Gulf War: The Press and Democracy in Wartime.* Washington, D.C.: Seven Locks Press.

Smith, Jean Edward. 1992. *George Bush's War.* New York: Holt.

Smith, R. Jeffrey. 1991. Congress to investigate U.S. intelligence on Iraq: Hearings will review apparent shortcomings. *Washington Post,* March 18, A16.

Smith, Tom W. 1985. The polls: America's most important problem. *Public Opinion Quarterly* 49, no. 2 (Summer): 264–74.

Solarz, Stephen J. 1991. The stakes in the Gulf. *New Republic,* January 7 and 14, 18–25.

Solomon, Norman. 1991. The media protest too much. *New York Times,* May 24, A31.

Stanley, Harold W., and Richard G. Niemi. 1992. *Vital Statistics on American Politics.* 3d. ed. Washington, D.C.: Congressional Quarterly Press.

Stein, Janice Gross. 1992. Deterrence and compellence in the Gulf, 1990–91: A failed or impossible task? *International Security* 17, no. 2 (Fall): 147–79.

Stein, Robert M. 1992. Correspondence: Patriot experience in the Gulf War. *International Security* 17, no. 1 (Summer): 199–225.

Stouffer, Samuel A. 1955. *Communism, Conformity, and Civil Liberties.* Garden City, N.Y.: Doubleday.

Summers, Harry G., Jr. 1992. *On Strategy II: A Critical Analysis of the Gulf War.* New York: Dell.

Taylor, Philip M. 1992. *War and the Media: Propaganda and Persuasion in the Gulf War.* Manchester: Manchester University Press.

Taylor, William J., and James Blackwell. 1991. The ground war in the Gulf. *Survival* 33, no. 3 (May/June): 230–45.

Telhami, Shibley. 1992. Did we appease Iraq? *New York Times,* June 29, A15.

Thomas, Evan. 1990. "No Vietnam": The lessons of Southeast Asia shape the president's strategy in the Gulf. *Newsweek,* December 10, 24–31.

Toner, Robin. 1991a. Dark skies for Bush: Rain on his parade buoys Democrats. *New York Times,* November 18, A10.

———. 1991b. Democrats don't need sacrificial lamb for '92. *New York Times,* March 11, A12.

———. 1991c. Did someone say "Domestic Policy"? *New York Times,* March 3, 4–1.

Towle, Philip. 1991. *Pundits and Patriots: Lessons from the Gulf War.* London: Institute for European Defence and Strategic Studies.

Tsouras, Peter, and Elmo C. Wright, Jr. 1991. The ground war. Pp. 81–120 in *Military Lessons of the Gulf War,* ed. Bruce W. Watson, Bruce George, Peter Tsouras, and B. L. Cyr. Novato, Calif: Presidio Press.

Tucker, Robert W. 1991. Justice and the war. *National Interest,* Fall, 108–12.

Tucker, Robert W., and David C. Hendrickson. 1992. *The Imperial Temptation: The New World Order and America's Purpose.* New York: Council on Foreign Relations Press.

Turner, Lynn W. 1971. Elections of 1816 and 1820. Pp. 299–321 in *History of American Presidential Elections, 1789–1968,* ed. Arthur M. Schlesinger, Jr. New York: Chelsea House.

Tyler, Patrick E. 1991. Health crisis said to grip Iraq in wake of war's destruction. *New York Times,* May 22, A16.

U.S. News and World Report. 1992. *Triumph Without Victory: The Unreported History of the Persian Gulf War.* New York: Times Books/Random House.

Viorst, Milton. 1991a. Report from Baghdad. *New Yorker,* June 24, 55–73.

———. 1991b. After the liberation. *New Yorker,* September 30, 37–72.

———. 1992. Blaming Bush unfairly for the Persian Gulf War: His policy with Saddam Hussein was right. *Washington Post National Weekly Edition,* November 2–8, 25.

Walsh, Elsa, and Paul Valentine. 1991. War protest draws tens of thousands here. *Washington Post,* January 27, 1A.

Wilcox, Clyde, Joe Ferrarra, and Dee Allsop. 1991. Before the rally: The dynamics of attitudes toward the Gulf crisis before the War. Paper presented at the annual meeting of the American Political Science Association, Washington, D.C., September.

Wines, Michael. 1991. U.S. is building up a picture of vast Iraqi atom program. *New York Times,* September 27, A8.

Wittkopf, Eugene R. 1990. *Faces of Internationalism: Public Opinion and American Foreign Policy.* Durham, N.C.: Duke University Press.

Woodward, Bob. 1991a. *The Commanders.* New York: Simon & Schuster.

———. 1991b. 100,000 Iraqi troops may have deserted. *Washington Post,* March 17, A24.

Yang, Frederick. 1991. After the storm: The political impact of the Gulf War. *The Polling Report* 7, no. 7 (April 1): 1–3.

Zaller, John. 1992. *The Nature of Origins of Mass Opinion.* New York: Cambridge University Press.

NAME INDEX ....

ABC News, 57
Achenbach, Joel, 55, 124, 340n.1
Adams, William C., 160
Albright, David, 118
Aldrich, John H., 102
Alford, John R., 19
Allsop, Dee, 43
Anderson, Jack, 154, 347n.12
Apple, R. W., Jr., 21, 124, 160
Ascherio, Alberto, 158
Aspin, Les, 55, 57, 154, 156
Atkinson, Rick, xviii

Barnes, Fred, 19, 20, 51, 52, 96, 153,
    337n.3, 338nn. 4, 5
Bay, Austin, 75, 155, 343n.4
Beeston, Richard, 126
Binder, David, 345n.3
Binstein, Michael, 154, 347n.12
Blackwell, James, 347n.13
Blair, Clay, 161
Borgida, Eugene, 102
Bosso, Christopher, 133
Braestrup, Peter, 137, 345n.1
Brennan, John, 337n.1
Brody, Richard A., 130
Brzezinski, Zbigniew, 146
Bundy, McGeorge, 100
Bush, George, xviii, 22, 41, 52, 54, 90

Cantril, Hadley, 28, 61, 73, 123,
    340nn. 5, 6
Carpenter, Ted Galen, 146
Chadwick, Frank, 343n.4
Chase, Robert, 158

Claiborne, William, 135, 155
Clark, Ramsey, 153
Clarke, Harold D., 101
Clarke, I. F., 46
Cockburn, Alexander, 149, 338n.4
Congressional Quarterly, 104
Copper, Andrew Fenton, 342n.2
Cordesman, Anthony H., 155, 157,
    343n.4
Coté, Tim, 158
Council of Economic Advisors, 152
Couturié, Bill, 347n.2
Cranford, John R., 346n.9
Crucé, Eméric, 347n.3
Curran, Tim, 97
Cushman, John H., 346n.11

Dannreuther, Roland, 57, 85, 147
Daponte, Beth Osborne, 157, 158
Delli Carpini, Michael X., 5
Department of Defense, 126, 154, 156,
    338n.4, 346nn. 11, 12
Dickinson, William, 154, 156
Dionne, E. J., Jr., 29
Doherty, Carroll J., 70
Dowd, Maureen, 104, 144, 338n.9
Drew, Elizabeth, 20, 21, 22, 52, 96,
    159
Drogin, Bob, 136
Duffy, Michael, 60, 118, 119, 138
Dunnigan, James F., 75, 155, 343n.4
Dupuy, Trevor N., 124, 127

Edwards, George C., III, 91
Elliot, Kimberly A., 19

363

SUBJECT INDEX

Citations in boldface are to table numbers, not page numbers.

FIGURES ....

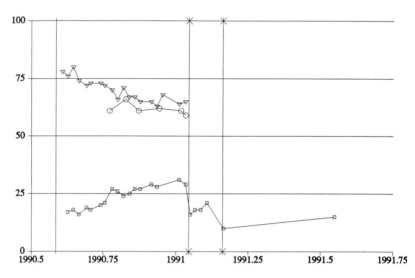

Fig. 1. Approval of Gulf policy.
        Triangles, table 20, Approve sending troops
        Circles, table 36, Right thing to send troops
        Squares, table 34, Mistake to send troops

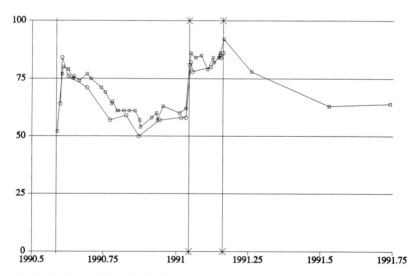

Fig. 2. Bush handling the Gulf.
        Squares, table 8, Approve Bush handling situation
        Circles, table 9, Approve Bush handling invasion

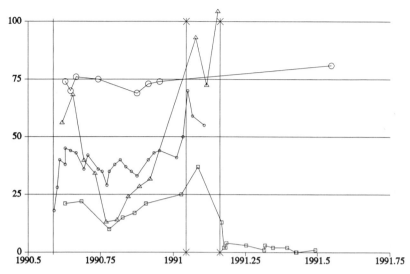

Fig. 3. Concern about the Gulf.
    Large Circles, table 50, clear idea why involved
    Triangles, table 48, News coverage index
    Small Circles, table 46, Follow Gulf news very closely
    Squares, table 45, Gulf most important problem

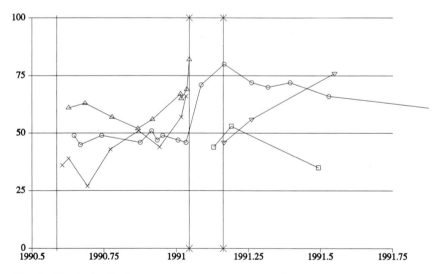

Fig. 4. War in the Gulf.
    Triangles, table 223, War will be short
    Circles, table 40, Worth going to war
    Crosses, table 232, Expect war
    Inverted triangles, table 164, Should have removed Saddam
    Squares, table 256, Mideast more secure now

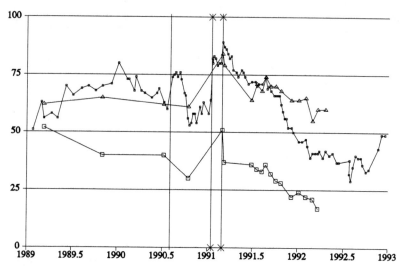

Fig. 5. Approval of Bush.
> *Small Squares,* table 1, Approve handling job
> *Triangles,* table 3A, Approve handling foreign policy
> *large Squares,* table 3B, Approve handling economy

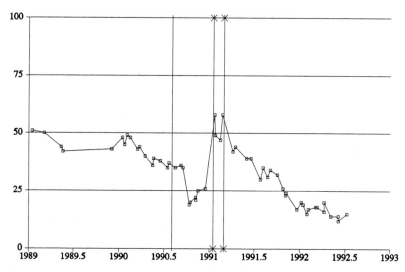

Fig. 6. Country going in right direction (table 198).

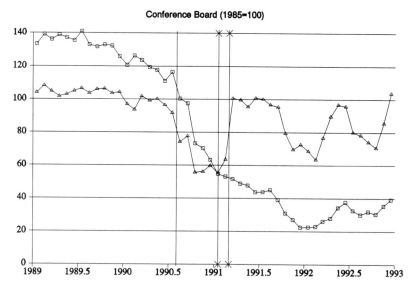

Fig. 7. Consumer confidence (table 203, Conference Board 1985 = 100).
Squares, Present situation
Triangles, Expectations in six months

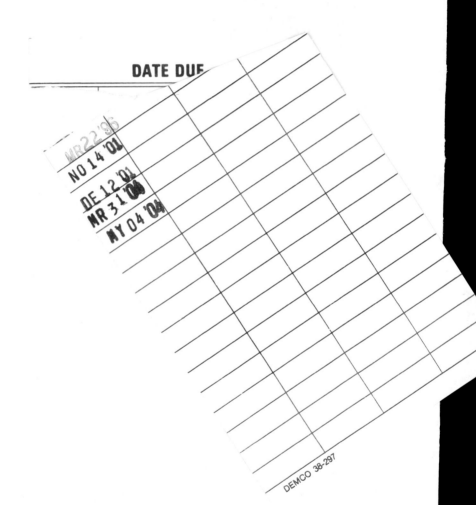

DATE DUE

MR22'96
NO 14'01
DE 12'01
MR 31'04
MY 04'04

DEMCO 38-297